World Intellectual Property Indicators 2017

WIPO
WORLD
INTELLECTUAL PROPERTY
ORGANIZATION

© WIPO, 2017

First published 2017

World Intellectual Property Organization
34, chemin des Colombettes, P.O. Box 18
CH-1211 Geneva 20, Switzerland

ISBN: 978-92-805-2903-6

Attribution 3.0 IGO license (CC BY 3.0 IGO)

Photo credits: phongphan5922/Getty Images/iStockphoto and MF3d/Getty Images/iStockphoto

Printed in Switzerland

Table of contents

SPECIAL SECTION

PATENTS

TRADEMARKS

INDUSTRIAL DESIGNS

PLANT VARIETIES

GEOGRAPHICAL INDICATIONS

ADDITIONAL INFORMATION

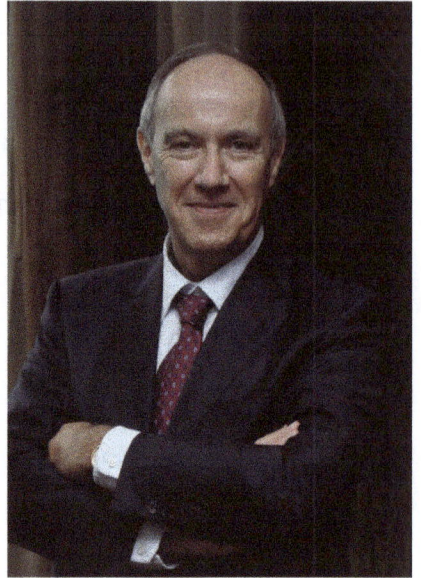

Foreword

With the world economy on a firmer footing than in recent years, global intellectual property (IP) filings have reached new highs. Global patent filings grew by 8.3% and global trademark filing activity by 13.5% – making for seven years of straight increases. Following an 8% decline in 2014 and 1% growth in 2015, industrial design filing activity rebounded strongly in 2016 with 8.3% growth.

As seen in previous years, China remained the main driver of global growth in filings. From already high levels, patent applications in China increased by 21.5%, as did filing activity for trademarks (+30.8%) and industrial designs (+14.3%). The United States of America also saw increases in filing activity for patents, trademarks and industrial designs, which grew by 2.7%, 5.5% and 12.1%, respectively. Other notable trends include large increases in trademark filing activity in Japan (+30.8%), the Russian Federation (+14.8%) and India (+8.3%), and rapid growth in industrial design filing activity in the Russian Federation (+9.4%) and at the European Union Intellectual Property Office (EUIPO; +6.5%). For the first time, however, the Republic of Korea saw declines in filing activity for all three intellectual property (IP) rights – patents (-2.3%), trademarks (-1.7%) and industrial designs (-4.6%).

The 2017 edition of WIPO's *World Intellectual Property Indicators* documents these and many other developments that shaped the global IP system in 2016. This year's special theme presents new statistics on certain dimensions of the operational performance of IP offices, including the size of their examiner workforce, application pendency times and patent examination outcomes. We are mindful that differences in IP filing procedures limit direct comparability of operational statistics across offices, but believe nonetheless that they can usefully inform decision-makers, especially when monitoring trends over time.

For the first time ever, this year's edition also publishes statistics on geographical indications (GIs). Noting the absence of statistical information on this form of IP, we initiated a new statistical survey and received responses from 54 national and regional authorities responsible for administering GIs. Correctly capturing the number of GIs in force in different jurisdictions is challenging due to the multiple ways in which GIs can be protected. We recognize that the statistics collected are incomplete but view them as a first step toward establishing a more complete picture of GI activity worldwide in the future.

Readers wishing to go beyond the statistics presented in this report can use the statistical tools on WIPO's website (*www.wipo.int/ipstats*), notably the IP Statistics Data Center and the Statistical Country Profiles.

Finally, I would like to thank our Member States as well as national and regional IP authorities for sharing their annual statistics with WIPO. Their invaluable cooperation makes the *World Intellectual Property Indicators* possible.

Francis GURRY
Director General

Acknowledgements

World Intellectual Property Indicators 2017 was prepared under the direction of Francis Gurry (Director General) and supervised by Carsten Fink (Chief Economist). The report was prepared by a team led by Mosahid Khan and comprising Kyle Bergquist, Ryan Lamb, Bruno Le Feuvre, Julio Raffo, Kritee Sharrma and Hao Zhou, all from the Economics and Statistics Division. The geographical indications section was prepared by Matteo Gragnani and benefited greatly from the inputs contributed by David Muls and Alexandra Grazioli, all from the Brands and Designs Sector. Peter Button of the International Union for the Protection of New Varieties of Plants (UPOV) provided comments and suggestions for the plant varieties section.

Samiah Do Carmo Figueiredo and Caterina Valles Galmes provided administrative support. Gratitude is also due to editorial and design colleagues in the Communications Division for leading the production of the report, especially Toby Boyd for his editing work. Thanks go to staff in the Printing Plant for their services.

Key numbers

Patents	2015	2016	Annual growth (%)	2016 share (%)
Applications worldwide	**2,887,300**	**3,127,900**	**8.3**	**100.0**
China	1,101,864	1,338,503	21.5	42.8
U.S.	589,410	605,571	2.7	19.4
Japan	318,721	318,381	-0.1	10.2
Trademarks				
Application class count worldwide	**8,609,500**	**9,768,200**	**13.5**	**100.0**
China	2,828,083	3,697,916	30.8	37.9
U.S.	517,083	545,587	5.5	5.6
Japan	344,946	451,320	30.8	4.6
Industrial designs				
Application design count worldwide	**1,145,200**	**1,240,600**	**8.3**	**100.0**
China	569,059	650,344	14.3	52.4
EUIPO (EU Office)	98,162	104,522	6.5	8.4
Rep. of Korea	72,458	69,120	-4.6	5.6
Utility models				
Applications worldwide	**1,205,400**	**1,553,300**	**28.9**	**100.0**
China	1,127,577	1,475,977	30.9	95.0
Germany	14,274	14,030	-1.7	0.9
Russian Federation	11,906	11,112	-6.7	0.7
Plant varieties				
Applications worldwide	**15,240**	**16,510**	**8.3**	**100.0**
Community Plant Variety Office (EU)	3,111	3,299	6.0	20.0
China	2,342	2,923	24.8	17.7
U.S.	1,634	1,604	-1.8	9.7

Overview of IP filing activity

Table 1
Ranking of total (resident and abroad) IP filing activity by origin, 2016

Origin	Patents	Marks	Designs	Origin	Patents	Marks	Designs
China	1	1	1	Bulgaria	58	43	36
U.S.	2	2	4	Morocco	71	47	19
Germany	5	4	2	Philippines	51	44	45
Japan	3	3	7	Colombia	49	37	66
Rep. of Korea	4	8	3	Chile	47	30	78
France	6	5	8	Greece (e)	44	73	39
U.K.	7	7	11	Pakistan	68	35	56
Italy	11	11	5	Slovakia	57	51	54
Switzerland	8	13	9	Indonesia	112	24	28
India	12	6	14	Belarus	41	66	59
Turkey	23	10	6	Cyprus	63	54	58
Iran (Islamic Republic of)	16	12	12	Liechtenstein (d)	42	76	57
Russian Federation	10	9	23	Slovenia (d, e, f)	53	72	50
Netherlands	9	19	16	Kazakhstan	40	57	84
Spain	22	15	10	Bangladesh	86	59	37
Sweden	14	26	13	Serbia	66	64	53
Australia	21	16	20	Croatia	72	67	46
Canada	13	18	27	United Arab Emirates (a, f)	52	52	81
Austria	17	25	18	Uzbekistan	60	68	62
Brazil	24	14	22	Sri Lanka	64	65	69
Poland (f)	26	20	17	Malta (f)	56	70	73
Ukraine	33	23	15	Estonia	67	78	65
Belgium	18	29	33	Latvia	72	79	60
Denmark	20	36	25	Peru	84	45	83
Mexico	34	17	34	Lithuania	77	69	70
China, Hong Kong SAR	36	27	26	Mongolia	96	62	64
Finland (c)	19	38	32	Sudan	65	100	63
Portugal	38	33	24	Barbados	61	103	68
Singapore	25	31	40	Kenya (b)	78	71	84
Czech Republic	35	32	30	Monaco	76	75	82
Viet Nam	50	22	29	Azerbaijan	55	82	104
Israel	15	56	31	Republic of Moldova	103	80	61
Thailand (d)	54	28	21	Panama	99	60	89
Argentina	45	21	42	Côte d'Ivoire (d, e, f)	68	112	72
South Africa	30	40	38	Ecuador	113	58	87
Luxembourg	31	34	44	Ghana	93	110	55
Norway	27	46	43	Jordan	88	81	89
New Zealand	32	39	48	Cameroon (d, e, f)	48	116	95
Malaysia	37	41	49	Iceland	74	93	92
Hungary	39	49	41	Georgia	95	86	79
Egypt (c)	46	50	35	Armenia	80	85	97
Romania	43	42	47	Syrian Arab Republic (a, c, e)	75	120	67
Ireland (e)	28	53	52	Tunisia (e)	70	117	75
Saudi Arabia (b)	29	55	51	Jamaica	109	87	74

Origin	Patents	Marks	Designs
China, Macao SAR	100	96	77
Dominican Republic	119	61	93
Costa Rica	110	63	102
Algeria (b, f)	93	48	142
Qatar (e, f)	87	105	94
Senegal (d, e, f)	59	122	107

Origin	Patents	Marks	Designs
Bosnia and Herzegovina	107	104	80
Uruguay (a, b, c)	101	74	120
Mauritius (f)	97	90	111
Cuba	85	91	126
Bahamas (f)	102	98	104
Iraq (a, e, f)	62	125	117

Note: Rankings are based on the total numbers of applications filed by origin. Patent data refer to numbers of equivalent patent applications. Trademark data refer to numbers of equivalent trademark applications based on class counts – the number of classes specified in applications. Industrial design data refer to numbers of equivalent industrial design applications based on design counts – the number of designs contained in applications. This table lists origins for which at least two types of IP filing data are available.

a. 2015 patent data.

b. 2015 trademark data.

c. 2015 industrial design data.

d. Data on patent applications at the national IP office are not available.

e. Data on trademark applications at the national IP office are not available.

f. Data on industrial design applications at the national IP office are not available.

Source: WIPO Statistics Database, September 2017.

Table 2
Ranking of resident IP filing activity by origin, 2016

Origin	Patents	Marks	Designs
China	1	1	1
Japan	3	2	6
U.S.	2	3	7
Germany	5	6	2
Rep. of Korea	4	9	3
France	7	4	9
Turkey	14	7	4
India	10	5	12
Iran (Islamic Republic of)	9	10	10
Italy	11	13	5
U.K.	8	11	11
Russian Federation	6	8	22
Spain	18	15	8
Brazil	16	12	18
Poland (f)	17	20	14
Netherlands	12	21	19
Switzerland	13	24	16
Ukraine	26	23	13
Thailand	..	25	17
Australia	25	17	23
Indonesia	..	22	24
Sweden	15	30	25
Mexico	30	14	28
Austria	19	33	21

Origin	Patents	Marks	Designs
Canada	20	16	43
Belgium	22	32	31
Portugal	39	27	20
Viet Nam	45	19	26
Denmark	21	44	27
Argentina	38	18	38
South Africa	24	35	39
Czech Republic	36	34	30
Finland (c)	23	46	35
Egypt (c)	37	45	29
Morocco	56	42	15
Romania	35	36	42
Malaysia	32	39	44
China, Hong Kong SAR	58	28	33
Norway	27	47	47
Singapore	28	50	46
New Zealand	33	40	53
Hungary	41	48	40
Philippines	51	37	41
Bulgaria	55	41	34
Israel	31	69	37
Pakistan	59	29	49
Saudi Arabia (b)	29	57	51
Colombia	46	31	61

Origin	Patents	Marks	Designs
Luxembourg	43	55	50
Chile	47	26	79
Slovakia	54	49	52
Bangladesh	76	52	32
Greece (e)	42	83	36
Uzbekistan	49	60	53
Kazakhstan	34	53	79
Croatia	62	63	45
Algeria (b)	71	43	..
Sri Lanka	53	58	60
Ireland (e)	40	75	57
Belarus	44	65	66
Syrian Arab Republic (a, c)	60	..	59
Mongolia	68	54	58
Tunisia	57	..	72
Peru	79	38	78

Origin	Patents	Marks	Designs
Lithuania	66	66	68
Serbia	61	70	69
Republic of Moldova	74	72	55
Sudan	52	93	56
Kenya (b)	64	64	79
Latvia	70	81	62
Ecuador	84	51	83
United Arab Emirates (a)	86	61	..
Estonia	77	76	69
Slovenia (d, e, f)	67	98	63
Liechtenstein (d)	48	110	74
Malta (f)	73	88	73
Cyprus	82	77	76
Georgia	72	86	77
Dominican Republic	94	56	86
Azerbaijan	63	78	96

Note: Rankings are based on the numbers of resident applications filed by origin. Patent data refer to numbers of equivalent patent applications. Trademark data refer to numbers of equivalent trademark applications based on class counts – the number of classes specified in applications. Industrial design data refer to numbers of equivalent industrial design applications based on design counts – the number of designs contained in applications. This table lists origins for which at least two types of IP filing data are available.

a. 2015 patent data.

b. 2015 trademark data.

c. 2015 industrial design data.

d. Data on patent applications at the national IP office are not available.

e. Data on trademark applications at the national IP office are not available.

f. Data on industrial design applications at the national IP office are not available.

.. indicates not available.

Source: WIPO Statistics Database, September 2017.

Special section

Patent office operations: application processing times, examination capacity and examination outcomes

Introduction

Patent offices examine applications and decide whether or not to grant patent rights. Examination processes differ across offices. For example, some offices such as South Africa conduct a purely formal examination of the application, whereas others such as Japan undertake both formal and substantial examination.

The substantive examination process usually consists of determining whether the claimed innovation is novel, non-obvious and industrially applicable. This may involve numerous interactions between applicants and examiners, and can be a lengthy process. For example, the patent grant procedure at the European Patent Office (EPO) takes three to five years from the date on which the application is filed. Annex S1 depicts the major phases of granting procedures at the five offices that receive the largest numbers of applications.

Procedures across offices may differ as regards:

- the patentability of subject matter;
- whether a request for examination must be made, and if so the time period within which such requests must be made;
- fee structure;
- whether and how an applicant may request accelerated examination;
- bilateral/multilateral work-sharing agreements such as a patent prosecution highway;
- the applicant-examiner communication process;
- management of workload, for example whether the prior art search is outsourced;
- the office's budget-setting procedure;
- the opposition system (e.g., pre-grant, post-grant, etc.);
- the training and experience of patent examiners, and incentives offered to them; and
- whether it may be possible to continue with an application after its initial rejection by filing continuation-in-parts, divisional application and so on.

Every effort has been made to compile procedural data based on common definitions and concepts, but the differences in procedures make it extremely difficult to fully harmonize such data. For instance, "rejection" is not recorded as a final decision in Canada. Applicants are informed what they must do/answer in order for their application to be considered, and if an applicant cannot provide the required information, they are regarded as having abandoned the application. A similar situation exists in Australia. To take another example, rejection of an application has a different meaning at offices, such as that of South Africa, which do not perform a substantive examination than at offices which do. At many offices, filing a national application does not imply a request for examination. For example, in China and Japan a request for examination can be made up to three years after the date the application was filed. In the U.S., filing an application implies an immediate request for examination.

This special section reports statistics on patent office examination capacity, application processing time and examination outcome. To shed light on these issues, WIPO has compiled patent procedural data from a number of patent offices (annex S2). This is the first time WIPO has collected such procedural data. As explained, it is challenging to compile comparable data and so one should exercise caution when making comparisons between offices. To address this data limitation, it is more meaningful to focus on trends at a given office.

A number of offices recorded large increases in patent applications received over the past two decades, with a threefold increase in patent applications filed worldwide between 1995 and 2016. The Republic of Korea and the U.S. each saw applications multiply by a factor of 2.7 (figure S1). The rapid growth in filings has led to an increased number of pending applications and considerable backlogs (see box for the definition of potentially pending applications). In 2016, the number of potentially pending applications stood at 1.1 million in the U.S., around 847,000 in Japan and about 668,000 at the EPO. Offices of middle-income countries Brazil and India also held large stocks of potentially pending applications (figure S2).

The growing number of applications has put pressure on offices to process applications in a timely manner while reducing backlogs. This has generated much discussion among academics, patent offices, policymakers and the press about pendency time, backlogs and the quality of issued patents.[1] Offices face the challenge of providing timely examination of patents while maintaining high examination quality.

How large has the increase in patent office workloads been?

The number of applications filed worldwide reached the 1 million mark in 1995, and has trended upward since then. In 2011, applications

exceeded 2 million. It then took only five years to reach 3 million. In 2016, more than 3.1 million applications were filed.

Applications filed in China increased from 18,700 in 1995 to 1.3 million in 2016, amounting to average yearly growth of 23%. Brazil, India and the Islamic Republic of Iran have also seen marked increases in applications filed in their countries over the past two decades (figure S1). The EPO, the Republic of Korea and the U.S. each saw average annual growth of around 5% over the same period.

Figure S1
Evolution of the number of patent applications filed at selected offices

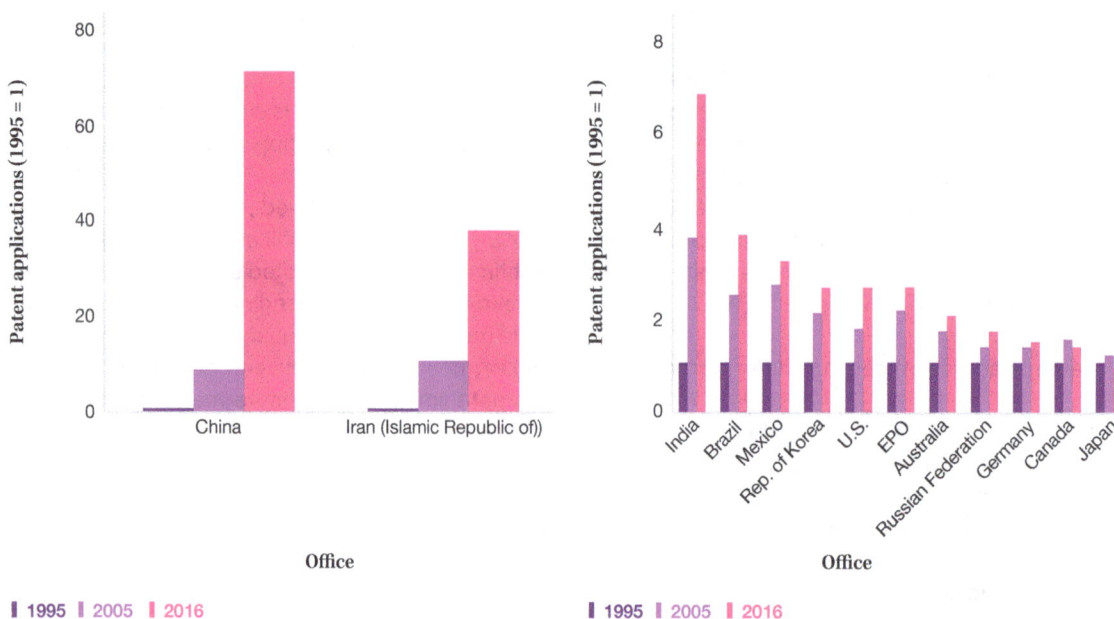

1995　2005　2016

Source: WIPO Statistics Database, September 2017.

In order to manage their incoming workload, patent offices need to adapt their processing capacity, particularly their examination capacity, according to the number of patent applications received. Strong growth in patent applications has the potential to increase the number of pending applications, resulting in backlogs, as hiring and training additional examiners takes time. While a certain level of pending applications is needed to fully occupy examiners, excessive backlogs can lead to longer pendency times.

Figure S2 shows the growth of potentially pending applications at the top 10 patent offices for which data are available. These top 10 offices were selected based on their total number of potentially pending applications in 2016. Potentially pending application data for China – the office that received by far the largest volume of applications – are not available. Figure S2 shows that all offices, except those of Canada and Japan, had substantially more potentially pending applications in 2016 than in 2005. The number of potentially pending applications in Australia and Brazil more than doubled between 2005 and 2016. India's volume of potentially pending applications in 2016 was 2.4 times higher than the level recorded in 2010. The decline in Japan was partly due to a substantial decrease in the number of patent applications filed.

Figure S2
Evolution of potentially pending applications

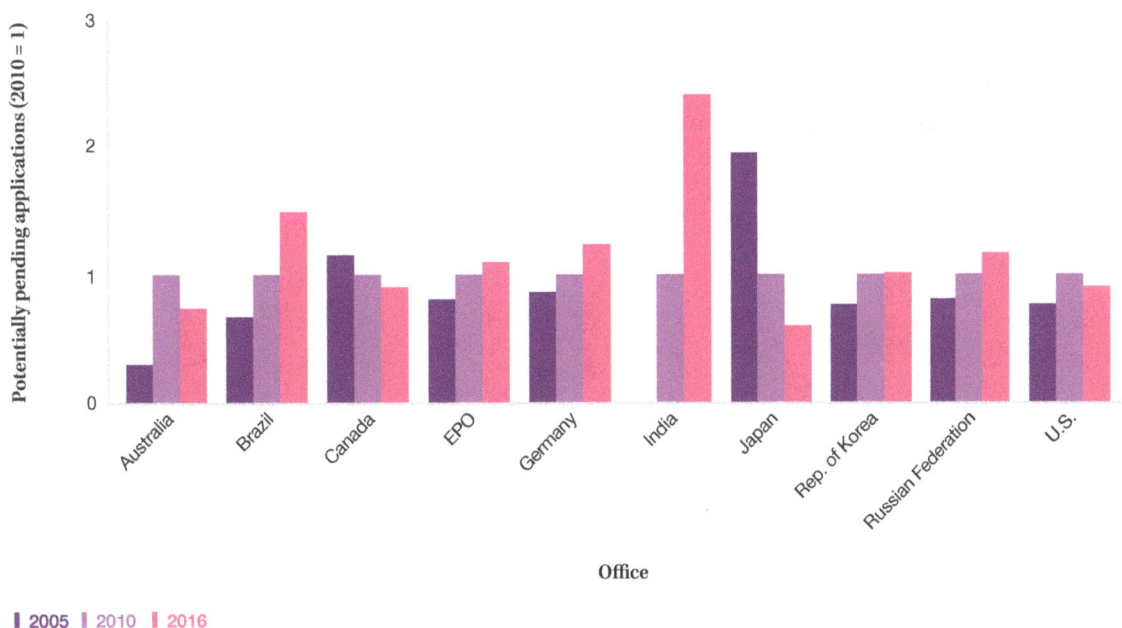

Office

■ 2005 ■ 2010 ■ 2016

Note: Data for Brazil includes both patent and utility models applications.

Source: WIPO Statistics Database, September 2017.

Potentially pending applications

Potentially pending applications include all patent applications, at any stage in the process, awaiting a final decision by a patent office, including those applications for which applicants have not filed a request for examination (where applicable). The concept of "potentially" pending applications is used rather than pending applications because, in many offices, the request for examination is filed at a later date than the application. Although the application is already at the office, it cannot start the examination process until the request for examination is filed. It is preferable to use the concept "potentially" pending applications to cover such cases.

To deal with the growing number of incoming applications and pending applications, offices need to have adequate examination capacity.[2] Figure S3 presents the trend in patent filings and the number of patent examiners at selected offices. It shows that the evolution of examination capacity – measured by number of examiners – at various offices generally has kept pace with the evolution of patent applications. For example, at the EPO, the Republic of Korea and the Russian Federation, patent applications and the number of examiners have grown at a similar rate, while at other reported offices the number of examiners has increased faster than patent filings.

Patent examiners

Data on the number of patent examiners consider those working full time and do not take into account other possible workforces provided by outsourcing companies and freelancers. However, examination work undertaken by affiliated institutions is included. At some offices, such as those of Japan and the Republic of Korea, patent examiners also process utility model applications, while in the U.S. patent examiners also deal with plant variety applications. These offices cannot provide breakdowns between patent examination and utility model/plant variety examination. The number of patent examiners at the office of Australia includes hearing staff, who account for a small proportion of the total staff.

Figure S3
Trends in the number of patent applications filed and the number of patent examiners for selected offices

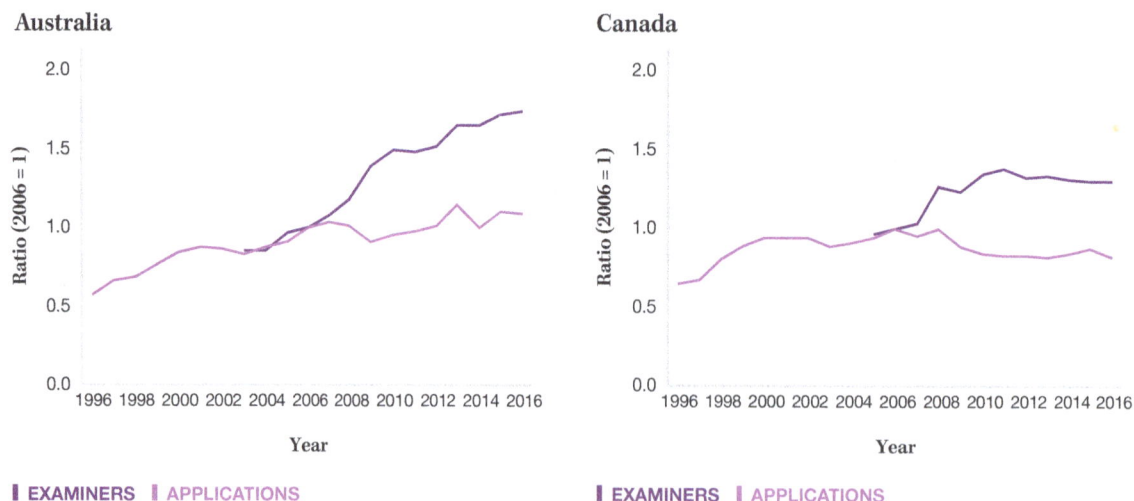

Australia

EXAMINERS   APPLICATIONS

Canada

EXAMINERS   APPLICATIONS

European Patent Office

Ratio (2006 = 1)

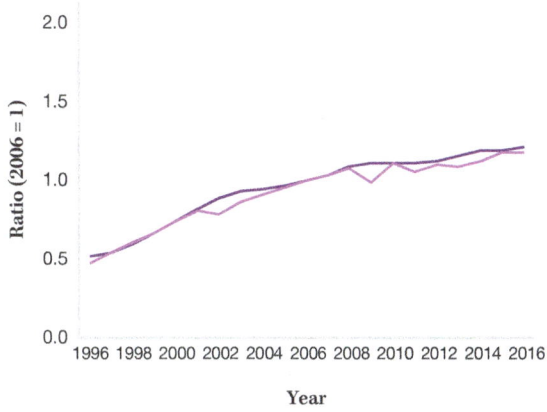

EXAMINERS **APPLICATIONS**

Finland

Ratio (2006 = 1)

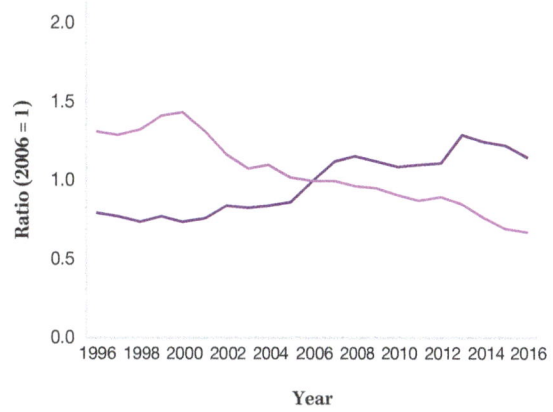

EXAMINERS **APPLICATIONS**

India

Ratio (2006 = 1)

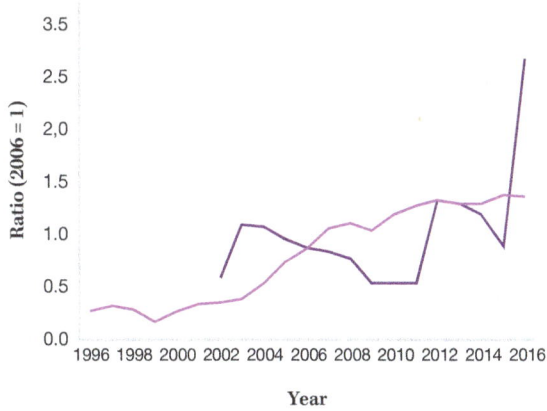

EXAMINERS **APPLICATIONS**

Japan

Ratio (2006 = 1)

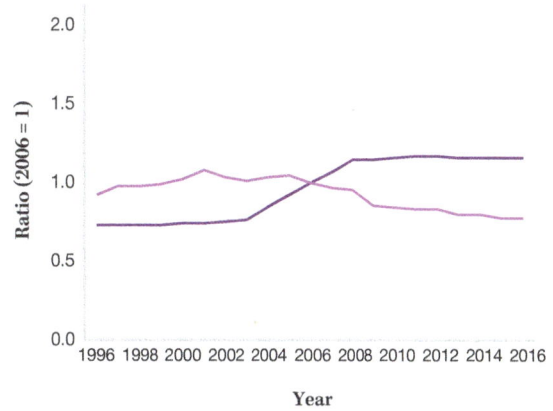

EXAMINERS **APPLICATIONS**

Philippines

Ratio (2006 = 1)

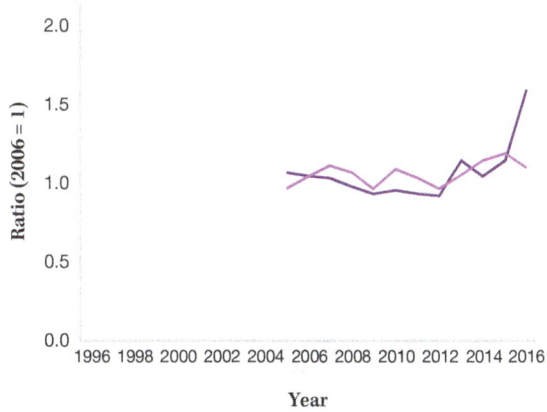

EXAMINERS **APPLICATIONS**

Republic of Korea

Ratio (2006 = 1)

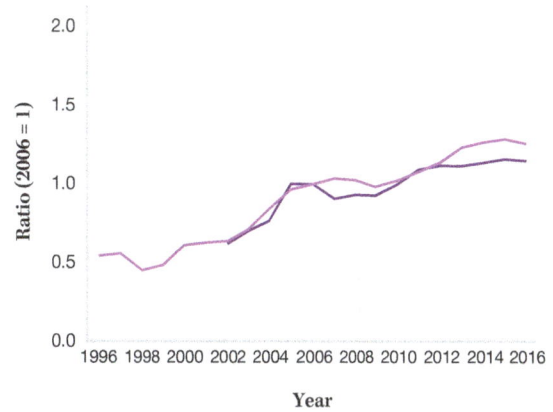

EXAMINERS **APPLICATIONS**

SPECIAL SECTION

Russian Federation

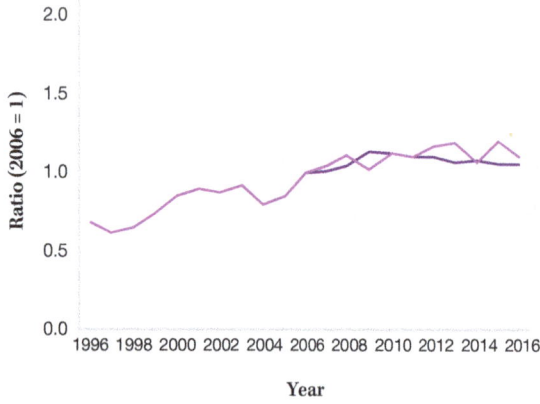

EXAMINERS **APPLICATIONS**

Spain

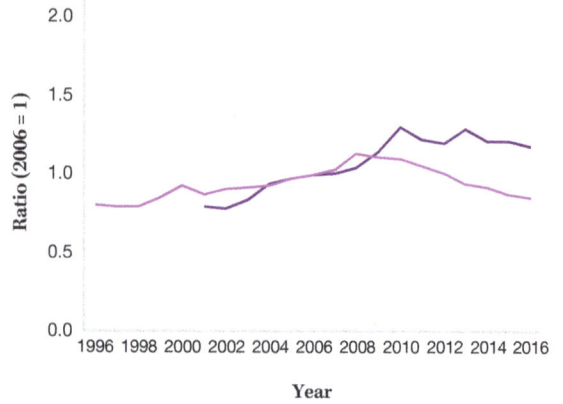

EXAMINERS **APPLICATIONS**

U.K.

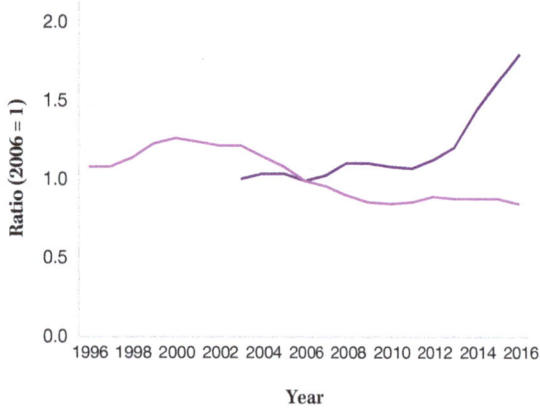

EXAMINERS **APPLICATIONS**

U.S.

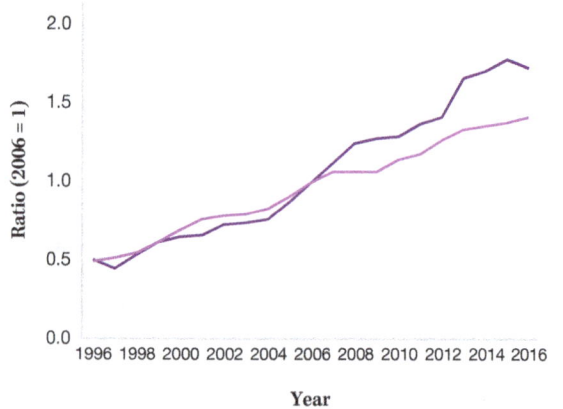

EXAMINERS **APPLICATIONS**

Note: The selection of offices is based on patent examiner data availability. Patent examiner data for India refer to head count rather than full-time equivalents.

Source: WIPO Statistics Database, September 2017

Figure S4 shows the average number of patent filings per examiner for selected offices.[3] Although the examination phase of an application usually occurs sometime after it has been filed, the average number of filings per examiner gives an indication of the examination capacity of offices relative to their numbers of incoming patent applications.

Thirteen of these 14 offices had fewer applications per examiner in 2016 than in 2005. For example, in the U.K. the average number of applications per examiner declined from 139 in 2005 to 63 in 2016. However, Japan had the largest drop in the number of applications per examiner, due mainly to a decrease in the number of patent applications filed in Japan. There was no change in the applications-per-examiner ratios

for Denmark and the EPO. The Republic of Korea saw a gradual increase in applications per examiner.

Japan and the Republic of Korea had the highest average applications per examiner among the selected offices. However, it is difficult to draw any conclusions from this, as the content of applications filed in Japan, the Republic of Korea and other offices might differ. For example, the average number of claims per application, the average number of pages per application and the complexity of application can vary across offices. In addition, an office's capacity to handle incoming applications depends on factors other than the number of examiners, such as outsourcing prior art searches, cooperation among offices and so on.

Figure S4
Average number of filings per examiner for selected patent offices

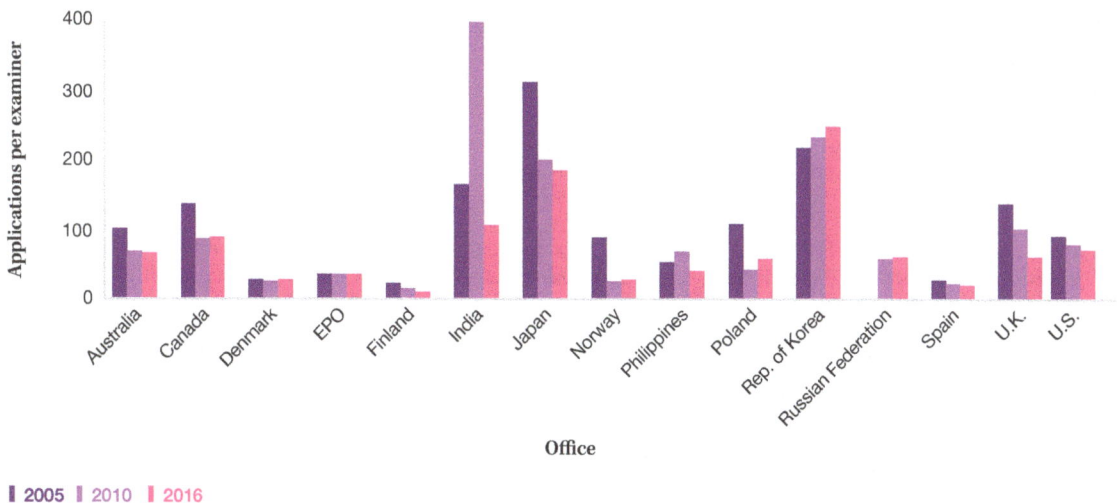

■ 2005 ■ 2010 ■ 2016

Note: Offices were selected based on the availability of patent examiner data. Patent examiner data for India refer to head count rather than full-time equivalents.

Source: WIPO Statistics Database, September 2017.

Pendency time

Measuring the time between the request for examination and the first office action, and between the request for examination and the final decision, provides an indication of the application processing delay. A long delay in processing applications at any given office does not necessarily imply that the office is processing applications too slowly. Among other factors, applicants can slow down the processing of applications at offices. For example, at the EPO applicants can amend their applications when they are undergoing search and examination. Similarly, at the United States Patent and Trademark Office (USPTO) applicants have many ways to delay prosecution from first action to final disposition. Paying for extensions of time to reply and filing requests for continued examination are the most often-used methods.

Figure S5 shows the average number of months that elapsed from the request for examination – or, where appropriate, patent filing – to the first action and the final decision for selected offices in 2016.

Pendency time for final decision was shortest in the Islamic Republic of Iran (9 months), Spain (11.2), Ukraine (13.5), Japan (15) and the Republic of Korea (16.2). China (22), the U.S. (22.6) and the EPO (23.3) all took roughly the same time on average to reach final decisions. The average time for final decision exceeded 50 months in Brazil (95.4), India (84), the Czech Republic (53) and Viet Nam (51.5).

Average pendency time for first office action was shortest at the offices of New Zealand (1.3 months), Mexico (3) and the Islamic Republic of Iran (4). In contrast, Brazil (84 months) and India (72 months) had the longest pendency times for first action.

Average pendency times for final office decision were longest in Brazil and India. However, the period between first office action and final decision at those offices was relatively short – 11.4 months in Brazil and 12 months in India. The average time between first office action and final decision was particularly short in Ukraine (3.1 months), the Islamic Republic of Iran (5) and Spain (5.4).

Pendency time

Pendency time for the first office action is calculated as the average time (months) from request for examination to the first office action. Where applicants are not required to request examination, it is calculated from the filing date to the date of first office action.

Pendency time for the final office decision is calculated as the average time (months) from request for examination to final decision. Where applicants are not required to request examination, it is calculated from the filing date to the date of examination decision.

Calculations of pendency time by offices can differ due to marked differences in their procedures. Therefore, caution should be exercised when comparing data across offices. Ideally, one should focus on the evolution of pendency time at a specific office.

Figure S5

Average pendency times for first office action and final decision at selected offices, 2016

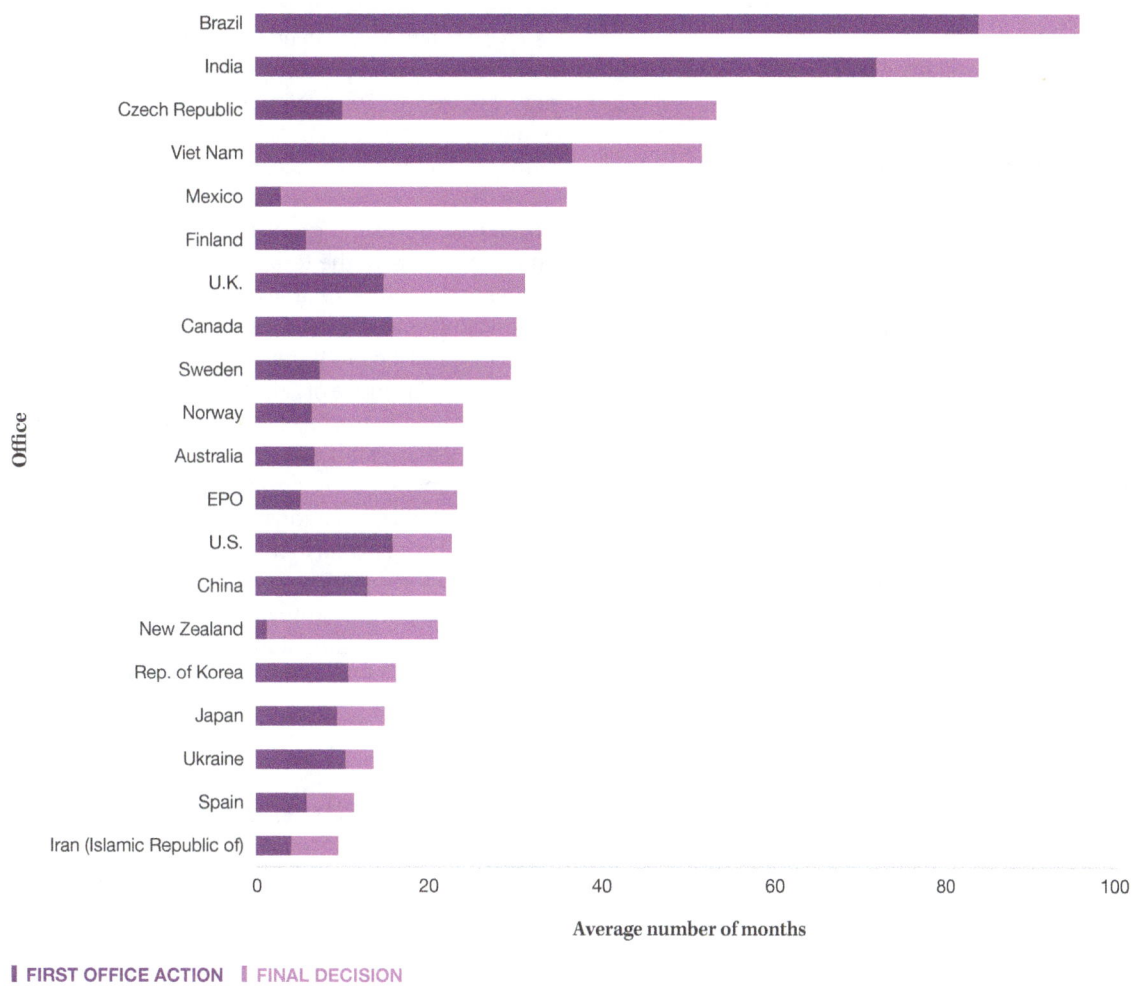

Average number of months

Office

FIRST OFFICE ACTION   **FINAL DECISION**

Source: WIPO Statistics Database, September 2017.

Figure S6 presents the changes in pendency times between 2011 and 2016 for selected offices, chosen based on data availability. On both measures, first office action and final decision, pendency time improved for all reported offices except China, where pendency time for the first office action increased marginally.

Japan saw the sharpest reduction in first office action pendency time, from 25.9 months in 2011 to 9.5 months in 2016. Canada and the U.S. also shortened their first office action pendency times considerably over the same period.

All the selected offices saw their final decision pendency times decrease, with New Zealand reporting the biggest fall. Canada, Japan and the U.S. also saw vast improvements over the same period.

Examination outcomes

The number of patents granted worldwide has increased rapidly during the past few years. In 2016, an estimated 1.35 million patents were granted worldwide, up 8.9% on 2015. The increase in the number of granted patents has generated some discussion in academic circles – mostly in the U.S. – on whether too many patents are being granted by offices.[4] Analyzing

patent grant rates over time would shed some light on this topic. However, calculating grant rates is a challenge because offices did not provide information on applications that are withdrawn, abandoned or rejected before publication. In addition, processing applications takes time – between three and five years on average, and even longer for filings in some specific fields of technology.[5] Furthermore, rejected patents can enter the system via continuation-in-parts or divisional application, making it hard to define the numerator and denominator precisely.

An alternative to the grant rate could be to focus on the outcome of the total number of applications processed by offices within a given year. The examination of a patent usually results in it being either granted, rejected, withdrawn or abandoned. Some offices, such as those of Australia and Canada, rarely reject patents. In the case of the office of Australia, only the hearing staff can reject applications. If the patent examiner has not granted the application by the end of the examination phase, the applicant can decide to proceed further, for example through a continuation-in-part. The office of Canada does not reject applications; a large proportion of abandoned files have a suspended status and, as a result, are still considered to be at the examination stage.

Figure S6
Average pendency times for first office action and final decision at selected offices, 2011 and 2016

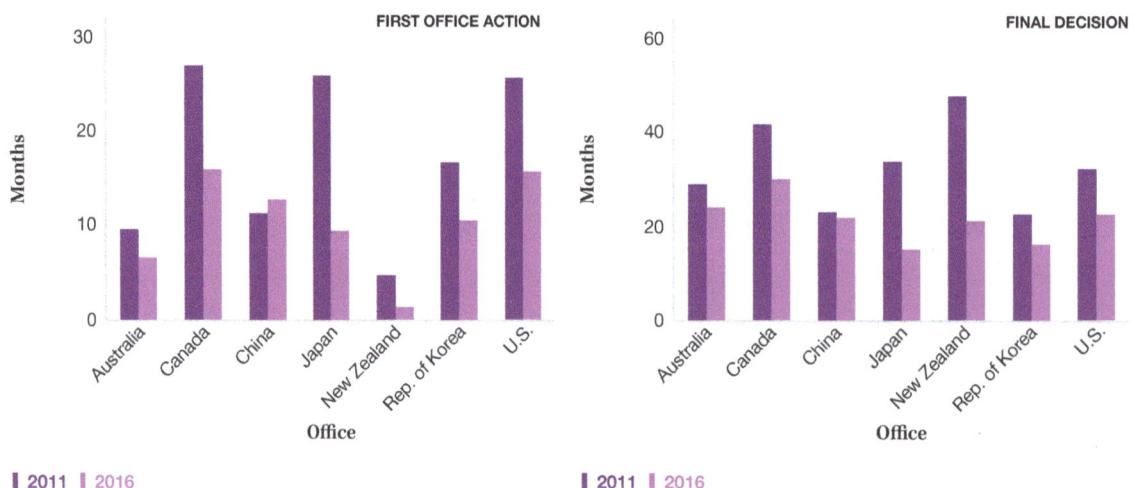

FIRST OFFICE ACTION

FINAL DECISION

Office

Office

■ 2011 ■ 2016

■ 2011 ■ 2016

Note: Offices were selected based on 2011 and 2016 data availability.

Source: WIPO Statistics Database, September 2017.

Figure S7 shows the distribution of examination outcomes for selected offices. The shares of applications granted should not be interpreted as grant rates, as they are based on the examination date rather than the date the application was filed. The number of grants in a given year relates to applications filed in previous years.

More than three-quarters of applications examined in 2016 resulted in patents being granted at the offices of Indonesia (81%), Spain (81%), the Russian Federation (79%) and Japan (75%). Among the 20 selected offices, seven granted patents for fewer than half of applications processed in 2016. The offices of Thailand (10%), Brazil (19%) and India (28%) had low proportions of patents granted for applications processed, primarily due to high proportions of withdrawn or abandoned applications. Around three-fifths of all applications processed by the office of the

Republic of Korea resulted in patents, while for the U.S. the ratio was just under a third. Data for China and the EPO are not available.

The shares of rejected applications were the highest in the U.S. (52%), Saudi Arabia (49%) and the Republic of Korea (38%). Several other offices had relatively high shares of rejected applications, including those of Colombia (34%), Germany (23%) and the Japan Patent Office (JPO); (23%). The share of processed applications that were rejected was low in Australia, Indonesia, Mexico and Norway. This can be explained in part by the high share of withdrawn/abandoned applications, where applicants decided to withdraw applications before they could be rejected. However, if an examiner does not grant a patent for an application, in many offices it is possible for applicants to amend their application and continue with the examination process (for example, through a continuation-in-part, divisional application, etc.).

Figure S7
Distribution of patent examination outcomes for selected offices, 2016

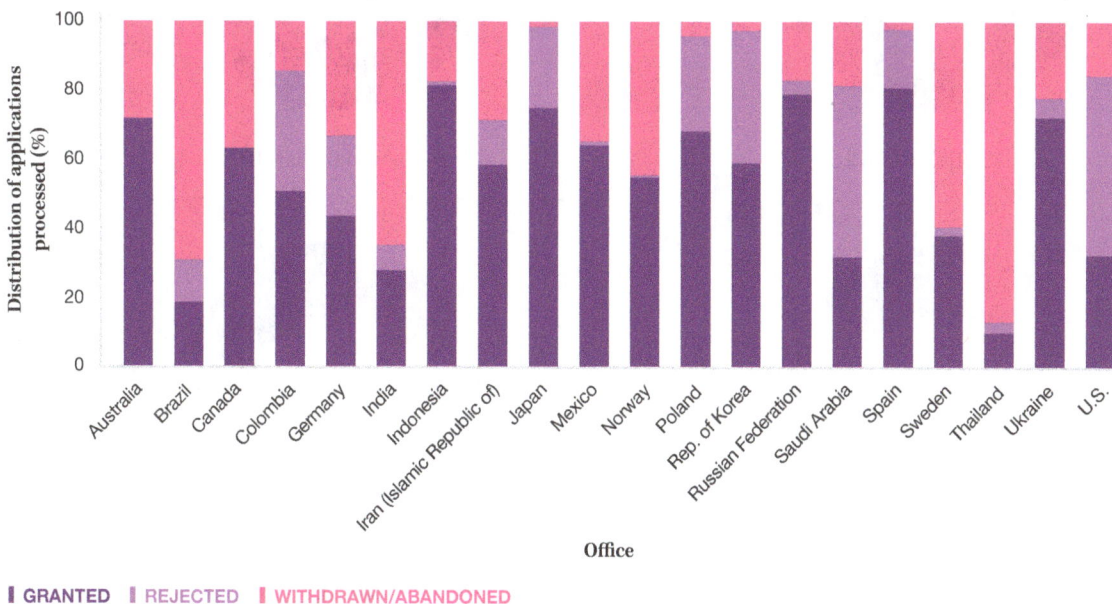

I GRANTED   **I** REJECTED   **I** WITHDRAWN/ABANDONED

Source: WIPO Statistics Database, September 2017.

Procedural differences limit cross-country comparison. Analyzing the distribution of examination outcomes at a given office over time is more meaningful. Figure S8 shows the distribution of examination outcomes for two intervals (2010-12 and 2014-16). Data going back to 2010 are available for only a small number of offices, so it is not possible to analyze longer time periods.

The share of the total number of processed applications granted increased in seven of the eight offices presented between 2010-12 and 2014-16. In Japan, the grant ratio increased from 59% to 71% (12 percentage points), and increased by 9 percentage points in Canada. Brazil saw an increase of 5.6 percentage points. Australia and the U.S. both saw an increase of around 4 percentage points, while for Germany and the Russian Federation the increase was only 1.7 and 1.2 percentage points respectively. The Republic of Korea is the only office where the grant ratio declined by 1.9 percentage points from 65% in 2010-12 to 63.1% in 2014-16.

Figure S8
Distribution of patent examination outcomes for selected offices

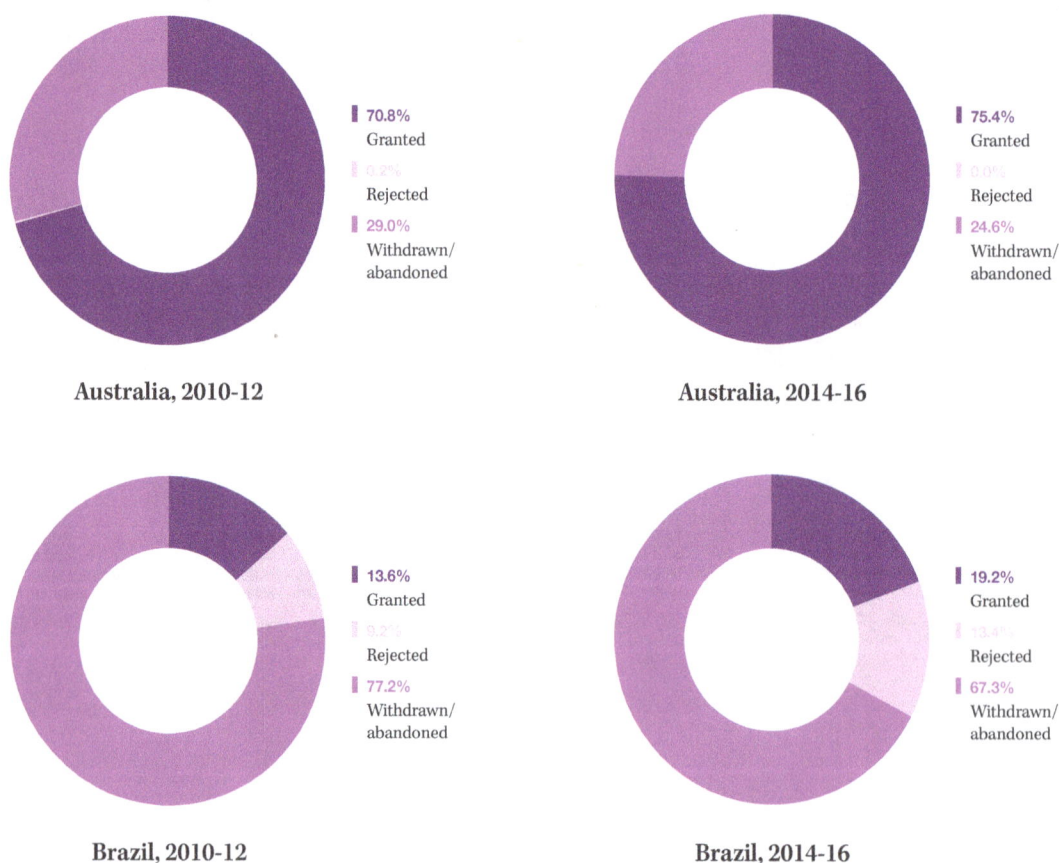

70.8%
Granted

0.2%
Rejected

29.0%
Withdrawn/
abandoned

Australia, 2010-12

75.4%
Granted

0.0%
Rejected

24.6%
Withdrawn/
abandoned

Australia, 2014-16

13.6%
Granted

9.2%
Rejected

77.2%
Withdrawn/
abandoned

Brazil, 2010-12

19.2%
Granted

13.6%
Rejected

67.3%
Withdrawn/
abandoned

Brazil, 2014-16

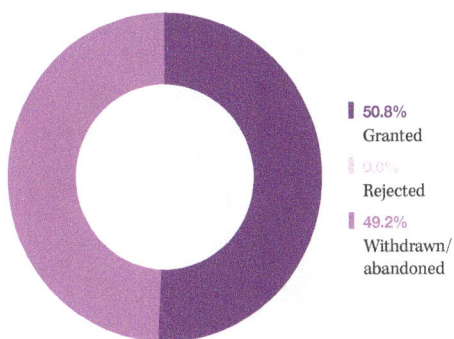

50.8%	Granted
0.0%	Rejected
49.2%	Withdrawn/ abandoned

Canada, 2010-12

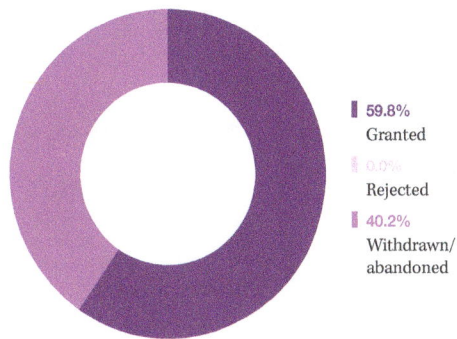

59.8%	Granted
0.0%	Rejected
40.2%	Withdrawn/ abandoned

Canada, 2014-16

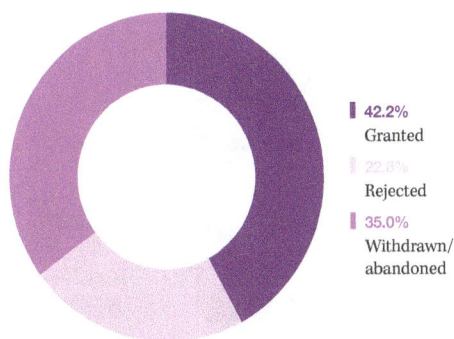

42.2%	Granted
22.8%	Rejected
35.0%	Withdrawn/ abandoned

Germany, 2010-12

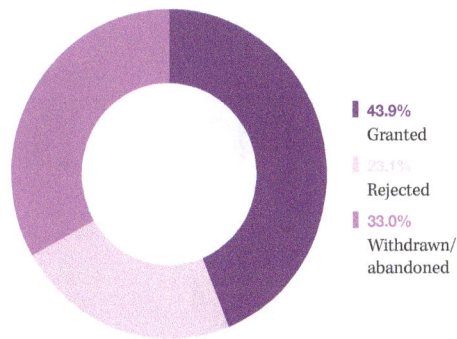

43.9%	Granted
23.1%	Rejected
33.0%	Withdrawn/ abandoned

Germany, 2014-16

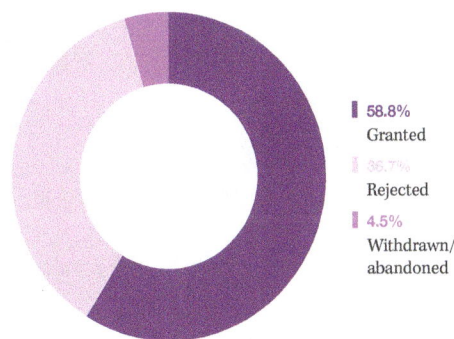

58.8%	Granted
36.7%	Rejected
4.5%	Withdrawn/ abandoned

Japan, 2010-12

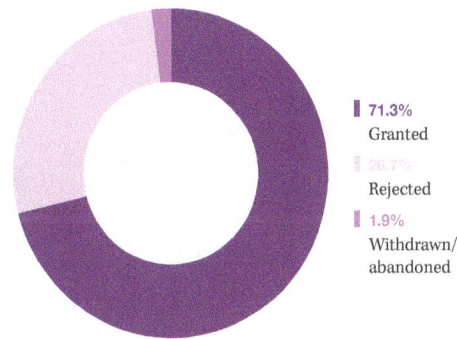

71.3%	Granted
26.7%	Rejected
1.9%	Withdrawn/ abandoned

Japan, 2014-16

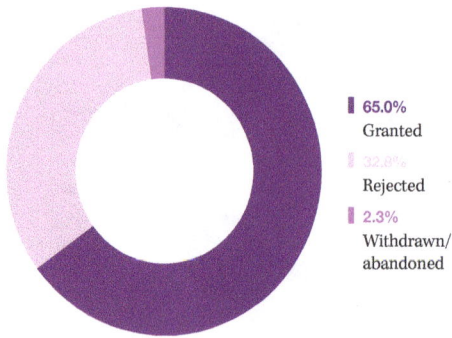

65.0%
Granted

32.8%
Rejected

2.3%
Withdrawn/
abandoned

Republic of Korea, 2010-12

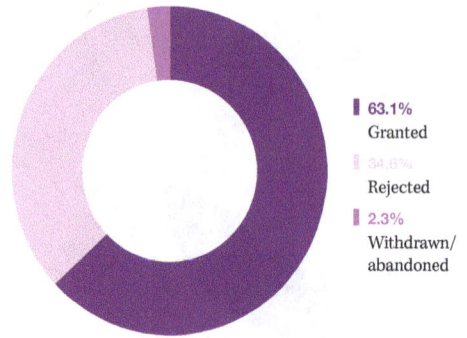

63.1%
Granted

34.6%
Rejected

2.3%
Withdrawn/
abandoned

Republic of Korea, 2014-16

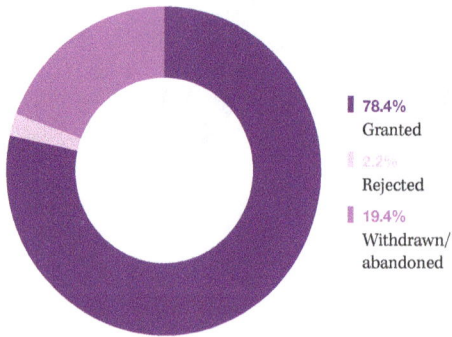

78.4%
Granted

2.2%
Rejected

19.4%
Withdrawn/
abandoned

Russian Federation, 2010-12

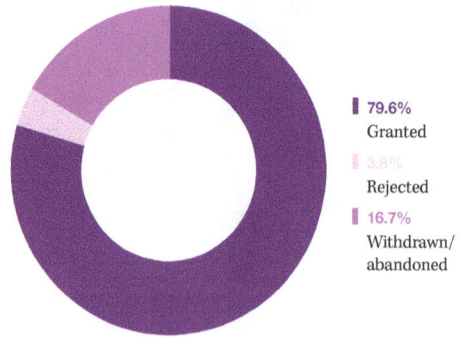

79.6%
Granted

3.8%
Rejected

16.7%
Withdrawn/
abandoned

Russian Federation, 2014-16

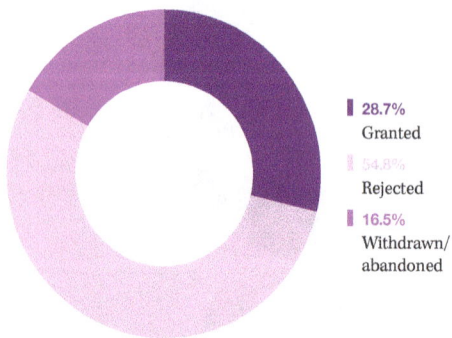

28.7%
Granted

54.8%
Rejected

16.5%
Withdrawn/
abandoned

U.S., 2010-12

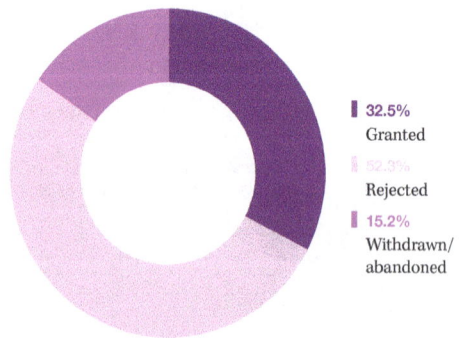

32.5%
Granted

52.3%
Rejected

15.2%
Withdrawn/
abandoned

U.S., 2014-16

Source: WIPO Statistics Database, September 2017.

Conclusions

The workload of patent offices as measured by the number of incoming patent applications has increased over time, but so has their examination capacity to process those applications. As documented in this section, the available data show there has been no significant increase in application-to-examiner ratios; in fact, for a number of offices, growth in numbers of examiners has outstripped the increase in applications.

Operational data on patent offices can contribute to evidence-based decision-making. However, procedures vary across offices and comparison should only be made among offices with similar procedures or, preferably, for a particular office over time.

WIPO will continue to collect these data to enable better monitoring of trends over time, and will expand the range of statistical indicators on operational dimensions.

WIPO is grateful to all offices that have shared their data. We encourage offices unable to share such data at present to make efforts to share them in the future.

Annex S1
Patent procedures at the world's five largest IP offices (the IP5)

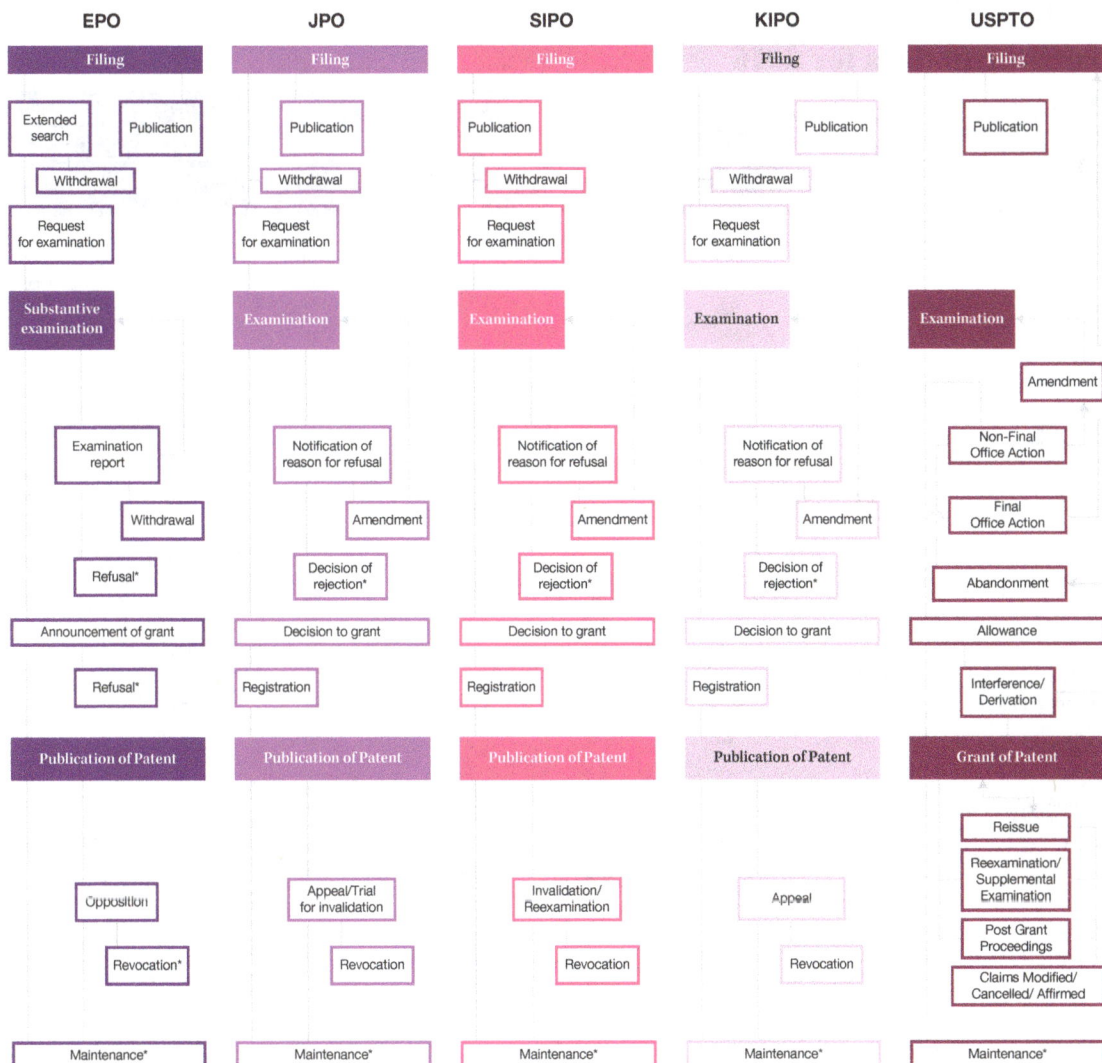

* Decision may be appealed.

Source: *IP5 Statistics Report*, 2015 edition.

Annex S2
Procedural data for 2016

WIPO added a new questionnaire to its annual IP statistics survey to compile the following data from offices across the world:

A. Number of patent examination decisions in the given year broken down by applications which are: granted, rejected, and withdrawn or abandoned.

B. Number of patent examiners (full-time equivalent, FTE), including persons conducting patent examination in affiliated institutions.

C. Average years of experience of examiners (number of years from recruitment including training period).

D. Average time (months) from the request for examination to the first office action (where applicants are not required to request examination, from the filing date to the date of first office action).

E. Average time (months) from the request for examination to the final decision (where applicants are not required to request examination, from the filing date to the date of examination decision).

The following offices provided data for 2016. In addition, several offices provided data going back to 2010.

Table S1
Procedural data for 2016

Office	Total applications processed	Granted	Rejected	Withdrawn or abandoned	Numbers of examiners (FTE)	First office action (months)	Final office decision (months)
Albania	..	..	..	..	..	3.0	18.0
Armenia	113	86	13	14	8	1.5	3.4
Australia	33,173	23,744	10	9,419	413	6.7	24.0
Bangladesh	206	106	10	90	5	11.0	18.0
Belarus	..	1,064	305	..	22	..	..
Bolivia (Plurinational State of)	163	86	72	5	..	..	..
Bosnia and Herzegovina	..	..	..	..	7	2.0	30.0
Brazil	22,401	4,228	2,731	15,442	201	84.0	95.4
Canada	41,651	26,424	..	15,227	386	16.0	30.2
China	..	404,208	..	..	..	12.9	22.0
China, Macao SAR	..	57	34	..	..	5.1	11.8
Colombia	1,861	948	640	273	44	..	..
Costa Rica	751	67	120	564	19	54.0	60.0
Cuba	194	93	6	95	11	32.0	38.0
Czech Republic	1,615	781	345	489	32	10.0	53.0
Denmark	1,760	409	1	1,350	62	6.0	32.0
Dominican Republic	120	20	69	31	10	12.0	26.0
Estonia	58	31	2	25	9	4.6	23.8
European Patent Office	..	95,940	5,464	..	4,310	5.1	23.3
Finland	1,824	815	13	996	111	6.0	33.0
Germany	35,759	15,651	8,228	11,880	837	..	..
Honduras	248	133	25	90	3	1.0	30.0
Hungary	1,094	271	61	762	47	6.0	19.7
Iceland	..	..	..	..	..	1.0	5.0

Office	Total applications processed	Granted	Rejected	Withdrawn or abandoned	Numbers of examiners (FTE)	First office action (months)	Final office decision (months)
India	29,574	8,248	2,144	19,182	416	72.0	84.0
Indonesia	4,393	3,578	41	774	..	..	..
Iran (Islamic Republic of)	5,583	3,268	722	1,593	24	4.0	9.0
Japan	254,678	191,032	58,638	5,008	1,702	9.5	15.0
Jordan	485	120	307	58	6	12.0	18.0
Kazakhstan	..	1,011	12	..	41	2.0	..
Kenya	..	26	..	96	10	..	..
Latvia	84	68	12	4	6	..	..
Lithuania	132	112	11	9	5	1.0	18.0
Madagascar	28	19	4	5	2	7.0	12.0
Mexico	14,039	9,026	128	4,885	122	3.0	36.0
Monaco	..	9	..	1	2	3.0	10.0
Mongolia	194	157	32	5	3	7.0	9.0
Montenegro	..	..	..	..	2	1.0	18.0
Morocco	441	306	93	42	18	7.0	..
New Zealand	..	3,881	..	1,981	34	1.3	21.1
Norway	4,585	2,526	16	2,043	73	6.5	24.0
Peru	..	..	..	..	26	30.3	34.5
Philippines	..	..	..	..	82	..	..
Poland	4,575	3,129	1,250	196	75	..	39.0
Portugal	..	119	178	..	17	22.2	30.3
Republic of Korea	172,053	101,678	66,055	4,320	836	10.6	16.2
Republic of Moldova	111	63	24	24	16	4.0	14.0
Romania	955	355	337	263	41	36.0	50.0
Russian Federation	43,303	34,283	1,613	7,407	666	..	10.3
Saudi Arabia	1,858	595	915	348	55	12.5	22.0
Singapore	..	..	..	..	102	..	..
Slovakia	306	122	69	115	25	..	..
Spain	2,849	2,308	480	61	140	5.9	11.2
Sri Lanka	409	123	272	14	9	0.5	24.0
Sudan	296	164	12	120	16	..	..
Sweden	2,253	866	50	1,337	114	7.3	29.4
Thailand	17,865	1,838	583	15,444	42	..	..
Ukraine	3,929	2,843	215	871	119	10.4	13.5
United Kingdom	9,540	5,602	..	3,938	349	15.0	31.0
United States of America	932,786	303,049	484,479	145,258	8,279	15.9	22.6
Uzbekistan	452	182	9	261	7	..	..
Viet Nam	..	..	..	..	56	36.5	51.5

Note: Patent examiner data for India refer to head count rather than full-time equivalents.

Grant data might slightly differ to grant data reported elsewhere in this report due to different dates of extraction.

Source: WIPO Statistics Database, September 2017.

Country notes

Australia

The number of examiners includes hearing staff.

Canada

In Canada, the abandon status is a suspension status only. It means that a fee or a response to a report from the client is outstanding and the deadline to pay the fee or respond to a letter has passed. A large proportion of abandoned files are caused by an agent/client not answering an examiner's report in time. A large proportion of abandoned files are actually still at the examination stage. Other than an allowance/grant of a patent, the patent office does not issue a final decision as "rejection." Applicants are informed what they must do/answer in order for their application to be allowed. If the applicant cannot answer this question, they are regarded as having abandoned the application.

European Patent Office

The first office action data include all kinds of searches done at the EPO, including searches on behalf of national offices. Final decision numbers are calculated as the time to decision to grant for patents for which the decision to grant was made in the given year. This definition was adopted in the 2016, which is why data are only available for 2015 and 2016.

Japan

The number of examiners includes both patent and utility model examiners. Examiners are responsible for processing both patent and utility model applications.

Republic of Korea

The number of examiners includes both patent and utility model examiners. Examiners are responsible for processing both patent and utility model applications.

U.S.

The rejected applications are applications with a non-final or final rejection that was neither patented nor abandoned. Data on the number of examiners and the time for patent examination include both patent and plant variety applications. However, the number of plant variety applications is low compared with patents – around 1,100 plant applications per year. So the number of examiners for the plant variety area is very small compared to the total number of examiners, and the impact on the time for patent examination is insignificant given the predominance of patent applications.

Patents

Highlights

More than 3 million patent applications were filed worldwide in 2016 – a record number

For the first time, more than 3 million patent applications were filed worldwide in a single year, up 8.3% from 2015 (figure 1). Driving such strong growth was an exceptional number of filings in China, which received about 236,600 or 98% of the additional filings. The next largest contributor was the United States of America (U.S.) with around 16,200 additional filings. Following a modest increase of 4.5% in 2014, the growth rate picked up in both 2015 (+7.7%) and 2016 (+8.3%), aligning with the annual growth rates of between 8% and 9% observed between 2011 and 2013. But when patent applications in China are excluded, applications filed in the rest of the world grew by only 0.2% in 2016.

China received more applications than the combined total for the EPO, Japan, the Republic of Korea and the U.S.

The State Intellectual Property Office of the People's Republic of China (SIPO) received 1.3 million patent applications in 2016 – more than the combined total for the United States Patent and Trademark Office (USPTO; 605,571), the Japan Patent Office (JPO; 318,381), the Korean Intellectual Property Office (KIPO; 208,830) and the European Patent Office (EPO; 159,358). Together, these top five offices accounted for 84% of the world total in 2016, which is nine percentage points higher than their combined share 10 years earlier. The list of top 10 offices in 2016 is almost the same as for 2015, except that Brazil was replaced by Australia as the tenth highest ranked office in 2016 (figure 2). Brazil moved down one position as a result of a 7.3% annual decline in filings.

Figure 1
Patent applications worldwide

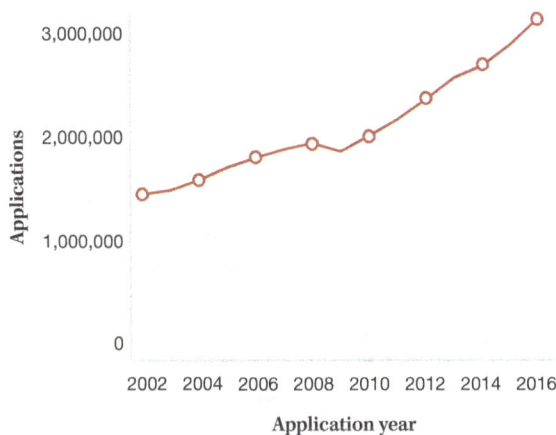

Source: Standard figure A1.

Figure 2
Patent applications at the top 10 offices, 2016

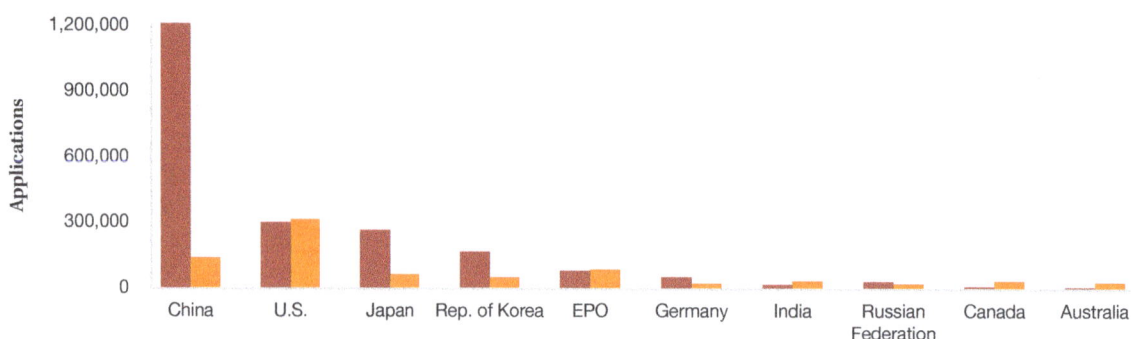

▌RESIDENT ▌NON-RESIDENT

Source: Standard figure A8.

Of the top 20 patent offices, 12 were located in high-income countries, six in upper middle-income countries and two in lower middle-income countries. In terms of geographical distribution, eight offices were located in Asia, six in Europe, two in North America, two in Latin America and the Caribbean (LAC), and one each in Africa and Oceania.

Eight of the top 20 offices received more applications in 2016 than in 2015, while 12 received fewer. South Africa (+29.5%), China (+21.5%) and China Hong Kong (SAR; +15.4%) all exhibited double-digit growth. The strong growth in filings in China Hong Kong (SAR) and South Africa followed small declines at those offices the previous year, while China has had double-digit growth each year since 2010. The increases in applications filed in China and South Africa were both driven mainly by growth in resident applications, whereas growth in China Hong Kong (SAR) came primarily from an increase in non-resident applications. Another office that showed notable growth in 2016 was that of the Islamic Republic of Iran (+9.5%).

Of the 12 offices among the top 20 that received fewer applications in 2016 than in 2015, the Russian Federation (-8.6%), Brazil (-7.3%), Indonesia (-6.7%), and Canada (-6%) reported the most substantial declines. Applications in Brazil fell for a third consecutive year. Following strong growth in applications received in 2015, Canada, Indonesia and the Russian Federation all saw decreases in 2016. A decline in resident applications was the primary reason for the decrease in total applications for the Russian Federation, whereas a decline in non-resident applications was the main driver for Canada and Brazil.

Among the top five offices, the JPO (-0.1%) saw a small drop in applications, continuing a trend that started in 2006 and mainly reflects a persistent fall in resident applications. The number of resident applications filed at the JPO has declined from around 347,000 in 2006 to around 260,200 in 2016. Following two consecutive years of growth, the EPO's filings declined by 0.4% in 2016 due to a drop in non-resident applications. KIPO has enjoyed solid growth in applications received each year since 2010, but filings there declined by 2.4% in 2016 primarily due to a decline in resident applications. SIPO, however, continues to experience very strong growth in applications received and retains top spot. The USPTO has seen seven consecutive years of growth.

Among offices of low- and middle-income countries, Morocco (+27.6%), the Republic of Moldova (+25%), Sri Lanka (+19.1%) and Turkey (+17.2%) recorded particularly rapid growth in 2016. Growth in resident applications was the main driver of total growth in the Republic of Moldova, Sri Lanka and Turkey, while non-resident applications were the main driver in

Morocco. The three regional offices – the African Intellectual Property Organization (OAPI), the African Regional Intellectual Property Organization (ARIPO) and the Eurasian Patent Organization (EAPO) – have seen applications fall for two successive years, mainly due to a drop in resident applications. At most offices of low- and middle-income countries, the bulk of applications is filed by non-residents. As a result, overall increases or decreases in applications received by these offices are determined mainly by the filing behavior of non-resident applicants.

Asia became the first region to receive 2 million applications in a single year

Offices located in Asia received just over 2 million applications in 2016, representing a 13% increase on 2015. Asia's share of all applications filed worldwide increased from 49.7% in 2006 to 64.6% in 2016, primarily driven by strong growth in filings in China (figure 3), which accounted for around two-thirds of all applications filed in the region. Excluding China, the share of the rest of Asia in the world total actually decreased from around 37.9% to 21.8% over the same period, mainly due to a decrease in applications filed in Japan.

Offices in North America accounted for one-fifth of the 2016 world total, while those in Europe accounted for just over one-tenth. The combined share for Africa, Latin America and the Caribbean (LAC) and Oceania was 3.6%. The shares of all world regions except Asia have gradually declined over the past decade due to the rapid growth in applications filed in China.

Offices of high-income countries received almost half of all applications filed worldwide in 2016 – considerably lower than their 78.3% share in 2006 – while the share for offices of upper middle-income countries rose from 18.3% in 2006 to 47.6% in 2016 (figure 4). This shift in distribution of applications toward the upper middle-income group is largely explained by the strong growth in filings in China and the decline in Japan. Applications filed in China increased from just over 210,000 in 2006 to around 1.3 million in 2016, whereas those filed in Japan decreased from around 408,000 to around 318,000 over the same period. China accounted for 90% of the upper middle-income group total in 2016; excluding China, the remaining upper middle-income countries received just 4.8% of total worldwide filings.

The combined share of the low- and lower middle-income groups was 2.8% in 2016, which is slightly below the 3.4% observed in 2006. However, the number of applications received by offices of these two income groups rose from 61,200 to 86,000 during the same period.

Figure 3
Patent applications by region

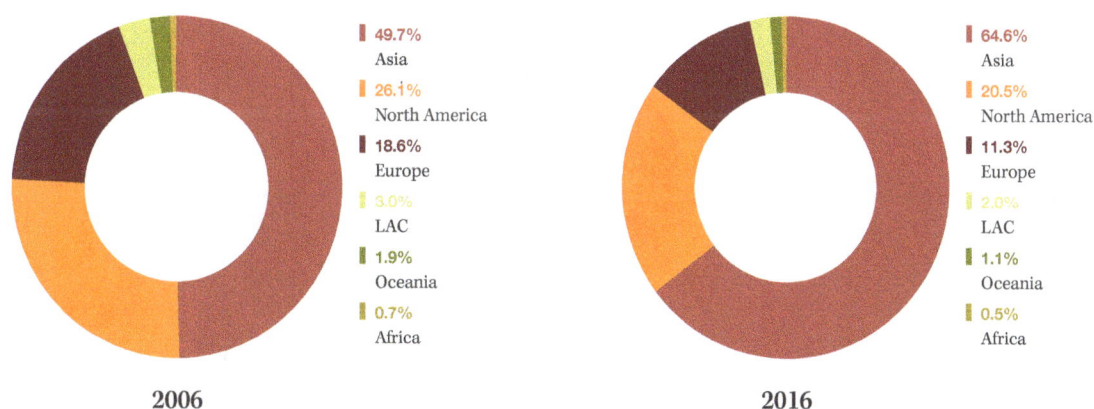

2006

49.7%	Asia
26.1%	North America
18.6%	Europe
3.0%	LAC
1.9%	Oceania
0.7%	Africa

2016

64.6%	Asia
20.5%	North America
11.3%	Europe
2.0%	LAC
1.1%	Oceania
0.5%	Africa

Source: Standard figure A6.

Figure 4
Patent applications by income group

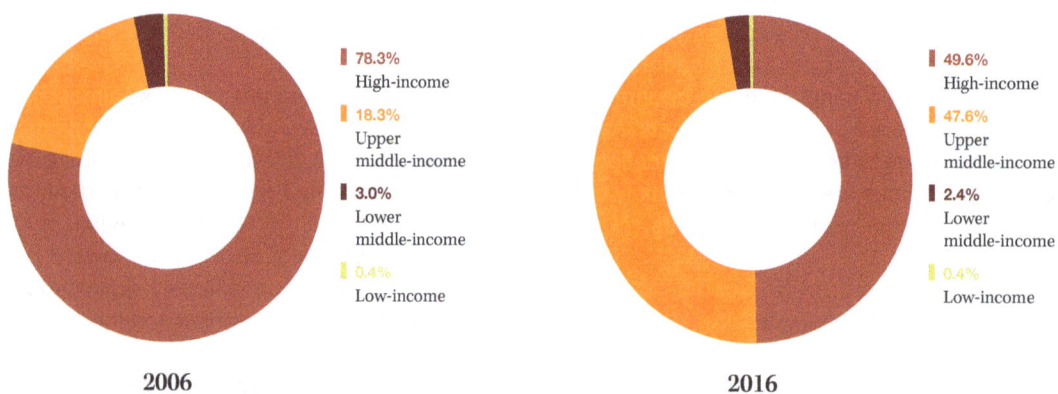

2006

- **78.3%** High-income
- **18.3%** Upper middle-income
- **3.0%** Lower middle-income
- **0.4%** Low-income

2016

- **49.6%** High-income
- **47.6%** Upper middle-income
- **2.4%** Lower middle-income
- **0.4%** Low-income

Source: Standard figure A5.

Patent filings since 1883

From 1883 to 1963, the patent office of the U.S. was the leading office for world filings. Application numbers in Japan and the U.S. were stable until the early 1970s, when Japan began to see rapid growth, a pattern also observed for the U.S. from the 1980s onward. Among the top five offices, Japan surpassed the U.S. in 1968 and maintained the top position until 2005. Since the early 2000s, however, the number of applications filed in Japan has trended downward. Both the EPO and the Republic of Korea have seen increases each year since the early 1980s, as has China since 1995. China surpassed the EPO and the Republic of Korea in 2005, Japan in 2010 and the U.S. in 2011 – and it now receives the largest number of applications worldwide. There has been a gradual upward trend in the combined share of the top five offices in the world total – from 74% in 2006 to 84% in 2016.

Trend in patent applications for the top five offices

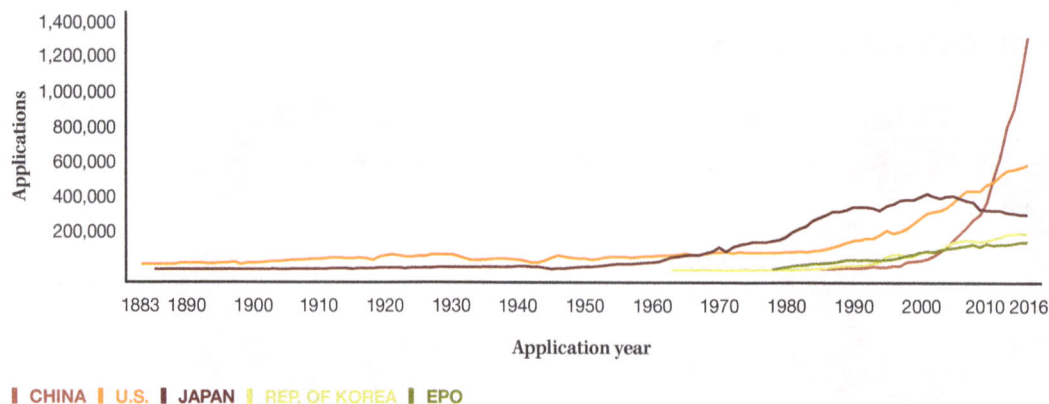

CHINA   U.S.   JAPAN   REP. OF KOREA   EPO

Note: The IP office of the Soviet Union, not represented in this figure, was the leading office in the world in terms of filings from 1964 to 1969. Like Japan and the U.S., the office of the Soviet Union saw stable application numbers until the early 1960s, after which it recorded rapid growth in applications filed.

Source: Standard figure A7.

Equivalent application class count

Applications at regional intellectual property (IP) offices are equivalent to multiple applications in the countries that are members of the organizations establishing those offices. In particular, to calculate the number of equivalent applications for the African Intellectual Property Organization (OAPI), the Eurasian Patent Organization (EAPO) and the Patent Office of the Cooperation Council for the Arab States of the Gulf (GCC Patent Office), each application is multiplied by the corresponding number of member states. For African Regional Intellectual Property Organization (ARIPO) and the European Patent Office (EPO) data, each application is counted as one application abroad if the applicant does not reside in a member state or as one resident application and one application abroad if the applicant resides in a member state. The equivalent application concept is used for reporting data by origin.

Residents of the U.S. filed more than four times as many patent applications abroad as Chinese residents

Applications received by offices from resident and non-resident applicants are referred to as office data, whereas applications filed by applicants at a national/regional office (resident applications) or at foreign offices (applications abroad) are referred to as origin data. Here, patent statistics based on the origin of residence of the first named applicant are reported in order to complement the picture of patent activity worldwide.

Applicants from China filed around 1.26 million equivalent patent applications in 2016 – more than the combined total for applicants from the U.S. (520,877), Japan (453,640) and the Republic of Korea (233,625)

(map 1). China has been the largest origin of patent applications since 2012, when it surpassed Japan. However, it should be noted that around 96% of all applications from China are filed in China and only 4% filed abroad. In contrast, filings abroad constitute around 43% of total applications from Japan and the U.S.

Twelve of the top 20 origins are located in Europe. Their combined total equivalent patent applications (523,605) is slightly higher than that from U.S.-based applicants. All top 20 origins, with the exception of China, India, the Islamic Republic of Iran and the Russian Federation, are high-income countries.

Among the top 20 origins, China (+24.4%), India (+7.7%), Belgium (+4.7%) and Israel (+4.3%) recorded the fastest growth in 2016. Almost all the growth in

Map 1
Equivalent patent applications by origin, 2016

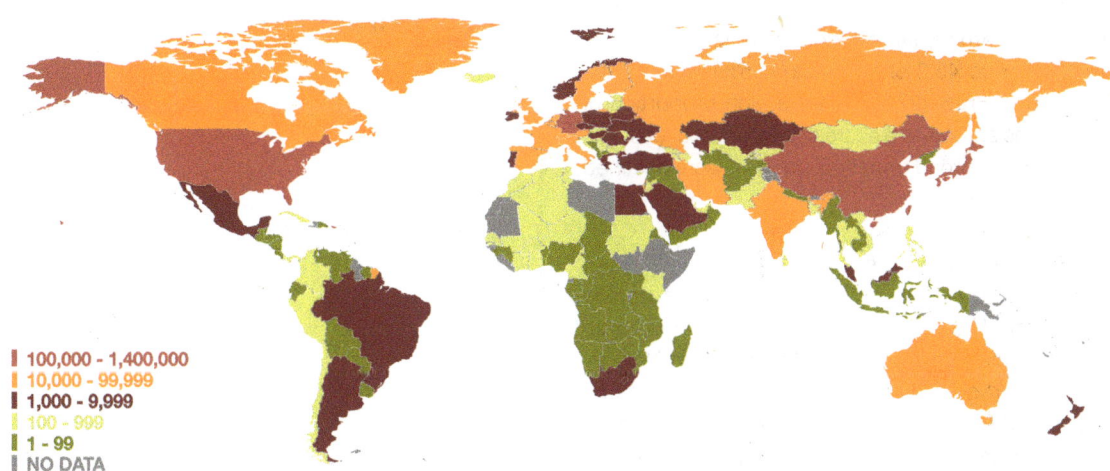

100,000 - 1,400,000
10,000 - 99,999
1,000 - 9,999
100 - 999
1 - 99
NO DATA

Source: Standard map A17.

filings from applicants from China was driven by increases in resident filings – of 246,700 additional filings by Chinese applicants, 236,700 were filed in China and only 10,000 abroad. For both India and Israel, growth in applications abroad (mainly in the U.S.) was the main source of overall growth.

A number of origins not among the top 20, such as South Africa (+96.9%), the United Arab Emirates (+38.8%), Colombia (+34.6%), Saudi Arabia (+33.8%) and Argentina (+28.5%), recorded double-digit growth. The overall growth in Argentina, Colombia, Saudi Arabia and South Africa was due to increases in resident applications, while growth in equivalent applications abroad drove overall growth in the United Arab Emirates.

Filing abroad reflects the globalization of intellectual property (IP) protection and a desire to commercialize technology in foreign markets. The costs of filing abroad can be substantial, so the patents for which applicants seek international protection are likely to confer higher values. Among the top 20 origins, applications filed abroad made up a large share of the totals for Canada, Israel and Switzerland. However, in absolute numbers, the U.S. had the most with 215,918, followed by Japan (191,819) and Germany (75,378). Germany saw growth in applications abroad, whereas these decreased for both Japan and the U.S.

Applicants residing in China, while ranking first in terms of resident applications, filed considerably fewer applications abroad (51,522). However, applications filed abroad from China have increased markedly in recent years – from around 7,000 in 2006 to the 51,522 filed in 2016. Among large middle-income origins, India (47.5%), Mexico (45.2%), Malaysia (42.5%), South Africa (28.9%) and Brazil (27.3%) have a high proportion of applications abroad as a share of total applications. The bulk of filings abroad from these origins were destined for the USPTO.

Among other factors, technological specialization, proximity and market size influence cross-border applications. U.S. applicants accounted for more than half of all non-resident applications filed in Norway (72.4%), Turkey (57.4%), Canada (52.8%), Mexico (51.3%) and Australia (50.1%). At many offices, applicants from Germany, Japan or the U.S. accounted for the highest non-resident shares. For example, applicants from Germany had the highest share of non-resident filings in Italy (33.2%), Switzerland (31.4%) and France (26.3%). Japanese applicants accounted

for a high share of the total in Germany (35.2%), the Republic of Korea (32.5%) and Indonesia (29.4%).

More than 1.4 million patent applications for unique inventions were filed worldwide in 2014

Patent applicants traditionally file at their national offices and then subsequently abroad. This means some inventions are recorded more than once. To take this into account, WIPO has developed indicators for patent families, and the trend in patent families mirrors that for patent applications. The total number of patent families worldwide increased from around 1 million in 2010 to just over 1.42 million in 2014. Applicants from China (47.3%), Japan (16.7%) and the U.S. (11.9%) accounted for three-quarters of all patent families in 2014.

Over the past 20 years, the ratio of families to applications has remained more or less stable at around 0.52. This means that just over half of all applications are initial filings and the others repetitive filings, mostly at foreign offices (figure 5). Belgium, Denmark, Norway, Switzerland and Turkey have low family-to-application ratios – around 0.17 for the period from 2012 to 2014 – indicating substantial multiplication due to high numbers of cross-border filings. Conversely, China and the Russian Federation have high ratios of around 0.8, indicating less duplication due to low numbers of cross-border filings.

Figure 5
Patent applications and patent families worldwide

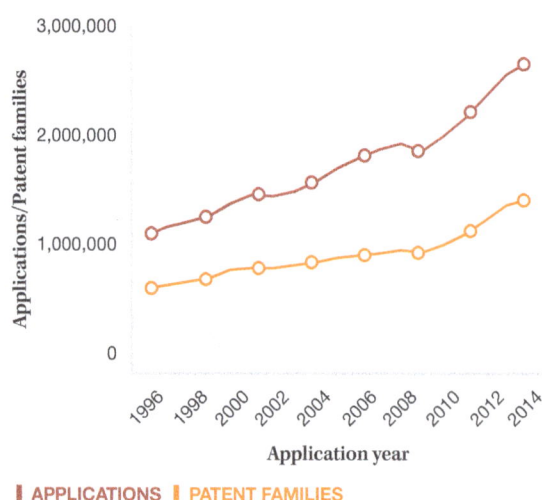

APPLICATIONS PATENT FAMILIES

Source: Standard figures A1 and A23.

Patent families

A patent family is a set of interrelated patent applications filed in one or more offices to protect the same invention. The patent applications in a family are interlinked by one or more of: priority claim, Patent Cooperation Treaty (PCT) national phase entry, continuation, continuation-in part, internal priority and addition or division. A special subset comprises foreign-oriented patent families, that is, those patent families that have at least one filing office different from the office of the applicant's country of origin. Some foreign-related patent families include only one filing office because applicants may choose to file only with a foreign office. For example, if a Canadian applicant files a patent application directly with the USPTO without having previously filed with the patent office of Canada, that patent family will constitute a foreign-oriented patent family with just one office.

The size of patent families (i.e., the number of offices) reflects their geographical coverage. Around 81% of patent families created worldwide between 2012 and 2014 were filed in a single office. There is considerable variation among top origins, however. For example, around one-third of all patent families originating from the Netherlands, Sweden and Switzerland cover a single office, whereas single-office patent families account for 97% of all families for China and the Russian Federation. Focusing exclusively on foreign-oriented patent families shows that on average such families cover three foreign offices. Among the top origins, applicants from Switzerland tend to cover four offices when filing abroad, whereas those from Canada cover two on average.

The top 10 patent applicants worldwide are Asia-based multinationals

Canon Inc. of Japan was the top applicant for the period from 2011 to 2014, with 30,476 patent families worldwide. It was followed by Samsung Electronics (26,609) of the Republic of Korea and Japanese companies Panasonic (22,899), Toshiba (22,627) and Toyota Jidosha (22,190). The top 10 applicants are all located in Asia. The highest-ranking non-Asian applicant was Robert Bosch of Germany (16,582) at number 12.

More than a quarter (26.9%) of Canon's patent families during this period related to optics technology, while computer technology accounted for the highest share of families belonging to Samsung Electronics (26%) and Toshiba (16.1%). For Panasonic, electrical machinery (22.7%) was the most important technology field. Transport (24.2%) saw the highest share of all patents for Toyota Jidosha.

Applicants from just nine origins make up the top 100 list for the period from 2011 to 2014. Japan (40) had the highest number of applicants in this list, followed by China (26), the Republic of Korea (15),

the U.S. (9), Germany (6) and one each from France, the Netherlands, Sweden and Taiwan, Province of China. The top 100 list mainly comprises multinational companies. However, 14 Chinese universities also feature. Combined, these 14 applicants accounted for 9% of all patent families held by the top 100 applicants.

The Republic of Korea filed the highest number of patents per unit of GDP

Variations in patenting activity across countries reflect differences in their levels of economic growth and development. It is therefore informative to examine resident patent activity with regard to population, R&D spending, GDP and other variables. These are commonly referred to as "patent activity intensity" indicators.

Since 2004, the Republic of Korea has had the highest number of patent applications per unit of USD 100 billion GDP. Its ratio of resident applications to GDP is considerably higher than those of China and Japan, ranked second and third, respectively (figure 6). For the first time since 2010, the top five ranking has changed. After surpassing Germany in 2010, China has moved ahead of Japan to rank second. The gap between China and the Republic of Korea has narrowed rapidly. Reflecting strong growth in resident applications, China's resident applications per unit of GDP increased from 1,455 in 2006 to 6,069 in 2016 – the fastest growth among the top origins. Germany and Switzerland are ranked fourth and fifth, respectively. Between 2006 and 2016, Germany's resident patent applications per GDP unit fell from 2,260 to 2,019, while those of Switzerland rose from 1,768 to 1,841.

The list of the top 20 origins is predominantly comprised of high-income countries. However, three middle-income countries – China, the Russian Federation and Ukraine – also feature. The rank of the top 20 origins has been stable for the past 10 years, with little movement in country rankings except that of China.

Figure 6
Resident patent applications per USD 100 billion GDP for the top 10 origins

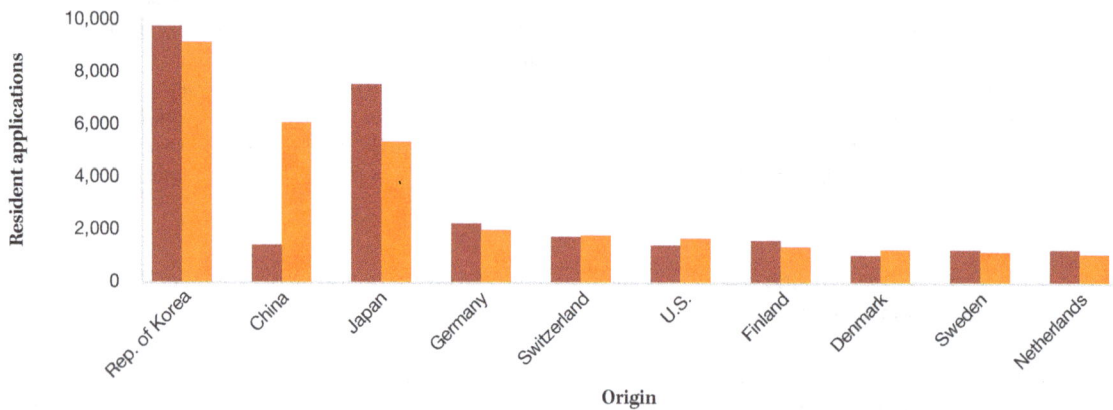

2006 2016

Source: Standard figure A41.

Despite sizable increases in their resident patent application to GDP ratios between 2006 and 2016, large middle-income countries such as Brazil, India, Malaysia and Mexico exhibit low numbers of resident applications per unit of GDP. Brazil, with 406 resident applications per unit of GDP, is the highest-placed origin in Latin America and the Caribbean, while South Africa ranks highest in Africa with 179.

The profile of resident applications per million population is similar to that adjusted by GDP, but shows some subtle differences. The Republic of Korea retains its lead. However, Japan ranks second in this regard. China ranks much lower – sixth, after Germany – due to its high population. Small high-income countries of origin such as Finland, Luxembourg, Norway and Singapore rank high when resident patent applications are adjusted by population or GDP. Among the large middle-income countries of origin, India and Mexico each filed 10 resident applications per million population, despite India's number of resident applications being 10 times higher than that of Mexico. Similarly, Chile has a higher ratio of resident applications to population than Argentina, even though Argentina has twice as many resident applications as Chile.

Computer technology remains the most frequently featured technology field in applications

In 2015 – the latest year for which complete data are available due to the delay between application and publication – computer technology was the most frequently featured technology in published patent applications worldwide with around 187,000 published applications. It was followed by electrical machinery (176,400), measurement (124,000), digital communication (123,300) and medical technology (110,100). These five fields accounted for 28.6% of all published applications worldwide.

Among the top 20 technology fields, food chemistry (+10.9%), digital communication (+8.7%), materials metallurgy (+8.1%) and basic materials chemistry (+7.7%) witnessed the fastest average annual growth between 2005 and 2015. Food chemistry rose from around 22,400 published applications in 2005 to around 63,200 in 2015, while digital communication increased from 53,600 to 123,300 over the same period. In contrast, there was a slight decline in published patent applications for optics (-0.9%), audio-visual technology (-1.5%) and telecommunications (-1.8%).

Among the top 10 origins in the period from 2013 to 2015, China, Japan and the Republic of Korea filed most heavily in electrical machinery; France and Germany in transport; Switzerland and the United Kingdom (U.K.) in pharmaceuticals; the Netherlands in medical technology; the Russian Federation in food chemistry; and the U.S. in computer technology. The combined share of the top three technologies for the top 10 origins ranged from 15.4% for the U.K. to 27.2% for the U.S.

Among the large middle-income countries in the period from 2013 to 2015, applicants residing in India filed most heavily in computer technology (17.4% of total published applications); Turkey (12.7%) and Mexico (11%) in pharmaceuticals; and South Africa in civil engineering (8.3%).

The top technology field – computer technology – accounted for a high share of published patent applications originating from Barbados (16.2%), Bermuda (14.5%), Israel (13%), China Hong Kong SAR (10.8%) and Singapore (10.7%) for the period from 2013 to 2015.

Patents granted by the EPO grew by 40% in 2016 – the fastest growth since 1983

Offices carry out a formal and substantive examination to decide whether or not to issue a patent. The procedure for granting a patent varies across offices, and differences in the numbers of granted patents among offices depend on factors such as examination capacity and procedural delays. For this reason, application data for a given year should not be compared with grant data from the same year.

In 2016, an estimated 1.35 million patents were granted worldwide, up 8.9% on 2015 (figure 7). Growth in 2016 was the fastest since 2012. This was due mainly to the increase at both the EPO and SIPO. The EPO granted 27,500 more patents in 2016 than in 2015, while SIPO issued 48,900 additional patents.

SIPO granted 404,208 patents in 2016, followed by the USPTO (303,049), the JPO (203,087), KIPO (108,875)

and the EPO (95,956). These five offices issued more than 1.1 million patents between them – 83% of the world total. Patents granted by the EPO grew by 40.2% in 2016 – the fastest growth since 1983. SIPO (+12.5%), the JPO (+7.3%), KIPO (+6.9%) and the USPTO (+1.6%) also issued more patents in 2016 than in 2015.

Figure 7
Patent grants worldwide

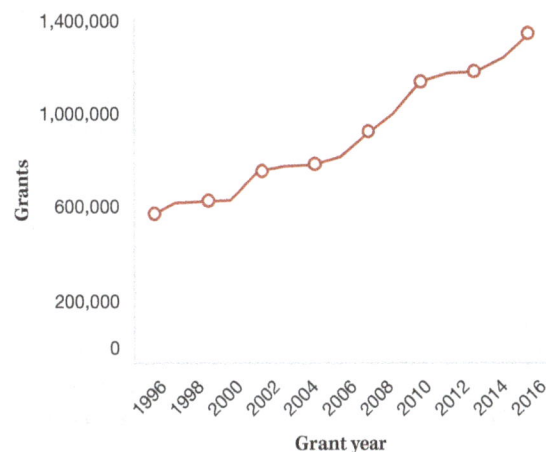

Source: Standard figure A3.

Among the top 20 offices, the Philippines saw the fastest growth (+82.1%), with grants increasing from 2,200 in 2015 to 4,006 in 2016. This reflected a substantial increase in the number of non-resident grants. India (+37%), Brazil (+23%) and Canada (+19%) were the other top 20 offices to exhibit double-digit growth in 2016. Again, growth in non-resident grants drove overall growth for these offices.

Beyond the top 20 list, Indonesia granted 3,674 patents in 2016, almost double the number for the previous year. The Islamic Republic of Iran and Malaysia each issued around 3,300 patents, while around 1,800 patents each were granted by Argentina and Turkey. All these offices saw strong annual growth in patent grants.

Asia's share of worldwide patent grants was 57% in 2016 – considerably below its share of applications (64.6%). However, its share of grants has increased from 48.8% in 2006 to 57% in 2016. Offices located in North America accounted for a quarter of patent grants worldwide in 2016, which is similar to the region's 2006 share. Offices in Europe accounted for 14.5% of the 2016 world total, while the combined share for Africa, Latin America and the Caribbean and Oceania was 4.1%.

Around 2.8 million patents are in force in the U.S.

Patent rights generally last for up to 20 years from the date the application was filed. The estimated number of patents in force worldwide rose from 7.8 million in 2009 to 11.8 million in 2016.

The USPTO recorded the most, with 2.8 million patents in force in 2016, followed by the JPO (2 million), SIPO (1.8 million) and KIPO (1 million). Just these four jurisdictions cover around 63% of all patents in force worldwide. The top 20 list includes 16 offices from high-income countries and four from upper middle-income countries, namely China, Mexico, the Russian Federation and South Africa. Offices of other large middle-income countries with substantial numbers of patents in force are Turkey (63,500), India (50,000), Malaysia (25,000) and Brazil (24,000). Denmark (55,700), Singapore (48,600) and Finland (48,600) – three small high-income countries – had large numbers of patents in force in their jurisdictions.

Holders must pay maintenance/renewal fees to maintain the validity of their patents, and may opt to let a patent lapse before the end of its full term. For the 72 offices that reported their in-force data broken down by year of filing, between 40% and 43% of patents granted remained in force for at least 6 to 10 years after the filing date, and about one-fifth lasted the full 20 years.

Although patents can be maintained for 20 years, the average age of patents varied across offices. For example, the average age of all patents in force 2016 in India was 12.8 years, while in China it was 7.2 years. Along with India, Germany (11.6 years), Canada (11)

and Denmark (10.9) also have high average ages of patents in force.

The top four offices had fewer potentially pending applications in 2016 than in 2015

Patent offices must assess whether the claims in applications meet the standards of novelty, non-obviousness and industrial applicability defined in national laws. Processing patents therefore consumes time and resources.

The number of applications that were potentially pending globally fell from 5.6 million in 2009 to 5 million in 2016. This estimate is based on data from 108 offices. However, the figure would be higher if data from SIPO were available. The decline in applications pending worldwide was driven mainly by Japan, which saw potentially pending applications decline from around 1.6 million in 2009 to 0.8 million in 2016.

The USPTO had the most potentially pending applications in 2016 with 1.1 million, followed by the JPO (around 847,000) and the EPO (668,000). However, the USPTO has seen eight successive years of reduction in the number of potentially pending applications, while the JPO has reported declines each year since 2005. The EPO saw 2.3% fewer potentially pending applications, representing the first decrease since at least 2004. This was partly due to a substantial increase in the number of patent applications processed and granted in 2016. A large share of the EPO's (70%) and the JPO's (79%) potentially pending applications was awaiting request for examination. In such cases, even if these offices have resources to process and reduce the number of pending applications, they will be unable to do so until they receive a request for examination from applicants.

Among middle-income countries, Brazil had the largest number of potentially pending applications: they almost doubled, from around 123,200 in 2006 to around 243,800 in 2016. India saw a 6.1% increase in its potentially pending applications in 2016. However, 80% of the total (242,800) were awaiting request for examination.

Potentially pending applications

Potentially pending applications include all patent applications, at any stage in the process, awaiting a final decision by a patent office, including those applications for which applicants have not filed a request for examination (where applicable).

A record number of international patent applications were filed through the PCT System in 2016

An international treaty administered by WIPO, the Patent Cooperation Treaty (PCT), allows applicants to seek patent protection for an invention simultaneously in a large number of countries by filing a single PCT international application. The granting of patents remains under the control of national and regional patent offices and is carried out in what is called the "national phase" or "regional phase."

The number of PCT applications grew by 7.2% in 2016 – the fastest increase since 2011 and the seventh consecutive year of growth. Around 233,000 PCT applications were filed in 2016. Applicants based in the U.S. filed the largest number of PCT applications with 56,590, followed by applicants from Japan (45,214), China (43,094), Germany (18,305) and the Republic of Korea (15,552).

Fourteen of the top 20 origins filed more PCT applications in 2016 than in 2015. China recorded extraordinary growth (+44.4%), while Italy (+9.4%), Israel (+9.1%), India (+8.2%) and the Netherlands (+7.9%) also saw strong increases. In contrast, for the second successive year Canada (-17.3%) saw a substantial decline in filings, linked to a declining number of applications filed by Research in Motion and Nortel.

Utility model applications worldwide increased by 28.9%

A utility model is a special form of patent right granted by a state or jurisdiction to an inventor or the inventor's assignee for a fixed period of time. The terms and conditions for granting a utility model are slightly different from those for normal patents, including a shorter term of protection and less stringent patentability requirements.

In 2016, utility model applications increased by 28.9%, amounting to 1.55 million applications. This strong growth was primarily due to a 30.9% increase in applications filed at SIPO. In 2016, SIPO received nearly 95% of all utility model applications filed in the world – the remaining 73 offices accounted for just 5% of the world total. China (1.48 million) was followed by Germany (14,030) and the Russian Federation (11,112). Ukraine (9,584) exhibited rapid growth and surpassed

the Republic of Korea (7,764) as the fourth highest office for utility model applications.

Among the top 20 offices, the Philippines (+42.3%), Kazakhstan (+35.1%) and Indonesia (+32.2%) witnessed sharp growth in 2016 – albeit from a low base. The numbers of applications filed in Japan and the Republic of Korea have declined drastically over the past 10 years. Applications filed in Japan fell from 10,965 in 2006 to 6,480 in 2016, while those in the Republic of Korea declined from 32,908 to 7,767.

Utility model applications are rarely filed abroad: resident applications made up about 99% of all applications filed worldwide in 2016. Among the top 10 offices, resident shares varied between 95% and 99%, except in Germany (72%) and Japan (76%), which had lower resident shares.

Women's participation rate in patent applications tends to be high in technology fields related to life sciences

The share of PCT applications with women inventors increased from 21.7% in 2002 to 29.7% in 2016. The 2016 figure is one percentage point higher than that for 2015. The total number of PCT applications with women inventors almost tripled, from around 22,600 to around 62,400, over the same period. Women's participation rate varied across countries. Among the top 20 origins, the Republic of Korea (46.9%) and China (46.8%) were the most gender-equal. Spain (36%), the U.S. (31.5%) and France (31.5%) also had relatively high shares of PCT applications with women inventors.

Technology fields related to the life sciences have relatively high shares of women inventors in PCT applications. Biotechnology (58.3%) had the highest share, followed by pharmaceuticals (56.4%), organic fine chemistry (54.7%) and food chemistry (51%).

The women's participation rate based on national/regional patent office application data is lower than that based on PCT application data. Among offices for which data were available, the share of resident patent applications with women inventors ranged from 11.1% at the German patent office to 38.7% at the Russian patent office in 2014. That Germany has the largest gender gap could be due in part to the fact it has a high number of patent filings in fields of technology, such as transport and mechanical engineering, for which the participation rates for women are low.

Standard figures and tables

PATENTS

PATENTS

Patent applications and grants worldwide

Figure A1
Trend in patent applications worldwide

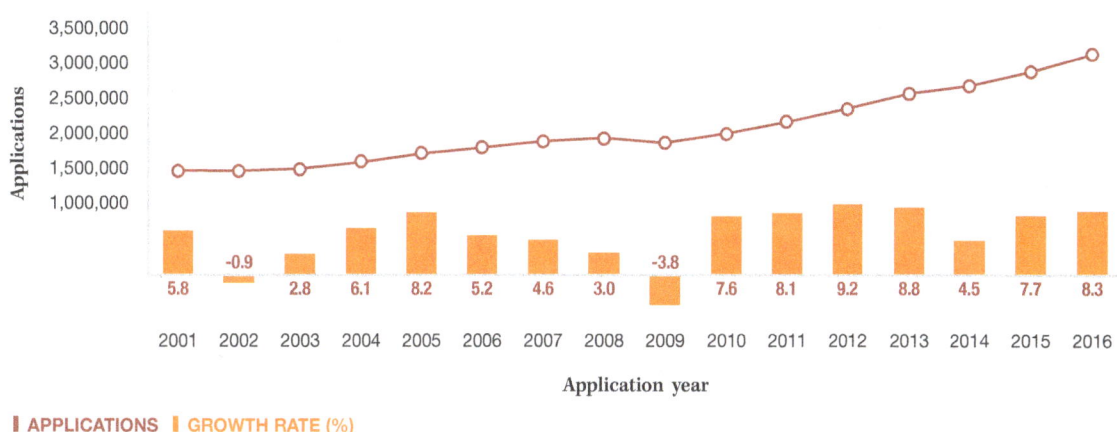

	2001	2002	2003	2004	2005	2006	2007	2008	2009	2010	2011	2012	2013	2014	2015	2016
Growth rate	5.8	-0.9	2.8	6.1	8.2	5.2	4.6	3.0	-3.8	7.6	8.1	9.2	8.8	4.5	7.7	8.3

Application year

| APPLICATIONS | GROWTH RATE (%)

Note: World totals are WIPO estimates using data covering 154 patent offices. These totals include applications filed directly with national and regional offices and applications entering offices through the Patent Cooperation Treaty national phase (where applicable).

Source: WIPO Statistics Database, September 2017.

Figure A2
Resident and non-resident patent applications worldwide

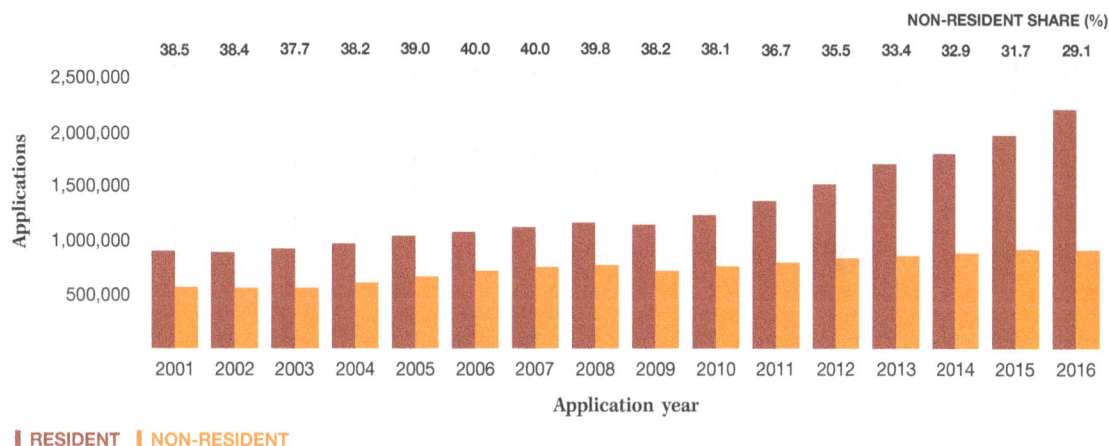

NON-RESIDENT SHARE (%)

| 38.5 | 38.4 | 37.7 | 38.2 | 39.0 | 40.0 | 40.0 | 39.8 | 38.2 | 38.1 | 36.7 | 35.5 | 33.4 | 32.9 | 31.7 | 29.1 |

Application year

| RESIDENT | NON-RESIDENT

Note: World totals are WIPO estimates using data covering 154 patent offices. These totals include applications filed directly with national and regional offices and applications entering offices through the Patent Cooperation Treaty national phase (where applicable). See the glossary for definitions of resident and non-resident.

Source: WIPO Statistics Database, September 2017.

PATENTS

Figure A3
Trend in patent grants worldwide

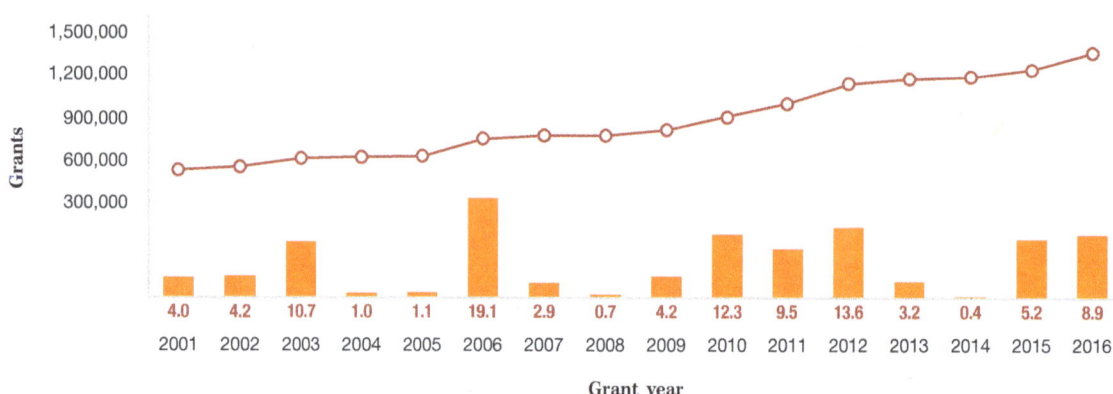

■ GRANTS   ■ GROWTH RATE (%)

Note: World totals are WIPO estimates using data covering 148 patent offices. These totals include patent grants based on applications filed directly with national and regional offices and patents granted by offices on the basis of the Patent Cooperation Treaty national phase (where applicable).

Source: WIPO Statistics Database, September 2017.

Figure A4
Resident and non-resident patent grants worldwide

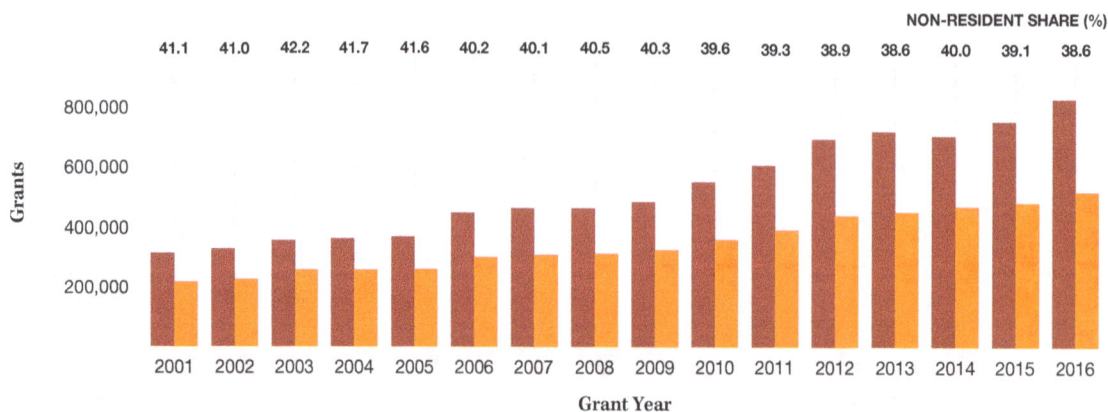

■ RESIDENT   ■ NON-RESIDENT

Note: World totals are WIPO estimates using data covering 148 patent offices. These totals include patent grants based on applications filed directly with national and regional offices and patents granted by offices on the basis of the Patent Cooperation Treaty national phase (where applicable). See the glossary for definitions of resident and non-resident.

Source: WIPO Statistics Database, September 2017.

Patent applications and grants by office

Figure A5
Patent applications by income group

Income group	Number of applications		Resident share (%)		Share of world total (%)		Average growth (%)
	2006	2016	2006	2016	2006	2016	2006-16
High-income	1,402,100	1,552,800	63.3	59.1	78.3	49.6	1.0
Upper middle-income	327,700	1,489,100	51.8	85.3	18.3	47.6	16.3
Lower middle-income	53,800	76,000	21.7	26.7	3.0	2.4	3.5
Low-income	7,400	10,000	86.5	86.0	0.4	0.4	3.1
World	**1,791,000**	**3,127,900**	**60.0**	**70.9**	**100.0**	**100.0**	**5.7**

Note: Totals by income group are WIPO estimates using data covering 154 offices. Each category includes the following number of offices: high-income countries/economies (58), upper middle-income (43), lower middle-income (37) and low-income (16). European Patent Office data are allocated to the high-income group because most of its member states are high-income countries. For similar reasons, data for the African Regional Intellectual Property Organization and the African Intellectual Property Organization are allocated to the low-income group, while those for the Eurasian Patent Organization are allocated to the lower middle-income group. For information on income group classification, see the Data description section.

Source: WIPO Statistics Database, September 2017.

Figure A6
Patent applications by region

Region	Number of applications		Resident share (%)		Share of world total (%)		Average growth (%)
	2006	2016	2006	2016	2006	2016	2006-16
Africa	12,700	17,500	11.0	28.0	0.7	0.5	3.3
Asia	889,800	2,019,100	69.9	83.3	49.7	64.6	8.5
Europe	333,100	354,900	63.9	61.3	18.6	11.3	0.6
Latin America & the Caribbean	54,000	61,300	11.9	14.2	3.0	2.0	1.3
North America	468,000	640,300	48.6	46.8	26.1	20.5	3.2
Oceania	33,400	34,800	15.0	10.6	1.9	1.1	0.4
World	**1,791,000**	**3,127,900**	**60.0**	**70.9**	**100.0**	**100.0**	**5.7**

Note: Totals by geographic region are WIPO estimates using data covering 154 offices. Each region includes the following number of offices: Africa (29), Asia (43), Europe (45), Latin America & the Caribbean (30), North America (2) and Oceania (5).

Source: WIPO Statistics Database, September 2017.

PATENTS

Figure A7
Trend in patent applications for the top five offices

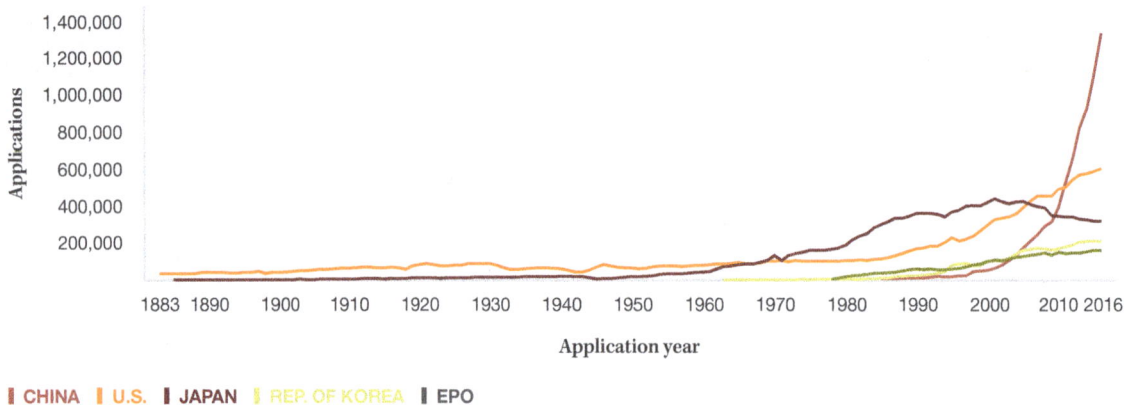

| CHINA | U.S. | JAPAN | REP. OF KOREA | EPO

Note: EPO is the European Patent Office. The top five offices were selected based on their 2016 totals.

Source: WIPO Statistics Database, September 2017.

Figure A8
Patent applications at the top 20 offices, 2016

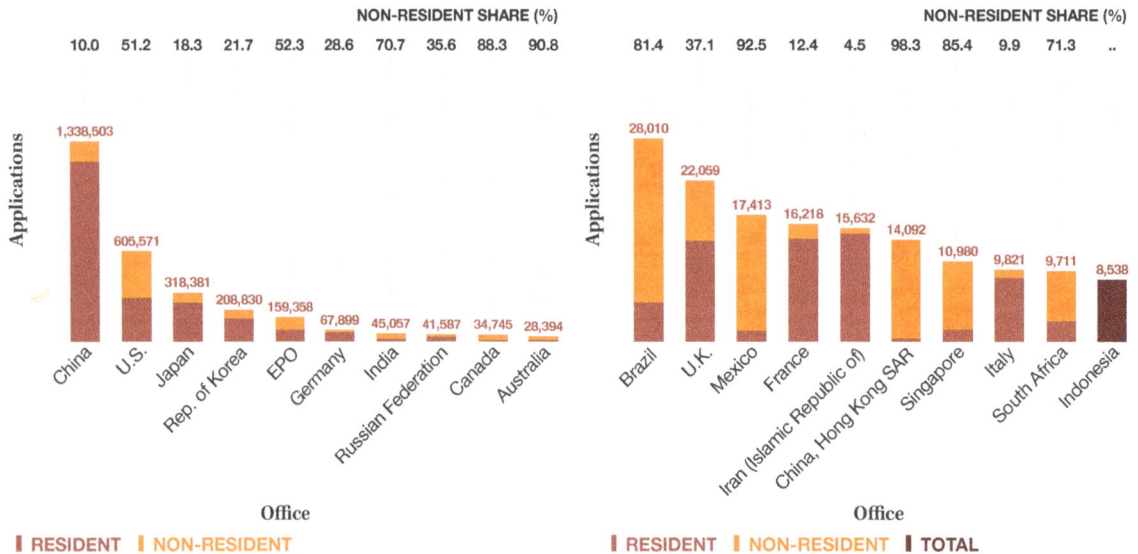

| RESIDENT | NON-RESIDENT

| RESIDENT | NON-RESIDENT | TOTAL

.. indicates not available.

Note: EPO is the European Patent Office. In general, national offices of European Patent Office (EPO) member states receive lower volumes of applications because applicants may apply via the EPO to seek protection within any EPO member state. The number of applications broken down by resident and non-resident is not available for Indonesia.

Source: WIPO Statistics Database, September 2017.

46

Figure A9

Contribution of resident and non-resident applications to total growth for the top 20 offices, 2015-16

TOTAL GROWTH RATE (%)

21.5	2.7	-0.1	-2.3	-0.4	1.5	-1.3	-8.6	-6.0	-0.7	-7.3	-3.3	-3.6	-0.5	..	15.4	1.5	..	29.5	-6.7

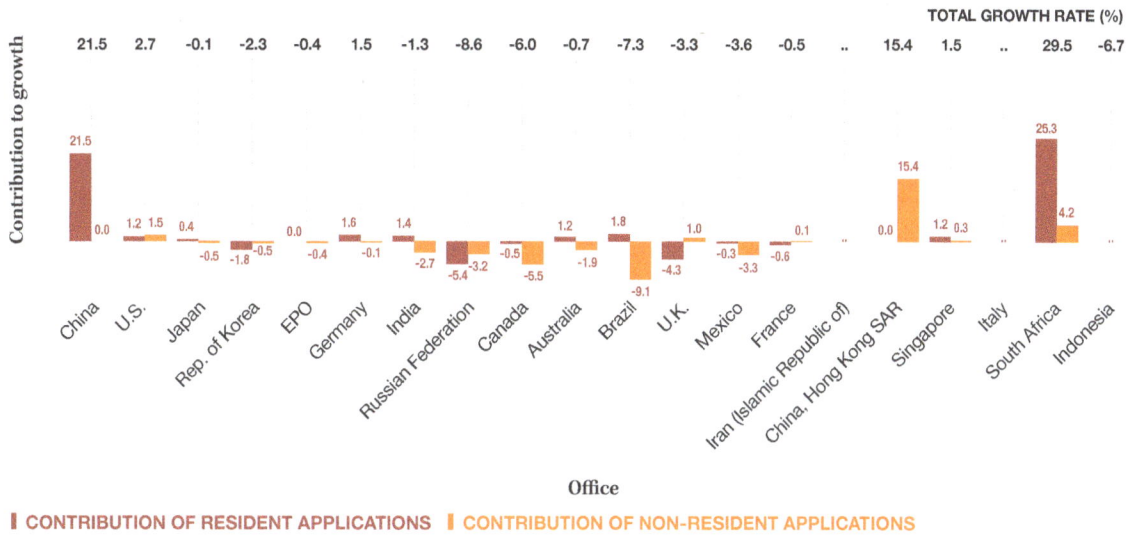

■ CONTRIBUTION OF RESIDENT APPLICATIONS   ■ CONTRIBUTION OF NON-RESIDENT APPLICATIONS

.. indicates not available.

Note: EPO is the European Patent Office. This figure shows total growth or decrease in applications at each office broken down by the respective contributions of resident and non-resident applications. For example, applications filed in the U.S. grew by 2.7%. Growth in resident applications accounted for 1.2 percentage points of this increase, whereas the remaining 1.5 percentage points reflected growth in non-resident applications. Resident and non-resident contributions are not available for Indonesia, the Islamic Republic of Iran and Italy.

Source: WIPO Statistics Database, September 2017.

Figure A10

Patent applications at offices of selected low- and middle-income countries, 2016

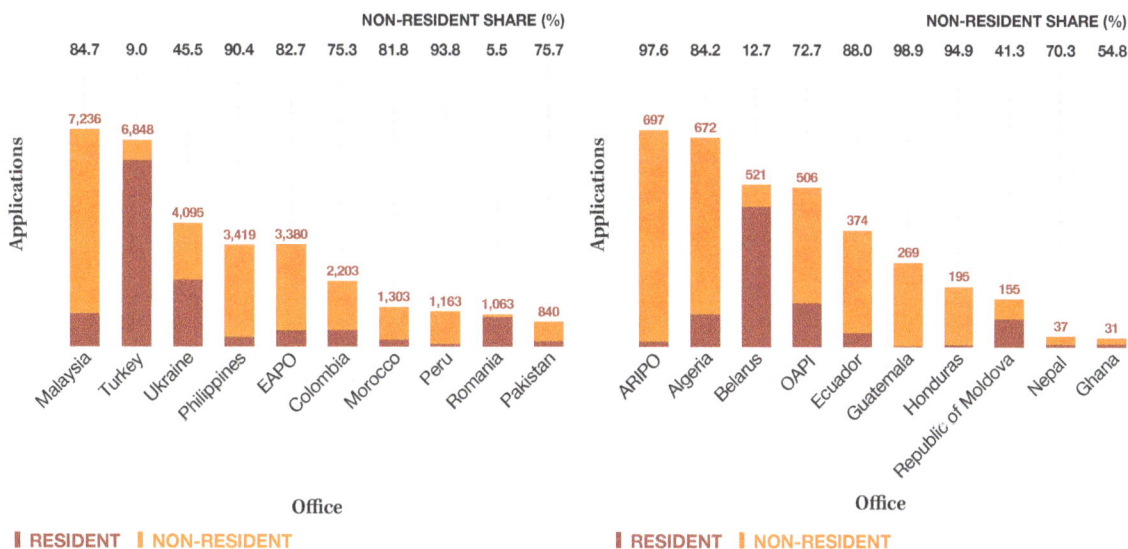

■ RESIDENT   ■ NON-RESIDENT   ■ RESIDENT   ■ NON-RESIDENT

Note: ARIPO is the African Regional Intellectual Property Organization, EAPO is the Eurasian Patent Organization and OAPI is the African Intellectual Property Organization. The selected offices are from different world regions and income groups (low-income, lower middle-income and upper middle-income). Where available, data for all offices are presented in the statistical table at the end of this section.

Source: WIPO Statistics Database, September 2017.

PATENTS

Figure A11
Contribution of resident and non-resident applications to total growth for offices of selected low- and middle-income countries, 2015-16

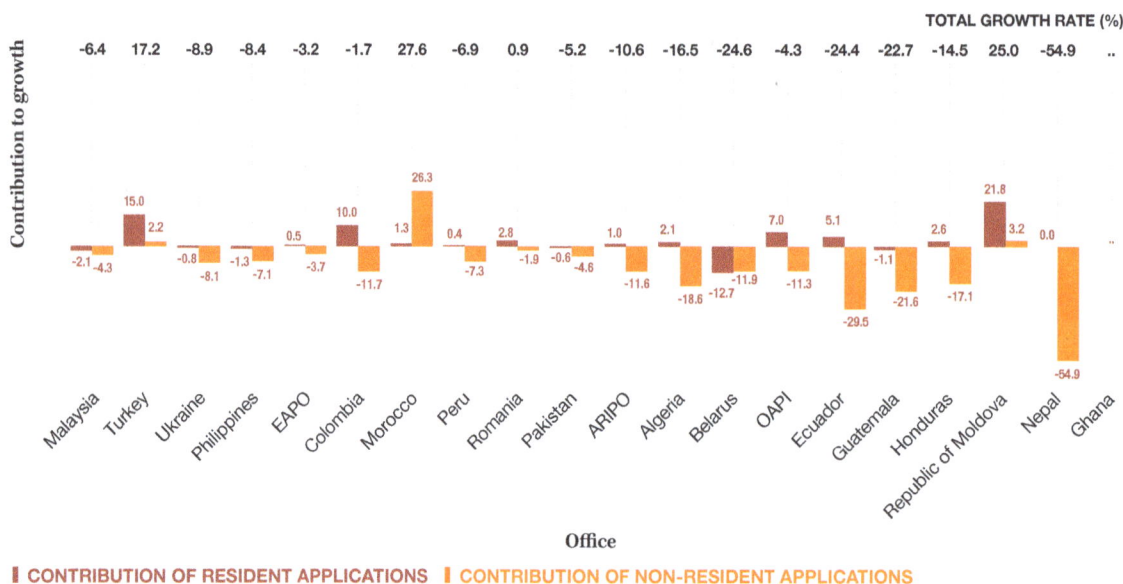

TOTAL GROWTH RATE (%)

| -6.4 | 17.2 | -8.9 | -8.4 | -3.2 | -1.7 | 27.6 | -6.9 | 0.9 | -5.2 | -10.6 | -16.5 | -24.6 | -4.3 | -24.4 | -22.7 | -14.5 | 25.0 | -54.9 | .. |

Contribution to growth

Office

█ CONTRIBUTION OF RESIDENT APPLICATIONS   █ CONTRIBUTION OF NON-RESIDENT APPLICATIONS

.. indicates not available.

Note: ARIPO is the African Regional Intellectual Property Organization, EAPO is the Eurasian Patent Organization and OAPI is the African Intellectual Property Organization. The selected offices are from different world regions and income groups (low-income, lower middle-income and upper middle-income). Data for all available offices are presented in the statistical table at the end of this section. This figure shows total growth or decrease in applications at each office broken down by the respective contributions of resident and non-resident applications. For example, applications filed in Turkey grew by 17.2%. Growth in resident applications accounted for 15 percentage points of this increase, whereas the remaining 2.2 percentage points came from growth in non-resident applications.

Source: WIPO Statistics Database, September 2017.

Figure A12
Patent grants by income group

Income group	Number of grants		Resident share (%)		Share of world total (%)		Average growth (%)
	2006	2016	2006	2016	2006	2016	2006-16
High-income	614,900	847,600	63.0	57.4	81.4	62.7	3.3
Upper middle-income	116,500	474,400	46.2	70.2	15.4	35.1	15.1
Lower middle-income	19,000	22,100	32.1	16.7	2.5	1.6	1.5
Low-income	4,800	7,500	87.5	88.0	0.6	0.6	4.6
World	**755,200**	**1,351,600**	**59.8**	**61.4**	**100.0**	**100.0**	**6.0**

Note: Totals by income group are WIPO estimates using data covering 148 offices. Each category includes the following number of offices: high-income countries/economies (56), upper middle-income (42), lower middle-income (35) and low-income (15). European Patent Office data are allocated to the high-income group because most of its member states are high-income countries. For similar reasons, data for the African Regional Intellectual Property Organization and the African Intellectual Property Organization are allocated to the low-income group, while those for the Eurasian Patent Organization are allocated to the lower middle-income group. For information on income group classification, see the Data description section.

Source: WIPO Statistics Database, September 2017.

Figure A13
Patent grants by region

Region	Number of grants		Resident share (%)		Share of world total (%)		Average growth (%)
	2006	2016	2006	2016	2006	2016	2006-16
Africa	4,500	7,800	31.1	14.1	0.6	0.6	5.7
Asia	368,500	771,000	69.3	72.8	48.8	57.0	7.7
Europe	163,100	195,900	62.0	59.6	21.6	14.5	1.8
Latin America & the Caribbean	17,600	19,600	6.3	7.7	2.3	1.5	1.1
North America	188,700	329,500	48.4	44.6	25.0	24.4	5.7
Oceania	12,800	27,800	10.2	6.1	1.7	2.1	8.1
World	**755,200**	**1,351,600**	**59.8**	**61.4**	**100.0**	**100.0**	**6.0**

Note: Totals by geographic region are WIPO estimates using data covering 148 offices. Each region includes the following number of offices: Africa (28), Asia (41), Europe (44), Latin America & the Caribbean (29), North America (2) and Oceania (4).

Source: WIPO Statistics Database, September 2017.

Figure A14
Trend in patent grants for the top five offices

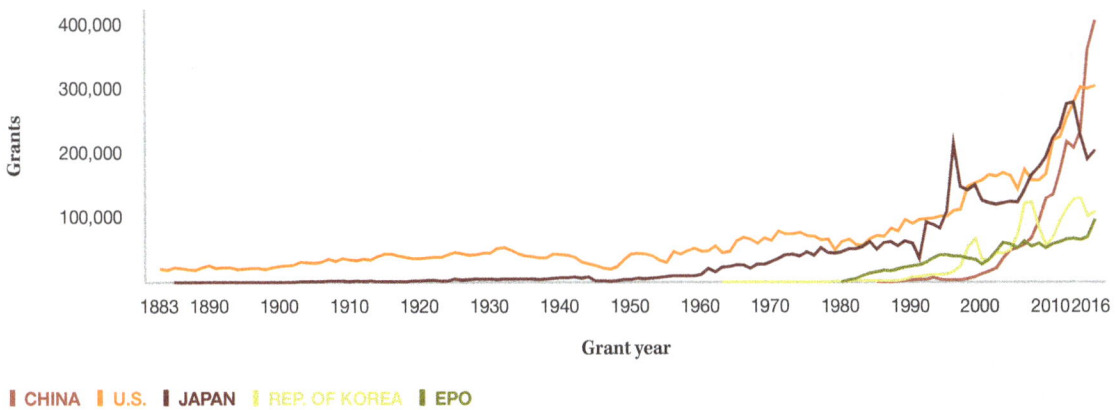

CHINA U.S. JAPAN REP. OF KOREA EPO

Note: EPO is the European Patent Office. The top five offices were selected based on their 2016 totals.

Source: WIPO Statistics Database, September 2017.

Figure A15
Patent grants for the top 20 offices, 2016

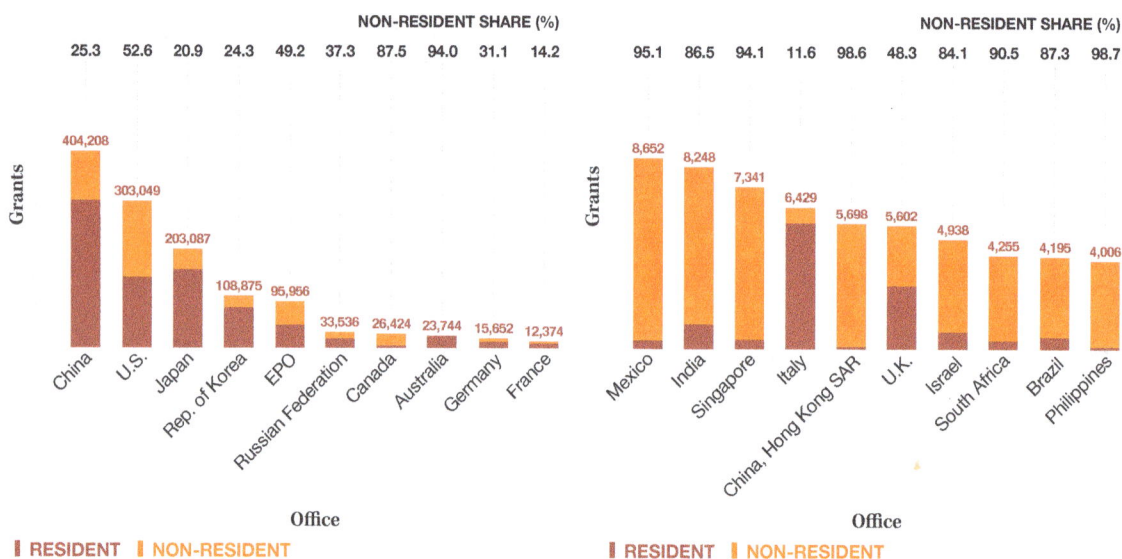

NON-RESIDENT SHARE (%)											NON-RESIDENT SHARE (%)									
25.3	52.6	20.9	24.3	49.2	37.3	87.5	94.0	31.1	14.2		95.1	86.5	94.1	11.6	98.6	48.3	84.1	90.5	87.3	98.7

Left chart grants: China 404,208; U.S. 303,049; Japan 203,087; Rep. of Korea 108,875; EPO 95,956; Russian Federation 33,536; Canada 26,424; Australia 23,744; Germany 15,652; France 12,374

Right chart grants: Mexico 8,652; India 8,248; Singapore 7,341; Italy 6,429; China, Hong Kong SAR 5,698; U.K. 5,602; Israel 4,938; South Africa 4,255; Brazil 4,195; Philippines 4,006

Office

▮ RESIDENT ▮ NON-RESIDENT

Note: EPO is the European Patent Office. The procedure for issuing patents varies across offices, and differences in the numbers of patents granted among offices depend on factors such as examination capacity and procedural delays. The examination process can also be lengthy, so there is a time lag between application and grant dates. For this reason, data on applications for a given year should not be compared with data on grants for the same year.

Source: WIPO Statistics Database, September 2017.

Figure A16
Patent grants for offices of selected low- and middle-income countries, 2016

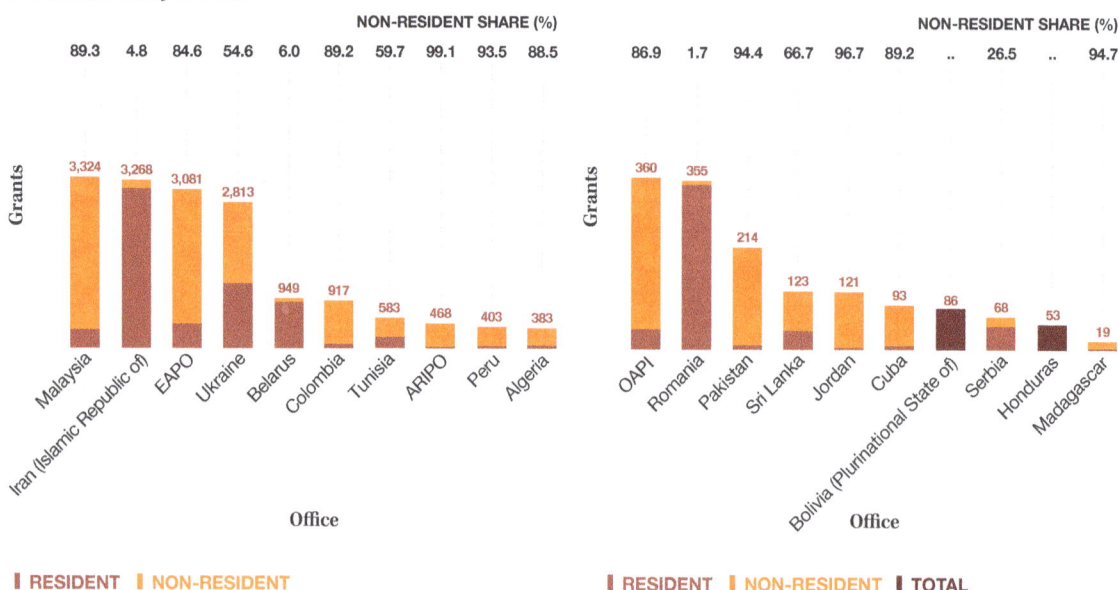

NON-RESIDENT SHARE (%)											NON-RESIDENT SHARE (%)									
89.3	4.8	84.6	54.6	6.0	89.2	59.7	99.1	93.5	88.5		86.9	1.7	94.4	66.7	96.7	89.2	..	26.5	..	94.7

Left chart grants: Malaysia 3,324; Iran (Islamic Republic of) 3,268; EAPO 3,081; Ukraine 2,813; Belarus 949; Colombia 917; Tunisia 583; ARIPO 468; Peru 403; Algeria 383

Right chart grants: OAPI 360; Romania 355; Pakistan 214; Sri Lanka 123; Jordan 121; Cuba 93; Bolivia (Plurinational State of) 86; Serbia 68; Honduras 53; Madagascar 19

Office

▮ RESIDENT ▮ NON-RESIDENT ▮ TOTAL

.. indicates not available.

Note: ARIPO is the African Regional Intellectual Property Organization, EAPO is the Eurasian Patent Organization and OAPI is the African Intellectual Property Organization. The selected offices are from different world regions and income groups (low-income, lower middle-income and upper middle-income). Where available, data for all offices are presented in the statistical table at the end of this section.

Source: WIPO Statistics Database, September 2017.

Patent applications and grants by origin

Figure A17
Equivalent patent applications by origin, 2016

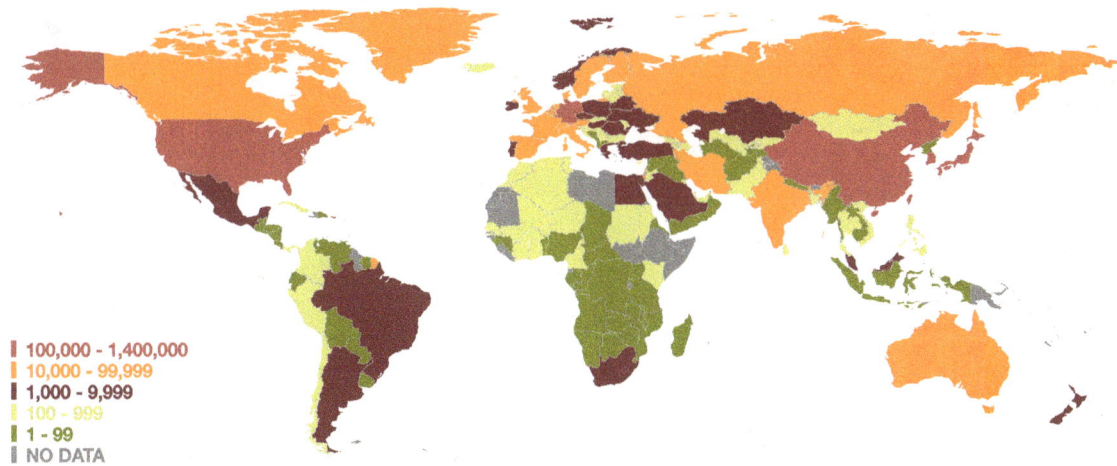

- 100,000 - 1,400,000
- 10,000 - 99,999
- 1,000 - 9,999
- 100 - 999
- 1 - 99
- NO DATA

Note: Patent filing activity by origin includes resident applications and applications filed abroad. The origin of a patent application is determined by the residence of the first named applicant. Applications filed at regional offices are considered equivalent to multiple applications in the relevant member states. See the glossary for the definition of equivalent application.

Source: WIPO Statistics Database, September 2017.

Figure A18
Equivalent patent applications for the top 20 origins, 2016

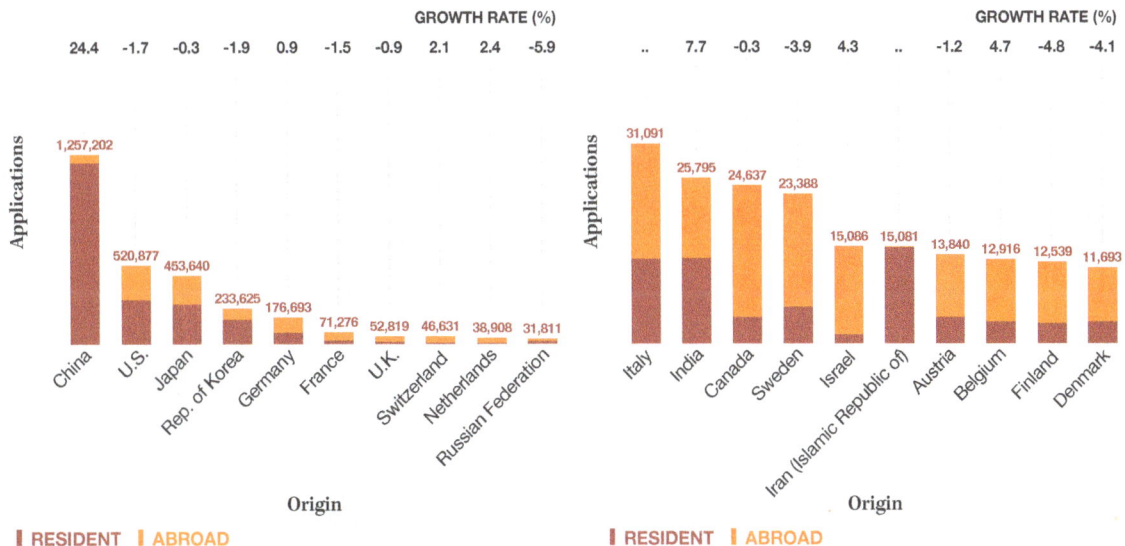

GROWTH RATE (%)

24.4	-1.7	-0.3	-1.9	0.9	-1.5	-0.9	2.1	2.4	-5.9

China 1,257,202
U.S. 520,877
Japan 453,640
Rep. of Korea 233,625
Germany 176,693
France 71,276
U.K. 52,819
Switzerland 46,631
Netherlands 38,908
Russian Federation 31,811

GROWTH RATE (%)

..	7.7	-0.3	-3.9	4.3	..	-1.2	4.7	-4.8	-4.1

Italy 31,091
India 25,795
Canada 24,637
Sweden 23,388
Israel 15,086
Iran (Islamic Republic of) 15,081
Austria 13,840
Belgium 12,916
Finland 12,539
Denmark 11,693

RESIDENT   ABROAD

RESIDENT   ABROAD

.. indicates not available.

Note: Patent activity by origin includes resident applications and applications filed abroad. The origin of a patent application is determined by the residence of the first named applicant. Applications filed at regional offices are considered equivalent to multiple applications in the relevant member states. See the glossary for the definition of equivalent application.

Source: WIPO Statistics Database, September 2017.

Figure A19

Patent applications for the top 25 offices and origins, 2016

Origin	Australia	Brazil	Canada	China	China, Hong Kong SAR	EPO	France	Germany	India	Indonesia	Iran (Islamic Republic of)	Israel
Australia	2,620	160	430	624	189	776	2	25	248	99	8	68
Austria	204	219	249	946	34	2,039	12	976	273	54	24	33
Belgium	254	318	305	700	109	2,186	103	54	281	58	21	81
Brazil	57	5,200	54	134	10	207		17	59	16	1	5
Canada	545	208	4,078	985	275	1,576	8	91	312	60	14	106
China	893	799	777	1,204,981	804	7,152	151	552	2,171	519	41	65
Denmark	206	200	260	858	71	1,870	2	26	313	63	19	44
Finland	179	178	296	1,007	143	1,818	9	77	248	112	5	15
France	808	1,452	1,695	4,631	422	10,508	14,206	270	1,138	280	71	263
Germany	1,394	2,219	2,023	14,158	864	25,094	530	48,480	2,871	446	101	363
India	207	159	159	288	45	759	6	29	13,199	91	4	52
Iran (Islamic Republic of)			3	1		4	2	4	3		14,930	
Israel	394	185	393	800	181	1,211		31	304	20		1,300
Italy	343	640	567	1,610	200	4,171	66	170	560	108	54	109
Japan	1,607	1,829	1,864	39,207	1,379	21,006	160	6,839	4,228	2,508	30	215
Netherlands	608	965	555	3,155	173	6,838	30	209	1,400	310	37	149
Rep. of Korea	468	290	330	13,764	170	6,824	36	1,204	1,533	367	56	46
Russian Federation	34	44	69	135	20	173	3	15	80	39	6	15
Singapore	121	46	95	769	67	433	2	132	131	65	2	20
Spain	141	200	189	393	73	1,562	87	26	171	39	12	57
Sweden	491	604	403	1,919	139	3,555	20	517	780	131	13	72
Switzerland	1,151	1,347	1,249	3,453	940	7,267	251	951	1,466	426	51	365
Turkey	19	30	18	80	6	510	4	11	27	14	8	17
U.K.	1,176	697	1,141	2,372	512	5,133	49	225	1,014	248	9	173
U.S.	12,909	9,100	16,191	35,895	5,856	40,046	315	5,859	10,441	2,096	47	2,486
Others/Unknown	1,565	921	1,352	5,638	1,410	6,640	164	1,109	1,806	369	68	300
Total	**28,394**	**28,010**	**34,745**	**1,338,503**	**14,092**	**159,358**	**16,218**	**67,899**	**45,057**	**8,538**	**15,632**	**6,419**

Origin						Office							
	Italy	Japan	Malaysia	Mexico	New Zealand	Rep. of Korea	Russian Federation	Singapore	South Africa	Turkey	U.K.	U.S.	Viet Nam
Australia	3	415	103	118	594	204	76	181	189	1	111	3,666	40
Austria	14	403	47	135	30	306	193	70	101	2	41	2,596	20
Belgium	8	433	52	130	59	274	132	79	84	1	163	2,644	30
Brazil	2	70	6	71	2	34	26	6	39	3	7	931	1
Canada	2	545	44	224	117	342	126	108	119	2	159	13,493	31
China	29	3,810	333	558	124	2,829	1,171	343	389	35	659	26,026	492
Denmark		380	60	128	58	166	170	54	68		45	2,202	24
Finland	2	407	34	85	28	283	148	40	121	2	117	3,085	66
France	33	3,237	192	594	183	1,766	896	338	379	3	150	12,863	94
Germany	323	6,388	427	1,153	275	4,111	1,726	593	669	49	499	31,201	238
India	3	227	79	112	58	121	46	66	137	5	60	8,739	39
Iran (Islamic Republic of)						1				1		129	
Israel	3	528	14	114	55	238	118	121	79	4	98	8,253	14
Italy	8,848	802	65	301	74	467	448	101	136	9	57	5,209	60
Japan	101	260,244	1,481	1,181	195	14,773	1,416	1,719	268	58	562	86,021	1,334
Netherlands	19	2,272	165	447	142	913	794	189	204	2	278	5,456	124
Rep. of Korea	7	5,216	208	222	42	163,424	394	162	72	22	78	37,341	576
Russian Federation		115	22	19	2	55	26,795	13	28	4	8	1,219	25
Singapore	1	488	96	34	19	146	50	1,601	26	1	99	1,988	49
Spain	17	260	32	204	41	138	121	44	66	2	42	1,790	12
Sweden	19	817	105	229	64	591	325	82	177	5	157	5,206	50
Switzerland	116	2,539	411	968	388	1,411	877	497	508	19	296	5,225	233
Turkey	2	38	4	10	2	23	28	3	10	6,230	15	373	2
U.K.	39	1,718	209	319	249	902	451	318	424	3	13,876	14,074	45
U.S.	126	23,979	1,607	8,262	2,251	13,643	4,323	3,707	2,248	355	2,864	295,327	786
Others/ Unknown	104	3,050	1,440	1,795	1,334	1,669	737	545	3,170	30	1,618	30,514	843
Total	9,821	318,381	7,236	17,413	6,386	208,830	41,587	10,980	9,711	6,848	22,059	605,571	5,228

Note: EPO is the European Patent Office. Origin data are based on absolute counts, not equivalent counts. The top 25 offices and origins are selected based on the available 2016 data broken down by country of origin.

Source: WIPO Statistics Database, September 2017.

PATENTS

Figure A20
Flow of non-resident patent applications between the top five origins and the top 10 offices, 2016

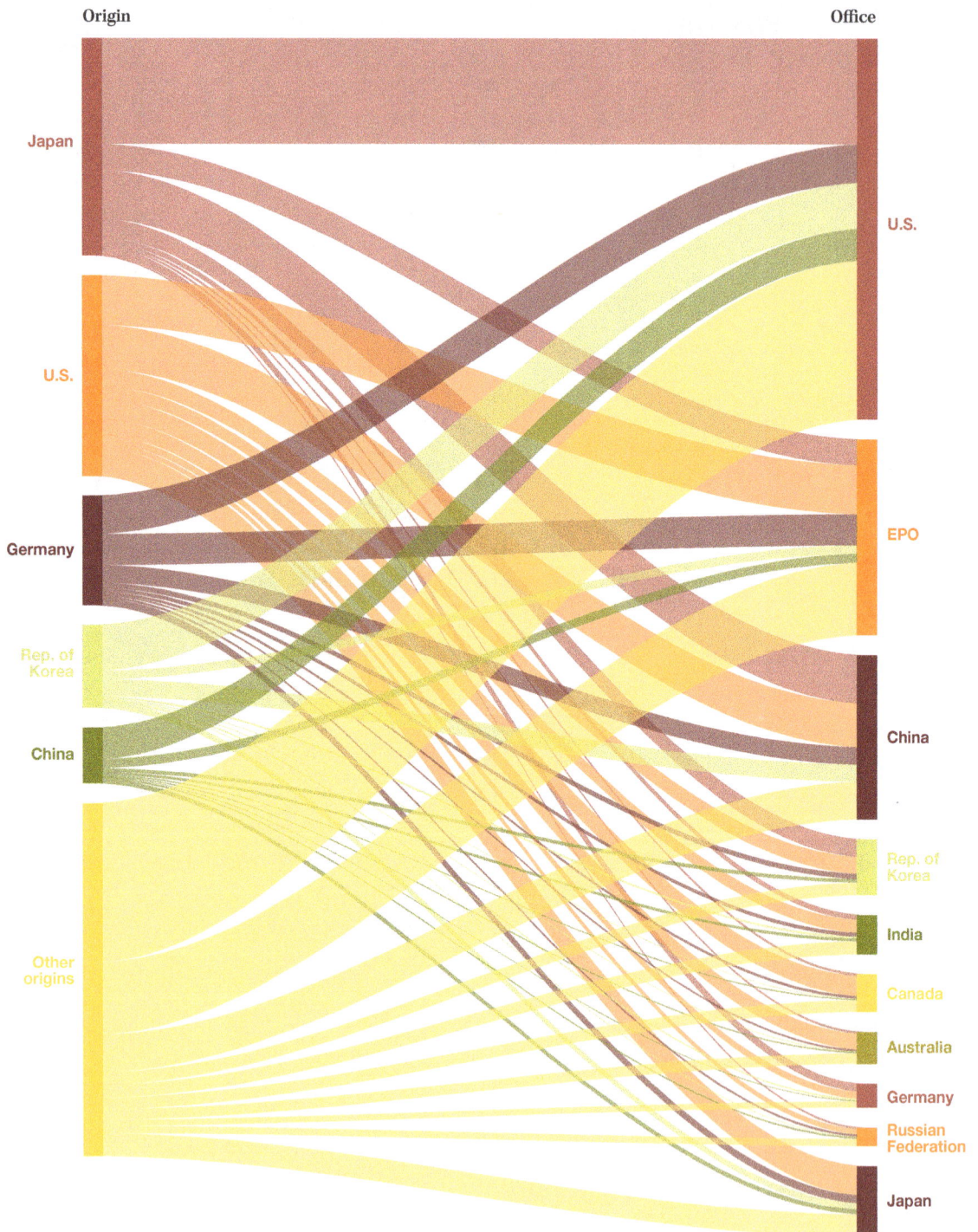

Note: EPO is the European Patent Office. Origin data are based on absolute counts, not equivalent counts.

Source: WIPO Statistics Database, September 2017.

Figure A21
Distribution of patent applications for the top 15 offices and selected origins, 2016

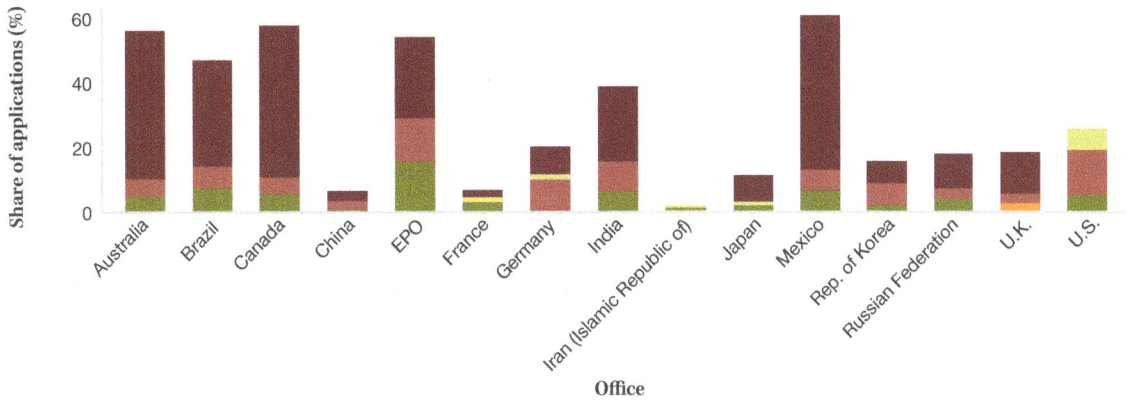

CHINA | **FRANCE** | **GERMANY** | **JAPAN** | **REP. OF KOREA** | **SWITZERLAND** | **U.S.**

Note: EPO is the European Patent Office. Origin data are based on absolute counts, not equivalent counts.

Source: WIPO Statistics Database, September 2017.

Figure A22
Equivalent patent grants for the top 20 origins, 2016

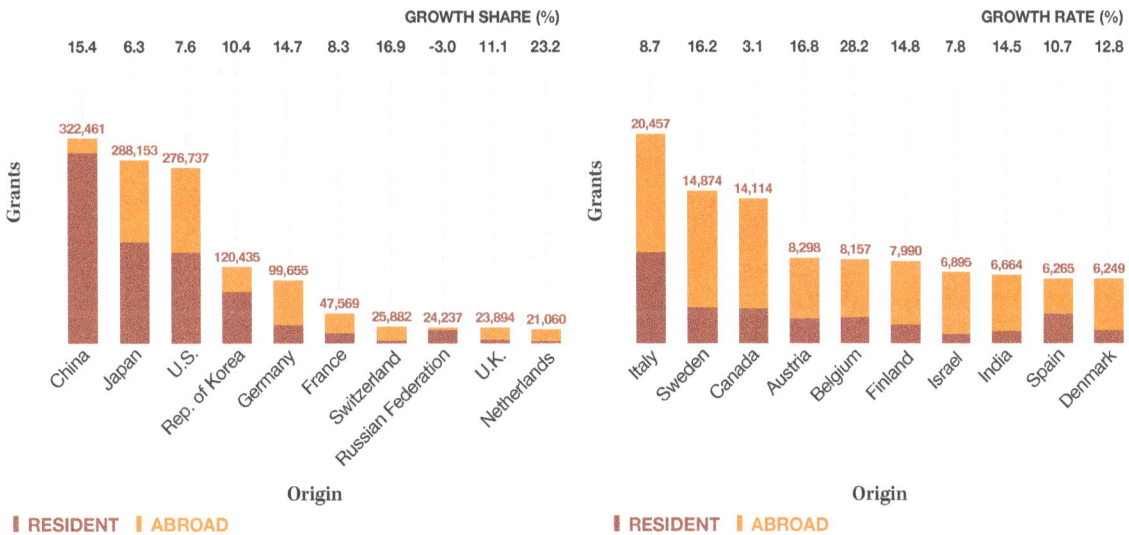

RESIDENT | **ABROAD**

Note: See the glossary for the definition of equivalent grants.

Source: WIPO Statistics Database, September 2017.

Patent families

Figure A23
Trend in patent families worldwide

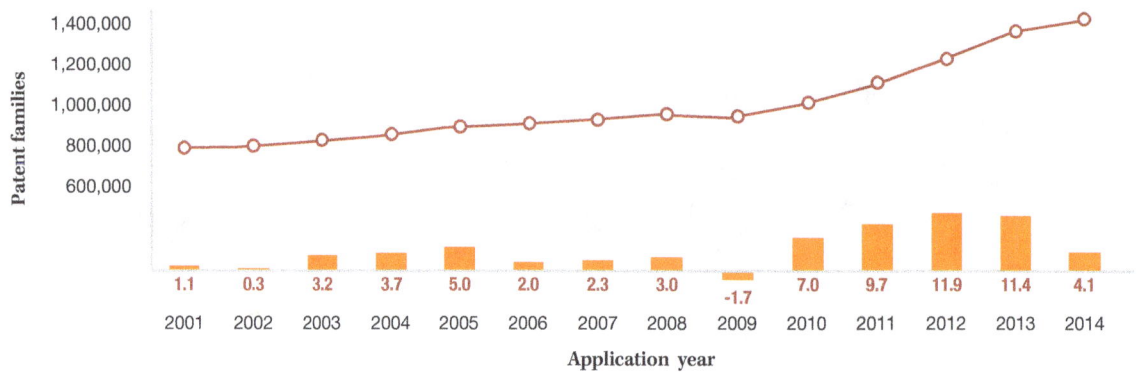

PATENT FAMILIES **GROWTH RATE (%)**

Note: Applicants often file patent applications in multiple jurisdictions, so some inventions are recorded more than once. To take this into account, WIPO has indicators related to patent families, defined as patent applications interlinked by one or more of: priority claim, Patent Cooperation Treaty national phase entry, continuation, continuation-in-part, internal priority and addition or division. Patent families here include only those associated with patent applications for inventions and exclude patent families associated with utility model applications.

Sources: WIPO Statistics Database and EPO PATSTAT database, October 2017.

Figure A24
Trend in foreign-oriented patent families worldwide

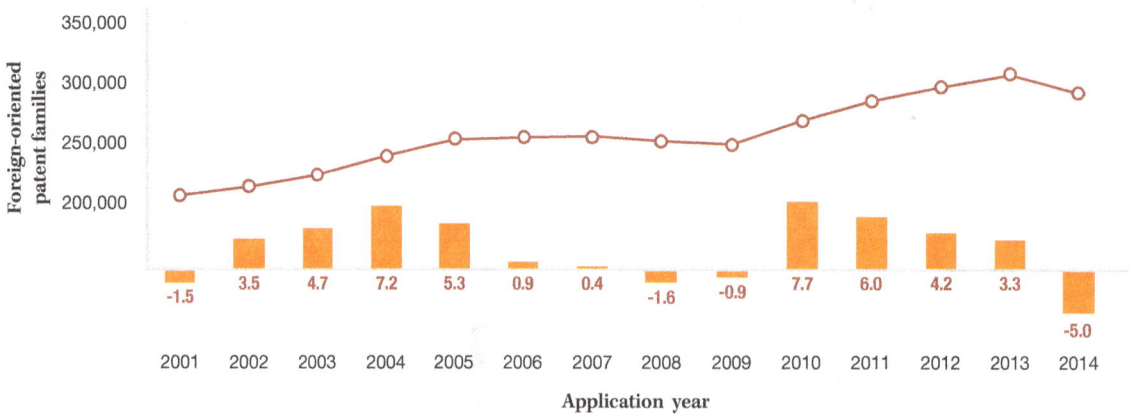

FOREIGN-ORIENTED PATENT FAMILIES **GROWTH RATE (%)**

Note: A special subset of patent families comprises foreign-oriented patent families: this includes only patent families that have at least one filing office different from the office of the applicant's country of origin. Some foreign-oriented patent families include only one filing office, because applicants may choose to file directly with a foreign office. For example, if a Canadian applicant files a patent application directly with the USPTO without previously filing with the patent office of Canada, that application and applications filed subsequently with the USPTO will form a foreign-oriented patent family. The sharp drop in foreign-oriented patent families in 2014 shown here may partly reflect incomplete data.

Sources: WIPO Statistics Database and EPO PATSTAT database, October 2017.

Figure A25
Domestic and foreign-oriented patent families for the top 20 origins, 2012-14

FOREIGN-ORIENTED SHARE (%)

| 2.9 | 29.4 | 45.9 | 20.3 | 56.3 | 3.1 | 64.1 | 46.2 | 87.5 | 55.8 |

FOREIGN-ORIENTED SHARE (%)

| 89.3 | 85.4 | 84.9 | 12.7 | 55.7 | 92.4 | 12.6 | 62.5 | 47.7 | 82.4 |

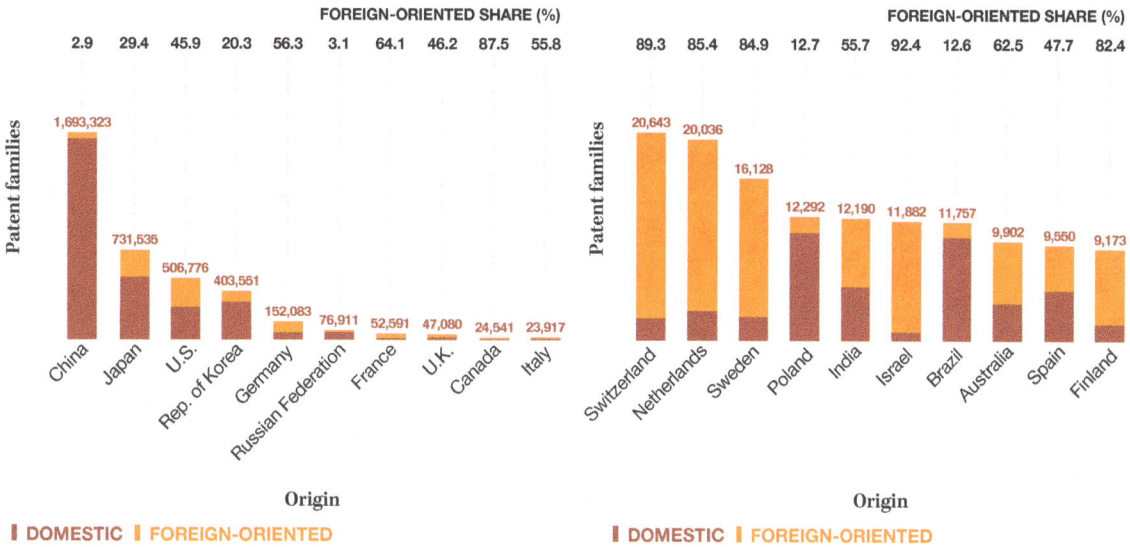

Left chart — Patent families by Origin:
- China: 1,693,323
- Japan: 731,535
- U.S.: 506,776
- Rep. of Korea: 403,551
- Germany: 152,083
- Russian Federation: 76,911
- France: 52,591
- U.K.: 47,080
- Canada: 24,541
- Italy: 23,917

Right chart — Patent families by Origin:
- Switzerland: 20,643
- Netherlands: 20,036
- Sweden: 16,128
- Poland: 12,292
- India: 12,190
- Israel: 11,882
- Brazil: 11,757
- Australia: 9,902
- Spain: 9,550
- Finland: 9,173

DOMESTIC **FOREIGN-ORIENTED**   **DOMESTIC** **FOREIGN-ORIENTED**

Note: A patent family is defined as patent applications interlinked by one or more of: priority claim, Patent Cooperation Treaty national phase entry, continuation, continuation-in-part, internal priority and addition or division. Patent families here include only those associated with patent applications for inventions and exclude patent families associated with utility model applications.

Sources: WIPO Statistics Database and EPO PATSTAT database, October 2017.

Figure A26
Distribution of patent families by number of offices for the top 20 origins, 2012-14

AVERAGE NUMBER OF OFFICES IN FOREIGN-ORIENTED FAMILIES

| 2.6 | 2.8 | 2.6 | 3.0 | 3.2 | 3.2 | 3.2 | 3.3 | 3.6 | 3.1 | 2.2 | 3.3 | 3.4 | 4.0 | 3.3 | 2.9 |

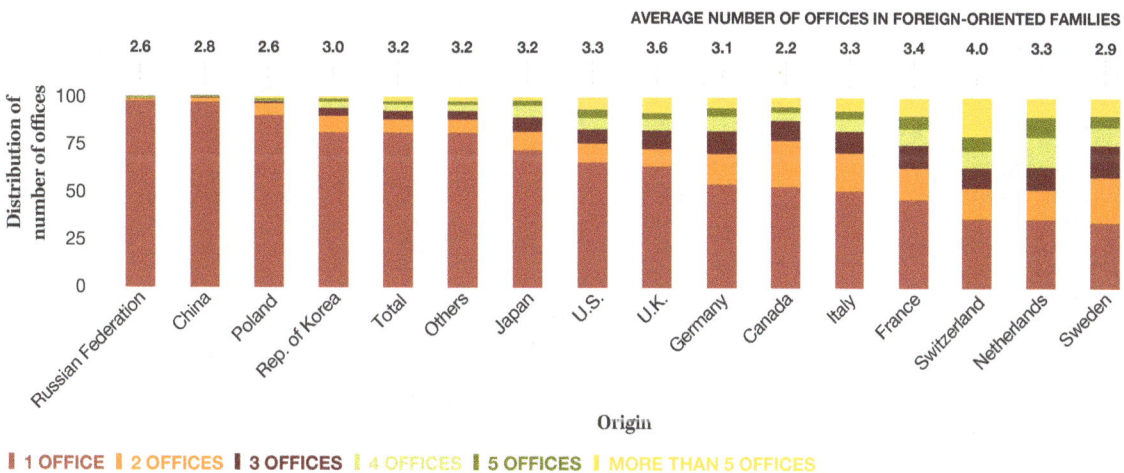

Origins: Russian Federation, China, Poland, Rep. of Korea, Total, Others, Japan, U.S., U.K., Germany, Canada, Italy, France, Switzerland, Netherlands, Sweden

1 OFFICE **2 OFFICES** **3 OFFICES** **4 OFFICES** **5 OFFICES** **MORE THAN 5 OFFICES**

Note: A patent family is defined as patent applications interlinked by one or more of: priority claim, Patent Cooperation Treaty national phase entry, continuation, continuation-in-part, internal priority and addition or division. Patent families here include only those associated with patent applications for inventions and exclude patent families associated with utility model applications.

Sources: WIPO Statistics Database and EPO PATSTAT database, October 2017.

Figure A27
Top 100 patent applicants worldwide, based on total number of patent families

Applicant	Origin	2011	2012	2013	2014	Total number of patent families 2011-14
CANON INC	Japan	6,871	7,473	7,829	8,303	30,476
SAMSUNG ELECTRONICS CO., LTD.	Rep. of Korea	5,139	6,254	7,635	7,581	26,609
PANASONIC CORPORATION	Japan	10,284	7,904	4,282	429	22,899
TOSHIBA KK	Japan	6,165	6,105	5,543	4,814	22,627
TOYOTA JIDOSHA KABUSHIKI KAISHA	Japan	6,980	5,487	4,824	4,899	22,190
MITSUBISHI ELECTRIC CORP	Japan	5,327	5,796	5,416	5,089	21,628
HUAWEI TECHNOLOGIES CO., LTD.	China	3,339	4,717	5,377	4,744	18,177
LG ELECTRONICS INC	Rep. of Korea	4,235	4,095	4,313	4,971	17,614
STATE GRID CORPORATION OF CHINA	China	193	671	6,875	9,494	17,233
SEIKO EPSON CORP	Japan	5,303	3,843	3,742	4,080	16,968
SHARP CORP	Japan	4,766	5,835	3,054	3,165	16,820
ROBERT BOSCH GMBH	Germany	3,658	4,335	4,433	4,156	16,582
RICOH CO LTD	Japan	4,130	3,981	4,550	3,652	16,313
CHINA PETROLEUM & CHEMICAL CORPORATION	China	3,076	3,318	3,721	4,044	14,159
FUJITSU LTD	Japan	3,508	3,513	3,520	3,282	13,823
ZTE CORPORATION	China	4,536	3,594	2,231	3,422	13,783
DENSO CORP	Japan	2,993	3,054	3,341	3,366	12,754
INTERNATIONAL BUSINESS MACHINES CORPORATION	U.S.	528	1,907	4,621	4,492	11,548
SIEMENS AG	Germany	3,001	2,899	2,731	2,886	11,517
HONDA MOTOR CO LTD	Japan	2,748	2,711	2,945	2,537	10,941
SONY CORP	Japan	3,273	2,760	2,363	2,491	10,887
HYUNDAI MOTOR CO LTD	Rep. of Korea	2,512	2,449	2,641	3,134	10,736
HITACHI LTD	Japan	2,720	2,844	2,591	2,486	10,641
ZHEJIANG UNIVERSITY	China	2,147	2,301	2,674	2,629	9,751
NEC CORP	Japan	2,444	2,603	2,218	2,073	9,338
QUALCOMM INCORPORATED	U.S.	1,324	2,097	2,971	2,891	9,283
FUJIFILM CORP	Japan	3,139	2,234	1,938	1,953	9,264
DAINIPPON PRINTING CO LTD	Japan	2,076	2,340	2,194	2,178	8,788
DAIMLER AG	Germany	2,112	2,139	2,032	1,967	8,250
NIPPON TELEGRAPH & TELEPHONE	Japan	1,993	2,022	2,158	1,843	8,016
SAMSUNG DISPLAY CO LTD	Rep. of Korea	904	1,653	2,749	2,563	7,869
LG DISPLAY CO LTD	Rep. of Korea	1,860	1,804	1,869	2,020	7,553
SCHAEFFLER TECHNOLOGIES GMBH & CO KG	Germany	1,538	1,602	1,832	2,486	7,458
TSINGHUA UNIVERSITY	China	1,582	1,876	1,785	1,831	7,074
HONGFUJIN PRECISION INDUSTRY (SHENZHEN) CO., LTD.	China	2,681	2,312	1,714	313	7,020
PANASONIC IP MAN CORP	Japan	55	155	2,023	4,748	6,981
KONICA CORP	Japan	246	2,381	2,212	2,136	6,975
OCEAN'S KING LIGHTING SCIENCE & TECHNOLOGY CO., LTD.	China	1,148	2,032	3,609	185	6,974
KOREA ELECTRONICS TELECOMM	Rep. of Korea	1,502	2,094	1,637	1,734	6,967
POSCO	Rep. of Korea	1,661	1,896	1,769	1,629	6,955
HARBIN INSTITUTE OF TECHNOLOGY	China	1,123	1,547	2,036	2,230	6,936
BROTHER IND LTD	Japan	1,960	1,734	1,694	1,461	6,849
LG CHEMICAL LTD	Rep. of Korea	897	1,547	2,029	2,318	6,791
SAMSUNG ELECTRO MECH	Rep. of Korea	1,767	1,922	1,649	1,364	6,702
SOUTHEAST UNIVERSITY	China	1,255	1,374	1,873	2,109	6,611
KYOCERA CORP	Japan	1,953	1,875	1,542	1,234	6,604
LENOVO (BEIJING) CO., LTD.	China	614	1,856	1,798	2,316	6,584
MITSUBISHI HEAVY IND LTD	Japan	1,825	2,019	1,628	1,085	6,557
KONINKLIJKE PHILIPS ELECTRONICS N.V.	Netherlands	1,586	1,577	1,633	1,597	6,393
TENCENT TECHNOLOGY (SHENZHEN) CO., LTD.	China	830	1,888	1,905	1,700	6,323
LG INNOTEK CO LTD	Rep. of Korea	2,548	1,490	949	1,218	6,205

Applicant	Origin	2011	2012	2013	2014	Total number of patent families 2011-14
HYUN DAI HEAVY IND CO LTD	Rep. of Korea	1,391	1,953	1,438	1,325	6,107
TELEFONAKTIEBOLAGET LM ERICSSON (PUBL)	Sweden	1,369	1,552	1,531	1,655	6,107
SHANGHAI JIAO TONG UNIVERSITY	China	1,250	1,478	1,673	1,631	6,032
SANKYO CO	Japan	774	1,549	1,874	1,822	6,019
FUJI XEROX CO LTD	Japan	1,406	1,671	1,510	1,378	5,965
KYOCERA DOCUMENT SOLUTIONS INC	Japan	1,093	1,215	1,653	1,899	5,860
NISSAN MOTOR	Japan	1,226	1,814	1,505	1,280	5,825
INTEL CORP	U.S.	1,243	1,181	1,703	1,636	5,763
GEN ELECTRIC	U.S.	399	1,151	2,044	1,859	5,453
GOOGLE INC	U.S.	438	1,257	2,156	1,482	5,333
BOE TECHNOLOGY GROUP CO., LTD.	China	472	1,211	1,552	2,066	5,301
TIANJIN UNIVERSITY	China	990	1,271	1,503	1,497	5,261
SUMITOMO ELECTRIC INDUSTRIES	Japan	1,631	1,368	1,146	1,109	5,254
NIPPON KOGAKU KK	Japan	1,678	1,682	1,248	580	5,188
HONGHAI PRECISION INDUSTRY CO., LTD.	Taiwan, Province of China	1,386	1,221	1,758	695	5,060
SOUTH CHINA UNIVERSITY OF TECHNOLOGY	China	914	1,116	1,369	1,630	5,029
TOPPAN PRINTING CO LTD	Japan	1,307	1,268	1,246	1,194	5,015
HEWLETT PACKARD DEVELOPMENT CO	U.S.	694	924	1,562	1,754	4,934
SAMSUNG HEAVY IND	Rep. of Korea	1,051	1,313	1,119	1,279	4,762
JFE STEEL KK	Japan	1,534	1,205	986	1,011	4,736
JIANGNAN UNIVERSITY	China	962	1,234	1,164	1,349	4,709
BEIHANG UNIVERSITY	China	1,080	1,098	1,220	1,184	4,582
GM GLOBAL TECH OPERATIONS INC	U.S.	919	1,080	1,381	1,162	4,542
OLYMPUS CORP	Japan	1,160	921	954	1,470	4,505
MURATA MANUFACTURING CO	Japan	1,058	1,042	1,242	1,148	4,490
BASF SE	Germany	1,098	1,385	1,035	934	4,452
FORD GLOBAL TECH LLC	U.S.	214	446	1,607	2,039	4,306
APPLE INC	U.S.	280	1,091	1,251	1,543	4,165
YAZAKI CORP	Japan	1,080	1,035	1,128	906	4,149
BAYERISCHE MOTOREN WERKE AG	Germany	651	823	1,173	1,477	4,124
UNIVERSITY OF ELECTRONIC SCIENCE AND TECHNOLOGY OF CHINA	China	687	843	1,187	1,390	4,107
PEUGEOT CITROEN AUTOMOBILES SA	France	1,209	1,141	953	789	4,092
BEIJING UNIVERSITY OF TECHNOLOGY	China	597	732	1,249	1,468	4,046
KYORAKU SANGYO KK	Japan	865	740	1,074	1,367	4,046
HYUNDAI MOBIS CO LTD	Rep. of Korea	838	1,221	864	1,098	4,021
TOYOTA IND CORP	Japan	703	1,228	984	1,082	3,997
PETROCHINA COMPANY LIMITED	China	598	801	1,196	1,385	3,980
PEKING UNIVERSITY	China	888	887	1,154	1,022	3,951
SUMITOMO CHEMICAL CO	Japan	1,569	1,170	601	605	3,945
SEMICONDUCTOR MANUFACTURING INTERNATIONAL (SHANGHAI) CO., LTD.	China	645	834	1,054	1,398	3,931
JIANGSU UNIVERSITY	China	488	914	1,455	1,051	3,908
XI'AN JIAOTONG UNIVERSITY	China	813	865	1,064	1,162	3,904
DAIKIN IND LTD	Japan	1,033	1,158	874	832	3,897
BRIDGESTONE CORP	Japan	1,375	912	868	723	3,878
SK HYNIX INC	Rep. of Korea	1,053	1,176	789	846	3,864
NSK LTD	Japan	989	923	780	1,071	3,763
DAEWOO SHIPBUILDING & MARINE	Rep. of Korea	590	903	1,015	1,189	3,697
SANYO PRODUCT CO LTD	Japan	631	875	947	1,242	3,695
ZHUHAI GREE ELECTRIC APPLIANCES INC.	China	325	951	1,106	1,284	3,666

Note: A patent family is defined as patent applications interlinked by one or more of: priority claim, Patent Cooperation Treaty national phase entry, continuation, continuation-in-part, internal priority and addition or division. Patent families here include only those associated with patent applications for inventions and exclude patent families associated with utility model applications.

Sources: WIPO Statistics Database and EPO PATSTAT database, September 2017.

Figure A28
Distribution of technology fields for each top 10 applicant based on patent families, 2011-14

Field of technology	Canon Inc	Samsung Electronics	Panasonic Corp	Toshiba KK	Toyota Jidosha KK	Mitsubishi Electric Corp	Huawei Technologies	LG Electronics Inc	State Grid Corp of China	Seiko Epson Corp
Electrical machinery, apparatus, energy	3.1	4.6	22.7	11.0	23.1	19.8	3.2	4.5	31.5	3.5
Audio-visual technology	16.4	10.8	10.3	9.4	0.8	6.0	4.2	7.8	1.6	7.8
Telecommunications	6.4	8.1	4.5	3.3	0.2	4.5	10.4	19.7	2.2	2.3
Digital communication	2.4	14.5	2.9	3.5	0.5	4.3	57.9	29.8	4.1	0.6
Basic communication processes	0.4	1.7	1.4	2.0	0.2	1.8	1.4	0.3	0.3	3.5
Computer technology	14.9	26.0	5.1	16.1	1.8	6.7	18.2	10.1	7.8	6.2
IT methods for management	0.5	1.4	0.6	1.8	0.3	0.8	0.6	0.7	7.2	0.7
Semiconductors	3.3	12.3	7.5	14.4	3.1	8.0	0.4	3.4	0.3	5.8
Optics	26.9	4.0	3.5	2.9	0.1	3.1	1.2	1.9	0.6	11.7
Measurement	3.1	2.9	4.3	4.8	3.8	6.6	0.9	1.1	21.1	8.7
Analysis of biological materials	0.0	0.3	0.2	0.1	0.0	0.0	0.0	0.1	0.3	0.1
Control	0.4	0.8	1.6	3.1	2.6	4.3	0.4	0.7	5.6	1.2
Medical technology	4.1	2.6	2.7	7.4	0.5	0.6	0.1	0.4	0.1	3.2
Organic fine chemistry	0.2	0.2	0.0	0.0	0.0	0.0	0.0	0.0	0.0	0.1
Biotechnology	0.0	0.7	0.3	0.1	0.2	0.0	0.0	0.1	0.0	0.3
Pharmaceuticals	0.1	0.2	0.0	0.0	0.0	0.0	0.0	0.0	0.2	0.1
Macromolecular chemistry, polymers	0.4	0.2	0.5	0.1	0.1	0.1	0.0	0.0	0.3	0.3
Food chemistry	0.0	0.0	0.0	0.0	0.1	0.0	0.0	0.0	0.0	0.0
Basic materials chemistry	0.7	0.4	0.4	0.3	0.3	0.2	0.0	0.1	0.4	1.7
Materials, metallurgy	0.2	0.3	0.9	0.9	1.8	0.2	0.1	0.2	0.4	0.5
Surface technology, coating	0.5	0.5	1.2	0.9	1.2	0.5	0.0	0.2	0.4	1.5
Micro-structural and nano-technology	0.1	0.2	0.1	0.2	0.1	0.0	0.0	0.0	0.0	0.9
Chemical engineering	0.2	0.6	1.2	1.2	1.1	0.5	0.0	1.1	1.0	0.7
Environmental technology	0.6	0.3	0.9	1.8	3.7	0.6	0.0	0.3	0.5	0.0
Handling	3.3	0.5	0.6	1.0	1.0	5.2	0.0	0.4	2.2	6.3
Machine tools	0.2	0.2	1.2	0.7	2.1	1.6	0.0	0.1	2.3	0.7
Engines, pumps, turbines	0.2	0.2	2.6	4.0	17.2	3.4	0.1	1.5	0.8	0.4
Textile and paper machines	9.5	0.2	0.5	0.9	0.0	0.3	0.0	0.2	0.1	28.6
Other special machines	0.8	0.4	1.2	0.5	0.9	0.5	0.0	0.3	0.8	1.0
Thermal processes and apparatus	0.0	1.1	6.5	1.2	0.4	11.6	0.2	6.0	0.8	0.0
Mechanical elements	0.5	0.3	0.7	0.6	8.0	1.0	0.1	0.3	1.1	0.4
Transport	0.0	0.1	1.9	1.2	24.2	3.5	0.1	0.9	1.0	0.1
Furniture, games	0.0	0.8	3.8	1.0	0.2	2.1	0.0	1.6	0.3	0.6
Other consumer goods	0.1	2.0	5.2	3.1	0.1	1.4	0.2	5.3	0.8	0.3
Civil engineering	0.0	0.1	2.9	0.3	0.3	0.5	0.1	0.2	3.9	0.0

Note: WIPO's IPC technology concordance table was used to convert IPC symbols into 35 corresponding fields of technology (see Annex A for details).

Sources: WIPO Statistics Database and EPO PATSTAT database, September 2017.

Figure A29
Trend in university and PRO patent families worldwide

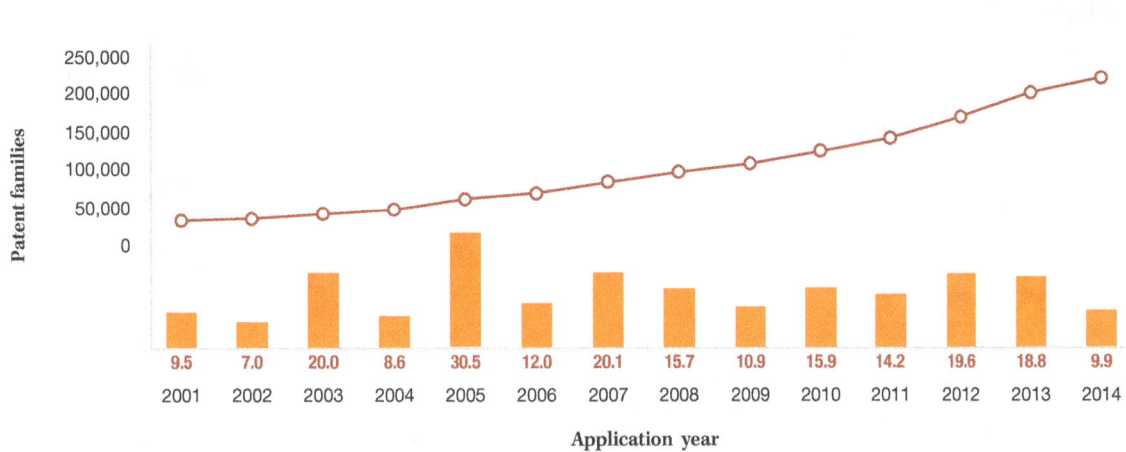

UNIVERSITY AND PRO   GROWTH RATE (%)

Note: PRO means public research organization. A patent family is defined as patent applications interlinked by one or more of: priority claim, Patent Cooperation Treaty national phase entry, continuation, continuation-in-part, internal priority and addition or division. Patent families here include only those associated with patent applications for inventions and exclude patent families associated with utility model applications.

Sources: WIPO Statistics Database and EPO PATSTAT database, October 2017.

Figure A30

Top five university and PRO patent applicants worldwide for selected origins, based on patent families

Origin	Applicant	2011	2012	2013	2014
China	ZHEJIANG UNIVERSITY	2,147	2,301	2,674	2,629
	TSINGHUA UNIVERSITY	1,582	1,876	1,785	1,831
	HARBIN INSTITUTE OF TECHNOLOGY	1,123	1,547	2,036	2,230
	SOUTHEAST UNIVERSITY	1,255	1,374	1,873	2,109
	SHANGHAI JIAO TONG UNIVERSITY	1,250	1,478	1,673	1,631
Germany	FRAUNHOFER GES FORSCHUNG	447	474	552	510
	DEUTSCH ZENTR LUFT & RAUMFAHRT	208	215	235	174
	TECH UNIVERSITY DRESDEN	59	56	71	91
	KARLSRUHER INST TECHNOLOGIE	50	63	50	49
	MAX PLANCK GESELLSCHAFT	70	61	32	40
France	COMMISSARIAT A L'ÉNERGIE ATOMIQUE ET AUX ÉNERGIES ALTERNATIVES	599	644	688	682
	CENTRE NATIONAL DE LA RECHERCHE SCIENTIFIQUE (CNRS)	229	205	161	178
	IFP ENERGIES NOUVELLES	169	172	161	168
	INSTITUT NATIONAL DE LA SANTE ET DE LA RECHERCHE MEDICALE	179	145	158	151
	CENTRE NATIONAL D'ÉTUDES SPATIALES	35	29	22	21
Japan	NAT INST OF ADV IND & TECHNOL	408	505	465	435
	TOKYO UNIVERSITY	196	197	293	252
	RAILWAY TECHNICAL RES INST	193	171	183	173
	TOHOKU UNIVERSITY	162	161	159	165
	KYOTO UNIVERSITY	132	137	141	164
Rep. of Korea	KOREA ELECTRONICS TELECOMM	1,502	2,094	1,637	1,734
	KOREA ADVANCED INSTITUTE OF SCIENCE AND TECHNOLOGY	908	1,040	745	766
	KOREA ELECTRONICS TECHNOLOGY	512	711	632	635
	YONSEI UNIVERSITY INDUSTRY ACADEMIC COOPERATION FOUNDATION	473	518	484	724
	SEOUL NAT UNIV IND FOUNDATION	469	513	484	541
U.S.	UNIVERSITY OF CALIFORNIA	585	638	732	666
	MASSACHUSETTS INSTITUTE TECHNOLOGY	218	294	386	327
	THE JOHNS HOPKINS UNIVERSITY	222	219	229	275
	STANFORD UNIVERSITY	186	202	287	198
	THE UNIVERSITY OF TEXAS SYSTEM	167	176	258	251

Note: PRO means public research organization. A patent family is defined as patent applications interlinked by one or more of: priority claim, Patent Cooperation Treaty national phase entry, continuation, continuation-in-part, internal priority and addition or division. Patent families include only those associated with patent applications for inventions and exclude patent families associated with utility model applications.

Sources: WIPO Statistics Database and EPO PATSTAT database, September 2017.

Figure A31

Distribution of technology fields for selected universities and PROs based on patent families, 2011-14

Field of technology	Applicant											
	Zhejiang Univ	Tsinghua Univ	Commissariat Energie Atomique	Centre national de la recherche scientifique (CNRS)	Fraunhofer Ges Forschung	Deutsch Zentr Luft & Raumfahrt	Nat Inst of Adv Ind & Tech	Tokyo Univ	Korea Electronics Telecomm	Korea Advanced Inst Sci & Tech	Univ of California	Massachusetts Inst Tech
Electrical machinery, apparatus, energy	6.7	8.0	12.3	4.9	6.4	5.4	9.6	10.2	2.8	9.7	3.6	6.9
Audio-visual technology	1.3	2.3	2.1	1.1	6.2	0.8	1.3	1.7	9.1	3.4	1.0	1.7
Telecommunications	1.2	2.2	2.0	1.5	2.8	3.5	0.6	1.3	11.7	4.9	0.8	1.9
Digital communication	2.9	7.8	1.9	0.2	2.5	3.2	0.6	1.2	28.8	6.9	0.8	2.3
Basic communication processes	0.7	1.5	1.8	1.7	2.1	4.2	0.4	0.3	2.2	2.4	0.9	1.3
Computer technology	10.0	13.3	7.1	2.4	8.7	2.7	2.7	4.6	21.5	15.9	5.1	5.7
IT methods for management	0.8	1.2	0.2	0.0	0.2	0.3	0.4	0.8	4.2	2.7	0.6	0.5
Semiconductors	1.7	5.9	17.5	4.7	7.4	0.9	14.8	3.5	3.7	6.9	4.7	5.7
Optics	2.1	3.4	3.9	3.8	5.3	1.6	4.0	3.0	3.2	3.0	2.1	3.8
Measurement	13.4	13.7	12.1	10.6	12.1	16.5	11.9	10.7	4.1	6.4	6.1	6.9
Analysis of biological materials	0.8	0.3	1.2	5.4	1.2	0.2	2.3	4.5	0.3	1.3	6.5	3.3
Control	3.1	2.5	0.7	0.5	0.8	6.3	0.8	1.0	2.6	1.5	0.4	1.1
Medical technology	2.6	2.4	2.1	2.7	3.4	2.6	2.2	4.8	1.2	3.3	11.4	8.0
Organic fine chemistry	4.5	1.4	0.9	8.8	0.9	0.0	3.7	5.4	0.0	0.7	5.9	3.6
Biotechnology	5.7	2.4	1.1	12.1	2.8	0.2	7.7	11.8	0.2	4.2	17.4	12.4
Pharmaceuticals	3.2	0.7	0.8	11.7	1.2	0.0	1.5	7.3	0.0	1.1	16.2	9.9
Macromolecular chemistry, polymers	2.4	0.6	0.8	2.1	2.4	0.2	2.9	4.1	0.1	0.6	1.4	1.3
Food chemistry	3.5	0.2	0.1	0.4	0.4	0.0	0.5	1.1	0.0	0.1	1.0	0.6
Basic materials chemistry	2.6	1.6	1.7	3.2	2.8	0.7	3.4	2.1	0.1	1.3	2.1	1.9
Materials, metallurgy	4.7	3.6	3.2	3.4	3.4	1.3	7.9	3.6	0.1	2.6	1.2	2.0
Surface technology, coating	1.7	1.6	4.0	2.1	4.3	1.1	3.8	1.1	0.3	1.4	1.8	3.1
Micro-structural and nano-technology	1.0	1.8	3.4	2.5	1.3	0.0	1.6	1.1	0.2	2.6	1.3	1.9
Chemical engineering	3.8	3.4	3.2	5.7	2.4	0.3	5.4	2.8	0.3	2.5	2.8	4.5
Environmental technology	3.3	3.3	2.3	1.8	0.7	0.9	2.2	1.0	0.0	1.0	0.7	1.7
Handling	1.0	1.3	1.1	0.6	1.1	4.8	0.7	0.3	0.3	1.6	0.2	0.8
Machine tools	1.5	2.1	1.4	0.9	4.5	0.4	1.0	0.8	0.0	0.6	0.2	0.3
Engines, pumps, turbines	2.1	3.3	3.6	1.0	1.3	6.5	1.1	1.2	0.1	1.4	0.7	1.0
Textile and paper machines	0.6	0.5	0.2	0.2	0.6	1.4	0.7	1.0	0.1	0.4	0.2	0.5
Other special machines	3.4	0.6	1.3	1.6	3.4	8.4	2.0	2.7	0.4	1.4	1.1	2.3
Thermal processes and apparatus	1.8	1.8	3.0	0.7	1.4	4.8	0.7	1.4	0.1	0.6	0.5	1.0
Mechanical elements	2.0	1.1	1.0	0.6	1.5	4.5	0.4	0.4	0.0	1.4	0.4	0.9
Transport	1.6	2.0	1.2	0.3	1.5	15.4	0.4	2.0	1.2	3.3	0.3	0.7
Furniture, games	0.4	0.1	0.2	0.1	0.7	0.2	0.3	0.2	0.3	0.9	0.3	0.2
Other consumer goods	0.3	0.2	0.3	0.5	1.1	0.4	0.1	0.4	0.2	0.5	0.3	0.3
Civil engineering	1.7	2.0	0.4	0.2	0.8	0.1	0.3	0.8	0.1	1.4	0.3	0.2

Note: PRO means public research organization. A patent family is defined as patent applications interlinked by one or more of: priority claim, Patent Cooperation Treaty national phase entry, continuation, continuation-in-part, internal priority and addition or division. Patent families here include only those associated with patent applications for inventions and exclude patent families associated with utility model applications. WIPO's IPC technology concordance table was used to convert IPC symbols into 35 corresponding fields of technology (see Annex A for details).

Sources: WIPO Statistics Database and EPO PATSTAT database, October 2017.

Published patent applications by field of technology

Figure A32
Published patent applications worldwide by field of technology

Field of technology	2005	2010	2015	Share (%) of 2015	Average growth (%) 2005-15
Electrical Engineering					
Electrical machinery, apparatus, energy	89,962	110,667	176,457	7.0	7.0
Audio-visual technology	87,442	72,811	75,133	3.0	-1.5
Telecommunications	60,638	54,162	50,786	2.0	-1.8
Digital communication	53,654	75,728	123,258	4.9	8.7
Basic communication processes	17,632	15,471	15,661	0.6	-1.2
Computer technology	105,158	121,224	187,007	7.4	5.9
IT methods for management	18,125	22,829	42,270	1.7	8.8
Semiconductors	67,453	71,547	77,542	3.1	1.4
Instruments					
Optics	69,650	60,613	63,590	2.5	-0.9
Measurement	61,548	75,815	123,986	4.9	7.3
Analysis of biological materials	12,524	11,422	15,200	0.6	2.0
Control	26,676	28,099	49,593	2.0	6.4
Medical technology	69,527	77,944	110,109	4.4	4.7
Chemistry					
Organic fine chemistry	57,323	54,253	63,603	2.5	1.0
Biotechnology	38,296	39,068	55,499	2.2	3.8
Pharmaceuticals	73,701	71,276	102,790	4.1	3.4
Macromolecular chemistry, polymers	27,965	28,531	45,576	1.8	5.0
Food chemistry	22,391	27,659	63,150	2.5	10.9
Basic materials chemistry	39,075	44,451	82,202	3.3	7.7
Materials, metallurgy	29,406	37,377	63,835	2.5	8.1
Surface technology, coating	27,962	32,222	42,671	1.7	4.3
Micro-structural and nano-technology	2,145	3,366	4,725	0.2	8.2
Chemical engineering	33,619	36,887	60,479	2.4	6.0
Environmental technology	20,880	25,776	42,979	1.7	7.5
Mechanical Engineering					
Handling	43,339	42,382	68,535	2.7	4.7
Machine tools	36,024	42,237	76,060	3.0	7.8
Engines, pumps, turbines	41,418	48,133	65,336	2.6	4.7
Textile and paper machines	38,280	30,643	38,380	1.5	0.0
Other special machines	46,948	49,107	89,750	3.6	6.7
Thermal processes and apparatus	24,238	29,092	42,876	1.7	5.9
Mechanical elements	42,620	45,746	69,589	2.8	5.0
Transport	65,748	66,359	105,294	4.2	4.8
Other fields					
Furniture, games	42,116	41,695	61,930	2.5	3.9
Other consumer goods	33,450	31,915	50,882	2.0	4.3
Civil engineering	51,225	56,268	90,185	3.6	5.8
Unknown	20,298	29,537	20,305	0.8	0.0
Total	**1,598,456**	**1,712,312**	**2,517,223**	**100.0**	**4.6**

Note: Data refer to published patent applications. There is a minimum delay of 18 months between the application date and the publication date. WIPO's IPC technology concordance table was used to convert IPC symbols into 35 corresponding fields of technology (see Annex A for details).

Sources: WIPO Statistics Database and EPO PATSTAT database, October 2017.

Figure A33
Trend in published patent applications for the top five technology fields

SHARE OF TOP FIVE TECHNOLOGIES (%)

| 23.8 | 24.5 | 25.2 | 26.0 | 26.5 | 26.9 | 27.4 | 28.1 | 28.7 | 29.3 | 28.6 |

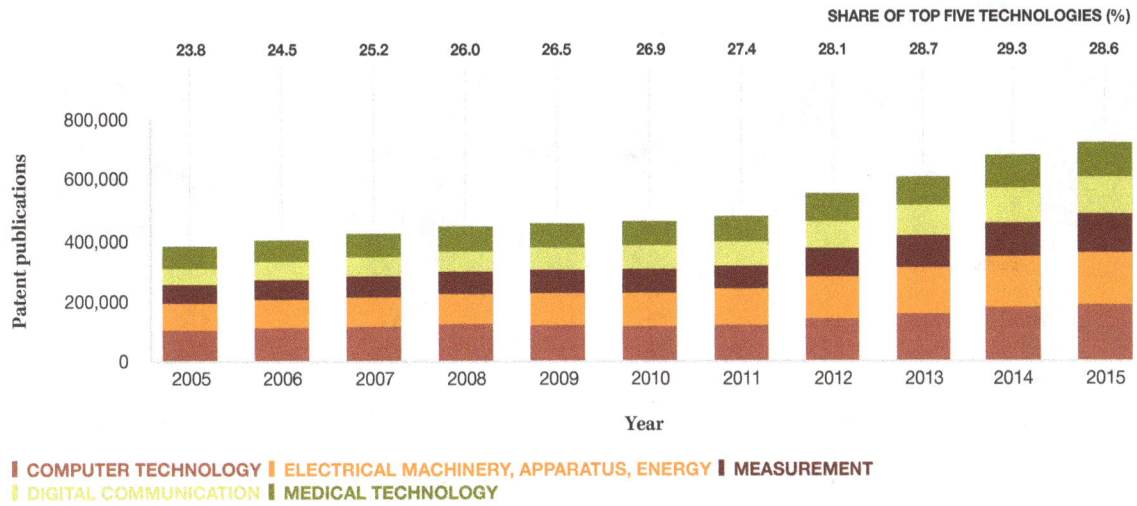

I COMPUTER TECHNOLOGY **I** ELECTRICAL MACHINERY, APPARATUS, ENERGY **I** MEASUREMENT
I DIGITAL COMMUNICATION **I** MEDICAL TECHNOLOGY

Note: Data refer to published patent applications. There is a minimum delay of 18 months between the application date and the publication date. WIPO's IPC technology concordance table was used to convert IPC symbols into 35 corresponding fields of technology (see Annex A for details).The top five fields were selected based on their 2015 totals.

Sources: WIPO Statistics Database and EPO PATSTAT database, October 2017.

Figure A34
Distribution of published patent applications by technology field for the top 10 origins, 2013-15

Field of technology	China	France	Germany	Japan	Netherlands	Rep. of Korea	Russian Federation	Switzerland	U.K.	U.S.
Electrical machinery, apparatus, energy	6.8	6.3	9.2	10.9	7.5	9.3	3.6	4.3	5.8	4.6
Audio-visual technology	2.0	2.5	1.5	5.4	3.0	5.7	0.7	1.0	1.8	3.0
Telecommunications	1.8	2.4	0.9	2.6	1.3	3.4	1.2	0.6	2.0	2.5
Digital communication	5.4	5.9	1.5	2.9	2.4	5.9	0.6	1.2	3.6	6.6
Basic communication processes	0.4	0.6	0.6	0.9	0.8	0.6	0.8	0.5	0.6	0.9
Computer technology	6.7	5.7	3.1	6.5	5.7	9.1	2.5	2.4	6.3	12.6
IT methods for management	1.0	0.9	0.4	1.1	0.7	3.4	0.4	0.7	1.5	3.4
Semiconductors	1.8	2.5	2.8	6.4	3.5	6.9	0.9	0.7	1.3	3.2
Optics	1.5	1.7	1.6	6.6	4.0	3.4	0.8	1.0	1.6	1.8
Measurement	6.3	5.3	5.6	4.3	5.1	3.5	7.5	7.8	5.2	3.9
Analysis of biological materials	0.4	0.9	0.6	0.3	0.8	0.4	2.1	1.5	1.4	0.9
Control	2.4	1.3	1.7	1.7	1.0	1.4	1.6	1.3	1.8	1.8
Medical technology	2.1	3.8	4.9	3.2	10.3	2.7	6.4	7.0	6.4	8.4
Organic fine chemistry	2.3	5.2	3.5	1.6	3.6	1.3	1.6	8.0	4.7	3.1
Biotechnology	1.8	2.9	1.7	0.9	3.8	1.4	1.8	5.7	3.9	3.5
Pharmaceuticals	4.3	4.4	2.7	1.2	3.4	1.9	4.3	11.5	6.4	5.6
Macromolecular chemistry, polymers	2.1	1.5	2.1	2.1	3.3	1.1	0.9	1.9	0.8	1.4
Food chemistry	4.5	0.9	0.5	0.8	3.5	1.7	13.2	4.0	1.3	1.2
Basic materials chemistry	4.4	2.1	3.5	2.1	4.9	1.5	3.6	3.5	3.4	2.9
Materials, metallurgy	4.0	2.2	1.9	2.3	1.0	2.0	5.6	1.5	1.4	1.1
Surface technology, coating	1.8	1.6	1.8	2.3	1.2	1.6	1.9	1.4	1.2	1.4
Micro-structural and nano-technology	0.2	0.3	0.2	0.1	0.2	0.2	0.8	0.2	0.1	0.2
Chemical engineering	3.0	2.4	2.7	1.4	2.8	2.0	3.2	2.5	3.0	2.0
Environmental technology	2.3	1.6	1.6	1.3	1.8	1.6	2.1	1.4	1.8	1.1
Handling	2.9	2.3	3.2	2.8	3.0	1.9	1.0	5.7	2.6	2.0
Machine tools	4.7	1.6	3.8	2.3	0.9	2.2	3.0	1.7	1.3	1.6
Engines, pumps, turbines	1.6	4.9	6.4	3.2	1.0	1.9	4.7	2.8	3.7	2.7
Textile and paper machines	1.8	0.7	1.5	2.5	1.3	0.9	0.4	2.3	0.8	1.0
Other special machines	4.3	3.4	3.4	2.7	4.6	2.7	5.5	2.5	2.6	2.5
Thermal processes and apparatus	2.1	1.6	1.8	1.8	1.0	2.0	1.7	1.4	1.4	0.9
Mechanical elements	2.4	3.7	7.0	2.9	1.6	2.0	3.0	1.9	3.1	2.0
Transport	2.5	9.6	9.6	5.4	2.5	5.2	4.3	1.6	4.8	2.9
Furniture, games	2.0	1.7	1.5	3.6	2.4	2.5	1.1	3.0	3.5	2.3
Other consumer goods	2.1	2.1	1.9	1.5	1.6	2.7	0.9	3.5	3.8	1.7
Civil engineering	4.0	3.3	3.2	2.2	4.0	4.0	6.3	2.0	5.1	3.1

Note: Data refer to published patent applications. There is a minimum delay of 18 months between the application date and the publication date. WIPO's IPC technology concordance table was used to convert IPC symbols into 35 corresponding fields of technology (see Annex A for details). The top 10 origins were selected based on their 2013-15 total published applications.

Sources: WIPO Statistics Database and EPO PATSTAT database, October 2017.

Figure A35
Trend in patent applications in energy-related technologies

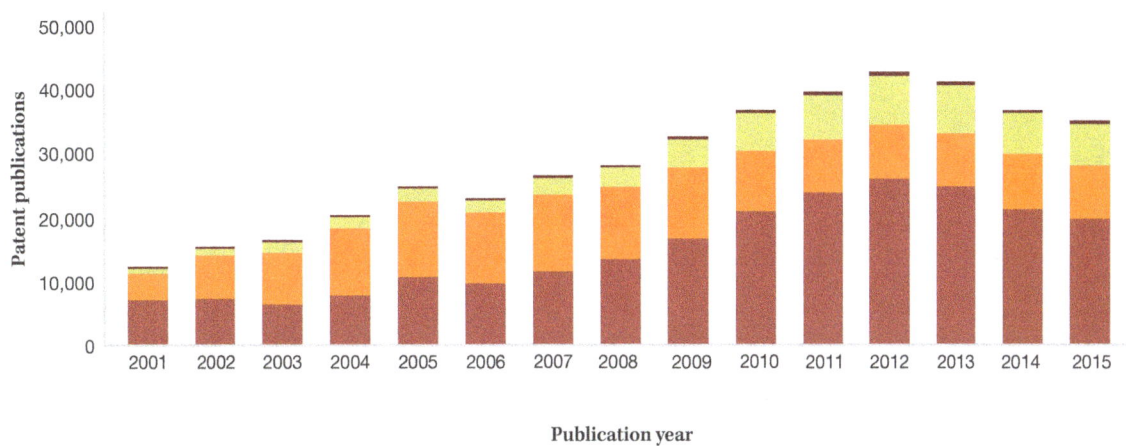

Publication year

SOLAR ENERGY | **FUEL CELL TECHNOLOGY** | WIND ENERGY TECHNOLOGY | **GEOTHERMAL ENERGY**

Note: For definitions of the technologies – fuel cells, geothermal, solar and wind energy – see Annex B. The correspondence between IPC symbols and technology fields is not always clear (there is no one-to-one relationship). It is thus difficult to capture all patents in a specific technology field. Even so, the IPC-based definitions are likely to capture the vast majority of patent applications in these areas. Data refer to published patent applications.

Sources: WIPO Statistics Database and EPO PATSTAT database, October 2017.

Patent applications by gender

Figure A36
Women inventors in PCT applications

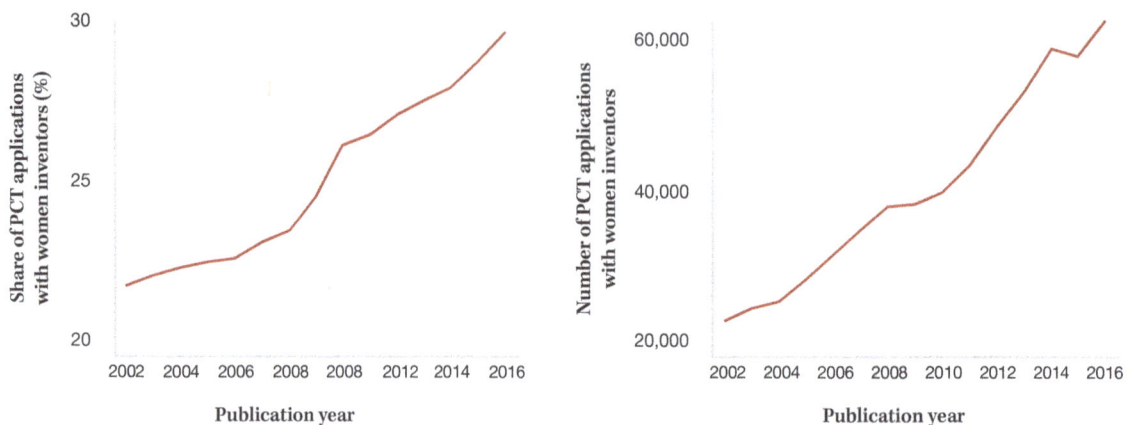

Note: In order to attribute gender to inventors' names recorded in PCT applications, WIPO produced a world gender-name dictionary based on information from 13 different public sources. Gender is attributed to a given name on a country-by-country basis because certain names can be considered male in one country but female in another.

Sources: WIPO Statistics Database, September 2017.

Figure A37
Share of PCT applications with women inventors for the top 20 origins, 2016

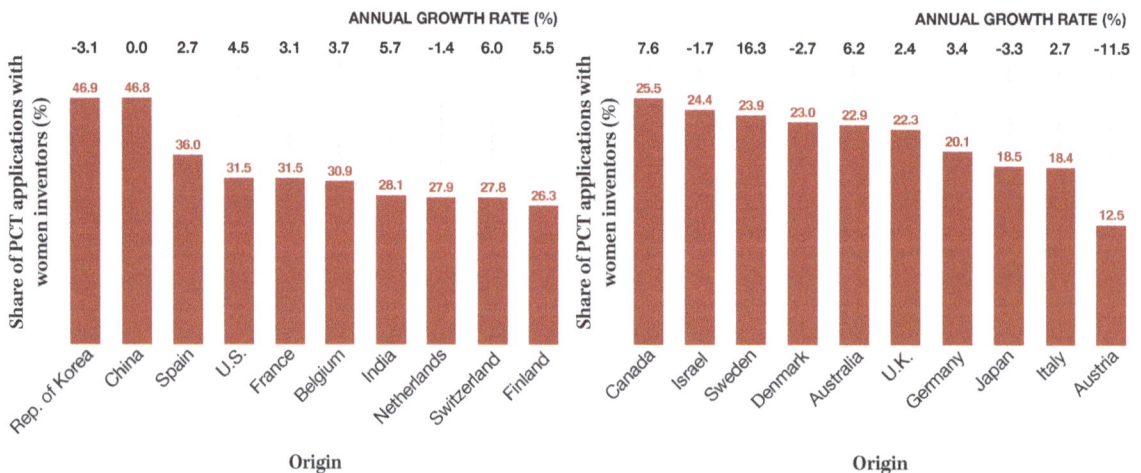

Note: In order to attribute gender to inventors' names recorded in PCT applications, WIPO produced a gender-name dictionary based on information from 13 different public sources. Gender is attributed to a given name on a country-by-country basis because certain names can be considered male in one country but female in another.

Sources: WIPO Statistics Database, September 2017.

Figure A38

Share of PCT international patent applications with women inventors by field of technology, 2016

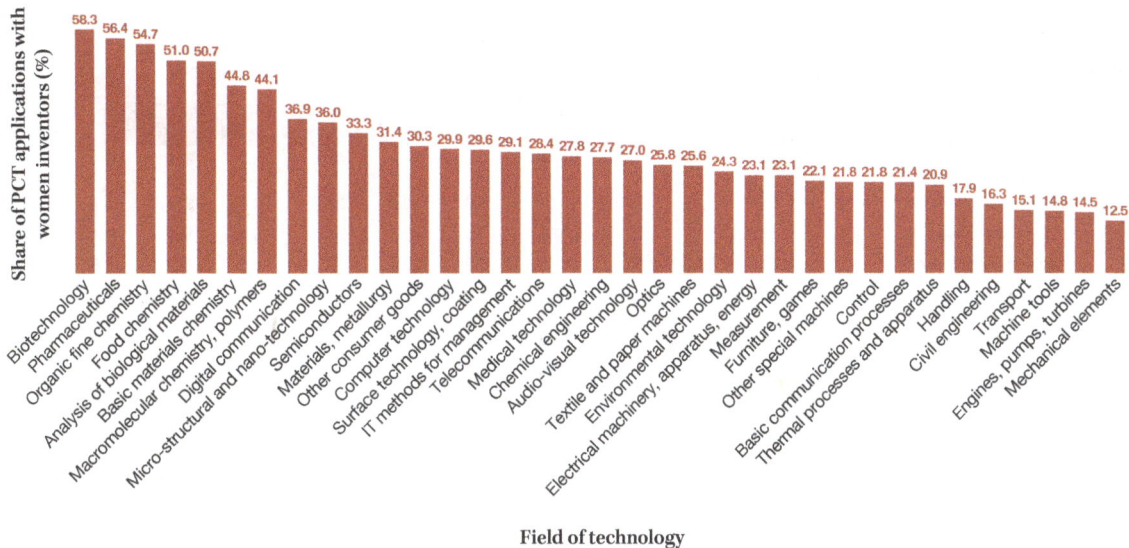

Field of technology

Note: In order to attribute gender to inventors' names recorded in PCT applications, WIPO produced a gender-name dictionary based on information from 13 different public sources. Gender is attributed to a given name on a country-by-country basis because certain names can be considered male in one country but female in another.

Sources: WIPO Statistics Database, September 2017.

Figure A39

Share of patent applications with women inventors for selected patent offices

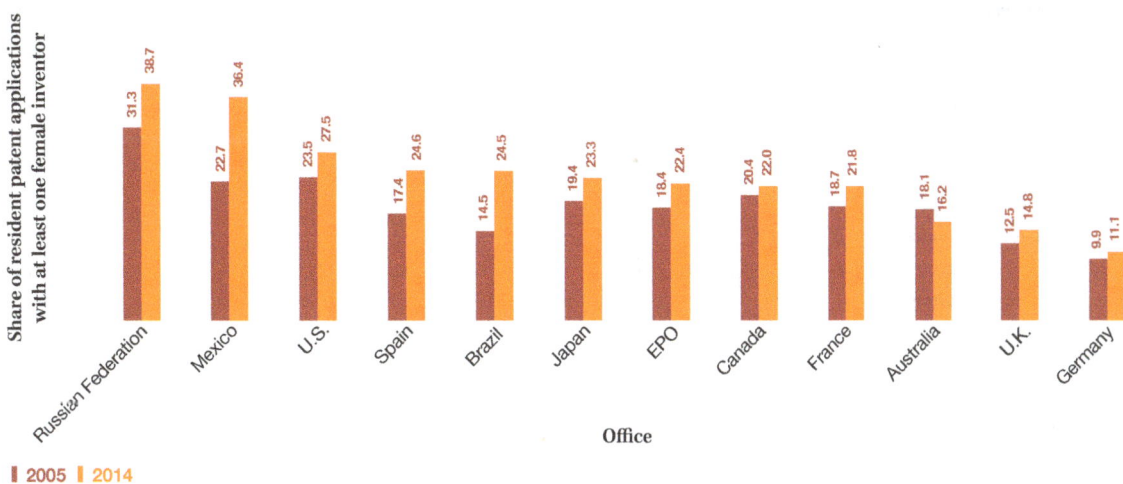

Office

█ 2005 █ 2014

Sources: WIPO Statistics Database and EPO PATSTAT database, September 2017.

69

Figure A40
Share of patent applications with women inventors for selected patent offices by field of technology, 2014

Field of technology	Australia	Brazil	Canada	EPO	France	Germany	Japan	Mexico	Russian Federation	Spain	U.K.	U.S.
Electrical machinery, apparatus, energy	9.7	17.5	22.1	16.1	18.1	9.5	21.7	14.3	25.2	27.9	12.1	21.3
Audio-visual technology	7.8	7.4	20.8	14.8	17.2	9.9	20.7	23.1	24.8	12.4	8.4	25.5
Telecommunications	10.4	27.5	14.6	18.0	17.8	7.6	20.2	26.3	19.5	15.9	11.1	24.8
Digital communication	10.3	12.9	20.1	21.4	17.6	7.3	22.0	25.0	16.0	21.7	15.8	28.2
Basic communication processes	9.1	0.0	5.7	12.6	14.5	6.0	14.9	25.0	18.1	21.4	6.5	23.8
Computer technology	18.4	17.4	20.8	19.2	21.3	11.4	23.4	26.1	23.5	30.7	11.2	27.5
IT methods for management	14.9	17.0	23.1	18.5	19.6	10.1	28.1	20.9	14.3	27.3	13.5	27.0
Semiconductors	40.9	54.5	44.8	26.1	30.9	18.5	24.8	22.2	41.1	43.3	27.7	37.6
Optics	18.9	23.2	19.2	21.6	24.8	13.0	23.4	12.5	29.4	35.6	15.0	25.6
Measurement	13.8	24.9	20.9	15.6	20.7	11.3	22.1	32.4	26.3	39.5	12.9	23.6
Analysis of biological materials	46.8	71.1	48.6	48.6	50.8	27.7	42.4	65.0	81.1	69.3	32.3	46.4
Control	8.4	16.0	20.8	12.3	17.9	10.5	22.8	29.4	31.9	15.5	7.8	21.2
Medical technology	27.7	25.4	31.8	22.5	20.7	16.5	27.2	41.8	56.0	30.6	21.1	26.4
Organic fine chemistry	42.0	70.4	53.5	59.8	63.8	58.4	43.6	73.6	70.2	74.2	52.6	50.7
Biotechnology	50.6	82.8	47.9	60.5	60.2	40.5	44.9	74.7	77.9	81.9	46.4	50.2
Pharmaceuticals	43.4	78.7	51.9	61.9	58.4	39.0	48.8	64.7	71.8	74.3	47.6	48.4
Macromolecular chemistry, polymers	18.4	50.0	35.7	48.3	51.3	36.1	32.3	60.0	73.2	53.8	41.3	43.4
Food chemistry	34.0	56.9	31.1	49.7	40.8	14.7	43.5	41.9	58.7	44.2	22.0	37.4
Basic materials chemistry	19.8	56.4	28.1	49.2	49.5	35.4	37.0	39.7	52.7	49.2	30.1	42.2
Materials, metallurgy	20.2	40.3	27.7	29.9	48.5	19.1	27.0	39.7	54.8	50	25.2	31.1
Surface technology, coating	21.9	32.6	21.9	25.0	35.8	16.7	26.8	38.2	42.9	28.8	16.6	31.2
Micro-structural and nano-technology	60.9	80.0	34.9	35.5	34.7	17.5	28.1	63.6	53.2	70.2	32.5	36.0
Chemical engineering	15.9	30.9	24.8	22.0	33.4	15.8	25.5	43.9	46.3	34.6	16.7	26.5
Environmental technology	14.9	34.5	15.7	19.9	25.5	12.7	24.4	42.9	32.4	26.9	13.1	21.8
Handling	2.6	15.3	12.2	10.0	12.9	7.0	20.1	23.7	19.8	15.5	8.9	18.1
Machine tools	4.6	17.7	14.3	8.4	11.0	7.2	20.5	27.3	27.5	18.5	5.2	16.6
Engines, pumps, turbines	1.2	8.9	16.8	11.4	20.0	9.6	19.0	19.2	15.6	14.1	5.6	14.0
Textile and paper machines	20.6	31.4	14.0	22.6	29.7	15.1	23.6	26.3	58.4	20.7	17.9	29.1
Other special machines	8.6	13.7	20.0	15.1	18.2	9.5	24.3	23.2	30.4	17.0	9.7	20.6
Thermal processes and apparatus	9.6	14.3	5.0	12.8	18.1	9.5	22.9	21.4	25.6	23.5	4.7	15.4
Mechanical elements	1.6	12.6	11.6	8.9	13.6	7.0	18.0	21.7	23.0	18.8	5.4	11.4
Transport	5.2	12.0	12.6	10.5	15.3	8.5	18.1	18.2	19.1	14.7	9.2	14.3
Furniture, games	17.0	12.7	15.9	13.1	17.4	12.8	20.0	17.5	14.2	16.2	12.8	20.0
Other consumer goods	20.3	18.7	31.3	22.6	28.6	20.1	26.3	23.7	39.8	24.8	23.8	28.6
Civil engineering	5.9	12.0	13.9	9.3	10.9	6.5	20.8	14.0	20.0	13.1	5.3	15.6

Sources: WIPO Statistics Database and EPO PATSTAT database, September 2017.

Patent applications in relation to GDP and population

Figure A41
Resident patent applications per USD 100 billion GDP for the top 20 origins

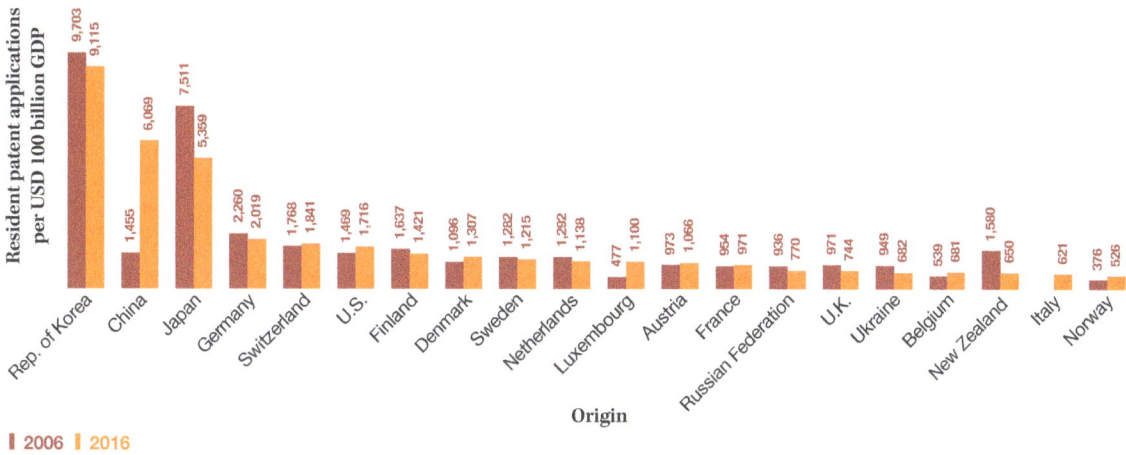

Resident patent applications per USD 100 billion GDP

Origin	2006	2016
Rep. of Korea	9,703	9,115
China	1,455	6,069
Japan	7,511	5,369
Germany	2,260	2,019
Switzerland	1,768	1,841
U.S.	1,469	1,716
Finland	1,637	1,421
Denmark	1,096	1,307
Sweden	1,282	1,215
Netherlands	1,292	1,138
Luxembourg	477	1,100
Austria	973	1,066
France	954	971
Russian Federation	936	770
U.K.	971	744
Ukraine	949	682
Belgium	539	681
New Zealand	1,580	650
Italy	621	
Norway	376	526

Origin

■ 2006 ■ 2016

Note: GDP data are in 2011 US PPP dollars. The top 20 origins were included if they had a GDP greater than USD 25 billion PPP and more than 100 resident patent applications. Due to space constraints, only the top 20 origins that fulfil these criteria are presented.

Sources: WIPO Statistics Database and World Bank, September 2017.

Figure A42
Resident patent applications per million population for the top 20 origins

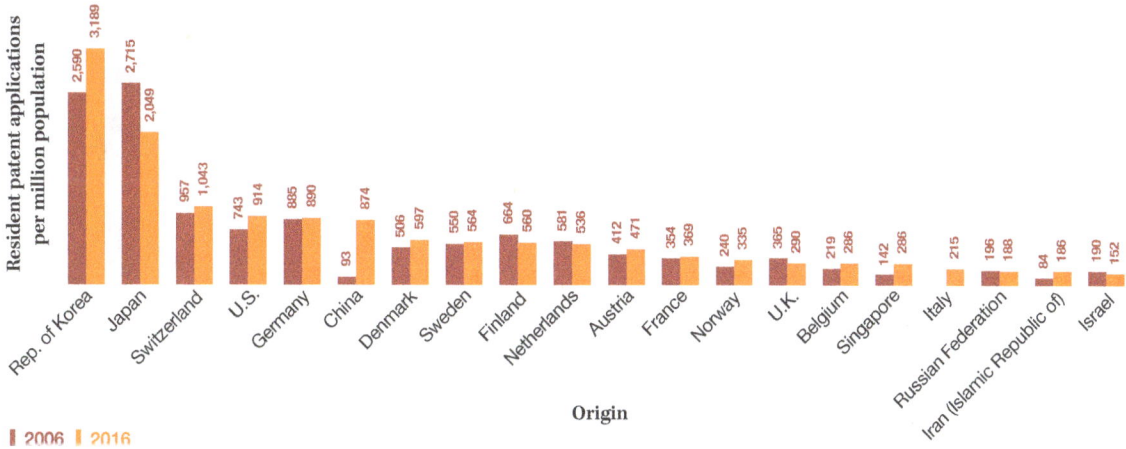

Resident patent applications per million population

Origin	2006	2016
Rep. of Korea	2,590	3,189
Japan	2,715	2,049
Switzerland	957	1,043
U.S.	743	914
Germany	885	890
China	93	874
Denmark	506	597
Sweden	550	564
Finland	664	560
Netherlands	581	536
Austria	412	471
France	354	369
Norway	240	335
U.K.	365	290
Belgium	219	286
Singapore	142	286
Italy		215
Russian Federation	196	188
Iran (Islamic Republic of)	84	186
Israel	190	152

Origin

■ 2006 ■ 2016

Note: The top 20 origins were included if they had a population greater than 5 million and if they had more than 100 resident patent applications. Due to space constraints, only the top 20 origins that fulfil these criteria are presented.

Sources: WIPO Statistics Database and World Bank, September 2017.

Patents in force

Figure A43
Trend in patents in force worldwide

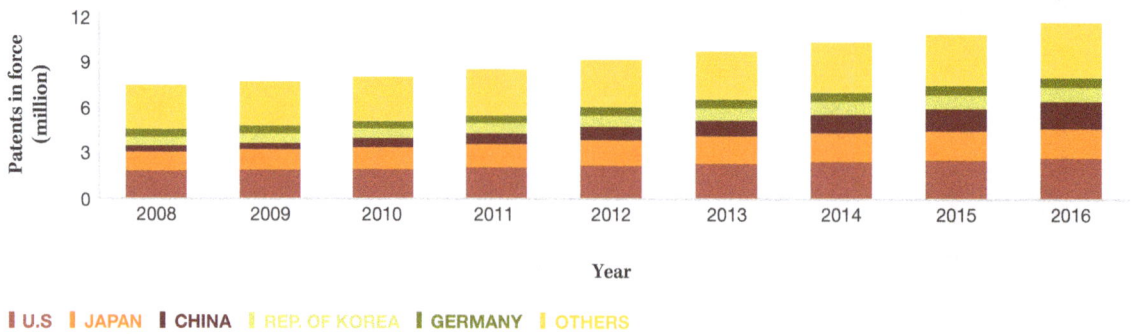

Note: World totals are WIPO estimates using data covering 107 offices.

Sources: WIPO Statistics Database, September 2017.

Figure A44
Patents in force at the top 20 offices, 2016

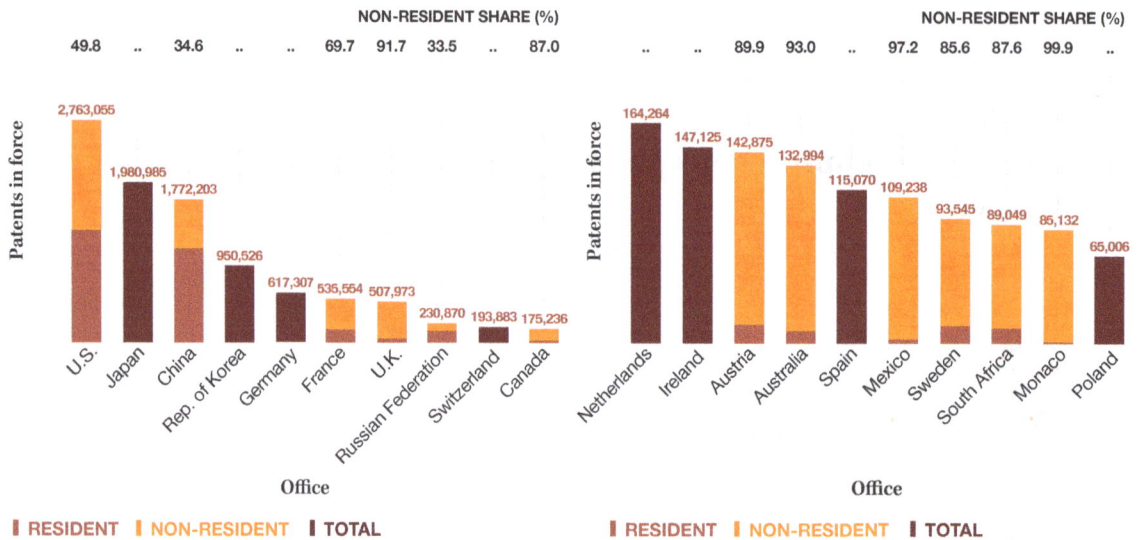

.. indicates not available.

Sources: WIPO Statistics Database, September 2017.

Figure A45
Patents in force in 2016 as a percentage of total applications

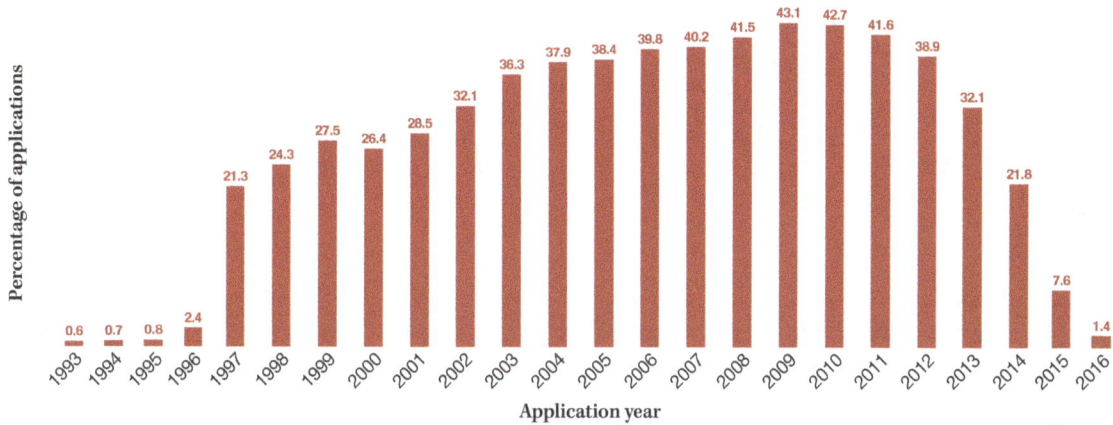

Note: Percentages are calculated as the number of patent applications filed in year *t* and in force in 2016, divided by the total number of patent applications filed in year *t*. Patent holders must pay maintenance fees to maintain the validity of their patents. Depending on technological and commercial considerations, patent holders may opt to let a patent lapse before the end of the full protection term. This figure shows the distribution of patents in force in 2016 as a percentage of total applications in the year of filing. But not all offices provide these data. Data for 72 offices show that 40-43% of the applications for which patents were eventually granted remained in force for at least 6 to 10 years after the application date. About 21% of these patents lasted the full 20-year patent term.

Sources: WIPO Statistics Database, September 2017.

Figure A46
Average age of patents in force at selected offices

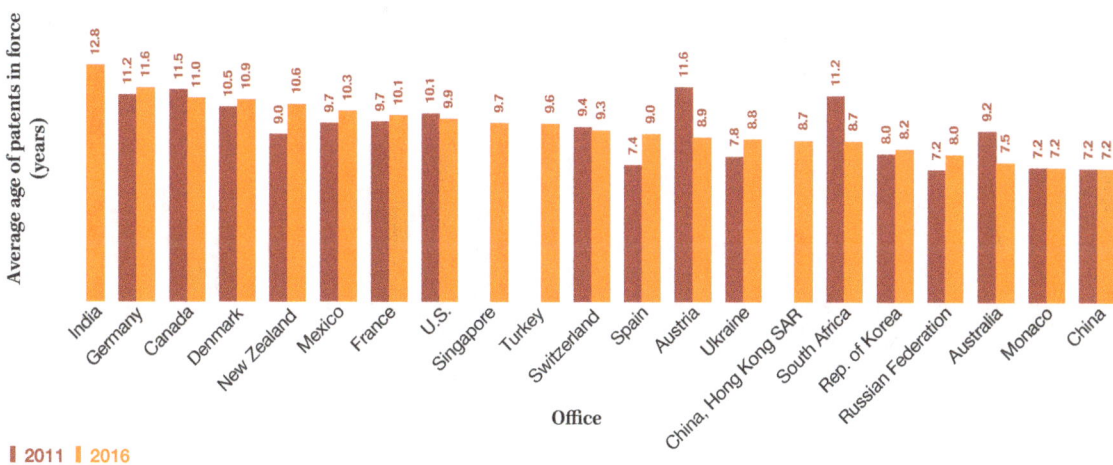

■ 2011 ■ 2016

Sources: WIPO Statistics Database, September 2017.

Pending patent applications

Figure A47
Potentially pending applications at the top offices

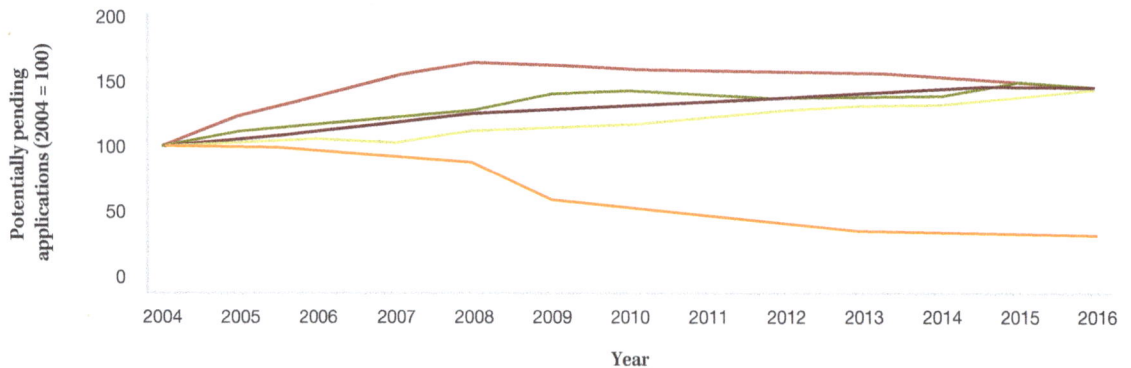

U.S. ┃ JAPAN ┃ EPO ┃ GERMANY ┃ REP. OF KOREA

Note: EPO is the European Patent Office. Application processing varies across offices, making it difficult to measure pending applications. In some offices patent applications automatically proceed to the examination stage unless applicants withdraw them; in others, applications do not proceed to examination unless applicants file a separate request for examination. To take account of procedural differences, pending application data are separated between (a) all patent applications, at any stage in the process, that are awaiting a final decision by a patent office, including those for which applicants have not filed a request for examination (where applicable) and (b) patent applications undergoing examination for which the applicant has requested examination (where such separate requests are necessary). Data for the State Intellectual Property Office of the People's Republic of China (SIPO), the office that receives the most applications, were unavailable.

Sources: WIPO Statistics Database, September 2017.

Figure A48
Potentially pending applications at the top 20 offices, 2016

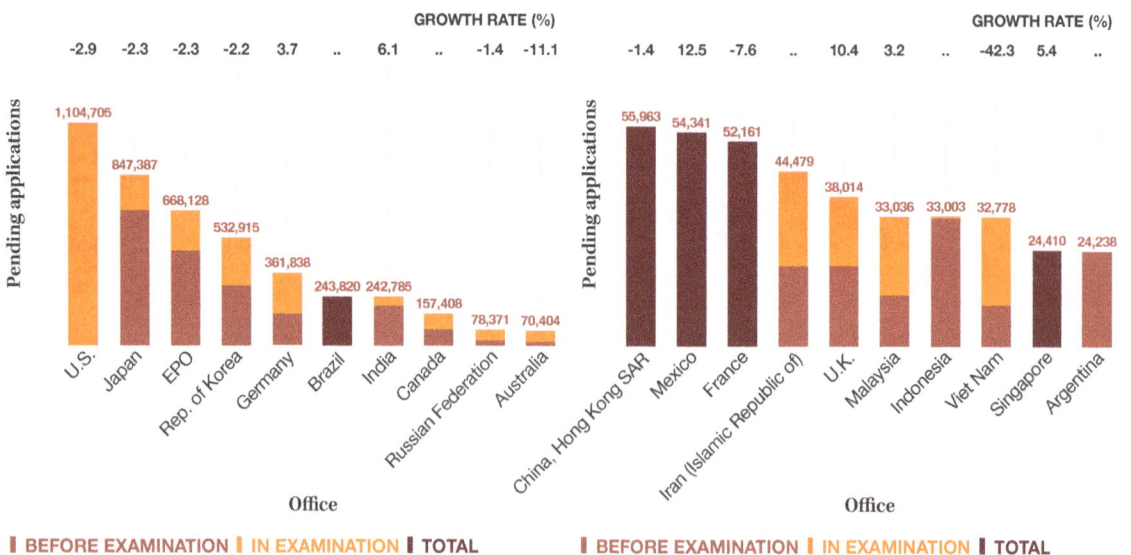

.. indicates not available.

Note: EPO is the European Patent Office. Potentially pending applications include all patent applications, at any stage in the process, awaiting a final decision by a patent office, including those for which applicants have not filed a request for examination (where applicable). Data for Brazil include both pending patent and utility model applications, and so are not comparable with other offices.

Sources: WIPO Statistics Database, September 2017.

Patent examination process

Figure A49
Distribution of patent examination decisions for selected offices, 2016

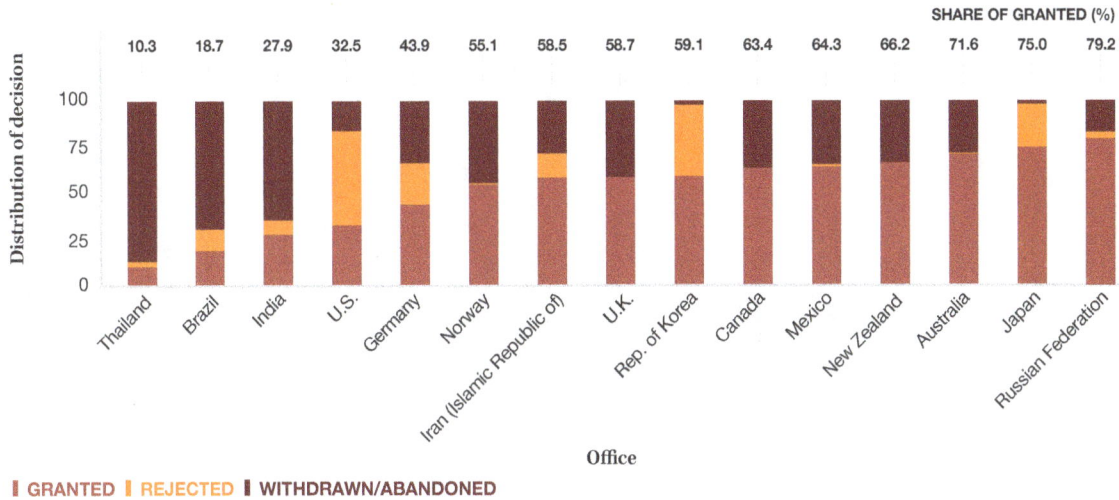

SHARE OF GRANTED (%)

| | 10.3 | 18.7 | 27.9 | 32.5 | 43.9 | 55.1 | 58.5 | 58.7 | 59.1 | 63.4 | 64.3 | 66.2 | 71.6 | 75.0 | 79.2 |

Distribution of decision

100
75
50
25
0

Thailand, Brazil, India, U.S., Germany, Norway, Iran (Islamic Republic of), U.K., Rep. of Korea, Canada, Mexico, New Zealand, Australia, Japan, Russian Federation

Office

❚ GRANTED ❚ REJECTED ❚ WITHDRAWN/ABANDONED

Note: WIPO collects data from IP offices using a common questionnaire and methodology. However, due to differences in patent procedures between offices, data cannot be fully harmonized. Therefore, one should exercise caution when making comparisons across offices.

Sources: WIPO Statistics Database, September 2017.

Figure A50
Average pendency time for first office action for selected offices, 2016

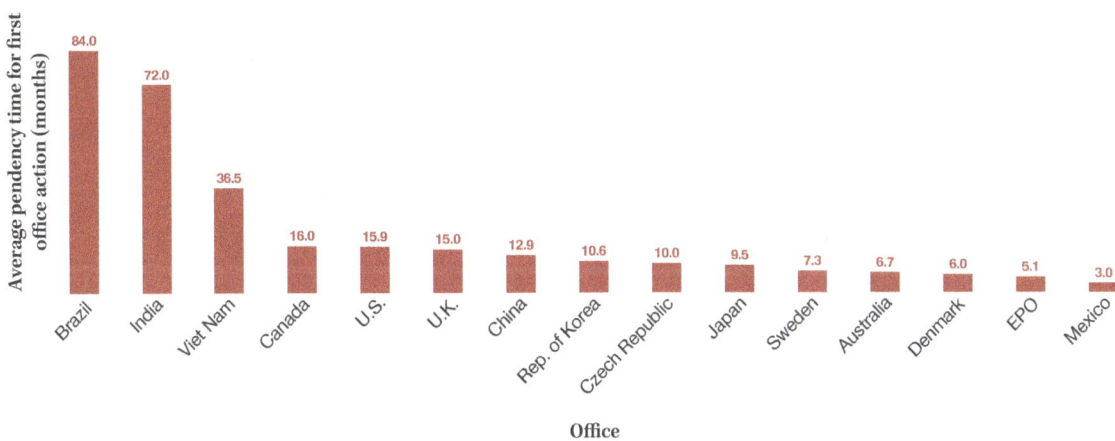

Average pendency time for first office action (months)

Office	Value
Brazil	84.0
India	72.0
Viet Nam	36.5
Canada	16.0
U.S.	15.9
U.K.	15.0
China	12.9
Rep. of Korea	10.6
Czech Republic	10.0
Japan	9.5
Sweden	7.3
Australia	6.7
Denmark	6.0
EPO	5.1
Mexico	3.0

Office

Note: WIPO collects data from IP offices using a common questionnaire and methodology. However, due to differences in patent procedures between offices, data cannot be fully harmonized. Therefore, one should exercise caution when making comparisons across offices.

Sources: WIPO Statistics Database, September 2017.

Figure A51
Average years of experience of patent examiners for selected offices, 2016

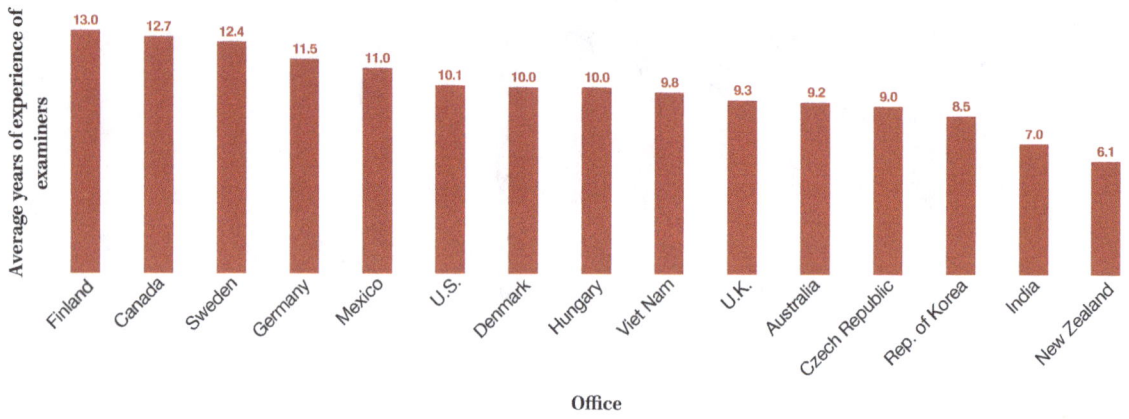

Average years of experience of examiners

Office	Years
Finland	13.0
Canada	12.7
Sweden	12.4
Germany	11.5
Mexico	11.0
U.S.	10.1
Denmark	10.0
Hungary	10.0
Viet Nam	9.8
U.K.	9.3
Australia	9.2
Czech Republic	9.0
Rep. of Korea	8.5
India	7.0
New Zealand	6.1

Office

Sources: WIPO Statistics Database, September 2017.

Patent applications filed through the Patent Cooperation Treaty (PCT) System

Figure A52
Trend in PCT applications

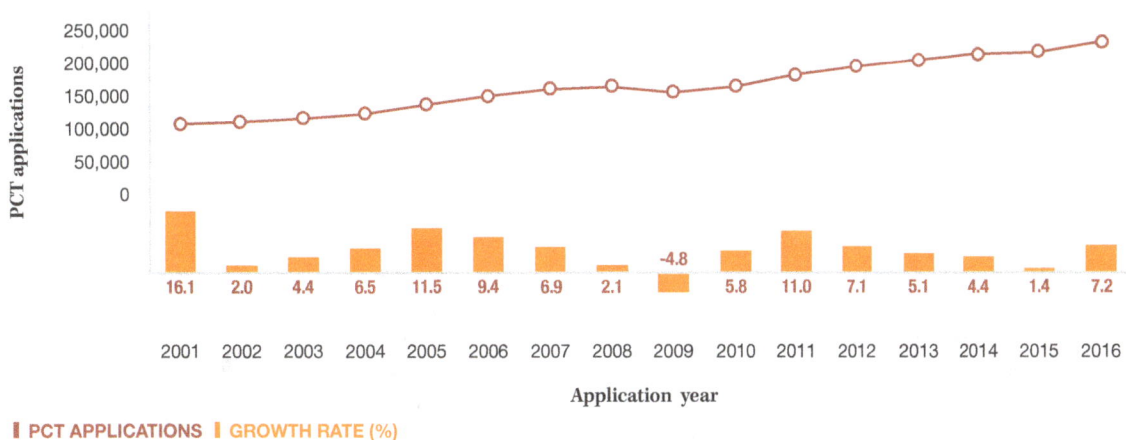

PCT APPLICATIONS   **GROWTH RATE (%)**

Year	2001	2002	2003	2004	2005	2006	2007	2008	2009	2010	2011	2012	2013	2014	2015	2016
Growth rate	16.1	2.0	4.4	6.5	11.5	9.4	6.9	2.1	-4.8	5.8	11.0	7.1	5.1	4.4	1.4	7.2

Application year

Note: Data refer to the international phase of the Patent Cooperation Treaty System. Counts are based on the international application date.

Source: WIPO Statistics Database, September 2017.

Figure A53
PCT applications by origin, 2016

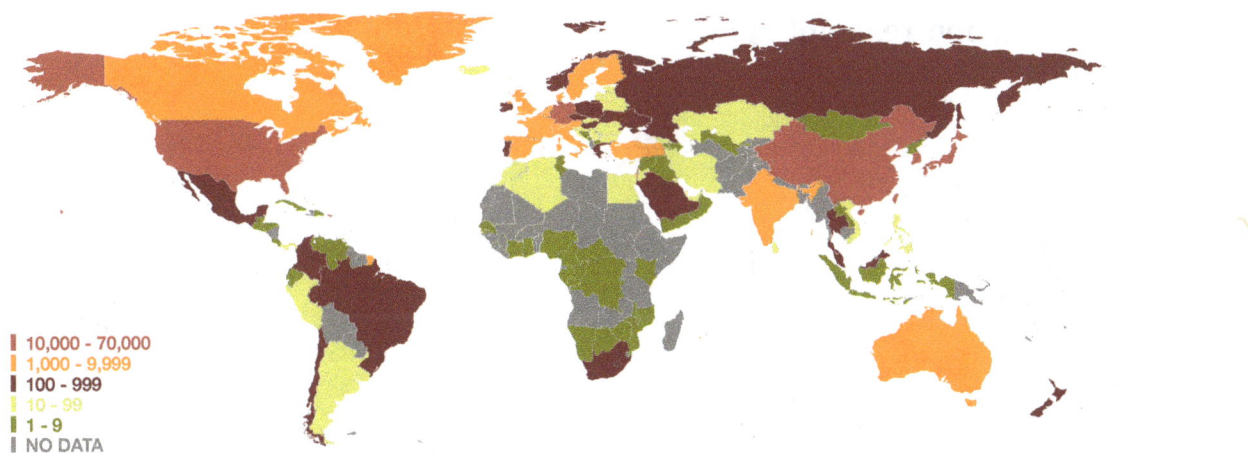

- 10,000 - 70,000
- 1,000 - 9,999
- 100 - 999
- 10 - 99
- 1 - 9
- NO DATA

Note: Data refer to the international phase of the Patent Cooperation Treaty System. Counts are based on the residency of the first named applicant and the international application date.

Source: WIPO Statistics Database, September 2017.

Figure A54
PCT applications for the top 20 origins, 2016

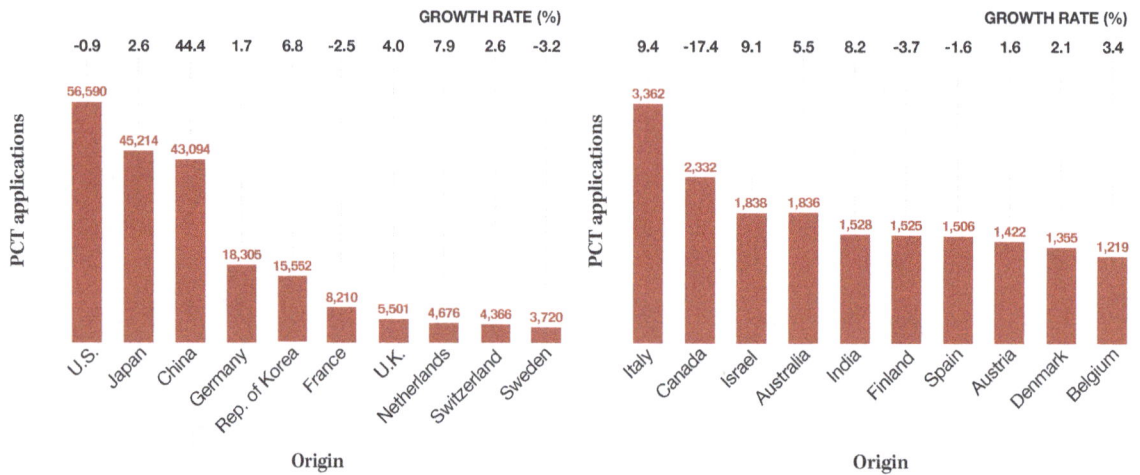

Note: Data refer to the international phase of the Patent Cooperation Treaty System. Counts are based on the residency of the first named applicant and the international application date.

Source: WIPO Statistics Database, September 2017.

Figure A55
Trend in non-resident applications by filing route

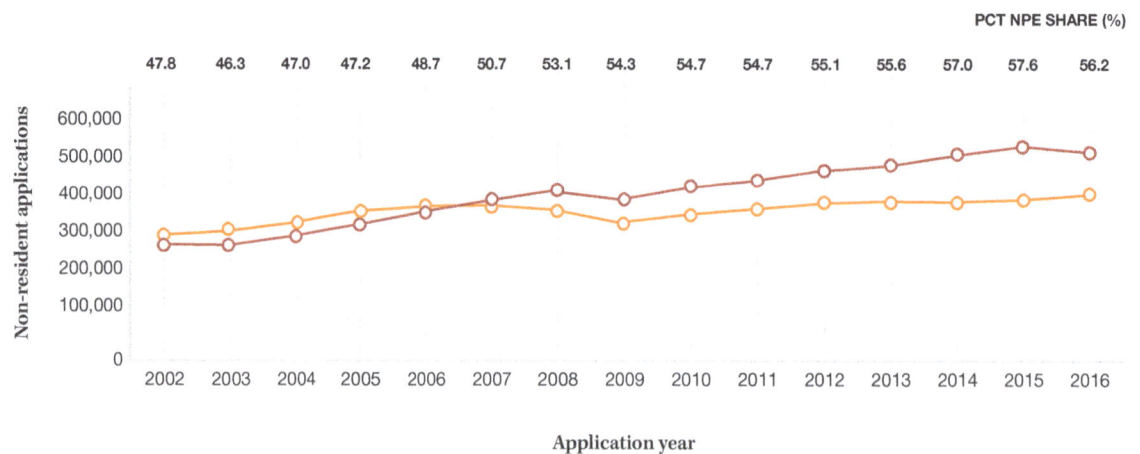

| PCT NATIONAL PHASE ENTRIES | DIRECT APPLICATIONS |

Note: A patent office may receive patent applications filed either directly with the office (known as the "Paris route") or through the Patent Cooperation Treaty System (Patent Cooperation Treaty national phase entries).

Source: WIPO Statistics Database, September 2017.

Figure A56
Non-resident applications by filing route for selected offices, 2016

SHARE OF NON-RESIDENT PCT NATIONAL PHASE ENTRIES IN TOTAL NON-RESIDENT APPLICATIONS (%)

Israel	South Africa	Viet Nam	Brazil	Malaysia	Canada	India	Mexico	Rep. of Korea	Russian Federation	Australia	Singapore	New Zealand	EPO	Japan	China	U.S.	U.K.	Germany
95.5	90.4	87.2	86.6	84.1	83.1	80.8	79.8	79.2	78.1	71.3	71.0	70.9	68.0	65.0	57.3	37.5	27.4	26.5

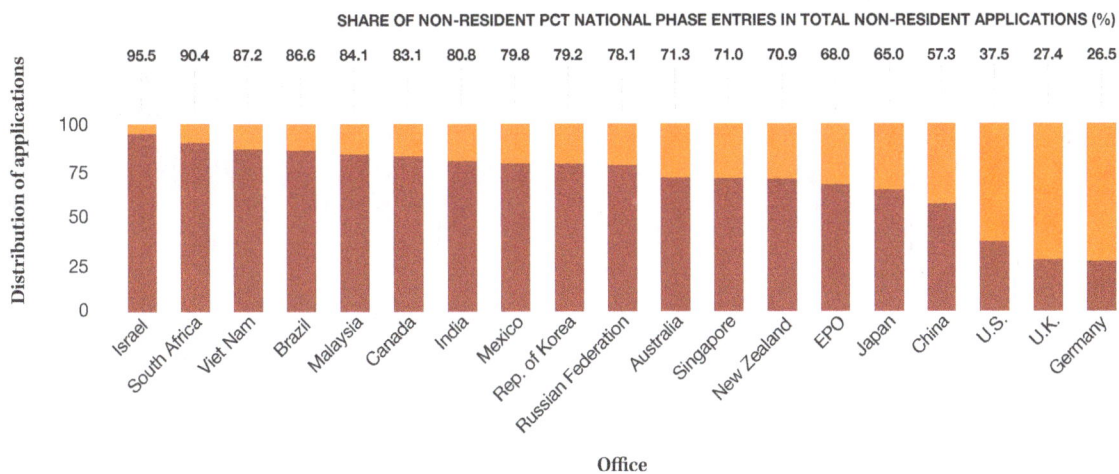

Office

❙ NON-RESIDENT PCT NATIONAL PHASE ENTRIES   ❙ NON-RESIDENT DIRECT APPLICATIONS

Note: EPO is the European Patent Office. A patent office may receive patent applications filed either directly with the office (known as the "Paris route") or through the Patent Cooperation Treaty System (Patent Cooperation Treaty national phase entries).

Source: WIPO Statistics Database, September 2017.

Patent Prosecution Highway (PPH)

Figure A57
PPH requests by office of first filing and offices of later examination, 2016

Office of later examination	Office of first filing																
	Australia	Austria	Canada	China	Denmark	EPO	Finland	Germany	Israel	Japan	Rep. of Korea	Russian Federation	Sweden	U.K.	U.S.	Others/Unknown	Total
Australia	9	2	1	11	2	26	1	7	5	102	5		17	39	864	40	1,131
Azerbaijan								2							7	14	23
Brazil															34		34
Canada	86	2	111	16	1	164	12	5	8	167	86	11	2	25	1,768	13	2,477
Chile																1	1
China			7		13	813	3	53	9	1,965	424	22	23	34	1,904	4	5,274
Colombia										13					60	2	75
EAPO										2							2
EPO	13		33	127					18	580	74				650	2	1,497
Finland							1			1			1		1		4
Germany	1	9		14	2					505	16	1		16	172		736
Indonesia										38						1	39
Israel	24		5	5		110			36	21	18		1	8	273	1	502
Japan*	16		14	113	12	773	5	15	7	1,205	161	9	5	39	1,832	3	4,209
Mexico	1	1	1	4		24		3		111	2			2	249	24	422
Norway										2				2	10	2	16
Singapore		2		3	1	4		1		21					6		38
Spain															2		2
Thailand										390							390
U.K.	2			15	1		1	2		14	6				117		158
U.S.	100	16	157	765	20	1,736	34	57	76	2,289	719	57	88	142	504	34	6,794
Viet Nam										100							100
Total	252	32	329	1,073	52	3,650	57	145	159	7,526	1,511	100	137	307	8,453	141	23,924

* indicates data based on office of earlier examination rather than office of first filing.

Note: EAPO is the Eurasian Patent Organization and EPO is the European Patent Office. A patent prosecution highway is a bilateral agreement between two offices that enables applicants to request a fast-track examination whereby patent examiners can use the work of the other office.

Source: WIPO Statistics Database, September 2017.

Figure A58
Flow of PPH requests between offices of first filing and offices of later examination, 2016

Office of first filing   Office of later examination

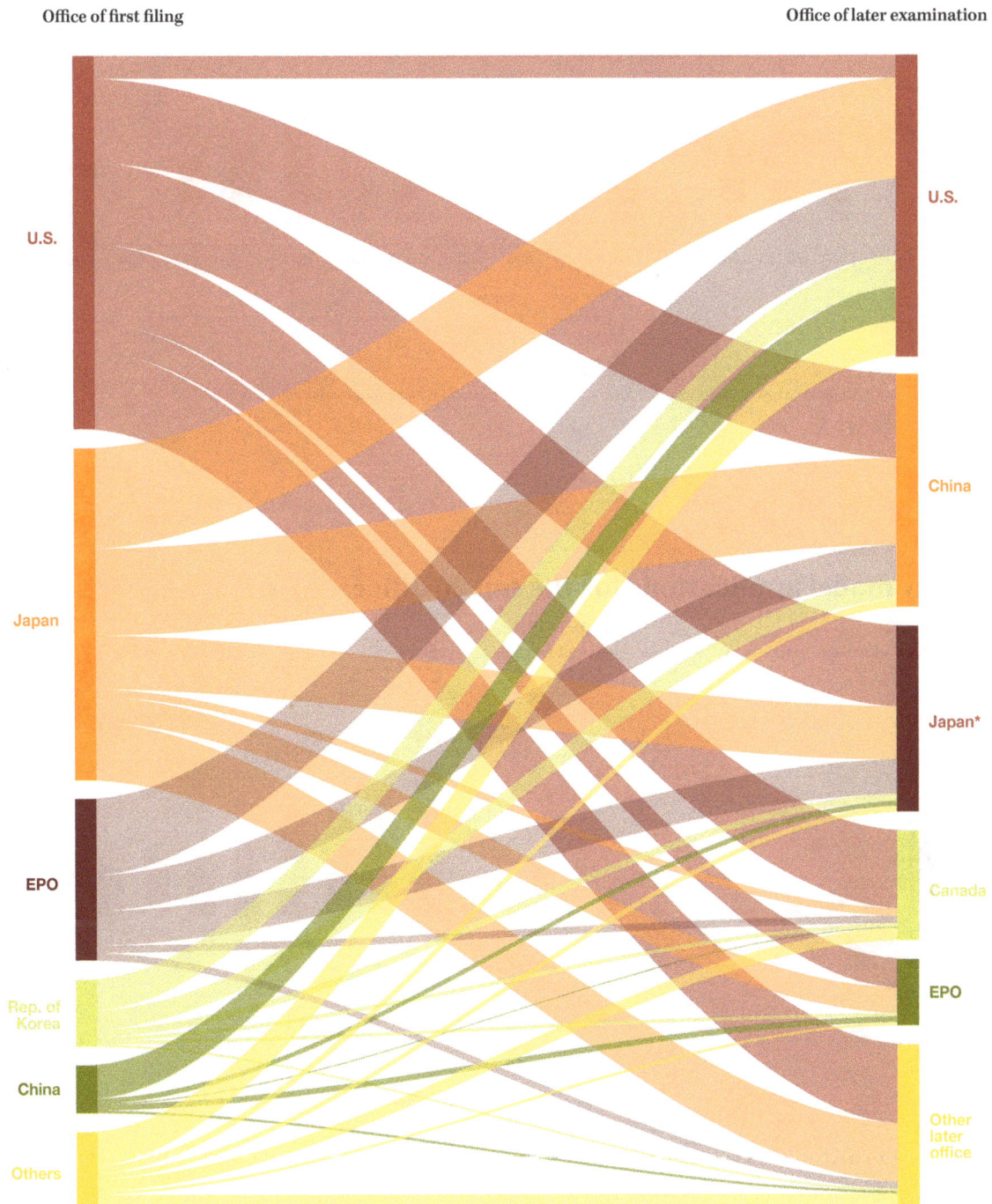

* indicates data based on office of earlier examination rather than office of first filing.

Note: EPO is the European Patent Office. Japan data refers to the office of earlier examination rather than the office of first filing. A patent prosecution highway is a bilateral agreement between two offices that enables applicants to request a fast-track examination whereby patent examiners can use the work of the other office. This graph shows the flows of PPH requests between offices of first filing and offices of later examination.

Source: WIPO Statistics Database, September 2017.

Utility model applications

Figure A59
Trend in utility model applications worldwide

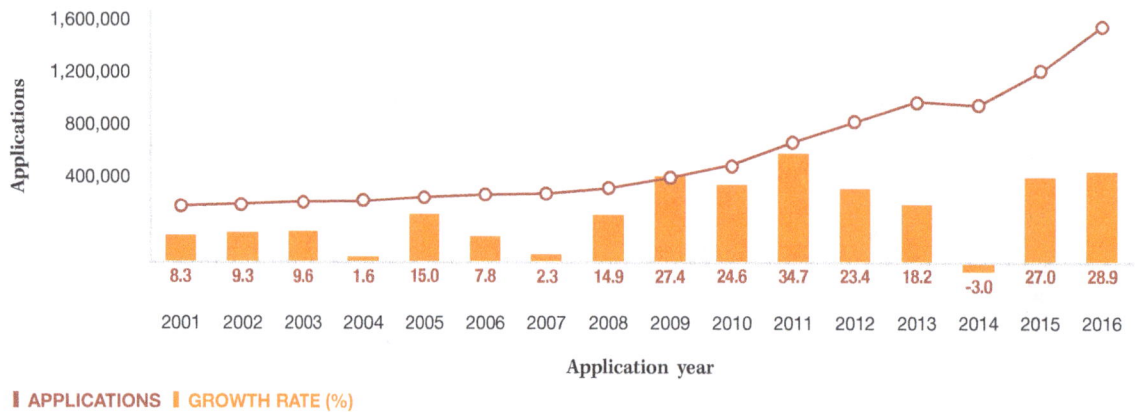

Year	2001	2002	2003	2004	2005	2006	2007	2008	2009	2010	2011	2012	2013	2014	2015	2016
Growth rate	8.3	9.3	9.6	1.6	15.0	7.8	2.3	14.9	27.4	24.6	34.7	23.4	18.2	-3.0	27.0	28.9

Application year

▮ APPLICATIONS ▮ GROWTH RATE (%)

Note: World totals are WIPO estimates using data covering 74 patent offices. These totals include applications filed directly with national and regional offices and applications entering offices through the Patent Cooperation Treaty national phase (where applicable).

Source: WIPO Statistics Database, September 2017.

Figure A60
Utility model applications for the top 20 offices, 2016

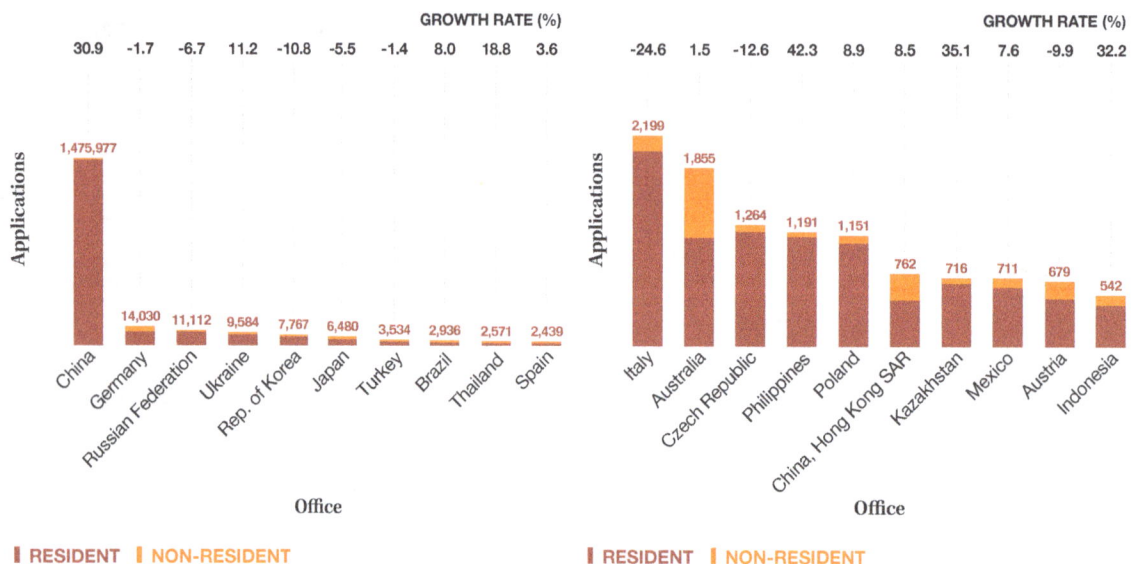

GROWTH RATE (%)									
30.9	-1.7	-6.7	11.2	-10.8	-5.5	-1.4	8.0	18.8	3.6

Office	China	Germany	Russian Federation	Ukraine	Rep. of Korea	Japan	Turkey	Brazil	Thailand	Spain
Applications	1,475,977	14,030	11,112	9,584	7,767	6,480	3,534	2,936	2,571	2,439

GROWTH RATE (%)									
-24.6	1.5	-12.6	42.3	8.9	8.5	35.1	7.6	-9.9	32.2

Office	Italy	Australia	Czech Republic	Philippines	Poland	China, Hong Kong SAR	Kazakhstan	Mexico	Austria	Indonesia
Applications	2,199	1,855	1,264	1,191	1,151	762	716	711	679	542

▮ RESIDENT ▮ NON-RESIDENT

▮ RESIDENT ▮ NON-RESIDENT

Source: WIPO Statistics Database, September 2017.

Figure A61
Utility model applications for offices of selected low- and middle-income countries, 2016

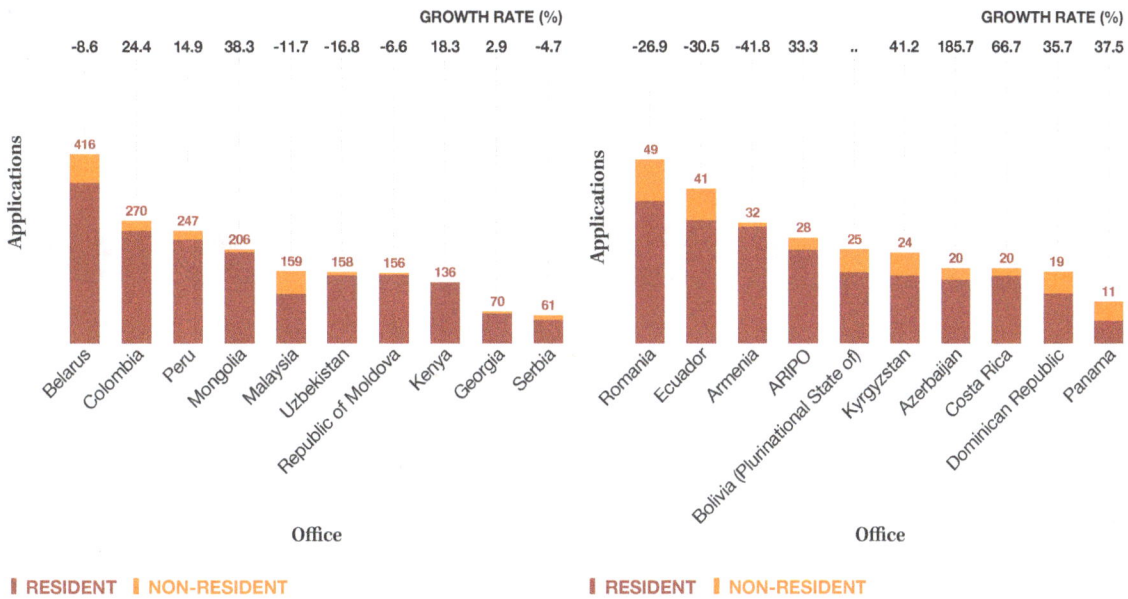

GROWTH RATE (%)

| -8.6 | 24.4 | 14.9 | 38.3 | -11.7 | -16.8 | -6.6 | 18.3 | 2.9 | -4.7 |

| Belarus | Colombia | Peru | Mongolia | Malaysia | Uzbekistan | Republic of Moldova | Kenya | Georgia | Serbia |
| 416 | 270 | 247 | 206 | 159 | 158 | 156 | 136 | 70 | 61 |

Office

GROWTH RATE (%)

| -26.9 | -30.5 | -41.8 | 33.3 | .. | 41.2 | 185.7 | 66.7 | 35.7 | 37.5 |

| Romania | Ecuador | Armenia | ARIPO | Bolivia (Plurinational State of) | Kyrgyzstan | Azerbaijan | Costa Rica | Dominican Republic | Panama |
| 49 | 41 | 32 | 28 | 25 | 24 | 20 | 20 | 19 | 11 |

Office

▌ RESIDENT ▌ NON-RESIDENT   ▌ RESIDENT ▌ NON-RESIDENT

.. indicates not available.

Note: ARIPO is the African Regional Intellectual Property Organization.

Source: WIPO Statistics Database, September 2017.

Microorganisms

Figure A62
Trend in microorganism deposits worldwide

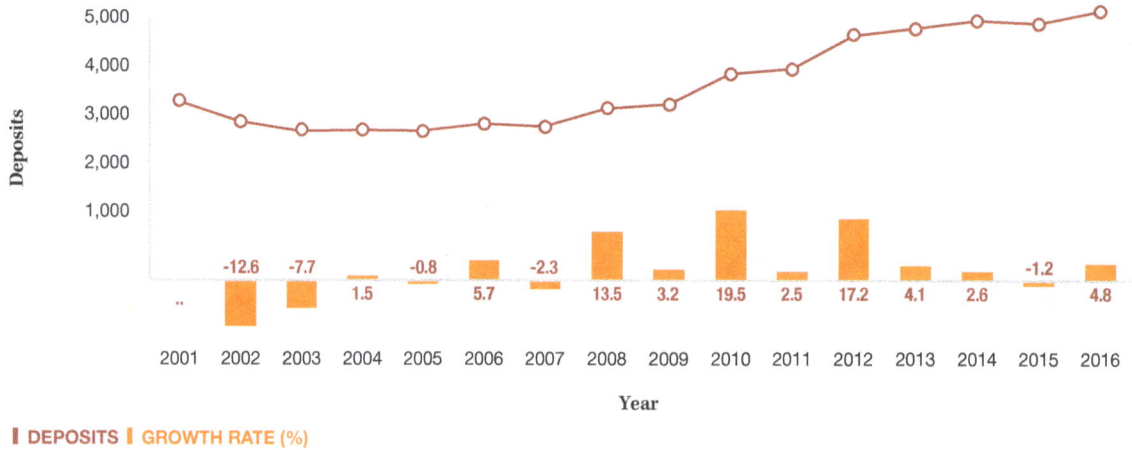

DEPOSITS   GROWTH RATE (%)

Note: Deposits of microorganisms for patent procedures are important for biotechnological inventions. Disclosing an invention is a requirement for receiving a patent.

Source: WIPO Statistics Database, September 2017.

Figure A63
Deposits at the top international depositary authorities, 2016

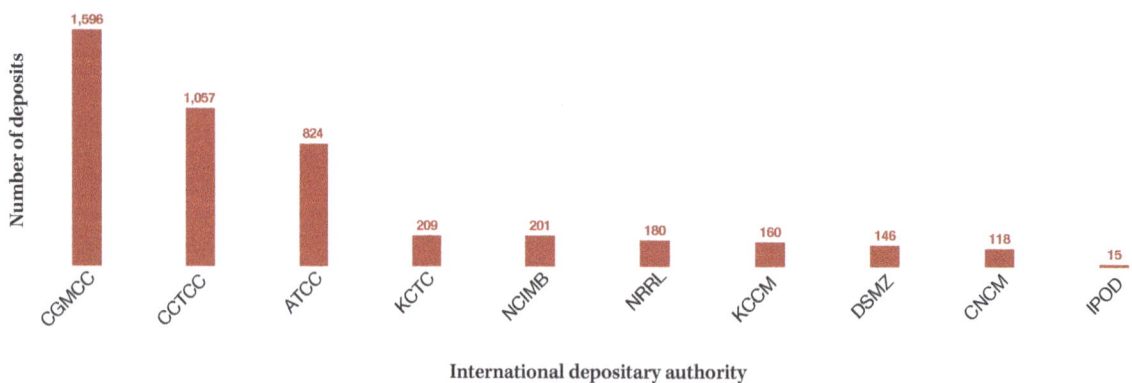

Note: ATCC is the American Type Culture Collection (U.S.), CCTCC is the China Center for Type Culture Collection, CGMCC is the China General Microbiological Culture Collection Center, CNCM is the Collection Nationale de Cultures de Micro-organismes (France), DSMZ is the Leibniz-Institut DSMZ (Deutsche Sammlung von Mikroorganismen und Zellkulturen GmbH; Germany), IPOD is the International Patent Organism Depositary (Japan), KCCM is the Korean Culture Center of Microorganisms (Rep. of Korea), KCTC is the Korean Collection for Type Cultures (Rep. of Korea), NCIMB is the National Collection of Industrial, Food and Marine Bacteria (U.K.) and NRRL is the Agriculture Research Services Culture Collection (U.S.).

Source: WIPO Statistics Database, September 2017.

Statistical tables

PATENTS

Figure A64
Patent applications by office and origin, 2016

| Name | Applications by office | | | Equivalent applications by origin | PCT international applications | | PCT national phase entry | |
	Total	Resident	Non-resident	Total (a)	Receiving office	Origin	Office	Origin
Afghanistan	..	..	..	8	n.a.	0	..	1
African Intellectual Property Organization	506	138	368	n.a.	2	n.a.	361	n.a.
African Regional Intellectual Property Organization	697	17	680	n.a.	0	n.a.	657	n.a.
Albania	25	21	4	53	0	0	2	16
Algeria	672	106	566	117	11	13	535	..
Andorra	3	0	3	15	n.a.	8	..	2
Angola (e)	..	..	..	3	n.a.	0	..	2
Antigua and Barbuda	12	0	12	84	0	0	12	..
Argentina	3,809	884	2,925	1,142	n.a.	46	..	84
Armenia	126	125	1	192	4	9	1	12
Aruba	..	..	..	3	n.a.	0	..	1
Australia	28,394	2,620	25,774	11,679	1,703	1,836	19,375	7,133
Austria	2,315	2,078	237	13,840	507	1,422	506	6,758
Azerbaijan	163	144	19	498	3	4	8	9
Bahamas	37	3	34	103	n.a.	5	..	37
Bahrain	177	6	171	33	0	6	170	4
Bangladesh	344	77	267	149	n.a.	0	..	13
Barbados (e)	41	0	41	357	n.a.	114	41	265
Belarus	521	455	66	1,473	8	14	44	46
Belgium	1,173	1,054	119	12,916	55	1,219	..	6,756
Belize	37	0	37	27	0	4	37	11
Benin (f,i)	n.a.	n.a.	n.a.	68	n.a.	0	n.a.	..
Bermuda	..	..	..	118	n.a.	0	..	46
Bolivia (Plurinational State of)	253	12	241	15	n.a.	0	..	3
Bosnia and Herzegovina	66	60	6	68	1	4	..	2
Botswana	7	1	6	11	0	1	..	1
Brazil	28,010	5,200	22,810	7,208	528	567	19,857	1,147
Brunei Darussalam	..	..	..	5	1	5	..	3
Bulgaria	241	230	11	428	29	58	5	82
Burkina Faso(f,i)	n.a.	n.a.	n.a.	155	n.a.	0	n.a.	1
Burundi	..	..	..	..	n.a.	2	..	..
Cabo Verde	..	..	..	3	n.a.	0	..	1
Cambodia (b,c)	65	0	65	4	0	0	..	2
Cameroon (f,i)	n.a.	n.a.	n.a.	816	n.a.	2	n.a.	..
Canada	34,745	4,078	30,667	24,637	1,855	2,332	27,021	9,512
Central African Republic (f,i)	n.a.	n.a.	n.a.	17	n.a.	0	n.a.	..
Chad (f,i)	n.a.	n.a.	n.a.	51	n.a.	0	n.a.	..

85

PATENTS

Name	Applications by office			Equivalent applications by origin	PCT international applications		PCT national phase entry	
	Total	Resident	Non-resident	Total (a)	Receiving office	Origin	Office	Origin
Chile	2,907	386	2,521	940	163	197	2,401	376
China	1,338,503	1,204,981	133,522	1,257,202	44,462	43,094	81,055	34,869
China, Hong Kong SAR	14,092	233	13,859	2,128	n.a.	0	..	338
China, Macao SAR	51	0	51	110	n.a.	0	..	5
Colombia	2,203	545	1,658	751	10	100	1,583	150
Congo (f,i)	n.a.	n.a.	n.a.	18	n.a.	1	n.a.	..
Costa Rica	505	9	496	58	1	4	477	12
Côte d'Ivoire (f,i)	n.a.	n.a.	n.a.	273	n.a.	2	n.a.	..
Croatia	188	175	13	255	27	39	6	50
Cuba	195	32	163	152	2	2	157	98
Curaçao	..	..	..	31	n.a.	0	..	7
Cyprus	4	3	1	335	2	37	..	152
Czech Republic	839	792	47	2,151	180	199	33	599
Democratic People's Republic of Korea	..	..	..	72	4	4	..	25
Democratic Republic of the Congo	..	..	..	4	n.a.	1	..	2
Denmark	1,850	1,552	298	11,693	524	1,354	106	6,452
Djibouti	..	..	..	..	1	0	..	..
Dominica	..	..	..	1	n.a.	0	..	..
Dominican Republic	273	16	257	27	5	6	234	1
Ecuador	374	45	329	51	2	9	284	2
Egypt	2,149	918	1,231	1,052	40	43	1,172	21
El Salvador	175	4	171	8	1	1	167	3
Eritrea	..	..	..	3	n.a.	0	..	3
Estonia	30	29	1	275	3	24	..	96
Eurasian Patent Organization	3,380	585	2,795	n.a.	3	n.a.	2,688	n.a.
European Patent Office	159,358	76,082	83,276	n.a.	35,288	n.a.	94,625	n.a.
Finland	1,368	1,260	108	12,539	969	1,525	27	7,120
France	16,218	14,206	2,012	71,276	3,606	8,210	..	37,793
Gabon (f,i)	n.a.	n.a.	n.a.	72	n.a.	1	n.a.	3
Gambia (h)	..	..	..	1	n.a.	0	..	1
Georgia	274	96	178	116	12	13	174	4
Germany	67,899	48,480	19,419	176,693	1,533	18,305	6,325	71,160
Ghana	31	14	17	117	0	2	17	11
Greece	646	606	40	1,226	68	111	..	384
Grenada	17	0	17	..	0	0	3	..
Guatemala	269	3	266	7	0	2	253	1
Guinea (f,i)	n.a.	n.a.	n.a.	19	n.a.	0	n.a.	..
Guyana	18	0	18	..	n.a.	0	..	..
Honduras	195	10	185	10	0	1	185	..
Hungary	665	616	49	1,533	148	178	17	663
Iceland	38	35	3	252	20	56	3	130

PATENTS

Name	Applications by office			Equivalent applications by origin	PCT international applications		PCT national phase entry	
	Total	Resident	Non-resident	Total (a)	Receiving office	Origin	Office	Origin
India	45,057	13,199	31,858	25,795	738	1,528	25,896	4,405
Indonesia	8,538	0	8,538	52	7	8	7	18
International Bureau	..	..	..	n.a.	10,020	n.a.	..	n.a.
Iran (Islamic Republic of)	15,632	14,930	702	15,081	3	63	582	11
Iraq (b,c)	437	335	102	343	n.a.	1	..	1
Ireland	287	202	85	5,356	23	441	..	2,167
Israel	6,419	1,300	5,119	15,086	1,425	1,838	5,430	7,061
Italy	9,821	8,848	973	31,091	309	3,362	..	13,964
Jamaica	78	19	59	63	n.a.	0	..	1
Japan	318,381	260,244	58,137	453,640	44,495	45,214	59,893	119,612
Jordan	278	22	256	140	0	1	..	56
Kazakhstan	1,224	993	231	1,526	19	21	190	29
Kenya	203	144	59	202	2	4	56	32
Kuwait (b,d)	228	..	..	122	n.a.	3	..	1
Kyrgyzstan	89	84	5	138	0	0	..	..
Lao People's Democratic Republic (e)	..	..	..	5	n.a.	2	..	3
Latvia	113	95	18	255	3	24	..	134
Lebanon (b,c)	304	110	194	158	n.a.	6	..	16
Liechtenstein (g)	..	..	..	1,327	n.a.	249	..	844
Lithuania	153	95	58	219	2	28	..	63
Luxembourg	444	143	301	3,408	1	431	..	2,151
Madagascar (e)	36	6	30	8	n.a.	0	30	1
Malawi	4	3	1	3	0	1	..	..
Malaysia	7,236	1,109	6,127	1,929	180	189	5,178	312
Mali (f,i)	n.a.	n.a.	n.a.	199	n.a.	0	n.a.	1
Malta	4	3	1	496	0	87	4	284
Marshall Islands	..	..	..	2	n.a.	0	..	2
Mauritius	38	2	36	113	n.a.	4	..	72
Mexico	17,413	1,310	16,103	2,403	214	289	12,884	539
Micronesia (Federated States of)	..	..	..	..	n.a.	2	..	..
Monaco	14	7	7	220	0	13	..	119
Mongolia	219	112	107	114	0	1	101	..
Montenegro (e)	10	10	0	17	0	3	..	..
Morocco	1,303	237	1,066	263	31	35	883	11
Mozambique (h)	40	15	25	17	n.a.	1	17	..
Myanmar	..	..	..	2	n.a.	0	..	..
Namibia (h)	..	..	..	5	n.a.	2	..	1
Nepal	37	11	26	11	n.a.	0	..	..
Netherlands	2,604	2,290	314	38,908	950	4,676	..	22,704
New Zealand	6,386	1,075	5,311	3,062	210	308	3,826	1,418
Nicaragua	..	..	..	2	0	0	..	..

PATENTS

Name	Applications by office			Equivalent applications by origin		PCT international applications	PCT national phase entry	
	Total	Resident	Non-resident	Total (a)	Receiving office	Origin	Office	Origin
Niger (f,i)	n.a.	n.a.	n.a.	121	n.a.	0	n.a.	1
Nigeria (e)	..	..	..	13	n.a.	4	..	3
Norway	2,060	1,227	833	5,899	300	653	745	3,184
Oman (e)	..	..	..	15	3	8	..	1
Pakistan	840	204	636	273	n.a.	0	..	3
Panama	417	68	349	112	4	60	330	31
Papua New Guinea (b,c)	47	1	46	4	0	0	41	1
Paraguay	..	..	..	3	n.a.	0	..	3
Patent Office of the Cooperation Council for the Arab States of the Gulf	1,949	286	1,663	n.a.	n.a.	n.a.	..	n.a.
Peru	1,163	72	1,091	153	25	24	1,025	71
Philippines	3,419	327	3,092	554	14	29	2,849	72
Poland	4,396	4,261	135	6,141	218	344	45	874
Portugal	751	724	27	1,675	46	184	8	671
Qatar	564	16	548	141	8	14	539	40
Republic of Korea	208,830	163,424	45,406	233,625	15,595	15,552	37,093	25,206
Republic of Moldova	155	91	64	101	7	10	64	2
Romania	1,063	1,005	58	1,254	27	44	6	102
Russian Federation	41,587	26,795	14,792	31,811	1,023	896	11,638	2,447
Rwanda	128	2	126	4	0	0	123	..
Saint Kitts and Nevis	..	..	..	14	n.a.	0	..	10
Saint Vincent and the Grenadines (b,c,e)	7	0	7	13	n.a.	0	7	13
Samoa (b,c)	4	1	3	25	n.a.	1	..	10
San Marino	458	4	454	47	6	8	..	22
Saudi Arabia	3,266	1,070	2,196	4,735	20	295	2,246	1,439
Senegal (f,i)	n.a.	n.a.	n.a.	392	n.a.	7	n.a.	..
Serbia	213	192	21	279	15	15	6	37
Seychelles	..	..	..	113	0	3	..	41
Singapore	10,980	1,601	9,379	6,684	646	864	7,040	2,894
Slovakia	235	220	15	458	19	55	6	105
Slovenia	..	..	..	513	29	69	..	322
South Africa	9,711	2,783	6,928	4,087	85	287	6,465	1,133
Spain	2,922	2,745	177	10,784	1,088	1,506	73	4,709
Sri Lanka (e)	573	280	293	315	n.a.	16	288	12
Sudan	285	284	1	291	0	0	..	..
Suriname	..	..	..	3	n.a.	0	..	..
Swaziland (b,c,h)	2	0	2	9	n.a.	0	..	3
Sweden	2,384	2,032	352	23,388	1,392	3,720	73	15,188
Switzerland	1,771	1,462	309	46,631	160	4,366	63	25,974
Syrian Arab Republic (c)	112	..	..	242	0	2	27	10
T F Y R of Macedonia	..	..	..	9	1	3	..	1

PATENTS

Name	Applications by office			Equivalent applications by origin	PCT international applications		PCT national phase entry	
	Total	Resident	Non-resident	Total (a)	Receiving office	Origin	Office	Origin
Tajikistan (b,c)	1	0	1	16	0	0	..	..
Thailand	..	..	..	503	108	155	..	232
Togo (f,i)	n.a.	n.a.	n.a.	170	n.a.	0	n.a.	..
Tonga	..	..	..	2	n.a.	0	..	2
Trinidad and Tobago	136	3	133	19	0	38	133	9
Tunisia	583	235	348	270	5	6	336	17
Turkey	6,848	6,230	618	8,364	805	1,065	300	1,524
Turkmenistan	..	..	..	19	0	0	..	1
Uganda (h)	16	16	0	17	n.a.	0	..	..
Ukraine	4,095	2,233	1,862	2,737	153	162	1,673	200
United Arab Emirates (c,e)	1,574	..	..	520	n.a.	81	1,336	158
United Kingdom	22,059	13,876	8,183	52,819	4,007	5,501	2,535	24,833
United Republic of Tanzania (b,c,h)	2	1	1	4	n.a.	0	..	1
United States of America	605,571	295,327	310,244	520,877	56,675	56,590	146,867	179,595
Uruguay (b,c)	558	26	532	108	n.a.	14	..	49
Uzbekistan	555	353	202	385	1	2	194	24
Vanuatu	..	..	..	1	n.a.	0	..	1
Venezuela (Bolivarian Republic of)	..	..	..	44	n.a.	1	..	7
Viet Nam	5,228	560	4,668	632	6	10	4,072	20
Yemen	32	16	16	16	n.a.	1	..	..
Zambia	..	..	..	1	0	0	..	..
Zimbabwe	13	8	5	10	0	2	..	..
Others/Unknown	..	..	..	34,358	n.a.	210	..	5,034
Total (2016 estimates)	**3,127,900**	**2,216,800**	**911,100**	**n.a.**	**232,904**	**232,904**	**615,400**	**n.a.**

(a) Equivalent applications by origin data are incomplete because some offices do not report by origin.

(b) 2015 data are reported for applications by office.

(c) 2015 data are reported for equivalent applications by origin.

(d) The office did not report resident applications so the equivalent applications by origin data may be incomplete.

(e) The International Bureau acts as the receiving office for PCT applications.

(f) The African Intellectual Property Organization (OAPI) acts as the receiving office for PCT applications.

(g) The Swiss Federal Institute of Intellectual Property acts as the receiving office for PCT applications.

(h) The African Regional Intellectual Property Organization (ARIPO) acts as the receiving office for PCT applications.

(i) The African Intellectual Property Organization (OAPI) is the competent office for processing applications.

.. indicates not available

n.a. is not applicable

Source: WIPO Statistics Database, September 2017.

Figure A65
Patent grants by office and origin, and patents in force, 2016

Name	Total	Resident	Non-resident	Equivalent grants by origin Total (a)	In force by office Total
Afghanistan	..	..	..	11	..
African Intellectual Property Organization	360	47	313	n.a.	2,220
African Regional Intellectual Property Organization	468	4	464	n.a.	3,421
Albania	5	5	0	6	..
Algeria	383	44	339	64	5,618
Andorra	..	..	..	15	..
Angola	..	..	..	1	..
Antigua and Barbuda	..	..	..	3	..
Argentina	1,879	201	1,678	377	..
Armenia	93	91	2	130	226
Aruba	..	..	..	1	..
Australia	23,744	1,433	22,311	6,176	132,994
Austria	1,135	984	151	8,298	142,875
Azerbaijan	131	117	14	466	345
Bahamas	47	0	47	212	1,077
Bahrain	..	..	..	11	..
Bangladesh	106	..	..	6	..
Barbados	26	0	26	366	..
Belarus	949	892	57	1,706	2,503
Belgium	1,620	1,368	252	8,157	..
Belize	4	0	4	7	132
Benin(e)	n.a.	n.a.	n.a.	51	..
Bermuda	..	..	..	169	..
Bolivia (Plurinational State of)	86	0	86	..	..
Bosnia and Herzegovina	12	0	12	3	375
Botswana	1	1	0	2	..
Brazil	4,195	533	3,662	1,472	24,153
Brunei Darussalam	..	..	..	10	..
Bulgaria	42	36	6	150	11,511
Burkina Faso (e)	n.a.	n.a.	n.a.	102	..
Cambodia (b,c)	1	0	1	1	..
Cameroon (e)	n.a.	n.a.	n.a.	206	..
Canada	26,424	3,295	23,129	14,114	175,236
Central African Republic (e)	n.a.	n.a.	n.a.	1	..
Chad(e)	n.a.	n.a.	n.a.	34	..
Chile	2,077	195	1,882	387	12,512
China	404,208	302,136	102,072	322,461	1,772,203

Name	Total	Resident	Grants by office Non-resident	Equivalent grants by origin Total (a)	In force by office Total
China, Hong Kong SAR	5,698	78	5,620	1,077	43,359
China, Macao SAR	57	1	56	31	467
Colombia	917	99	818	160	6,623
Congo (e)	n.a.	n.a.	n.a.	17	..
Costa Rica	67	3	64	19	678
Côte d'Ivoire (e)	n.a.	n.a.	n.a.	221	..
Croatia	35	11	24	80	6,606
Cuba	93	10	83	111	857
Curaçao	..	..	..	16	
Cyprus	..	..	..	285	79
Czech Republic	781	637	144	1,311	37,889
Democratic People's Republic of Korea	..	..	..	13	..
Denmark	409	236	173	6,249	55,715
Dominica	..	..	..	1	..
Dominican Republic	21	1	20	5	265
Ecuador	10	2	8	8	..
Egypt	450	72	378	124	3,189
El Salvador	40	0	40	3	..
Estonia	27	19	8	117	8,924
Eurasian Patent Organization	3,081	474	2,607	n.a.	n.a.
European Patent Office	95,956	48,733	47,223	n.a.	n.a.
Finland	815	709	106	7,990	48,588
France	12,374	10,623	1,751	47,569	535,554
Gabon(e)	n.a.	n.a.	n.a.	17	..
Georgia	177	62	115	69	1,394
Germany	15,652	10,792	4,860	99,655	617,307
Ghana	25	3	22	3	25
Greece	271	264	7	500	26,479
Grenada	14	0	14	..	..
Guatemala	52	0	52	..	883
Guinea (e)	n.a.	n.a.	n.a.	17	..
Guyana	57	0	57	..	29
Holy See	..	..	..	1	..
Honduras	53	0	53	..	82
Hungary	271	89	182	690	23,782
Iceland	22	2	20	116	5,941
India	8,248	1,115	7,133	6,664	49,575
Indonesia	3,674	393	3,281	440	..
Iran (Islamic Republic of)	3,268	3,111	157	3,155	..
Iraq (b,c)	312	197	115	199	..

PATENTS

Name	Total	Grants by office Resident	Non-resident	Equivalent grants by origin Total (a)	In force by office Total
Ireland	164	77	87	2,906	147,125
Israel	4,938	787	4,151	6,895	30,922
Italy	6,429	5,682	747	20,457	..
Jamaica	5	1	4	16	328
Japan	203,087	160,643	42,444	288,153	1,980,985
Jordan	121	4	117	53	463
Kazakhstan (c)	1,011	..	..	1,534	3,218
Kenya	26	5	21	8	..
Kuwait	..	..	..	66	..
Kyrgyzstan	120	118	2	135	274
Latvia	68	66	2	152	7,419
Lebanon (b,c)	279	85	194	105	..
Liechtenstein	..	..	..	579	..
Lithuania	103	86	17	168	522
Luxembourg	184	85	99	1,843	19,960
Madagascar	19	1	18	1	386
Malawi	7	6	1	6	..
Malaysia	3,324	355	2,969	937	25,117
Mali[e]	n.a.	n.a.	n.a.	18	..
Malta	6	6	0	238	423
Marshall Islands	..	..	..	5	..
Mauritius	2	0	2	35	..
Mexico	8,652	423	8,229	950	109,238
Monaco	9	7	2	79	85,132
Mongolia	157	57	100	58	4,324
Montenegro (d)	8	8	0	9	2,372
Morocco	352	109	243	141	..
Mozambique	35	10	25	10	..
Namibia	..	..	..	2	..
Nepal (b,c)	2	2	0	3	..
Netherlands	1,914	1,624	290	21,060	164,264
New Zealand	3,910	304	3,606	1,275	38,906
Nicaragua	..	..	..	1	..
Nigeria	..	..	..	2	..
Norway	2,525	543	1,982	3,572	27,930
Oman	..	..	..	7	..
Pakistan	214	12	202	30	1,848
Panama	13	2	11	51	1,734
Papua New Guinea (b,c,d)	70	0	70	..	71
Paraguay	..	..	..	5	..

PATENTS

Name	Total	Resident	Grants by office Non-resident	Equivalent grants by origin Total (a)	In force by office Total
Patent Office of the Cooperation Council for the Arab States of the Gulf	673	65	608	n.a.	4,308
Peru	403	26	377	60	2,779
Philippines	4,006	52	3,954	141	..
Poland	3,548	3,370	178	4,337	65,006
Portugal	38	36	2	365	35,649
Qatar	..	..	..	49	..
Republic of Korea	108,875	82,400	26,475	120,435	950,526
Republic of Moldova	70	54	16	110	343
Romania	355	349	6	498	18,906
Russian Federation	33,536	21,020	12,516	24,237	230,870
Rwanda(d)	..	..	..	..	108
Saint Kitts and Nevis	..	..	..	4	..
Saint Vincent and the Grenadines	..	..	..	9	..
Samoa (b,c,d)	64	0	64	14	64
San Marino	462	6	456	26	..
Saudi Arabia	595	124	471	1,475	3,104
Senegal(e)	n.a.	n.a.	n.a.	119	..
Serbia	68	50	18	85	3,790
Seychelles	..	..	..	69	..
Singapore	7,341	432	6,909	3,066	48,603
Sint Maarten (Dutch Part)	..	..	..	1	..
Slovakia	122	81	41	195	16,363
Slovenia	..	..	..	411	..
South Africa	4,255	403	3,852	1,085	89,049
Spain	2,308	2,137	171	6,265	115,070
Sri Lanka	123	41	82	54	710
Sudan	164	163	1	164	164
Suriname	..	..	..	1	..
Swaziland[b,c]	2	0	2	45	..
Sweden	866	736	130	14,874	93,545
Switzerland	617	416	201	25,882	193,883
Syrian Arab Republic (c)	32	..	..	17	..
T F Y R of Macedonia	..	..	..	7	..
Tajikistan (d)	..	..	..	32	237
Thailand (b,c)	1,364	83	1,281	240	..
Trinidad and Tobago	60	1	59	5	..
Tunisia	583	235	348	243	..
Turkey	1,764	1,609	155	2,667	63,575
Uganda	..	..	..	..	19
Ukraine	2,813	1,277	1,536	1,636	24,760

Name	Total	Resident	Non-resident	Grants by office Equivalent grants by origin Total (a)	In force by office Total
United Arab Emirates (c)	222	..	..	106	673
United Kingdom	5,602	2,897	2,705	23,894	507,973
United Republic of Tanzania (b,c)	1	0	1	1	..
United States of America	303,049	143,723	159,326	276,737	2,763,055
Uruguay (b,c,d)	19	4	15	23	606
Uzbekistan	166	102	64	104	977
Vanuatu	..	..	..	1	..
Venezuela (Bolivarian Republic of)	..	..	..	20	..
Viet Nam	1,423	76	1,347	118	14,398
Yemen (b,c)	15	2	13	2	..
Zimbabwe	..	..	..	1	..
Others/Unknown	..	..	..	17,982	..
Total (2016 estimates)	**1,351,600**	**829,600**	**522,000**	**n.a.**	**11,328,700**

(a) Equivalent grants by origin data are incomplete because some offices do not report by origin.

(b) 2015 data are reported for grants by office.

(c) 2015 data are reported for equivalent grants by origin.

(d) 2015 data are reported for patents in force.

(e) The African Intellectual Property Organization (OAPI) is the competent office for issuing grants.

n.a. is not applicable

.. indicates not available

Source: WIPO Statistics Database, September 2017.

Figure A66
Utility model applications and grants by office and origin, 2016

Name	Applications by office			Equivalent applications by origin	Grants by office		
	Total	Resident	Non-resident	Total (a)	Total	Resident	Non-resident
Afghanistan	..	..	..	6	..	..	..
African Regional Intellectual Property Organization	28	25	3	n.a.	2	2	0
Albania (b,c,d)	4	3	1	5	1	0	1
Andorra	..	..	..	2	..	..	..
Argentina	205	184	21	205	42	34	8
Armenia	32	31	1	34	44	44	0
Australia	1,855	1,125	730	1,243	1,920	1,032	888
Austria	679	496	183	901	575	419	156
Azerbaijan	20	17	3	21	10	8	2
Bangladesh	..	..	..	1	..	..	..
Barbados	..	..	..	7	..	..	..
Belarus	416	353	63	456	328	265	63
Belgium	..	..	..	102	..	..	..
Belize	..	..	..	11	..	..	..
Bermuda	..	..	..	3	..	..	..
Bolivia (Plurinational State of)	25	19	6	19	6	2	4
Bosnia and Herzegovina	..	..	..	11	..	..	..
Botswana	4	3	1	10	1	1	0
Brazil	2,936	2,814	122	2,858	564	549	15
Brunei Darussalam	..	..	..	2	..	..	..
Bulgaria	462	450	12	467	217	208	9
Cambodia (b,c)	7	0	7	..	..	..	..
Canada	..	..	..	74	..	..	..
Chile	110	89	21	108	44	28	16
China	1,475,977	1,468,295	7,682	1,470,004	903,420	897,035	6,385
China, Hong Kong SAR	762	483	279	564	485	275	210
China, Macao SAR	15	1	14	33	11	1	10
Colombia	270	248	22	258	72	61	11
Costa Rica (b,c,d)	20	18	2	18	1	1	0
Croatia	83	77	6	77	70	68	2
Cuba	1	1	0	1	..	..	..
Cyprus	..	..	..	127	..	..	..
Czech Republic	1,264	1,199	65	1,373	1,187	1,124	63
Denmark	144	111	33	157	126	91	35
Dominican Republic	19	13	6	15	19	13	6
Ecuador	41	33	8	33	6	1	5
Egypt	..	..	..	4	..	..	..
El Salvador (b,c,d)	7	5	2	5	13	12	1
Equatorial Guinea	..	..	..	1	..	..	..
Estonia	61	55	6	70	52	38	14
Finland	450	419	31	574	402	374	28

PATENTS

Name	Applications by office			Equivalent applications by origin	Grants by office		
	Total	Resident	Non-resident	Total (a)	Total	Resident	Non-resident
France	472	208	264	616	..	..	..
Georgia	70	67	3	73	38	38	0
Germany	14,030	10,099	3,931	11,104	12,441	8,777	3,664
Ghana	2	2	0	2	..	..	..
Greece	23	20	3	35	19	17	2
Guatemala (b,c,d)	8	7	1	10	1	1	0
Honduras	7	6	1	6	6	1	5
Hungary	304	282	22	297	108	98	10
Iceland	..	..	..	1	..	..	..
India	..	..	..	24	..	..	..
Indonesia	542	427	115	430	90	84	6
Iran (Islamic Republic of)	..	..	..	9	..	..	..
Iraq	..	..	..	1	..	..	..
Ireland	..	..	..	21	..	..	..
Israel	..	..	..	83	..	..	..
Italy	2,199	2,033	166	2,437	1,849	1,690	159
Japan	6,480	4,928	1,552	7,358	6,297	4,756	1,541
Kazakhstan (b,c,d)	716	654	62	680	166	102	64
Kenya	136	136	0	136	22	22	0
Kyrgyzstan	24	18	6	20	26	20	6
Latvia	..	..	..	4	..	..	..
Lebanon	..	..	..	2	..	..	..
Liechtenstein	..	..	..	14	..	..	..
Lithuania	..	..	..	2	..	..	..
Luxembourg	..	..	..	47	..	..	..
Malaysia	159	110	49	147	29	18	11
Mali	..	..	..	2	..	..	..
Malta	..	..	..	7	..	..	..
Mauritius	..	..	..	2	..	..	..
Mexico	711	612	99	619	175	138	37
Monaco	..	..	..	2	..	..	..
Mongolia	206	204	2	204	129	129	0
Montenegro	..	..	..	2	..	..	..
Mozambique	8	7	1	7	7	6	1
Netherlands	..	..	..	230	..	..	..
New Zealand	..	..	..	43	..	..	..
Norway	..	..	..	15	..	..	..
Panama (b,c,d)	11	6	5	10	4	3	1
Peru	247	231	16	237	83	78	5
Philippines	1,191	1,141	50	1,147	1,674	1,587	87
Poland	1,151	1,084	67	1,125	674	638	36
Portugal	118	87	31	93	82	51	31
Republic of Korea	7,767	7,395	372	8,367	2,854	2,694	160

Name	Applications by office			Equivalent applications by origin	Grants by office		
	Total	Resident	Non-resident	Total (a)	Total	Resident	Non-resident
Republic of Moldova	156	154	2	160	122	121	1
Romania	49	38	11	42	41	34	7
Russian Federation	11,112	10,643	469	10,845	8,875	8,474	401
Rwanda	3	3	0	3	..	..	..
Samoa	..	..	..	19	..	..	..
San Marino	..	..	..	4	..	..	..
Saudi Arabia	..	..	..	4	..	..	..
Serbia	61	54	7	56	40	36	4
Seychelles	..	..	..	15	..	..	..
Singapore	..	..	..	280	..	..	..
Slovakia	359	300	59	352	363	322	41
Slovenia	..	..	..	4	..	..	..
South Africa	..	..	..	15	..	..	..
Spain	2,439	2,299	140	2,552	2,291	2,159	132
Sweden	..	..	..	156	..	..	..
Switzerland	..	..	..	660	..	..	..
Tajikistan (b,c,d)	93	90	3	90	83	81	2
Thailand	2,571	2,462	109	2,507	1,288	1,223	65
Turkey	3,534	3,457	77	3,517	2,441	2,346	95
Turkmenistan	..	..	..	1	..	..	..
Uganda (b,c,d)	..	..	..	..	1	1	0
Ukraine	9,584	9,470	114	9,610	9,044	8,931	113
United Arab Emirates	8	..	..	9	..	..	..
United Kingdom	..	..	..	256	..	..	..
United States of America	..	..	..	3,608	..	..	..
Uruguay (b,c,d)	54	41	13	43	15	12	3
Uzbekistan	158	153	5	154	103	98	5
Viet Nam	478	326	152	327	138	114	24
Yemen	1	1	0	1	1	1	0
Others/Unknown	..	..	..	2,286	..	..	..
Total (2016 estimates)	**1,553,300**	**1,536,000**	**17,300**	**n.a.**	..	..	..

(a) Equivalent applications by origin data are incomplete because some offices do not report by origin.

(b) 2015 data are reported for applications by office.

(c) 2015 data are reported for equivalent applications by origin.

(d) 2015 data are reported for grants by office.

n.a. is not applicable

.. indicates not available

Source: WIPO Statistics Database, September 2017.

Trademarks

Highlights

Applications grew by 16.4% in 2016

An estimated 7 million trademark applications were filed worldwide in 2016, 16.4% more than in 2015 (figure 8). This marks the seventh consecutive year of growth. There are now almost three times as many trademark applications being filed around the world than in 2001 – applications have increased every year except for three during that period, and five years saw annual growth exceed 10%.

Trademark applications dipped in 2001, but returned to growth the following year. After slowing in 2007 and showing slight declines in 2008 and 2009, they rebounded in 2010 and have continued to increase year on year. For each year since 2010, large numbers of applications filed in China have accounted for between 50% and 85% of the increases in overall growth.

When differences in filing systems across national and regional offices are harmonized using the application class count, trademark filing activity in 2016 also saw a double-digit increase, up 13.5% on the previous year. The total number of classes specified in applications – known as the application class count – reached an estimated 9.77 million (figure 9). Excluding the 2016 application class count for China, trademark filing activity grew by a more moderate 5% in the rest of the world.

Figure 8
Trademark applications worldwide

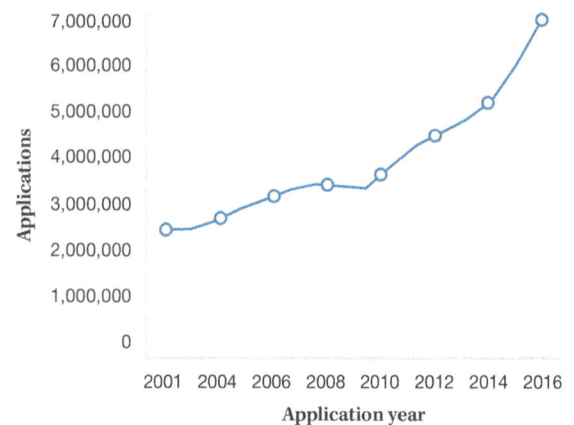

Source: Standard figure B1.

Figure 9
Trademark application class counts worldwide

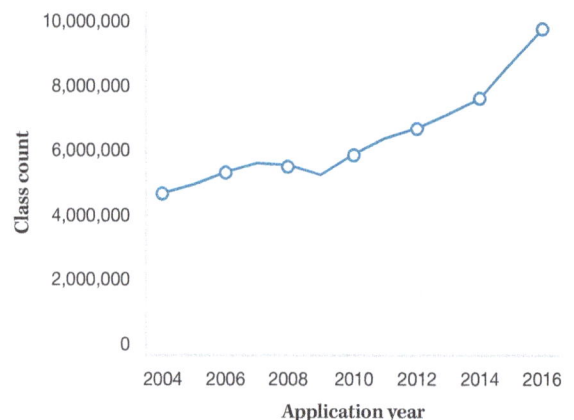

Source: Standard figure B2.

Class count

A trademark application may refer to different classes of goods or services. Many offices use the Nice Classification, an international classification of goods and services for registering trademarks and service marks. Applications received by these offices are classified in one or more of the 45 Nice classes (see *www.wipo.int/classifications/nice*). Some offices allow single-class filing only, meaning applicants have to file a separate application for each class. Others permit multi-class filings, enabling applicants to file a single application in which a number of classes can be specified. To improve international comparisons of the numbers of applications received, it helps to compare class counts across offices. Class counts are also used to make trademark registration activity internationally comparable. This method for comparing offices began in 2004, the first year for which complete class count data are available.

Offices with the most filing activity

As with other forms of intellectual property (IP), the increase in trademark filing activity (measured in application class counts) largely reflects high numbers of trademark applications filed in China. In 2016, the trademark office of China accounted for 75% of the annual increase in global trademark filing activity. It was followed by the office of Japan, which accounted for 9% of total growth.

The office of China's class count of almost 3.7 million was followed by a count of 545,587 at the office of the United States of America (U.S.) (figure 10). These have been the top two offices since the early 2000s, but since 2006 China's class count has grown from double that of the U.S. to over six times as much. These two offices were followed by that of Japan (451,320), the European Union Intellectual Property Office (EUIPO; 369,970) and that of India (313,623). The top five offices accounted for 55% of all trademark filing activity in 2016, up from 34% a decade earlier in 2006.

Among the top 20 offices, over half had more trademark filing activity in 2016 than in 2015, with the largest increases of 30.8% recorded in both China and Japan, followed by double-digit growth in Viet Nam (+21.1%), the United Kingdom (U.K.; +19.1%) and the Russian Federation (+14.8%). Conversely, the offices of France (-3.1%) and the Republic of Korea (-1.7%) saw declines.

For offices located in low- and middle-income countries, annual growth was particularly high in Madagascar (+22.1%), Pakistan (+28.8%) and Yemen (+33.7%). The offices of Morocco, the Philippines and Uzbekistan saw double-digit growth of about 12-14%.

At most offices, trademark applications are filed mainly by residents seeking protection within their domestic jurisdiction. In 2016, residents accounted for 79.8% of global filing activity. In fact, domestic filing is becoming increasingly pronounced as a share of total filing activity, with the world resident application class count having increased by 15.5% on the previous year; in contrast, that for non-residents increased by only 6%.

Due largely to the high number of resident trademark applications in China, the global non-resident share of filing activity declined by almost 13 percentage points from a peak of 33.1% in 2004 to 20.2% in 2016. However, when the figures for China are excluded, the non-resident share fell by only around 7 percentage points over the same period.

Of the top 20 offices, half had non-resident filing shares of around 20% or greater, with Australia (39.7%), Canada (47%), Mexico (30.3%), Switzerland (59%) and Viet Nam (33%) recording the highest. The lowest non-resident shares were recorded at the offices of China (4.6%), France (5.9%) and the Islamic Republic of Iran (6.9%). The low non-resident shares for France and other EU member state offices can be explained by the fact that many non-resident applicants file for protection in these countries via the EUIPO.

Resident filing activity drove the double-digit growth in China, Japan, the Russian Federation, the U.K. and Viet Nam as well as growth at several other top 20 offices, whereas non-resident filing activity accounted for most or all of the total growth in Australia, the EUIPO, Switzerland and the U.S. In Canada, France, Germany and the Republic of Korea, declines in total filing activity can be attributed entirely or mainly to a drop in resident applications.

Figure 10
Trademark application class counts for the top 10 offices, 2016

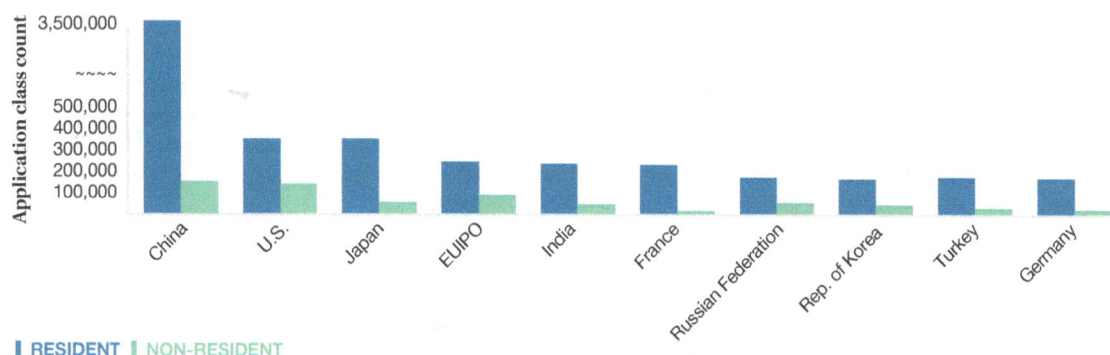

RESIDENT **NON-RESIDENT**

Source: Standard figure B10.

The list of top 20 offices in 2016 is largely similar to that in 2015, but with a somewhat different ranking and several new additions. Due to the recent provision of application class counts by the Islamic Republic of Iran, its office appears for the first time among the top 20 offices at number 11. Another new arrival is the office of Viet Nam, which enters the list at number 19. As for changes in ranking, Japan moved up one place ahead of the EUIPO, replacing it as the third largest office in terms of trademark filing activity. For the second year running, India ranks among the top five offices in trademark filing activity. The Russian Federation moved up two places to number seven, ahead of both the Republic of Korea and Turkey.

Total application class counts at offices of high-income economies grew only slightly (+2%) between 2006 and 2016. This is lower than the average annual growth rates for all other income groups. The highest growth (+11.3%) over this 11-year period was recorded for offices of upper middle-income countries. Offices of lower middle-income (+5.7%) and low-income (+4%) countries also saw growth over the same period.

Twelve of the top 20 offices are in high-income economies, six are in upper middle-income countries (Brazil, China, the Islamic Republic of Iran, Mexico, the Russian Federation and Turkey) and two are in lower middle-income countries (India and Viet Nam). In 2016, the offices of high-income countries together received 36.7% of total global filing activity, down from 55.5% in 2006. In contrast, the share for offices of upper middle-income countries rose from 33.7% in 2006 to 53.2% in 2016, due to their combined high average annual growth (figure 11). When China's statistics are removed from the upper middle-income group, the application class count for the other countries in this group still grew between 2006 and 2016, but at a lower rate of 4%. However, the combined share of the world total claimed by upper middle-income countries actually decreased from 19.3% to 15.4%. The shares of total filing activity for lower middle-income (9.4% in 2016) and low-income countries (0.7%) did not change much over the same period.

Eight of the top 20 offices in 2016 were located in Europe, seven in Asia, two each in Latin America and the Caribbean (LAC) and North America, and one in Oceania. Offices in Asia accounted for 60% of all trademark filing activity, up from 37% in 2006. This in part explains the decline in overall shares for the other five geographical regions over the same period (figure 12). Offices in Europe accounted for 21.5% of the world total in 2016, followed by North America (7.2%) and LAC (7%) – holding almost equal shares – and by Africa (2.4%) and Oceania (1.9%).

Figure 11
Trademark application class counts by income group

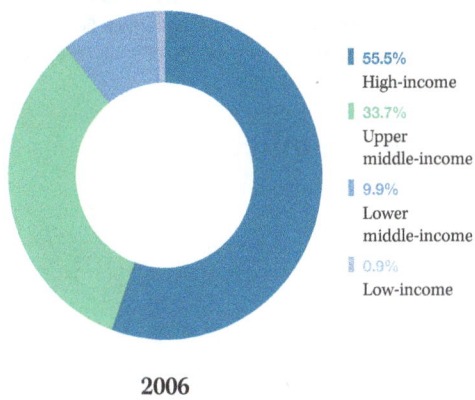

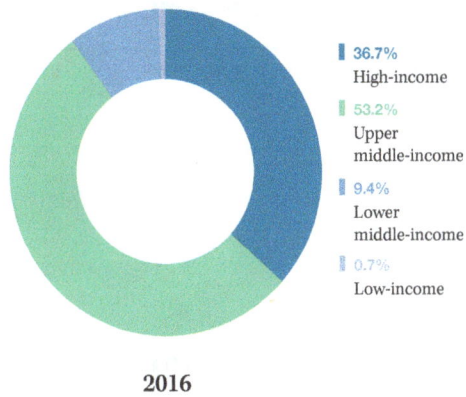

55.5%
High-income

33.7%
Upper middle-income

9.9%
Lower middle-income

0.9%
Low-income

2006

36.7%
High-income

53.2%
Upper middle-income

9.4%
Lower middle-income

0.7%
Low-income

2016

Source: Standard figure B7.

Figure 12
Trademark application class counts by region

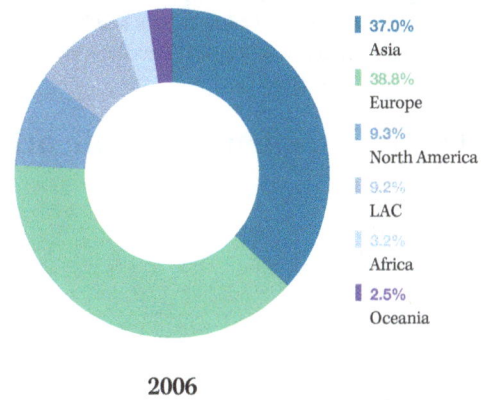

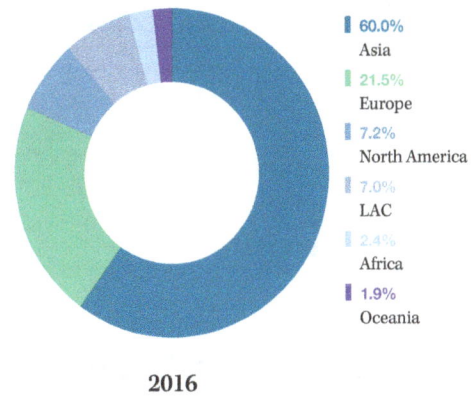

37.0%
Asia

38.8%
Europe

9.3%
North America

9.2%
LAC

3.2%
Africa

2.5%
Oceania

2006

60.0%
Asia

21.5%
Europe

7.2%
North America

7.0%
LAC

2.4%
Africa

1.9%
Oceania

2016

Source: Standard figure B8.

TRADEMARKS

Trademark filings since 1883

Trademark filings were fairly low and stable until the mid-1980s. Filings at China's office took off in the 1990s, and in 2001 they exceeded those received by that of the U.S., making China's office the largest in terms of applications received. Even so, filings in the U.S. have doubled since the mid-1990s despite declines at the end of the dot-com era in 2001 and 2002 and again during the financial crisis in 2008 and 2009. Having remained below 100,000 until 2006, India's trademark filings are now rapidly approaching 300,000. Trademark applications in the Republic of Korea stand at just over 180,000, and they are close to 170,000 in Brazil.

Trend in trademark applications for the top five offices

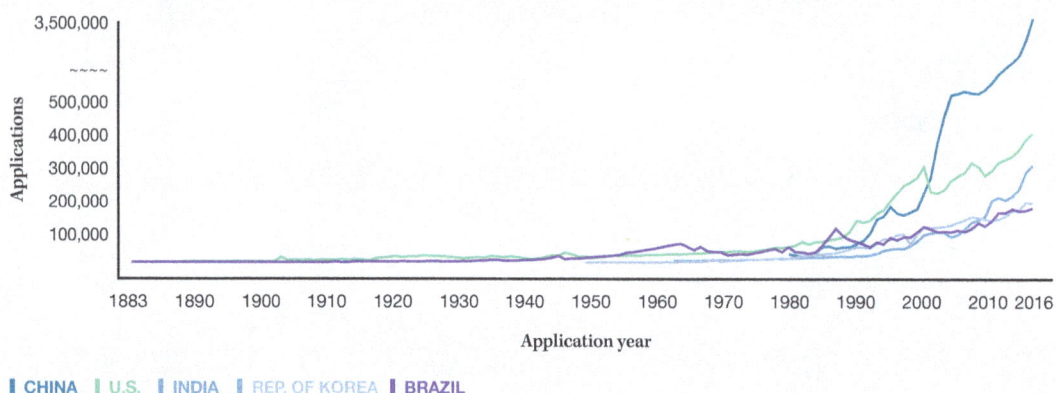

Source: Standard figure B9.

Map 2
Equivalent trademark application class counts by origin, 2016

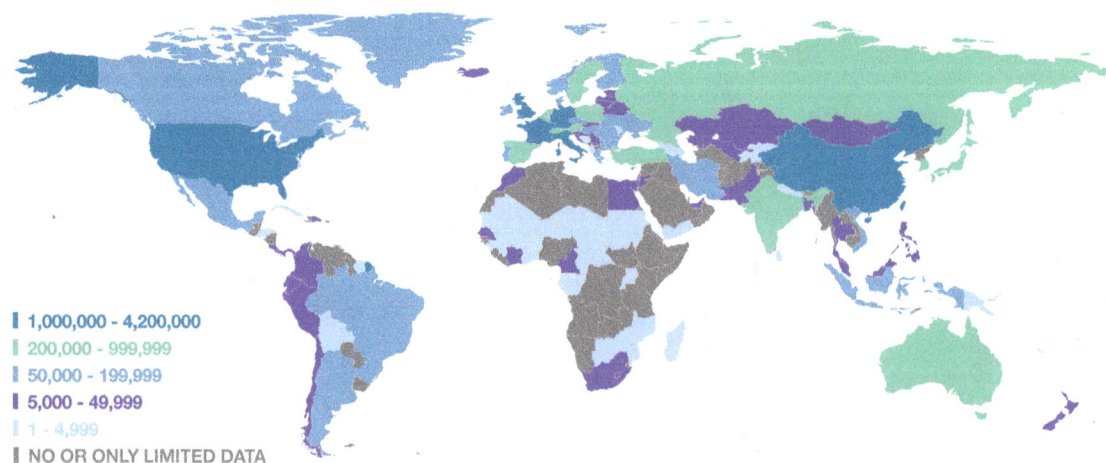

1,000,000 - 4,200,000
200,000 - 999,999
50,000 - 199,999
5,000 - 49,999
1 - 4,999
NO OR ONLY LIMITED DATA

Source: Standard map B19.

Equivalent application class count

Applications at some regional IP offices are equivalent to multiple applications in the countries that are members of the organizations establishing those offices. For example, to calculate the number of equivalent applications for the EUIPO, each application is multiplied by the corresponding number of EU member states. So an application filed with the EUIPO by an applicant residing outside the EU is counted as 28 applications abroad – equivalent to the 28 member countries of the EU in 2016. An application filed by an applicant residing in an EU country is counted as 1 resident application and 27 applications abroad. The same multiplier is applied to the classes specified in these applications. The equivalent application class count concept is used for reporting data by origin.

German applicants continue to file the most applications abroad

Trademark applications received by offices from resident and non-resident applicants are referred to as office data, whereas applications filed by applicants at a national/regional office (resident applications) or at foreign offices (applications abroad) are referred to as origin data. Here, trademark statistics based on the origin of the residence of the applicant are reported in order to complement the picture of trademark filing activity worldwide.

In terms of filing activity abroad based on equivalent class count, applicants from Germany seek protection for their marks outside their country more than those of any other origin, a position Germany has held since 2006. In 2016, German filing activity abroad reached an equivalent application class count of about 2.04 million, followed by applicants from the U.S. (1.22 million), the U.K. (1.07 million) and Italy (922,851).[1] The high equivalent class counts for applications abroad from these origins can be explained not only by their high application class counts at numerous offices abroad, but also their frequent use of the EUIPO – with its multiplier effect – to seek protection within the EU as a whole.

Looking at absolute counts – and so removing the EUIPO's multiplier effect – 95% of all filing activity (application class counts) by China-based applicants was in China alone, with only 5% attributed to those seeking protection abroad. The shares for resident filing and filing abroad were similar for applicants from Brazil, India and the Islamic Republic of Iran. Applicants residing in many other low- and middle-income countries also dedicated less than 10% of their trademark filing activity to seeking protection abroad.

Among the top 20 origins, about 77% of filing activity by Switzerland-based applicants occurred outside the country. This high share of applications abroad as a proportion of total filing activity was followed by that of applicants from the U.S. (46%) and Germany (45%).

Applicants from the upper middle-income countries Mauritius (57%) and Serbia (55%) sought protection abroad for a considerable share of their trademark filing activity. For upper middle-income countries Colombia, the Russian Federation, Thailand and Turkey and the lower-middle income country El Salvador, the share was 12-13%.

When deciding where to seek trademark protection, applicants consider such factors as market size and geographical proximity. For example, 36% of all non-resident filing activity in Mexico in 2016 came from U.S. applicants, 10% from applicants in Germany and 6% from applicants in Switzerland (figure 13). Applicants from China (22%) and the U.K. (10%) accounted for the largest shares of non-resident trademark filing activity in the U.S, followed by applicants from Germany (9%). In China, the three origins accounting for the largest shares of non-resident filing activity were the U.S. (21%), the Republic of Korea (12%) and Germany (9%). For non-resident filing activity at the EUIPO, it was applicants from the U.S. (34%), China (17%) and Switzerland (12%).

In 2016, applicants from China surpassed those from Switzerland (16%) to become the most active foreign filers at the German IP office, accounting for 18% of application class counts in filings it received from abroad.

TRADEMARKS

Figure 13
Share of total non-resident filing activity by origin at selected offices

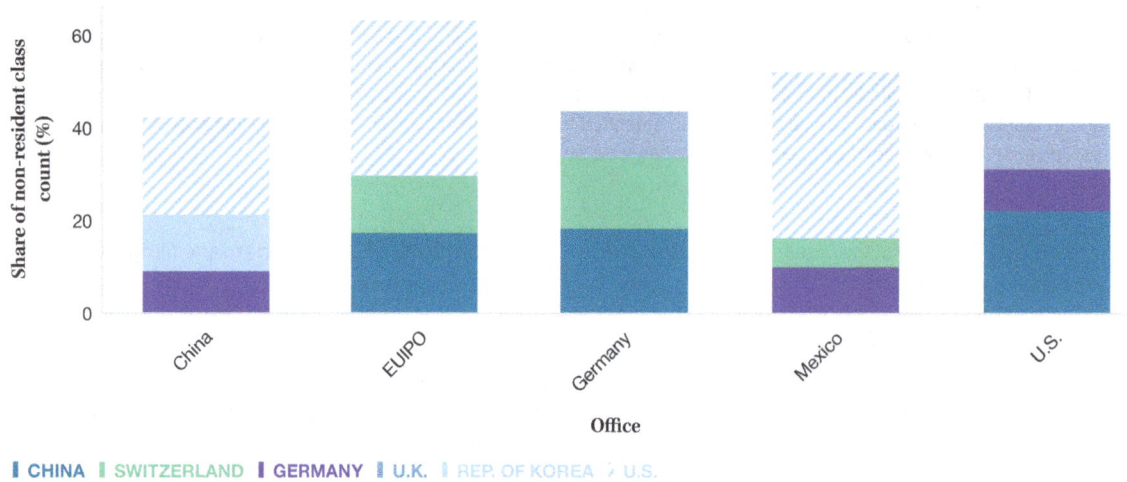

Note: EUIPO is the European Union Intellectual Property Office.

Source: Standard figure B25.

Adjusting for GDP and population

Differences in trademark filing activity across countries may reflect both the size of their economies and their level of economic development. To compare trademark filing intensity across countries, it helps to measure resident application class counts relative to GDP or population level.

When resident trademark applications are viewed as class counts and adjusted by GDP, countries with a lower number of classes specified in resident applications such as New Zealand, Switzerland and Ukraine may rank higher than some countries that otherwise show higher class counts (for example Australia and Germany). Of selected origins, China (17,764), Ukraine (14,021), the Republic of Korea (10,242), New Zealand (10,016) and Switzerland (7,755) exhibited among the highest ratios of resident application class count to GDP in 2016 (figure 14). China (+9,801), the Russian Federation (+2,374), Ukraine (+2,113) and Mexico (+2,002) saw particularly large increases in resident application class count per unit of GDP between 2006 and 2016. In the case of China, this was due to 2016 resident filing activity being over five times the level recorded in 2006. As for Ukraine, the increase in the ratio over this period was due to a 5.2% rise in resident filing activity coupled with a fall in GDP of 10.7%. In 2016, India, South Africa and Thailand each had a ratio of around 3,300, even though India's resident filing activity was close to 12 times that of residents of South Africa and about 7 times that of residents of Thailand.

Figure 14
Resident trademark application class count per USD 100 billion GDP for selected origins

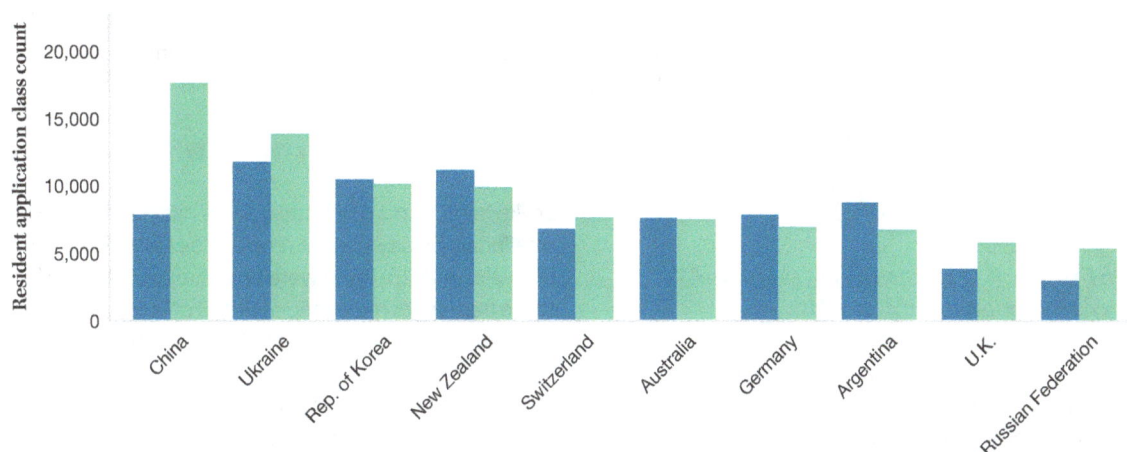

2006 **2016**

Source: Standard figure B33.

The data reflecting application class count per million population present a somewhat different picture. Iceland – with a population of about 334,300 – reported a resident application class count of 4,550 per million, one of the most intensive among all countries of origin in 2016. Among selected origins, Switzerland (4,391) – with a population of approximately 8.4 million – had a similar resident application class count, followed by the Republic of Korea (3,583), Australia (3,374) and Germany (3,114). Panama, the Russian Federation and the U.S. had ratios of about 1,200-1,300 each, while the ratio for Armenia and Mexico was around 800 (see standard figure B34).

Which classes and industries saw the most filing activity?

Trademarks are registered in relation to particular classes of goods or services. The Nice Classification of goods and services is used in the international trademark system and at certain national and regional offices. Nice Classification statistics offer insights into the relative importance of different goods and services. Service class 35 (advertising, business management, business administration and office functions) has been number one since 2004 – when complete class counts first became available – and in 2016 was represented in 10.5% of all reported trademark filing activity by class. Nice Class 35 is followed by goods class 9 (6.9%), which includes scientific, photographic, measuring instruments, recording equipment, computers and software; service class 41 (5.8%), which relates to education, entertainment and sports activities; and goods class 25 (5.7%), which includes articles of clothing.

The 11 service-related classes accounted for about 38% of all Nice classes specified in applications filed in 2016, up from 30% in 2004. Services classes accounted for just over a third of all filing activity in China, the Russian Federation and Viet Nam, and half or more in the offices of France, Japan and Spain.

It is useful to group the 45 Nice classes into 10 industry sectors. Agriculture, research and technology, and business services were the top three sectors in 2016, each accounting for between 13% and 18% of global reported trademark filing activity. In contrast, industries relating to chemicals (2.6%) and transportation (5.6%) accounted for the smallest shares (see standard figure B28). The distribution of total trademark applications across industries has remained stable for more than a decade.

Concordant with being the global top industry in terms of trademark filing activity, agriculture was

TRADEMARKS

the top sector at the offices of China (22%), the Republic of Korea (20%) and the Russian Federation (16%). Research and technology was the top industry sector at the EUIPO (21%) and the offices of France (19%), Germany (18%), Japan (26%) and the U.S. (20%). In Turkey, business services topped the list of industry sectors, accounting for 19% of all trademark filing activity. Among the top 10, only the offices of India (23%) and the Republic of Korea (16%) listed health among their top three industry sectors for trademark filing.

4.61 million trademark registrations recorded worldwide in 2016

After examination, an office may decide to register a trademark. The number of registrations issued can fluctuate greatly from year to year, due in part to the resources dedicated by offices to examining trademark applications. For this reason, one should not compare the number of applications filed at an office in a given year with the number of registrations issued by that office in the same year.

The estimated 4.61 million trademark registrations recorded worldwide in 2016 represents an increase of 4.3%, or 191,500 additional registrations, on the previous year's total.

Just as class counts make application activity internationally comparable, so they also permit a more meaningful comparison of registrations. In 2016, an estimated 6.55 million classes were specified in trademark registrations. After two years of double-digit growth, 2016 saw a return to a modest increase of 2.5%, similar to the level of growth recorded in 2013. India's office saw growth of 134% in trademark registration activity in 2016, accounting for 71% of the total global annual increase.

China's office registered trademarks in which about 2.27 million classes were specified, followed distantly by the EUIPO (330,379), and the offices of the U.S. (326,481) and Turkey (218,137).

Along with the very high annual growth in India, several other offices among the top 20 experienced large increases in registration activity, including Argentina (+16.5%), Canada (+14.9%) and the Russian Federation (+15.3%).

Many offices of EU countries – including the Benelux Office for Intellectual Property (BOIP) – have witnessed decreases in filing and registration activity in recent years. This is due in part to the alternative offered by the EUIPO, which provides a route to seek protection for trademarks not only in individual EU member countries, but in the EU as a whole.

Active trademarks increased by 8.7%

Unlike most forms of IP, trademarks can be maintained indefinitely by payment of renewal fees at defined time intervals. In 2016, there were an estimated 39.1 million active trademark registrations at 136 offices worldwide, representing an increase of 8.7% on 2015.

Once again, the office of China accounted for the most trademark registrations in force in 2016, with about 12.38 million – a 19.6% increase on 2015. It was followed by the offices of the U.S. (2.12 million), Japan (1.85 million) and India (1.33 million). With between 1 and 1.1 million trademark registrations in force each, the EUIPO and the offices of Mexico and the Republic of Korea also recorded high numbers of active trademarks. Australia (607,871) had about the same number of trademark registrations in force as Indonesia (605,397), while the Russian Federation (557,405) and Canada (555,571) too had similar figures.

About 13.8 million trademark registrations in force at 65 offices in 2016 can be distributed according to the year in which they were initially registered. This represents 53% of the approximately 26.1 million trademark registrations recorded at these offices between 1983 and 2016.

Sixteen percent of these trademarks registered in 1983 remained in force in 2016, reflecting the enduring value of marks. For those registered in 2006 and later, the percentage rises above 50%. About half of these 13.8 million registrations in force have a recent registration date dating back only to 2010.

Madrid international trademark applications exceeded 50,000 for the first time

To obtain trademark protection in multiple countries or jurisdictions, applicants can either file their applications directly at each individual office – known as the "Paris route" – or file an application for international registration through the Madrid System: the "Madrid route" (see the glossary). In 2016, the Madrid System offered trademark holders the ability to obtain protection for their branded products and services in an area covering a total of 114 countries.

Madrid international applications totaled 53,493 in 2016, up 9.1% on 2015, marking the seventh consecutive year of growth and the fastest recorded since 2010. In fact, since 2001 the number of applications has increased in all but three years, each coinciding with economic downturns in the early 2000s and 2009. This prevailing growth is due partly to the expanding membership of the Madrid System and partly to a general upward trend in trademark application volumes worldwide.

For the third year in a row, the U.S. remained the largest user of the Madrid System. International applications filed by applicants located in the U.S. reached 7,730. These were followed by applications from Germany (7,544), France (4,124) and China (3,820). Applicants domiciled in China filed about 1,860 more Madrid applications in 2016 than in 2015. This remarkably high growth of 94.7% pushed China up from eighth largest origin in 2015 to fourth largest in 2016.

Between 2006 and 2016, applicants for international registrations have accounted for between 63% and 77% of all non-resident trademark filing activity emanating from Madrid member jurisdictions at the IP offices of all Madrid members combined.

For many Madrid member offices, over half their non-resident trademark filing activity (application class counts) is received through the Madrid route. In 2016, this was the case for the offices of India (59.1%), Israel (76.3%), Japan (59.6%), the Republic of Korea (57.8%) and Turkey (73.2%), to name a few. The EUIPO (28.3%), and the offices of China (34.3%) and the U.S. (36%), however, received lower shares of total non-resident filing activity via the Madrid route. For further information and statistics, see the *Madrid Yearly Review 2017.*

Standard figures and tables

TRADEMARKS

TRADEMARKS

Trademark applications and registrations worldwide

Figure B1
Trend in trademark applications worldwide

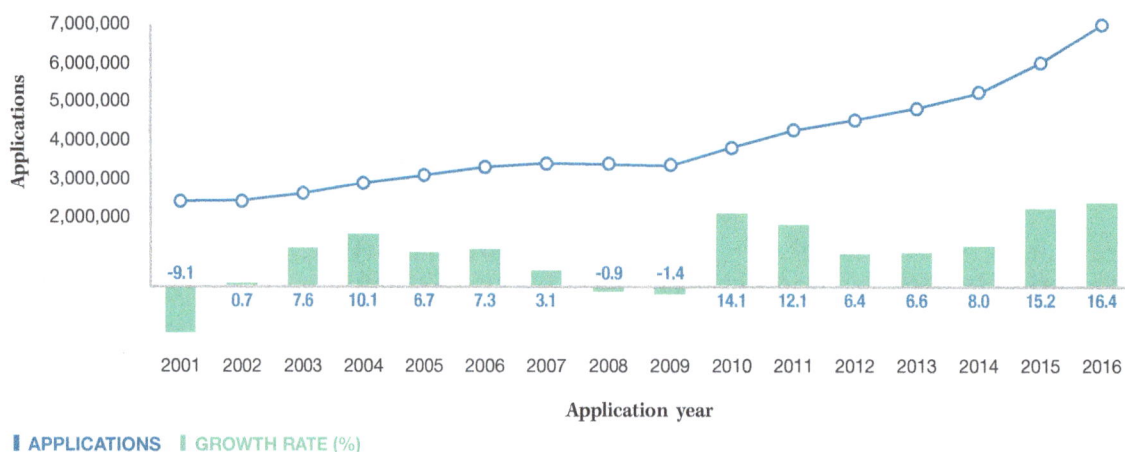

Applications (y-axis)

Application year	2001	2002	2003	2004	2005	2006	2007	2008	2009	2010	2011	2012	2013	2014	2015	2016
Growth rate (%)	-9.1	0.7	7.6	10.1	6.7	7.3	3.1	-0.9	-1.4	14.1	12.1	6.4	6.6	8.0	15.2	16.4

Application year (x-axis)

▮ APPLICATIONS ▮ GROWTH RATE (%)

Note: World totals are WIPO estimates using data covering 169 IP offices. Each total includes the number of applications filed directly with national and regional offices (known as the "Paris route") as well as the number of designations received by offices via the Madrid System (where applicable).

Source: WIPO Statistics Database, September 2017.

Figure B2
Trend in trademark application class counts worldwide

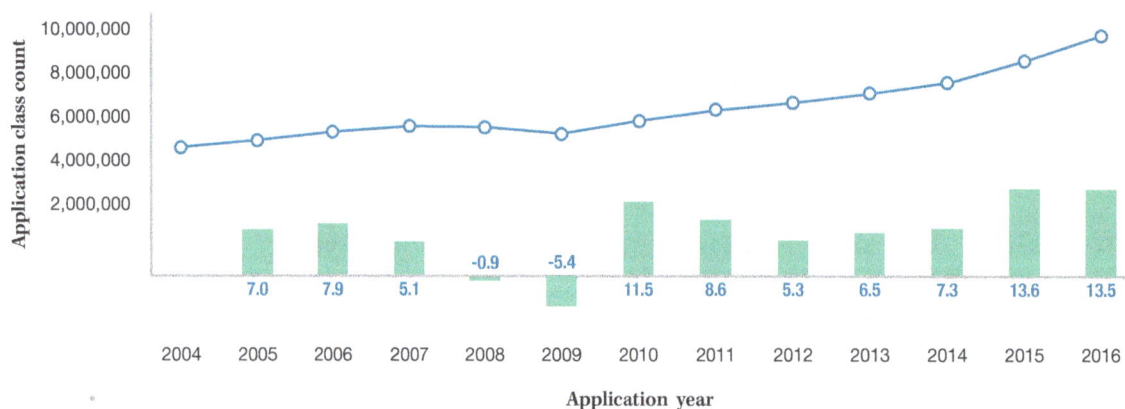

Application class count (y-axis)

Application year	2004	2005	2006	2007	2008	2009	2010	2011	2012	2013	2014	2015	2016
Growth rate (%)		7.0	7.9	5.1	-0.9	-5.4	11.5	8.6	5.3	6.5	7.3	13.6	13.5

Application year (x-axis)

▮ APPLICATION CLASS COUNT ▮ GROWTH RATE (%)

Note: World totals are WIPO estimates using data covering 166 IP offices. These totals include class counts in applications filed directly with national and regional offices (known as the "Paris route") as well as class counts in designations received by offices via the Madrid System (where applicable). See the glossary for the definition of class count.

Source: WIPO Statistics Database, September 2017.

TRADEMARKS

Figure B3
Resident and non-resident trademark application class counts worldwide

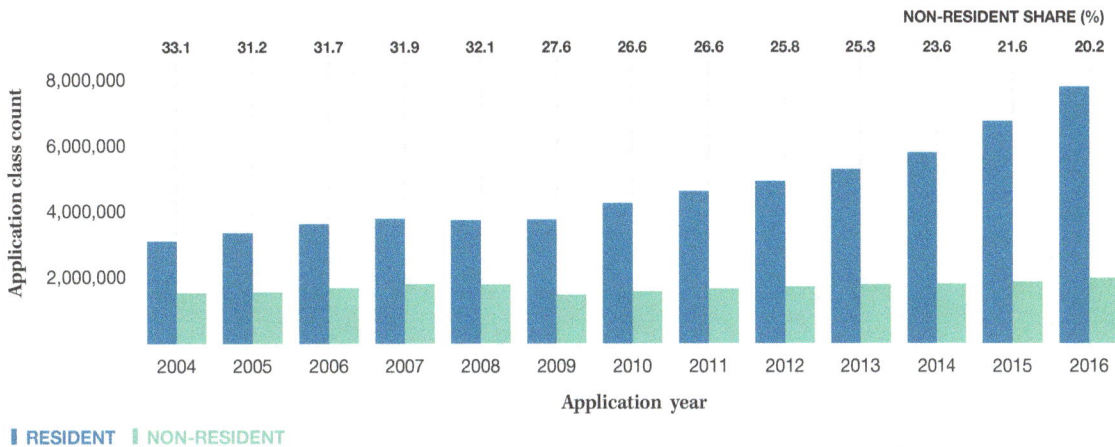

NON-RESIDENT SHARE (%)

| 33.1 | 31.2 | 31.7 | 31.9 | 32.1 | 27.6 | 26.6 | 26.6 | 25.8 | 25.3 | 23.6 | 21.6 | 20.2 |

Application class count / **Application year** (2004–2016)

■ RESIDENT ■ NON-RESIDENT

Note: World totals are WIPO estimates using data covering 166 IP offices. These totals include class counts in applications filed directly with national and regional offices (known as the "Paris route") as well as class counts in designations received by offices via the Madrid System (where applicable). See the glossary for definitions of class count and for resident and non-resident.

Source: WIPO Statistics Database, September 2017.

Figure B4
Trend in trademark registrations worldwide

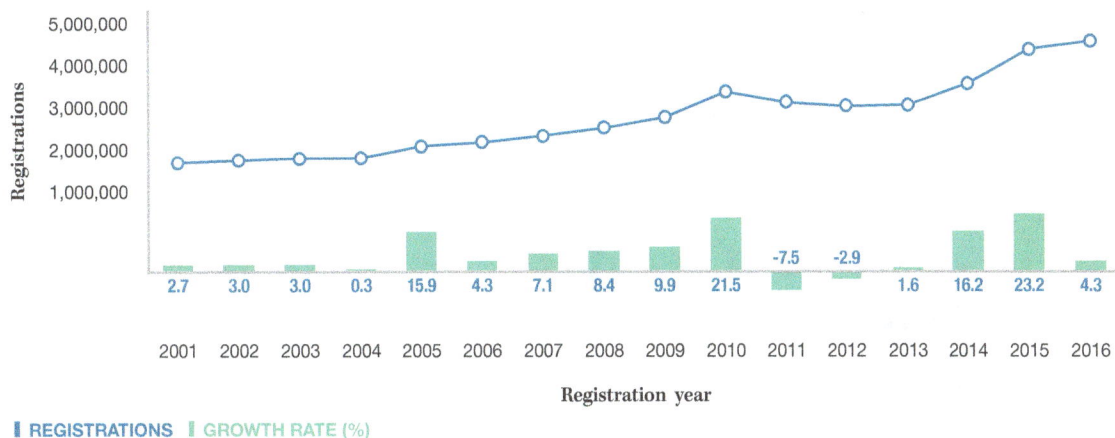

Registrations / **Registration year** (2001–2016)

| 2.7 | 3.0 | 3.0 | 0.3 | 15.9 | 4.3 | 7.1 | 8.4 | 9.9 | 21.5 | -7.5 | -2.9 | 1.6 | 16.2 | 23.2 | 4.3 |

■ REGISTRATIONS ■ GROWTH RATE (%)

Note: World totals are WIPO estimates using data covering 169 IP offices. Each total includes the number of registrations issued by national and regional offices for applications filed directly with offices (known as the "Paris route") as well as the number of designations received by offices via the Madrid System (where applicable).

Source: WIPO Statistics Database, September 2017.

TRADEMARKS

111

Figure B5
Trend in trademark registration class counts worldwide

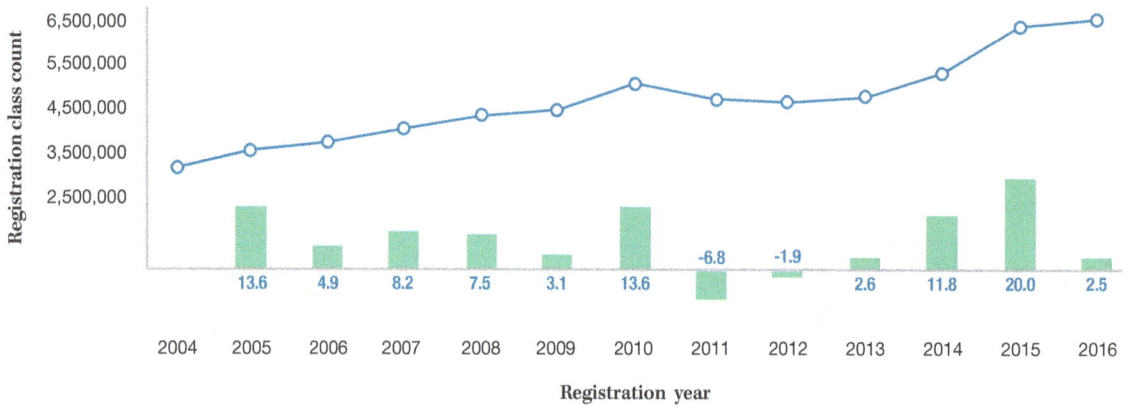

▌REGISTRATION CLASS COUNT   ▌GROWTH RATE (%)

Note: World totals are WIPO estimates using data covering 166 IP offices. These totals include class counts in registrations issued by national and regional offices for applications filed directly with offices (known as the "Paris route") as well as designations received by offices via the Madrid System (where applicable). See the glossary for the definition of class count.

Source: WIPO Statistics Database, September 2017.

Figure B6
Resident and non-resident trademark registration class counts worldwide

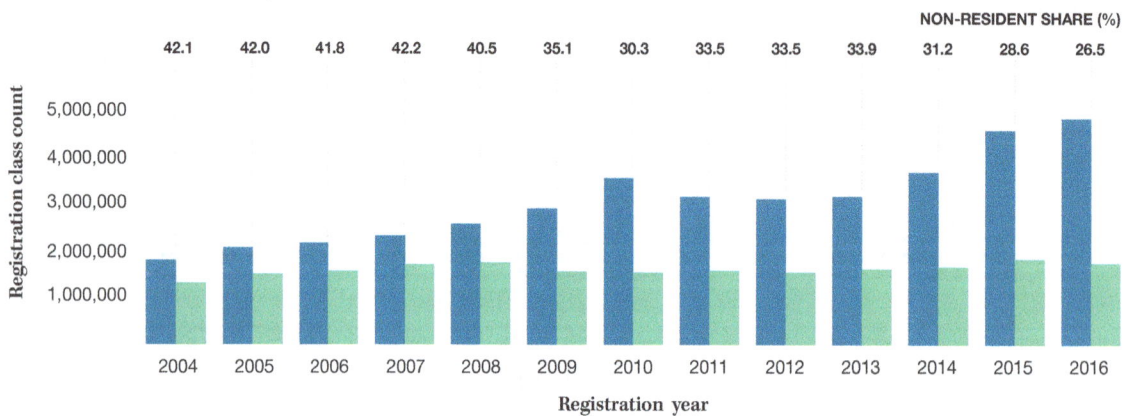

▌RESIDENT   ▌NON-RESIDENT

Note: World totals are WIPO estimates using data covering 166 IP offices. These totals include class counts in registrations issued by national and regional offices for applications filed directly with offices (known as the "Paris route") as well as for designations received by offices via the Madrid System (where applicable). See the glossary for definitions of class count and for resident and non-resident.

Source: WIPO Statistics Database, September 2017.

Trademark applications and registrations by office

Figure B7
Trademark application class counts by income group

Income group	Application class count		Resident share (%)		Share of world total (%)		Average growth (%)
	2006	2016	2006	2016	2006	2016	2006-16
High-income	2,932,300	3,584,200	68.2	72.1	55.5	36.7	2.0
Upper middle-income	1,778,200	5,201,000	72.6	88.2	33.7	53.2	11.3
...Upper middle-income without China	1,018,500	1,503,100	61.1	70.6	19.3	15.4	4.0
Lower middle-income	525,300	916,700	56.3	65.0	9.9	9.4	5.7
Low-income	44,800	66,300	44.9	43.0	0.9	0.7	4.0
World	**5,280,600**	**9,768,200**	**68.3**	**79.8**	**100.0**	**100.0**	**6.3**

Note: Totals by income group are WIPO estimates using data covering 166 IP offices. Each category includes the following number of offices: high-income (62), upper middle-income (46), lower middle-income (40) and low-income (18). Data for the European Union Intellectual Property Office (EUIPO) are allocated to the high-income group because most EU member states are high-income countries. For similar reasons, data for the African Regional Intellectual Property Organization (ARIPO) and the African Intellectual Property Organization (OAPI) are allocated to the low-income group. For information on income group classification, see the Data description section.

Source: WIPO Statistics Database, September 2017.

Figure B8
Trademark application class counts by region

Region	Application class count		Resident share (%)		Share of world total (%)		Average growth (%)
	2006	2016	2006	2016	2006	2016	2006-16
Africa	168,900	248,600	44.6	46.1	3.2	2.4	3.9
Asia	1,955,100	5,861,200	74.0	87.1	37.0	60.0	11.6
Europe	2,046,300	2,096,700	65.4	74.7	38.8	21.5	0.2
Latin America & the Caribbean	485,500	680,300	63.4	65.5	9.2	7.0	3.4
North America	490,200	699,300	73.2	67.2	9.3	7.2	3.6
Oceania	134,600	182,100	58.4	53.9	2.5	1.9	3.1
World	**5,280,600**	**9,768,200**	**68.3**	**79.8**	**100.0**	**100.0**	**6.3**

Note: Totals by geographical region are WIPO estimates using data covering 166 IP offices. Each region includes the following number of offices: Africa (33), Asia (46), Europe (43), Latin America & the Caribbean (37), North America (2) and Oceania (5).

Source: WIPO Statistics Database, September 2017.

TRADEMARKS

Figure B9
Trend in trademark applications for the top five offices

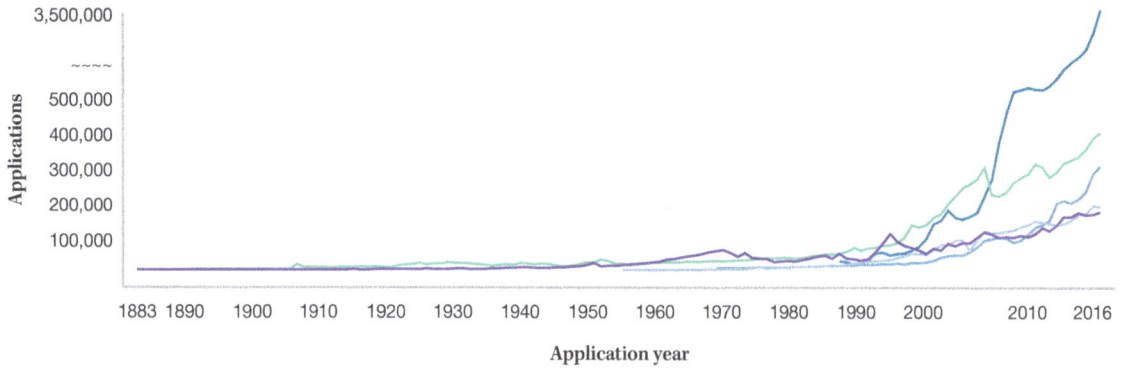

▮ CHINA   ▮ U.S.   ▮ INDIA   ▮ REP. OF KOREA   ▮ BRAZIL

Note: Data are based on the numbers of applications filed; that is, differences between single-class and multi-class filing systems across IP offices are not taken into account. The top five offices were selected based on their 2016 totals.

Source: WIPO Statistics Database, September 2017.

Figure B10
Trademark application class counts for the top 20 offices, 2016

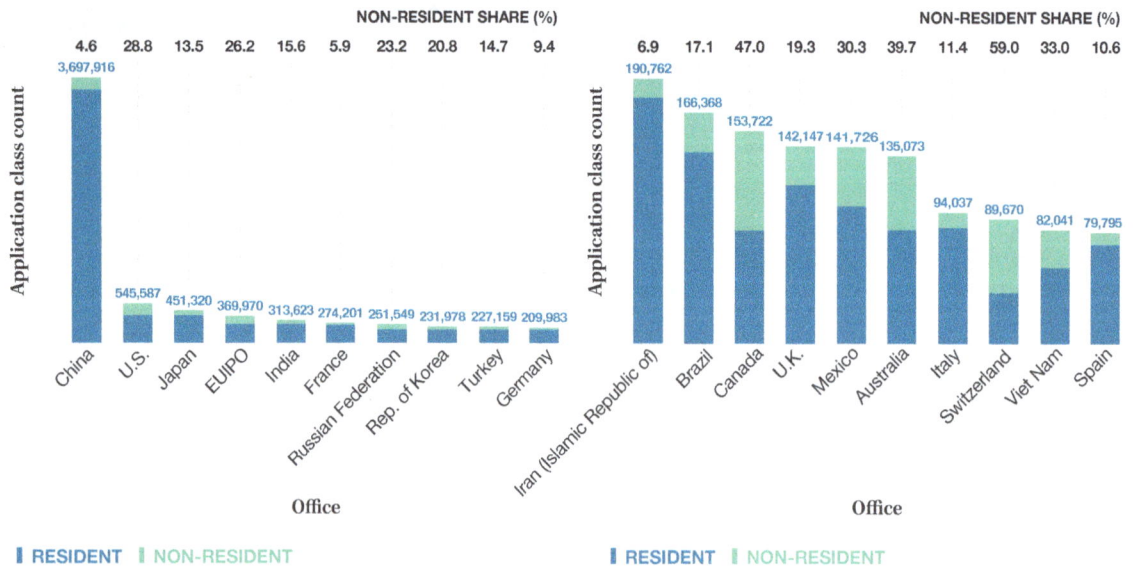

▮ RESIDENT   ▮ NON-RESIDENT   ▮ RESIDENT   ▮ NON-RESIDENT

Note: EUIPO is the European Union Intellectual Property Office.

Source: WIPO Statistics Database, September 2017.

Figure B11

Contribution of resident and non-resident application class counts to total growth for the top 20 offices, 2015-16

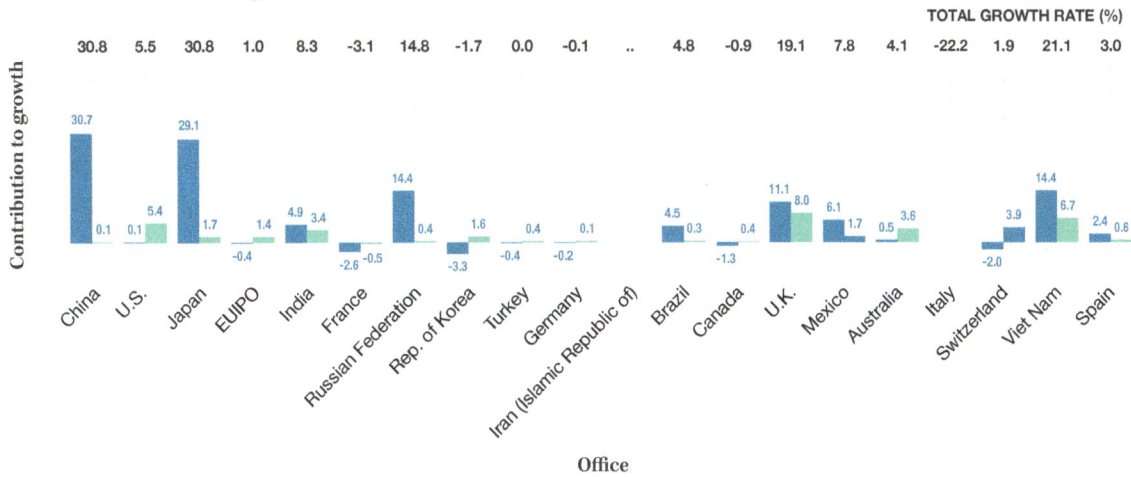

TOTAL GROWTH RATE (%)

	China	U.S.	Japan	EUIPO	India	France	Russian Federation	Rep. of Korea	Turkey	Germany	Iran (Islamic Republic of)	Brazil	Canada	U.K.	Mexico	Australia	Italy	Switzerland	Viet Nam	Spain
	30.8	5.5	30.8	1.0	8.3	-3.1	14.8	-1.7	0.0	-0.1	..	4.8	-0.9	19.1	7.8	4.1	-22.2	1.9	21.1	3.0

■ CONTRIBUTION OF RESIDENT APPLICATIONS   ■ CONTRIBUTION OF NON-RESIDENT APPLICATIONS

.. indicates not available.

Note: EUIPO is the European Union Intellectual Property Office. This figure shows, for each office, total growth or decreases in application class counts broken down by the respective contributions of resident and non-resident filing activity. For example, the total number of classes specified in trademark applications in India grew by 8.3%. Growth in resident filing activity accounted for 4.9 percentage points of this increase, whereas the remaining 3.4 percentage points came from non-resident filing activity. Resident and non-resident contributions are not available for the Islamic Republic of Iran and Italy.

Source: WIPO Statistics Database, September 2017.

Figure B12

Trademark application class counts for offices of selected low- and middle-income countries, 2016

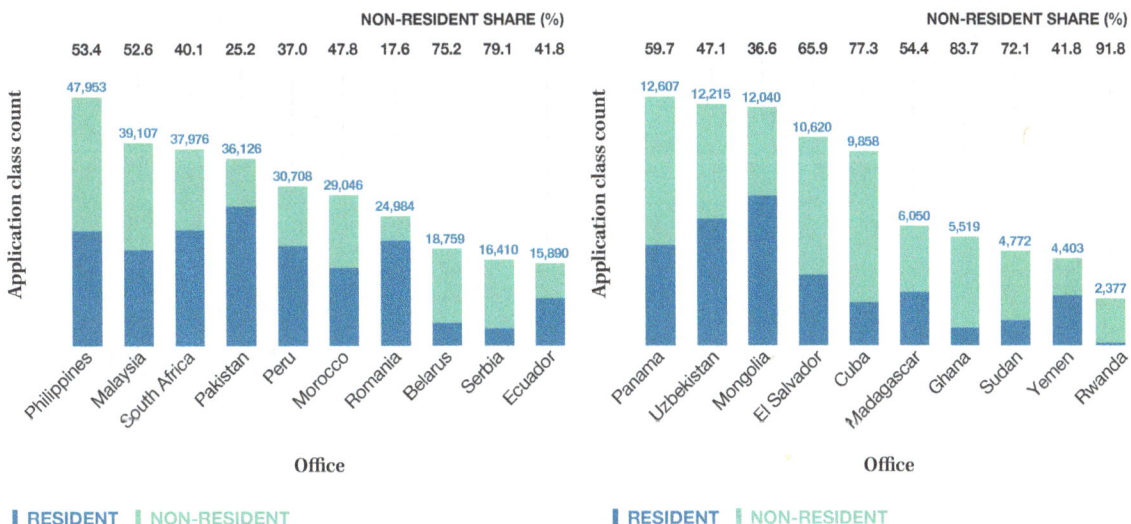

NON-RESIDENT SHARE (%)

	Philippines	Malaysia	South Africa	Pakistan	Peru	Morocco	Romania	Belarus	Serbia	Ecuador
	53.4	52.6	40.1	25.2	37.0	47.8	17.6	75.2	79.1	41.8

NON-RESIDENT SHARE (%)

	Panama	Uzbekistan	Mongolia	El Salvador	Cuba	Madagascar	Ghana	Sudan	Yemen	Rwanda
	59.7	47.1	36.6	65.9	77.3	54.4	83.7	72.1	41.8	91.8

■ RESIDENT ■ NON-RESIDENT   ■ RESIDENT ■ NON-RESIDENT

Note: The selected offices are from different world regions and income groups (low-income, lower middle-income and upper middle-income). Where available, data for all offices are presented in the statistical table at the end of this section.

Source: WIPO Statistics Database, September 2017.

TRADEMARKS

Figure B13

Contribution of resident and non-resident application class counts to total growth for offices of selected low- and middle-income countries, 2015-16

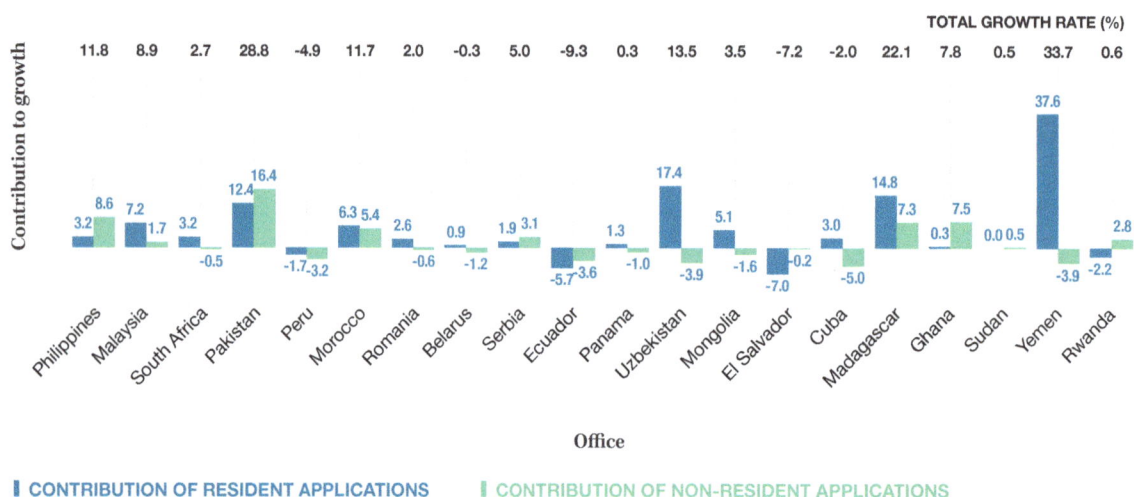

Note: The selected offices are from different world regions and income groups (low-income, lower middle-income and upper middle-income). Where available, data for all offices are presented in the statistical table at the end of this section. This figure shows, for each office, total growth or decrease in application class counts broken down by the respective contributions of resident and non-resident applications. For example, the total number of classes specified in trademark applications at the IP office of the Philippines grew by 11.8%. Growth in resident filing activity accounted for 3.2 percentage points of this increase, whereas the remaining 8.6 percentage points came from non-resident filing activity.

Source: WIPO Statistics Database, September 2017.

Figure B14

Trademark registration class counts by income group

Income group	Registration class count		Resident share (%)		Share of world total (%)		Average growth (%)
	2006	2016	2006	2016	2006	2016	2006-16
High-income	2,284,600	2,561,900	61.0	67.0	61.4	39.1	1.2
Upper middle-income	995,600	3,344,300	57.0	83.1	26.7	51.1	12.9
...Upper middle-income without China	702,700	1,073,400	48.2	61.4	18.9	16.4	4.3
Lower middle-income	412,000	593,800	47.8	51.9	11.1	9.1	3.7
Low-income	29,700	49,200	24.2	25.0	0.8	0.8	5.2
World	3,721,900	6,549,100	58.2	73.5	100.0	100.0	5.8

Note: Totals by income group are WIPO estimates using data covering 166 IP offices. Each category includes the following number of offices: high-income (62), upper middle-income (46), lower middle-income (40) and low-income (18). Data for the European Union Intellectual Property Office are allocated to the high-income group because most EU member states are high-income countries. For similar reasons, data for the African Regional Intellectual Property Organization and the African Intellectual Property Organization are allocated to the low-income group. For information on income group classification, see the Data description section.

Source: WIPO Statistics Database, September 2017.

Figure B15
Trademark registration class counts by region

Region	Registration class count		Resident share (%)		Share of world total (%)		Average growth (%)
	2006	2016	2006	2016	2006	2016	2006-16
Africa	127,300	159,900	29.8	29.1	3.4	2.4	2.3
Asia	1,182,500	3,713,500	61.7	80.8	31.8	56.7	12.1
Europe	1,698,400	1,611,400	57.3	70.6	45.6	24.6	-0.5
Latin America & the Caribbean	345,900	503,300	58.4	58.4	9.3	7.7	3.8
North America	285,400	422,200	63.0	64.6	7.7	6.4	4.0
Oceania	82,400	138,800	50.1	45.9	2.2	2.1	5.4
World	**3,721,900**	**6,549,100**	**58.2**	**73.5**	**100.0**	**100.0**	**5.8**

Note: Totals by geographical region are WIPO estimates based on data covering 166 offices. Each region includes the following number of offices: Africa (33), Asia (46), Europe (43), Latin America & the Caribbean (37), North America (2) and Oceania (5).

Source: WIPO Statistics Database, September 2017.

Figure B16
Trend in trademark registrations for the top five offices

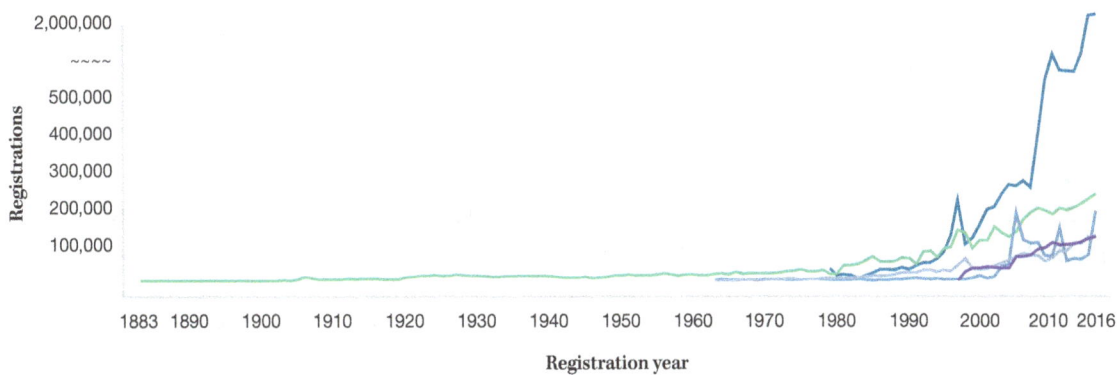

I CHINA I U.S. I INDIA I REP. OF KOREA I EUIPO

Note: EUIPO is the European Union Intellectual Property Office. Data are based on the numbers of registrations recorded; that is, differences between single-class and multi-class registration systems across IP offices are not taken into account. The top five offices were selected based on their 2016 totals.

Source: WIPO Statistics Database, September 2017.

TRADEMARKS

TRADEMARKS

Figure B17
Trademark registration class counts for the top 20 offices, 2016

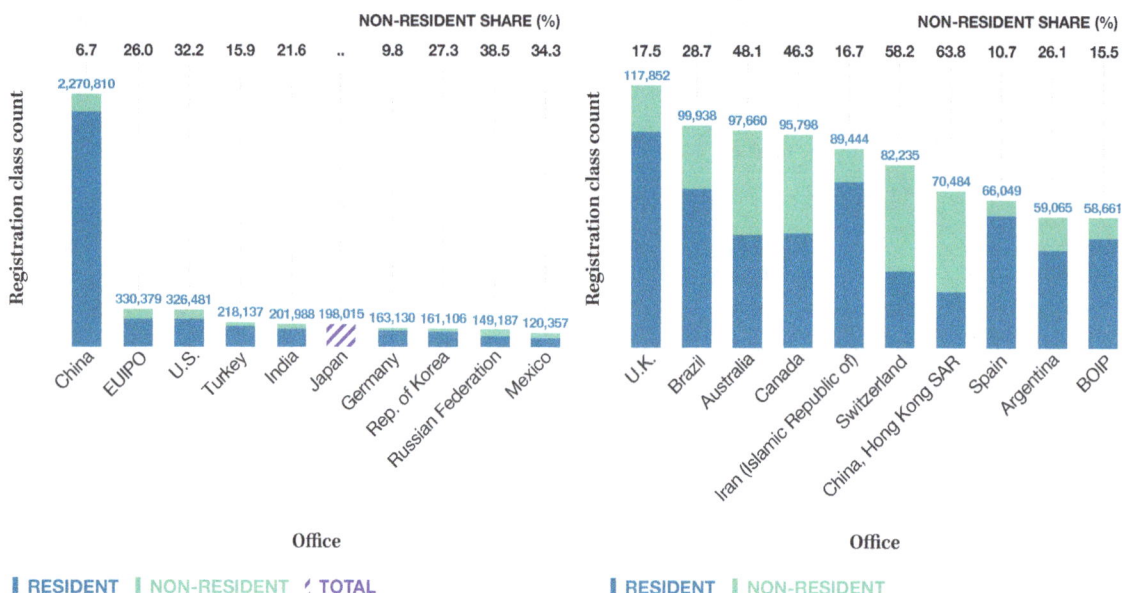

NON-RESIDENT SHARE (%)

| 6.7 | 26.0 | 32.2 | 15.9 | 21.6 | .. | 9.8 | 27.3 | 38.5 | 34.3 |

Registration class count

- China: 2,270,810
- EUIPO: 330,379
- U.S.: 326,481
- Turkey: 218,137
- India: 201,988
- Japan: 198,015
- Germany: 163,130
- Rep. of Korea: 161,106
- Russian Federation: 149,187
- Mexico: 120,357

Office

NON-RESIDENT SHARE (%)

| 17.5 | 28.7 | 48.1 | 46.3 | 16.7 | 58.2 | 63.8 | 10.7 | 26.1 | 15.5 |

Registration class count

- U.K.: 117,852
- Brazil: 99,938
- Australia: 97,660
- Canada: 95,798
- Iran (Islamic Republic of): 89,444
- Switzerland: 82,235
- China, Hong Kong SAR: 70,484
- Spain: 66,049
- Argentina: 59,065
- BOIP: 58,661

Office

▮ RESIDENT ▮ NON-RESIDENT ⟋ TOTAL   ▮ RESIDENT ▮ NON-RESIDENT

.. indicates not available.

Note: EUIPO is the European Union Intellectual Property Office, and BOIP is the Benelux Office for Intellectual Property. Figures for the office of France are not presented here because their data are not available. On the basis of an examination, a registration may be issued for a trademark application. The number of registrations issued may fluctuate greatly from one year to the next, in part reflecting the resources that IP offices dedicate to examining trademark applications.

Source: WIPO Statistics Database, September 2017.

Figure B18
Trademark registration class counts for offices of selected low- and middle-income countries, 2016

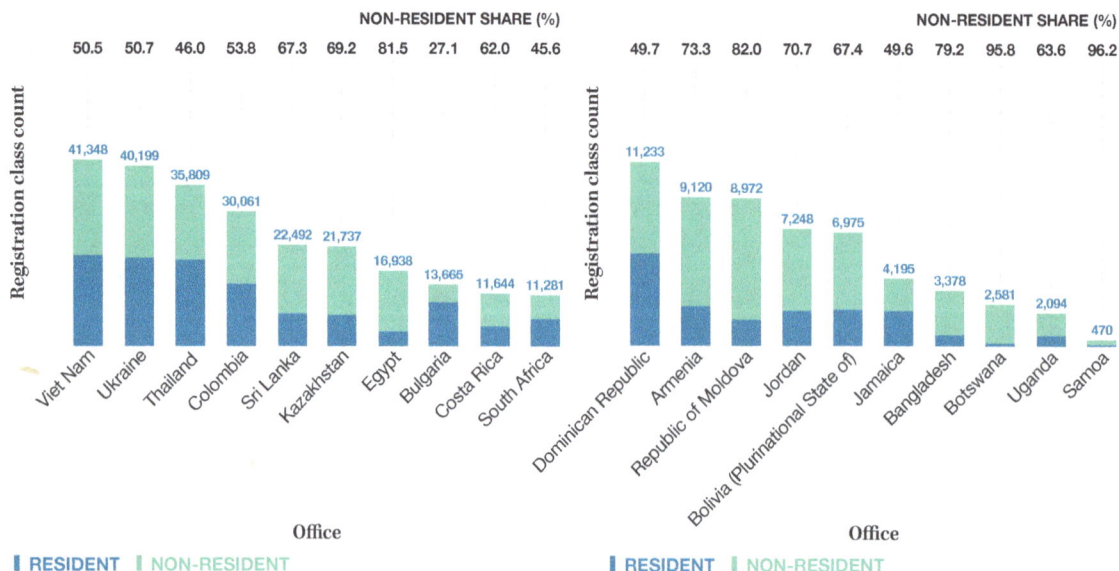

NON-RESIDENT SHARE (%)

| 50.5 | 50.7 | 46.0 | 53.8 | 67.3 | 69.2 | 81.5 | 27.1 | 62.0 | 45.6 |

Registration class count

- Viet Nam: 41,348
- Ukraine: 40,199
- Thailand: 35,809
- Colombia: 30,061
- Sri Lanka: 22,492
- Kazakhstan: 21,737
- Egypt: 16,938
- Bulgaria: 13,666
- Costa Rica: 11,644
- South Africa: 11,281

Office

NON-RESIDENT SHARE (%)

| 49.7 | 73.3 | 82.0 | 70.7 | 67.4 | 49.6 | 79.2 | 95.8 | 63.6 | 96.2 |

Registration class count

- Dominican Republic: 11,233
- Armenia: 9,120
- Republic of Moldova: 8,972
- Jordan: 7,248
- Bolivia (Plurinational State of): 6,975
- Jamaica: 4,195
- Bangladesh: 3,378
- Botswana: 2,581
- Uganda: 2,094
- Samoa: 470

Office

▮ RESIDENT ▮ NON-RESIDENT   ▮ RESIDENT ▮ NON-RESIDENT

Note: The selected offices are from different world regions and income groups (low-income, lower middle-income and upper middle-income). Where available, data for all offices are presented in the statistical table at the end of this section.

Source: WIPO Statistics Database, September 2017.

Trademark applications by origin

Figure B19
Equivalent trademark application class counts by origin, 2016

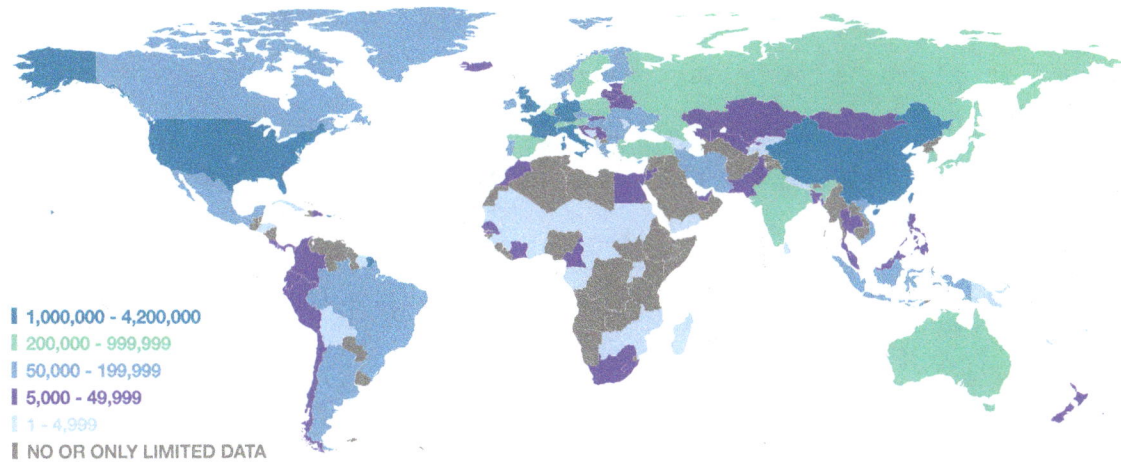

1,000,000 - 4,200,000
200,000 - 999,999
50,000 - 199,999
5,000 - 49,999
1 - 4,999
NO OR ONLY LIMITED DATA

Note: Trademark filing activity by origin includes the number of classes specified in resident applications and in applications filed abroad. The origin of a trademark application is determined by the residence of the applicant. Applications filed at regional offices are considered equivalent to multiple applications in the relevant member states, and the classes specified in these applications are multiplied accordingly. See the glossary for the definition of equivalent application.

Source: WIPO Statistics Database, September 2017.

Figure B20
Trademark application class counts for the top 20 origins, 2016

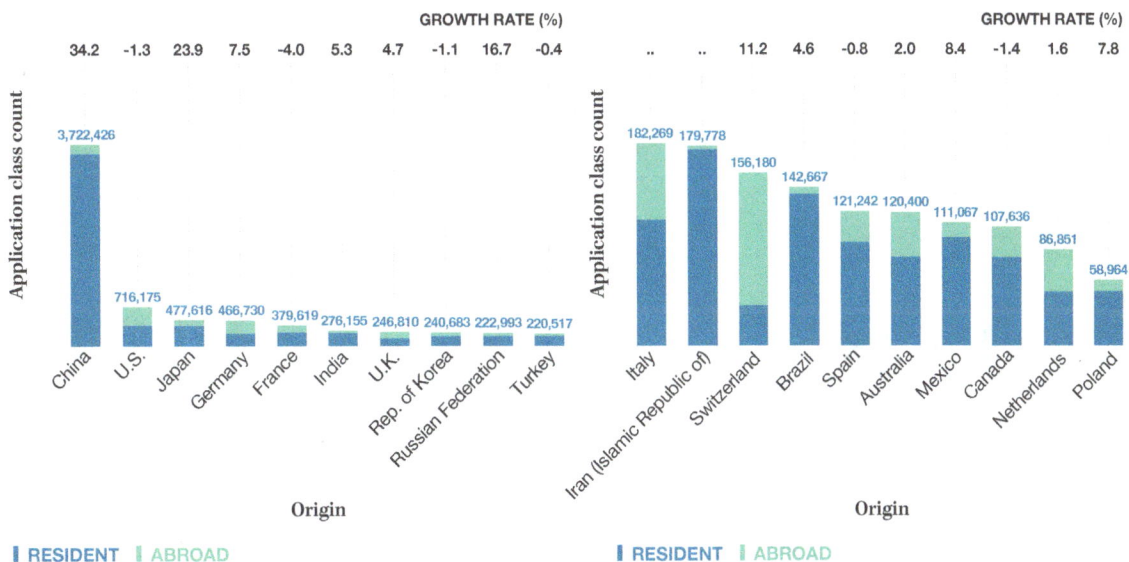

GROWTH RATE (%)

34.2	-1.3	23.9	7.5	-4.0	5.3	4.7	-1.1	16.7	-0.4

Application class count

- China: 3,722,426
- U.S.: 716,175
- Japan: 477,616
- Germany: 466,730
- France: 379,619
- India: 276,155
- U.K.: 246,810
- Rep. of Korea: 240,683
- Russian Federation: 222,993
- Turkey: 220,517

Origin

GROWTH RATE (%)

..	..	11.2	4.6	-0.8	2.0	8.4	-1.4	1.6	7.8

Application class count

- Italy: 182,269
- Iran (Islamic Republic of): 179,778
- Switzerland: 156,180
- Brazil: 142,667
- Spain: 121,242
- Australia: 120,400
- Mexico: 111,067
- Canada: 107,636
- Netherlands: 86,851
- Poland: 58,964

Origin

RESIDENT   ABROAD

RESIDENT   ABROAD

.. indicates not available.

Note: In this figure, trademark application filing activity by origin includes the number of classes specified in resident applications and in applications filed abroad, and is based on absolute count, not equivalent count. The origin of a trademark application is determined by the residence of the applicant. An application filed at a regional office is considered a resident filing if the applicant is a resident of one of the relevant member states.

Source: WIPO Statistics Database, September 2017.

Figure B21
Trademark application class counts for selected low- and middle-income origins, 2016

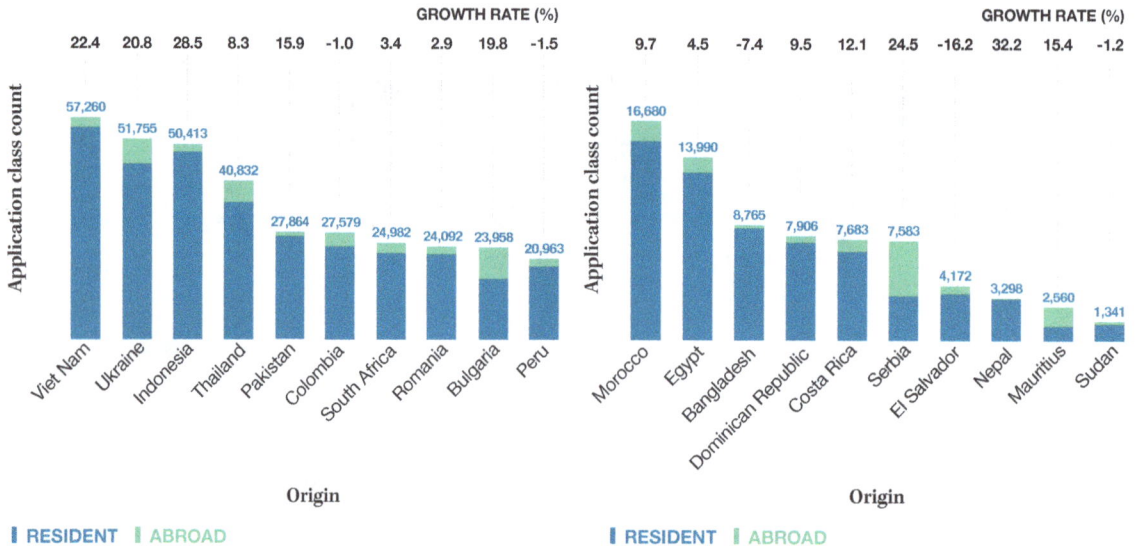

GROWTH RATE (%)

| 22.4 | 20.8 | 28.5 | 8.3 | 15.9 | -1.0 | 3.4 | 2.9 | 19.8 | -1.5 |

GROWTH RATE (%)

| 9.7 | 4.5 | -7.4 | 9.5 | 12.1 | 24.5 | -16.2 | 32.2 | 15.4 | -1.2 |

Left chart — Application class count:

- Viet Nam: 57,260
- Ukraine: 51,755
- Indonesia: 50,413
- Thailand: 40,832
- Pakistan: 27,864
- Colombia: 27,579
- South Africa: 24,982
- Romania: 24,092
- Bulgaria: 23,958
- Peru: 20,963

Right chart — Application class count:

- Morocco: 16,680
- Egypt: 13,990
- Bangladesh: 8,765
- Dominican Republic: 7,906
- Costa Rica: 7,683
- Serbia: 7,583
- El Salvador: 4,172
- Nepal: 3,298
- Mauritius: 2,560
- Sudan: 1,341

Origin

■ RESIDENT ■ ABROAD   ■ RESIDENT ■ ABROAD

Note: In this figure, trademark application filing activity by origin includes the number of classes specified in resident applications and in applications filed abroad, and is based on absolute count, not equivalent count. The origin of a trademark application is determined by the residence of the applicant. The selected origins are from different world regions and income groups (low-income, lower middle-income and upper middle-income). Where available, data for all origins are presented in the statistical table at the end of this section.

Source: WIPO Statistics Database, September 2017.

Figure B22
Trademark application class counts abroad for the top 20 origins, 2016

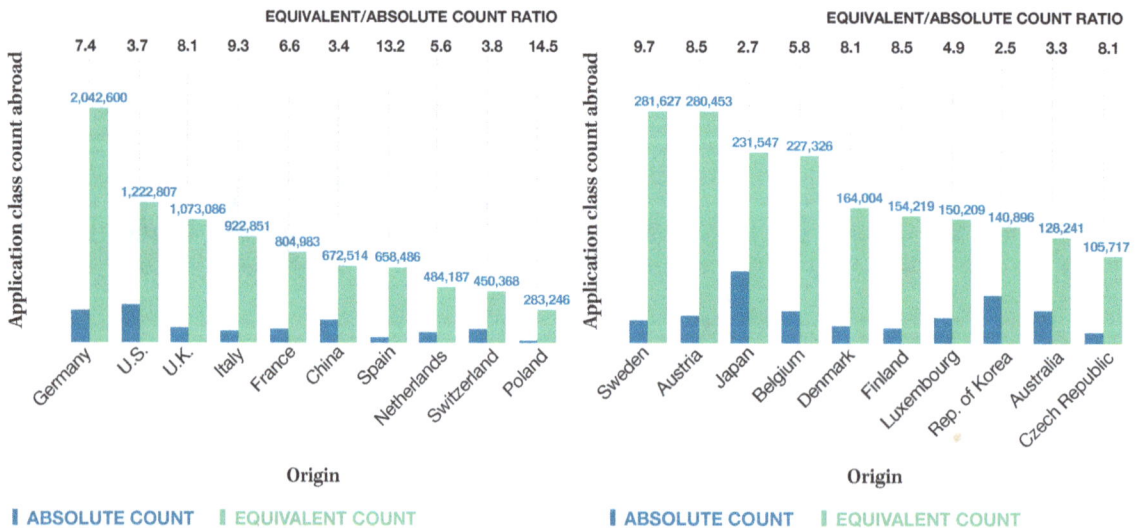

EQUIVALENT/ABSOLUTE COUNT RATIO

| 7.4 | 3.7 | 8.1 | 9.3 | 6.6 | 3.4 | 13.2 | 5.6 | 3.8 | 14.5 |

EQUIVALENT/ABSOLUTE COUNT RATIO

| 9.7 | 8.5 | 2.7 | 5.8 | 8.1 | 8.5 | 4.9 | 2.5 | 3.3 | 8.1 |

Left chart — Application class count abroad:

- Germany: 2,042,600
- U.S.: 1,222,807
- U.K.: 1,073,086
- Italy: 922,851
- France: 804,983
- China: 672,514
- Spain: 658,486
- Netherlands: 484,187
- Switzerland: 450,368
- Poland: 283,246

Right chart — Application class count abroad:

- Sweden: 281,627
- Austria: 280,453
- Japan: 231,547
- Belgium: 227,326
- Denmark: 164,004
- Finland: 154,219
- Luxembourg: 150,209
- Rep. of Korea: 140,896
- Australia: 128,241
- Czech Republic: 105,717

Origin

■ ABSOLUTE COUNT ■ EQUIVALENT COUNT   ■ ABSOLUTE COUNT ■ EQUIVALENT COUNT

Note: This figure distinguishes between absolute counts and equivalent counts for filing activity abroad – that is, resident applications are excluded. Based on equivalent application class counts, applicants from Germany had the highest level of trademark filing activity abroad. This was due not only to their high application class counts at numerous foreign offices, but also to their frequent use of the European Union Intellectual Property Office (EUIPO) – with its multiplier effect – to seek trademark protection within the entire EU. See the glossary for the definition of equivalent application. The origin of a trademark application is determined by the residence of the applicant.

Source: WIPO Statistics Database, September 2017.

Figure B23
Trademark application class counts for the top 25 offices and origins, 2016

Origin	China	U.S.	Japan	EUIPO	India	France	Russian Federation	Rep. of Korea	Turkey	Germany	Iran (Islamic Republic of)	Brazil
Argentina	120	263	41	178	3	15	27	25	3	22	1	295
Australia	6,397	5,791	1,448	3,264	1,075	123	478	979	214	118	50	163
Austria	1,210	1,515	503	9,496	518	153	1,063	318	695	1,454	189	256
Brazil	385	868	71	459	27	56	29	37	13	8	10	137,878
Canada	2,853	12,995	431	2,800	186	128	299	559	138	34	20	253
China	3,526,953	34,910	7,635	16,871	5,500	2,099	4,136	6,748	2,097	3,636	1,652	1,228
France	8,357	7,538	3,613	25,152	2,225	258,090	3,461	2,342	2,024	1,209	915	1,777
Germany	15,810	14,415	6,651	67,252	5,620	1,320	8,989	5,392	7,093	190,216	2,103	2,713
India	420	1,114	109	569	264,662	44	288	146	85	49	207	142
Indonesia	183	86	69	38	22	19	10	77	26	4	10	5
Iran (Islamic Republic of)	392	61	13	138	43	46	147	38	119	71	177,538	
Italy	7,036	5,811	2,948	31,550	1,858	373	3,722	2,183	2,042	325	842	959
Japan	14,847	6,647	390,525	5,264	2,150	477	1,902	6,047	1,136	314	367	1,128
Mexico	480	2,354	144	556	52	46	139	92	102	14	8	1,294
Netherlands	3,250	3,186	1,170	13,794	1,019	474	1,349	735	1,178	719	212	710
Poland	881	596	171	10,132	172	77	828	228	303	112	94	56
Rep. of Korea	20,715	4,665	3,474	3,023	493	178	1,158	183,620	482	225	306	980
Russian Federation	2,093	800	210	954	474	334	193,213	250	358	571	167	84
Spain	2,233	2,451	699	23,278	499	343	749	382	505	247	243	653
Switzerland	5,969	5,639	3,456	11,786	2,410	1,828	4,115	2,435	2,595	3,092	728	1,506
Turkey	806	1,051	229	2,001	419	421	985	162	193,824	827	1,211	46
U.K.	11,519	15,357	3,581	35,865	3,635	895	2,773	2,557	1,642	1,908	428	1,399
U.S.	35,910	388,504	14,474	32,502	11,785	1,311	7,113	10,503	4,617	1,418	891	8,450
Ukraine	244	259	42	235	90	100	744	19	101	179	28	5
Viet Nam	338	187	102	40	42	40	84	99	29	24	16	1
Others	28,515	28,524	9,511	72,773	8,644	5,211	13,748	6,005	5,738	3,187	2,526	4,387
Total	**3,697,916**	**545,587**	**451,320**	**369,970**	**313,623**	**274,201**	**251,549**	**231,978**	**227,159**	**209,983**	**190,762**	**166,368**

TRADEMARKS

121

Origin	Canada	U.K.	Mexico	Australia	Italy	Switzerland	Viet Nam	Spain	China, Hong Kong SAR	Argentina	Ukraine	BOIP	Indonesia
Argentina	44	22	242	13	4	8	17	32	24	55,739	4	9	
Australia	1,607	1,775	405	81,399	71	332	673	68	1,092	97	111	60	280
Austria	465	124	305	442	324	2,416	142	110	157	57	478	157	46
Brazil	66	20	291	29	25	9	22	13	28	477	8	6	30
Canada	81,540	360	606	817	21	134	144	29	369	116	78	33	100
China	3,373	3,456	2,301	4,283	1,762	1,960	3,348	1,332	12,290	620	1,614	946	1,640
France	3,788	1,442	1,995	2,093	1,329	5,382	1,136	1,220	1,590	851	1,161	2,039	496
Germany	5,047	1,966	4,388	5,279	1,005	19,577	2,375	800	2,192	1,186	3,702	1,479	671
India	257	241	109	313	15	123	314	16	72	102	291	20	154
Indonesia	13	6	8	53	6	11	208	1	36	3		12	48,756
Iran (Islamic Republic of)	21	37	5	15	31	128	6	25	4		4	2	2
Italy	1,645	410	1,402	1,701	83,358	2,933	860	266	1,113	488	1,194	164	269
Japan	2,206	724	1,252	2,209	233	1,199	3,085	249	4,264	410	487	140	1,817
Mexico	422	102	98,739	76	17	66	5	115	19	1,313	17	17	12
Netherlands	1,333	489	723	1,141	178	1,625	412	253	590	361	736	35,220	402
Poland	113	105	157	151	59	246	101	54	52	32	703	47	23
Rep. of Korea	801	271	1,097	1,191	148	214	2,055	99	1,732	197	260	114	834
Russian Federation	89	340	179	149	455	252	277	281	50	62	1,679	231	65
Spain	514	229	1,865	467	175	513	166	71,312	280	574	298	72	99
Switzerland	2,082	1,375	2,610	2,369	1,303	36,762	1,191	580	1,468	1,011	1,886	764	642
Turkey	191	440	153	183	363	364	189	296	47	17	645	487	31
U.K.	5,313	114,722	1,852	5,783	333	2,423	995	350	1,940	658	791	1,406	570
U.S.	34,090	6,818	15,420	14,486	851	5,816	3,554	699	7,249	4,143	2,094	767	2,323
Ukraine	15	96	33	45	122	59	12	101	1	4	45,880	105	5
Viet Nam	22	32	15	82	22	20	54,965	18	20		23	26	34
Others	8,665	6,545	5,574	10,304	1,827	7,098	5,789	1,476	35,036	2,540	5,467	22,191	4,420
Total	**153,722**	**142,147**	**141,726**	**135,073**	**94,037**	**89,670**	**82,041**	**79,795**	**71,715**	**71,058**	**69,611**	**66,514**	**63,721**

Note: EUIPO is the European Union Intellectual Property Office, and BOIP is the Benelux Office for Intellectual Property. The office and origin data shown here consist of absolute application class counts rather than equivalent application class counts.

Source: WIPO Statistics Database, September 2017.

Figure B24
Flow of non-resident trademark application class counts between selected top origins and offices, 2016

Non-resident origin   Office

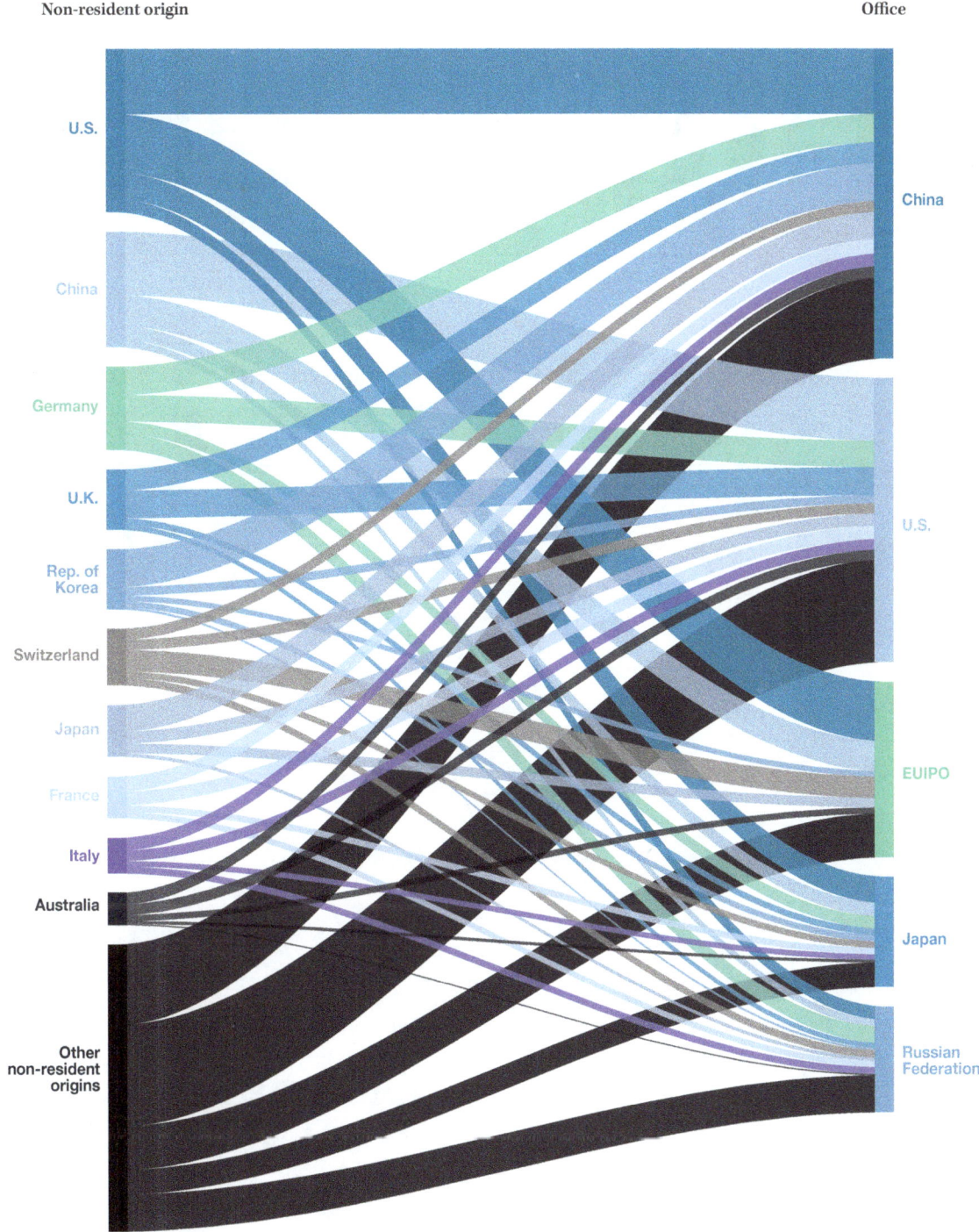

Note: EUIPO is the European Union Intellectual Property Office. The office and non-resident origin data shown here consist of absolute application class counts rather than equivalent application class counts.

Source: WIPO Statistics Database, September 2017.

TRADEMARKS

TRADEMARKS

Figure B25
Distribution of trademark application class counts for the top 15 offices and selected non-resident origins, 2016

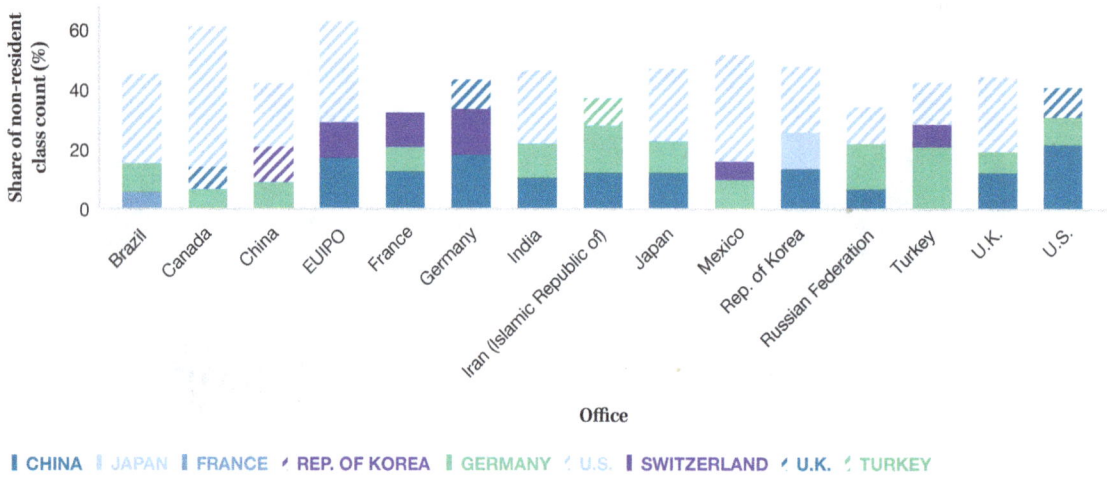

Office

■ CHINA ■ JAPAN ■ FRANCE ✔ REP. OF KOREA ■ GERMANY ✔ U.S. ■ SWITZERLAND ✔ U.K. ✔ TURKEY

Note: EUIPO is the European Union Intellectual Property Office. The office and origin data shown here consist of absolute application class counts rather than equivalent application class counts.

Source: WIPO Statistics Database, September 2017.

Trademark applications by Nice class and industry sector

Figure B26
Distribution of trademark applications by top Nice classes, 2016

Rank		Class	Class share (%)
1	35	Advertising, business management, business administration and office functions	10.5
2	9	Scientific, photographic, measuring instruments; recording equipment; computers and software	6.9
3	41	Education, entertainment, and sporting activities	5.8
4	25	Clothing	5.7
5	30	Coffee, tea, cocoa, rice, flour, bread, pastry and confectionery, sugar, honey, yeast, salt, mustard, vinegar, sauces (condiments) and spices	4.8
6	42	Scientific and technological services, design and development of computer hardware and software	4.6
7	5	Pharmaceutical preparations, baby food, dietary supplements for humans and animals, disinfectants, fungicides and herbicides	4.3
8	43	Services for providing food and drink; temporary accommodation	3.8
9	3	Bleaching preparations and other substances for laundry use; cleaning and abrasive preparations; scarps, perfumery and cosmetics	3.6
10	29	Foodstuffs of animal origin and vegetables	3.5
		Remaining classes	46.5

Note: These figures are based on filing data from 128 IP offices. Some classes listed are abbreviated. See Annex C for full definitions.

Source: WIPO Statistics Database, September 2017.

Figure B27
Trademark applications by goods and services classes, 2016

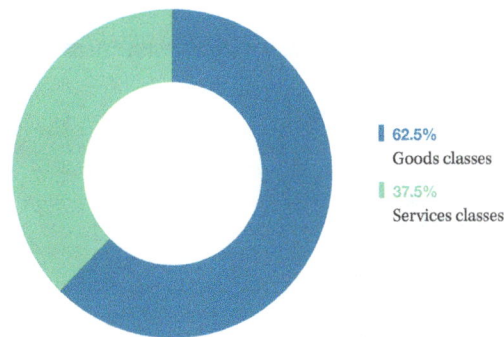

62.5% Goods classes

37.5% Services classes

Note: In the 45-class Nice Classification, the first 34 classes indicate goods and the remaining 11 refer to services. See Annex C for full definitions of classes. These figures are based on filing data from 128 IP offices.

Source: WIPO Statistics Database, September 2017.

Figure B28
Trademark applications by industry sector, 2016

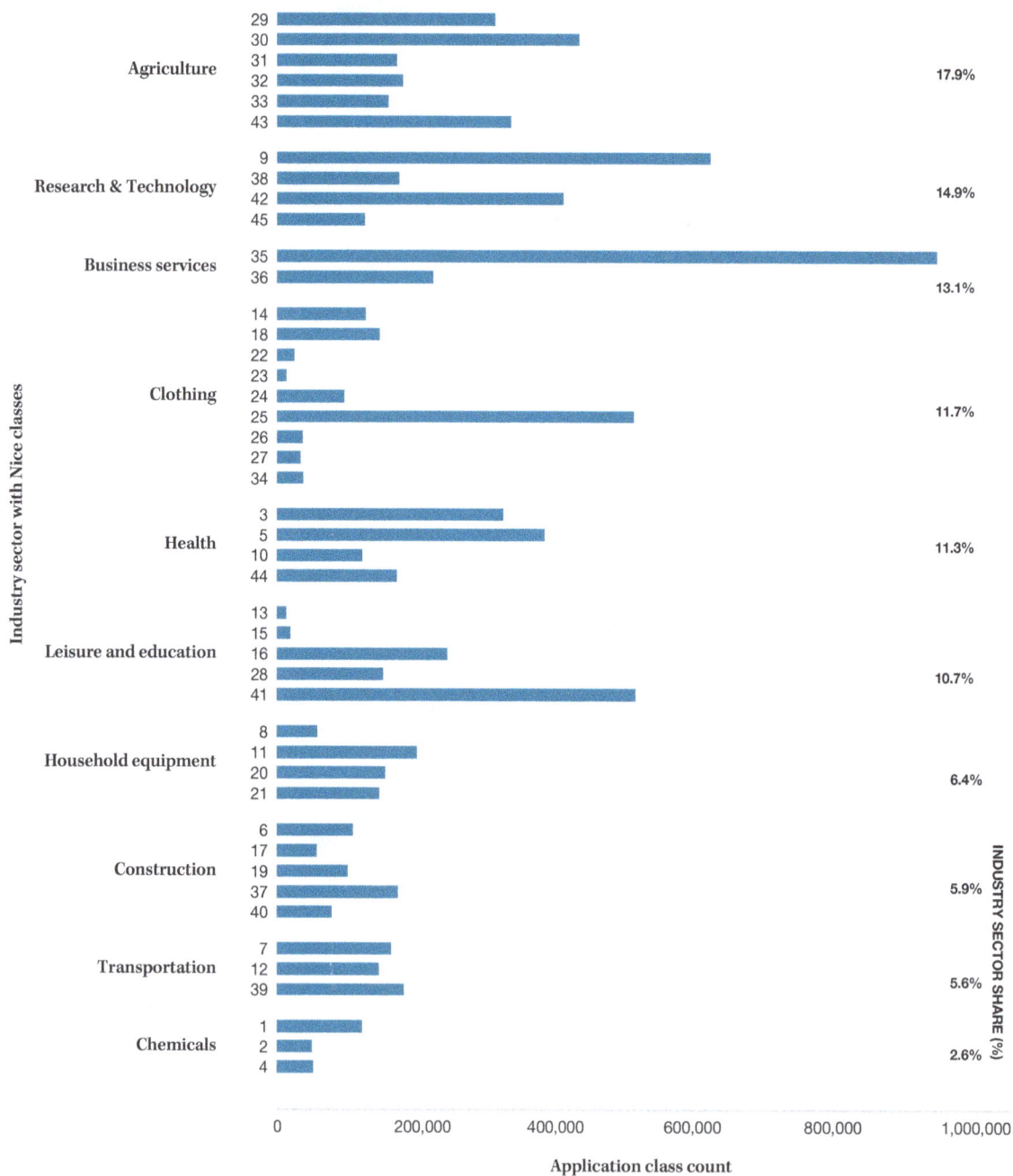

Note: Industry sectors based on class groups are those defined by Edital. Some industry sectors are abbreviated. See Annex C for full definitions. These figures are based on filing data from 128 IP offices.

Source: WIPO Statistics Database, September 2017.

STANDARD FIGURES AND TABLES

Figure B29
Trademark applications by top three sectors at the top offices, 2016

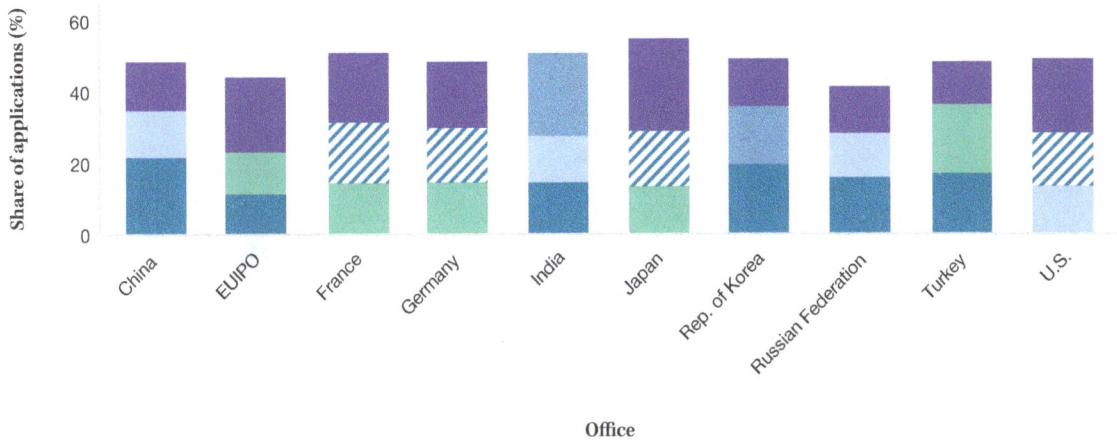

I AGRICULTURE **I** HEALTH **I** BUSINESS SERVICES **⁄** LEISURE & EDUCATION **I** CLOTHING **I** RESEARCH & TECHNOLOGY

Note: EUIPO is the European Union Intellectual Property Office. Industry sectors based on class groups are those defined by Edital. Some industry sectors are abbreviated. See Annex C for full definitions. The top three sectors and top offices were selected based on their 2016 totals.

Source: WIPO Statistics Database, September 2017.

Figure B30
Distribution of trademark applications by goods and services at the top offices, 2016

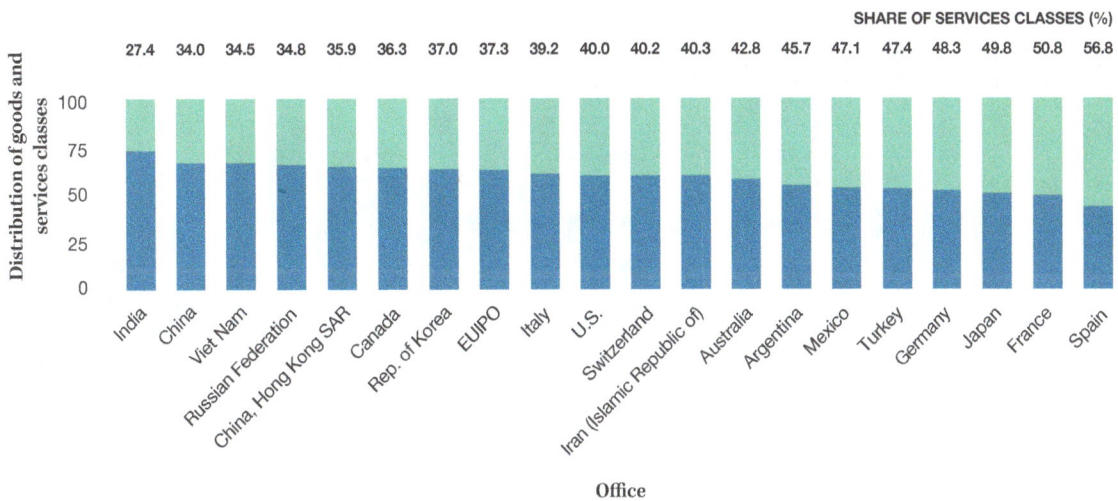

I GOODS CLASSES **I** SERVICES CLASSES

Note: EUIPO is the European Union Intellectual Property Office.

Source: WIPO Statistics Database, September 2017.

127

TRADEMARKS

Figure B31
Trademark applications by top three sectors for the top origins, 2016

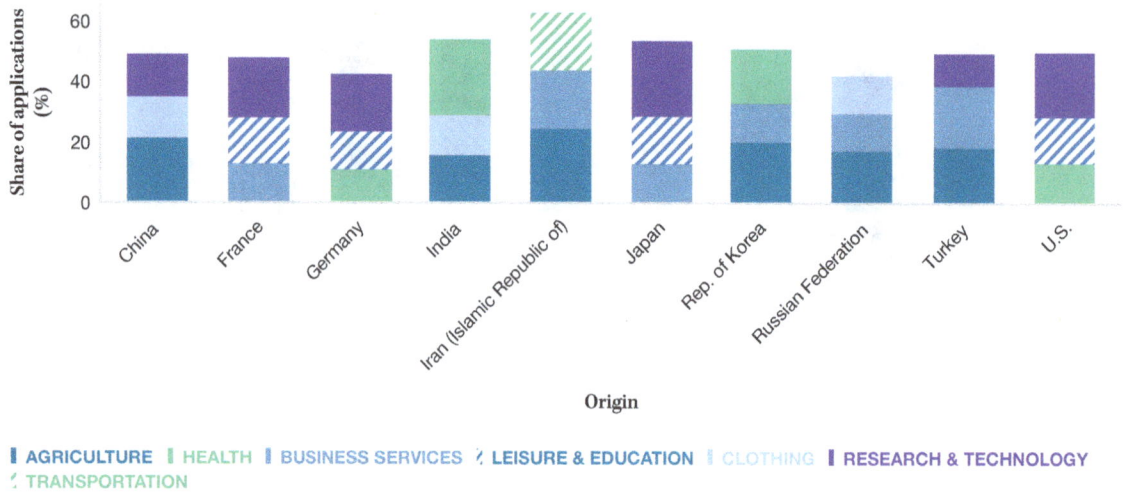

AGRICULTURE | HEALTH | BUSINESS SERVICES | LEISURE & EDUCATION | CLOTHING | RESEARCH & TECHNOLOGY | TRANSPORTATION

Note: Industry sectors based on class groups are those defined by Edital. Some industry sectors are abbreviated. See Annex C for full definitions. The top three sectors and top origins were selected based on their 2016 totals.

Source: WIPO Statistics Database, September 2017.

Figure B32
Distribution of trademark applications by goods and services for the top origins, 2016

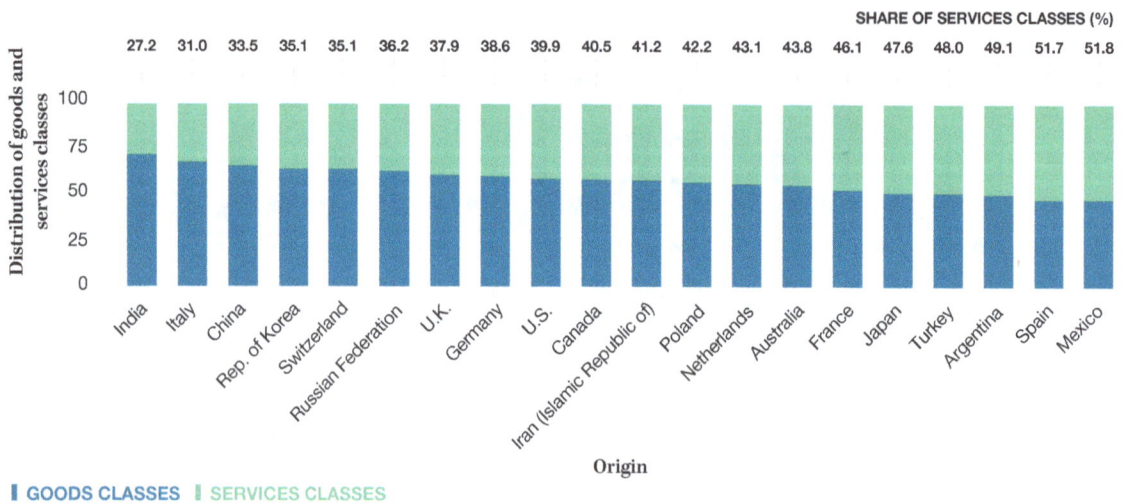

GOODS CLASSES | SERVICES CLASSES

Source: WIPO Statistics Database, September 2017.

Trademark application class count in relation to GDP and population

Figure B33

Resident trademark application class count per USD 100 billion GDP for selected origins

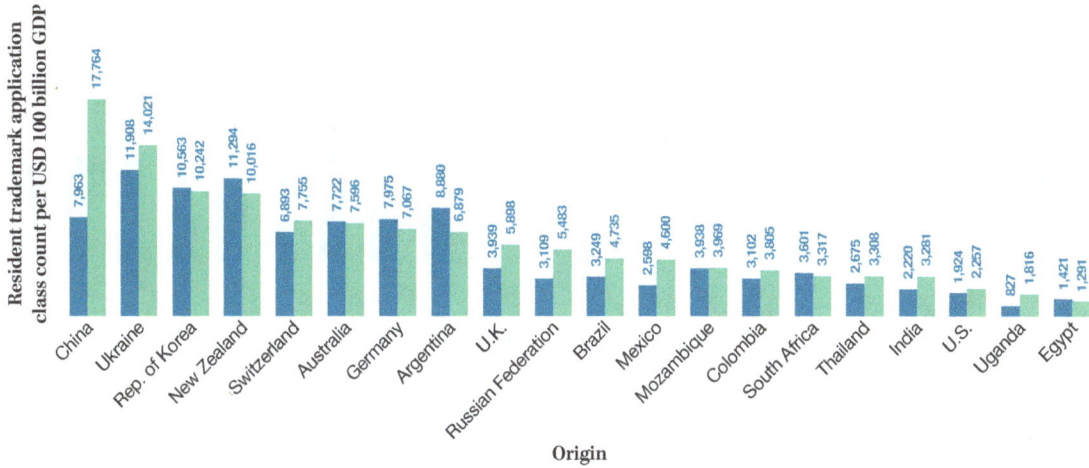

Resident trademark application class count per USD 100 billion GDP

China	7,963	17,764
Ukraine	11,908	14,021
Rep. of Korea	10,563	10,242
New Zealand	11,294	10,016
Switzerland	6,893	7,755
Australia	7,722	7,596
Germany	7,975	7,067
Argentina	8,880	6,879
U.K.	3,939	5,898
Russian Federation	3,109	5,483
Brazil	3,249	4,735
Mexico	2,598	4,600
Mozambique	3,938	3,969
Colombia	3,102	3,805
South Africa	3,601	3,317
Thailand	2,675	3,308
India	2,220	3,281
U.S.	1,924	2,257
Uganda	827	1,816
Egypt	1,421	1,291

Origin

■ 2006 ■ 2016

Note: GDP data are in constant 2011 U.S. PPP dollars. This figure does not provide an overall ranking of all origins; rather, it shows a selection across geographical regions and income groups.

Sources: WIPO Statistics Database and World Bank, September 2017.

Figure B34

Resident trademark application class count per million population for selected origins

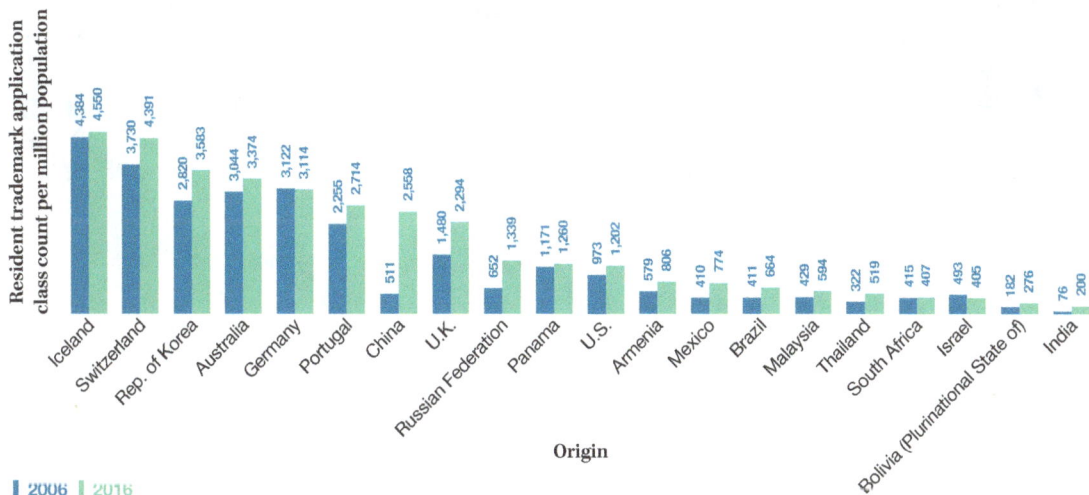

Resident trademark application class count per million population

Iceland	4,384	4,550
Switzerland	3,730	4,391
Rep. of Korea	2,820	3,583
Australia	3,044	3,374
Germany	3,122	3,114
Portugal	2,255	2,714
China	511	2,558
U.K.	1,480	2,294
Russian Federation	652	1,339
Panama	1,171	1,260
U.S.	973	1,202
Armenia	579	806
Mexico	410	774
Brazil	411	664
Malaysia	429	594
Thailand	322	519
South Africa	415	407
Israel	493	405
Bolivia (Plurinational State of)	182	276
India	76	200

Origin

■ 2006 ■ 2016

Note: This figure does not provide an overall ranking of all origins; rather, it shows a selection across geographical regions and income groups.

Sources: WIPO Statistics Database and World Bank, September 2017.

Collective and certification trademark applications by office

Figure B35
Collective trademark applications for the top 20 offices, 2016

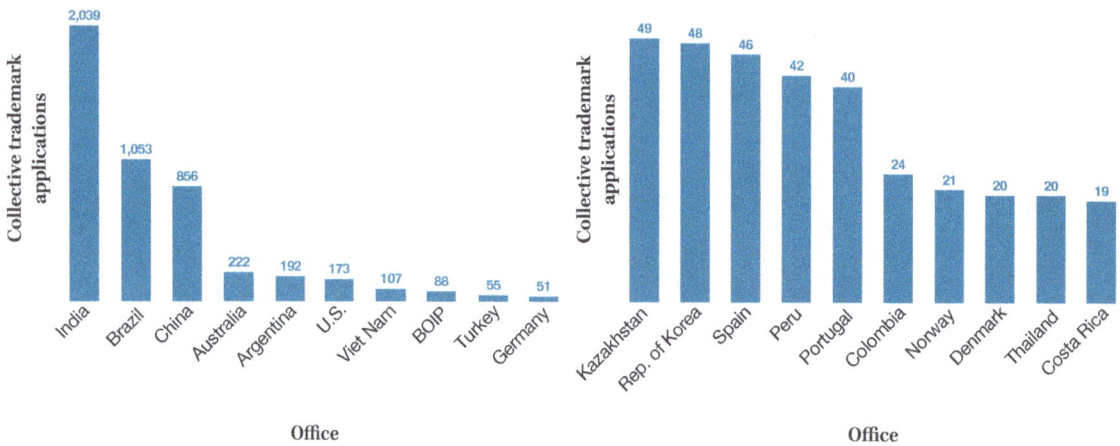

India 2,039
Brazil 1,053
China 856
Australia 222
Argentina 192
U.S. 173
Viet Nam 107
BOIP 88
Turkey 55
Germany 51

Kazakhstan 49
Rep. of Korea 48
Spain 46
Peru 42
Portugal 40
Colombia 24
Norway 21
Denmark 20
Thailand 20
Costa Rica 19

(y-axis: Collective trademark applications; x-axis: Office)

Note: BOIP is the Benelux Office for Intellectual Property.

Source: WIPO Statistics Database, September 2017.

Figure B36
Certification trademark applications for the top 20 offices, 2016

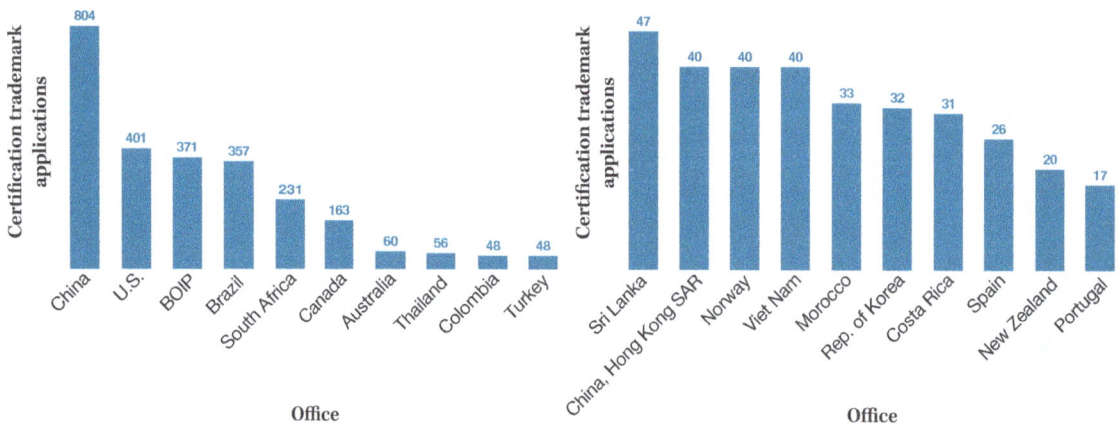

China 804
U.S. 401
BOIP 371
Brazil 357
South Africa 231
Canada 163
Australia 60
Thailand 56
Colombia 48
Turkey 48

Sri Lanka 47
China, Hong Kong SAR 40
Norway 40
Viet Nam 40
Morocco 33
Rep. of Korea 32
Costa Rica 31
Spain 26
New Zealand 20
Portugal 17

(y-axis: Certification trademark applications; x-axis: Office)

Note: BOIP is the Benelux Office for Intellectual Property.

Source: WIPO Statistics Database, September 2017.

Trademark registrations in force

Figure B37
Trend in trademark registrations in force worldwide

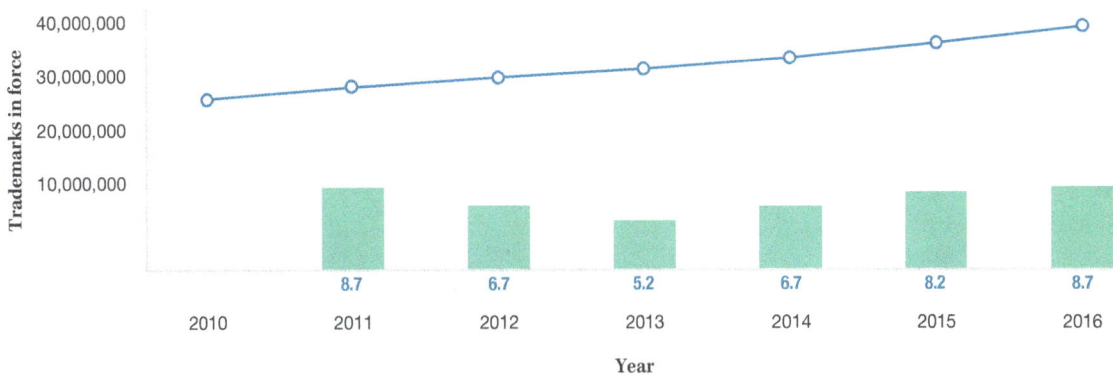

	2010	2011	2012	2013	2014	2015	2016
Growth rate (%)		8.7	6.7	5.2	6.7	8.2	8.7

▌ TRADEMARKS IN FORCE ▌ GROWTH RATE (%)

Note: World totals are WIPO estimates using data covering 136 IP offices. Data refer to the number of trademark registrations in force, not the number of classes specified in those registrations. Trademark rights can be maintained indefinitely by paying renewal fees at defined time intervals. Trademarks in force provide information on the volume of trademark registrations currently active as well as the historical trademark life cycle.

Source: WIPO Statistics Database, September 2017.

Figure B38
Trademark registrations in force at selected offices, 2016

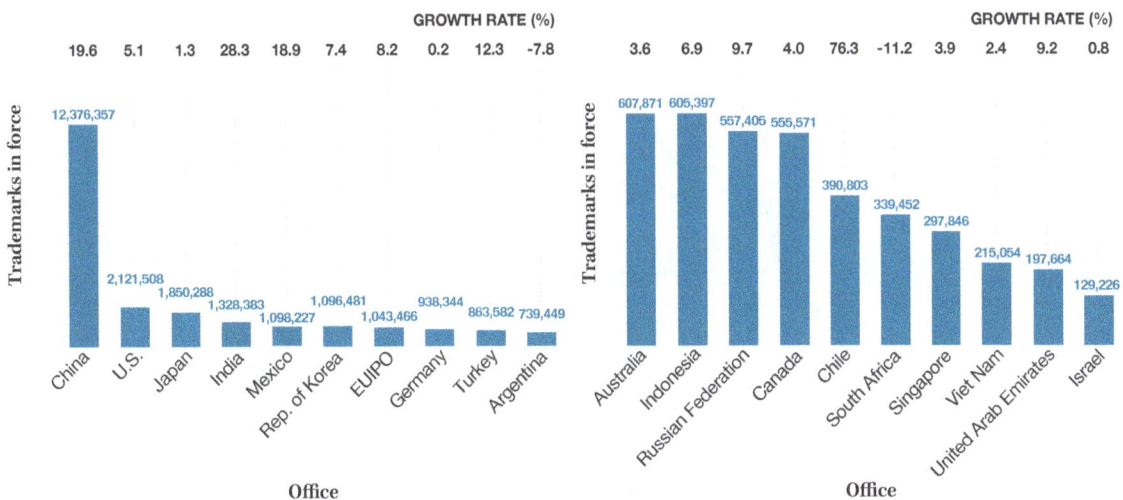

Note: EUIPO is the European Union Intellectual Property Office. Data refer to the number of trademark registrations in force, not the number of classes specified in those registrations.

Source: WIPO Statistics Database, September 2017.

Figure B39
Trademark registrations in force in 2016 as a percentage of total registrations

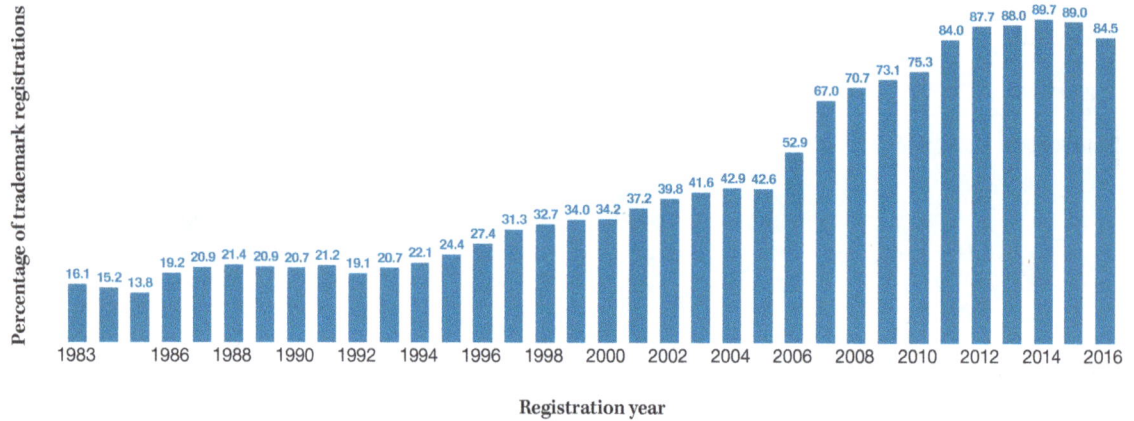

Percentage of trademark registrations

16.1 15.2 13.8 19.2 20.9 21.4 20.9 20.7 21.2 19.1 20.7 22.1 24.4 27.4 31.3 32.7 34.0 34.2 37.2 39.8 41.6 42.9 42.6 52.9 67.0 70.7 73.1 75.3 84.0 87.7 88.0 89.7 89.0 84.5

1983 1986 1988 1990 1992 1994 1996 1998 2000 2002 2004 2006 2008 2010 2012 2014 2016

Registration year

Note: Percentages are calculated as follows: the number of trademark registrations issued in year *t* and in force in 2016 divided by the total number of trademark registrations issued in year *t*. Trademark holders must pay renewal fees to maintain the validity of their marks, which in most cases can be maintained indefinitely. This figure is based on about 13.8 million active trademark registrations reported by 65 offices that provided a breakdown by year of registration. Detailed data for several larger offices, such as those of Brazil, China, France, Italy and Japan, are not available.

Source: WIPO Statistics Database, September 2017.

Figure B40
Average age of trademarks in force at selected offices

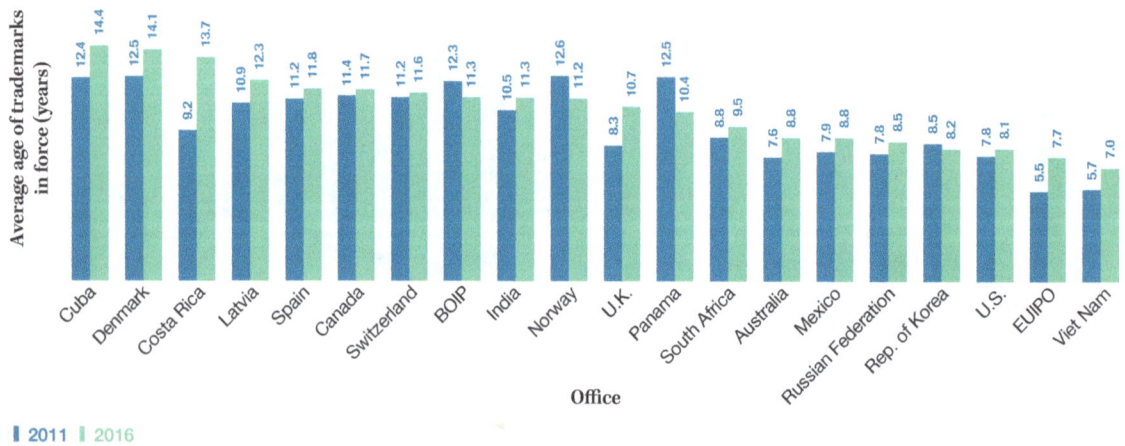

Average age of trademarks in force (years)

Office	2011	2016
Cuba	12.4	14.4
Denmark	12.5	14.1
Costa Rica	9.2	13.7
Latvia	10.9	12.3
Spain	11.2	11.8
Canada	11.4	11.7
Switzerland	11.2	11.6
BOIP	12.3	11.3
India	10.5	11.3
Norway	12.6	11.2
U.K.	8.3	10.7
Panama	12.5	10.4
South Africa	8.8	9.5
Australia	7.6	8.8
Mexico	7.9	8.8
Russian Federation	7.8	8.5
Rep. of Korea	8.5	8.2
U.S.	7.8	8.1
EUIPO	5.5	7.7
Viet Nam	5.7	7.0

Office

■ 2011 ■ 2016

Note: BOIP is the Benelux Office for Intellectual Property, and EUIPO is the European Union Intellectual Property Office.

Source: WIPO Statistics Database, September 2017.

Trademark application processing

Figure B41

Average number of days between the filing of an application and its recording as a registration for selected offices, 2016

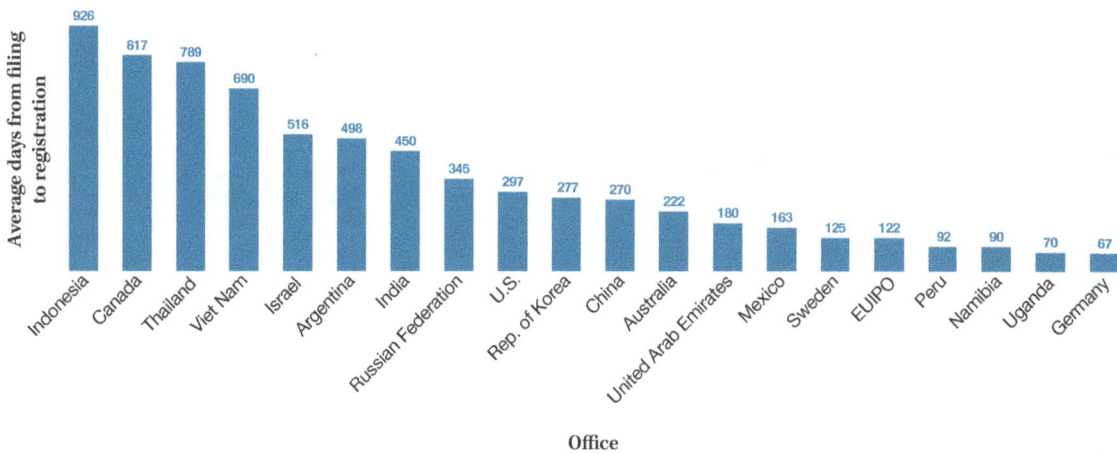

Note: EUIPO is the European Union Intellectual Property Office. WIPO collects data from IP offices using a common questionnaire and methodology. However, due to differences in application processing procedures between offices, data cannot be fully harmonized. Therefore, one should exercise caution when making comparisons across offices.

Source: WIPO Statistics Database, September 2017.

Trademark applications and registrations through the Madrid System

Figure B42

Trend in Madrid international applications

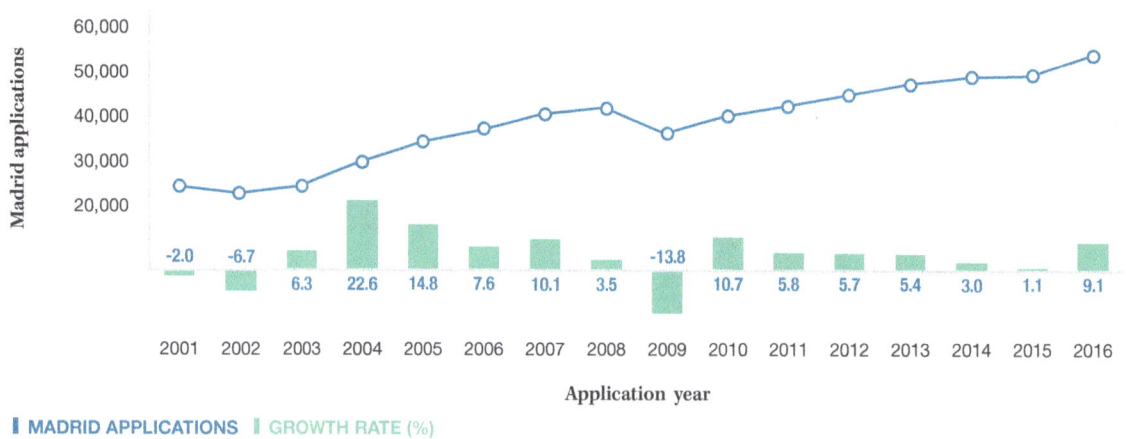

Madrid applications / Application year

MADRID APPLICATIONS   GROWTH RATE (%)

Source: WIPO Statistics Database, September 2017.

Figure B43

Madrid international applications by origin, 2016

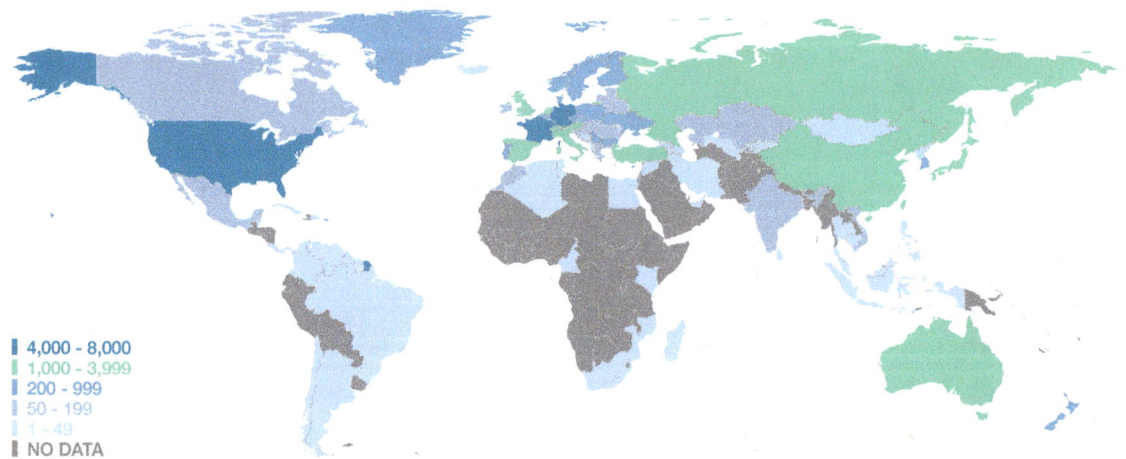

- 4,000 - 8,000
- 1,000 - 3,999
- 200 - 999
- 50 - 199
- 1 - 49
- NO DATA

Note: Counts are based on the country of the applicant's address, not the office of origin.

Source: WIPO Statistics Database, September 2017.

Figure B44
Madrid applications for the top 20 origins, 2016

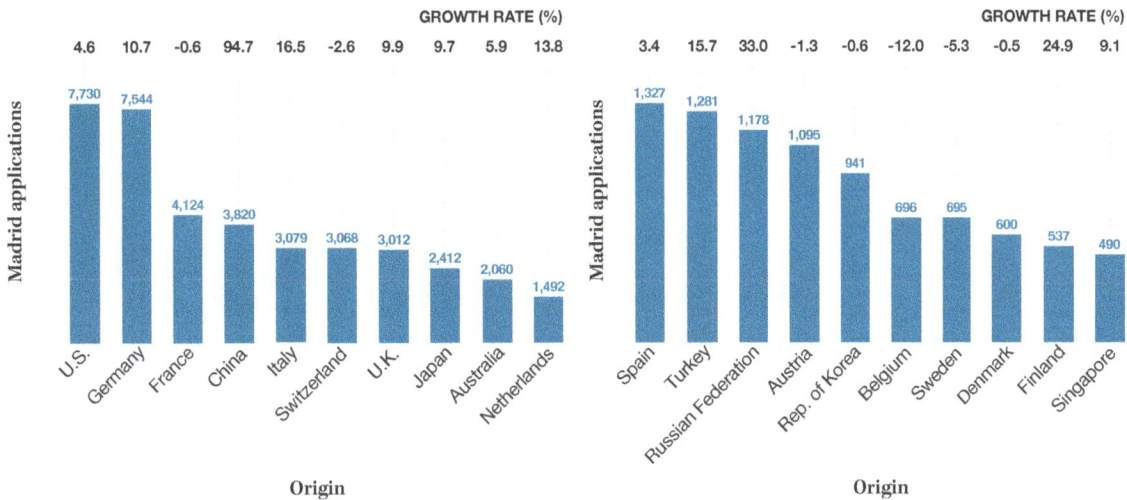

GROWTH RATE (%)

4.6	10.7	-0.6	94.7	16.5	-2.6	9.9	9.7	5.9	13.8

Madrid applications

- U.S. 7,730
- Germany 7,544
- France 4,124
- China 3,820
- Italy 3,079
- Switzerland 3,068
- U.K. 3,012
- Japan 2,412
- Australia 2,060
- Netherlands 1,492

Origin

GROWTH RATE (%)

3.4	15.7	33.0	-1.3	-0.6	-12.0	-5.3	-0.5	24.9	9.1

Madrid applications

- Spain 1,327
- Turkey 1,281
- Russian Federation 1,178
- Austria 1,095
- Rep. of Korea 941
- Belgium 696
- Sweden 695
- Denmark 600
- Finland 537
- Singapore 490

Origin

Note: Origin data are based on the country of the applicant's address.

Source: WIPO Statistics Database, September 2017.

Figure B45
Trend in non-resident filing activity by filing route (direct and Madrid)

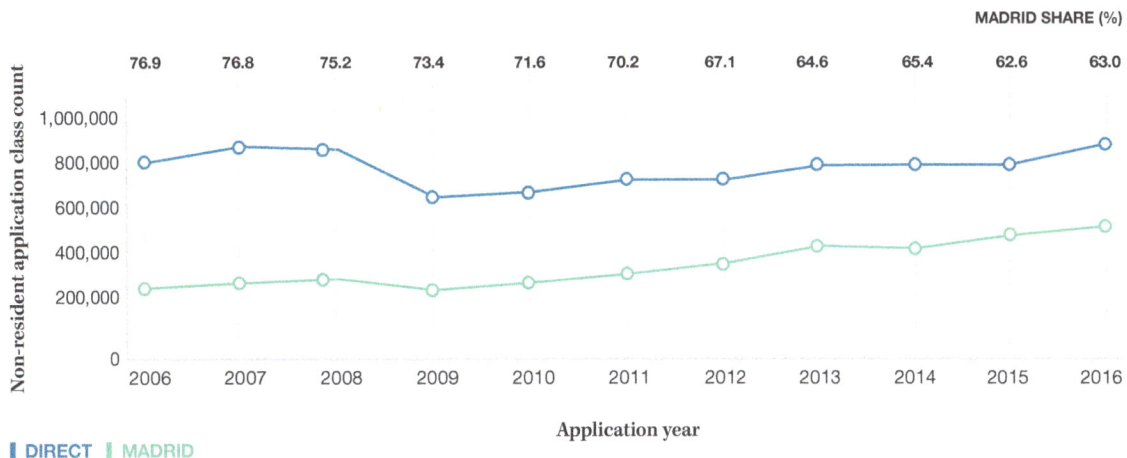

MADRID SHARE (%)

76.9	76.8	75.2	73.4	71.6	70.2	67.1	64.6	65.4	62.6	63.0

■ DIRECT ■ MADRID

Note: The direct route refers to classes specified in applications filed by non-residents of Madrid member origins directly with national or regional IP offices of Madrid members. This is also referred to as the "Paris route". The Madrid route refers to classes specified in designations received by offices via the Madrid System.

Source: WIPO Statistics Database, September 2017.

TRADEMARKS

Figure B46
Madrid share of non-resident filing activity for selected designated Madrid members, 2016

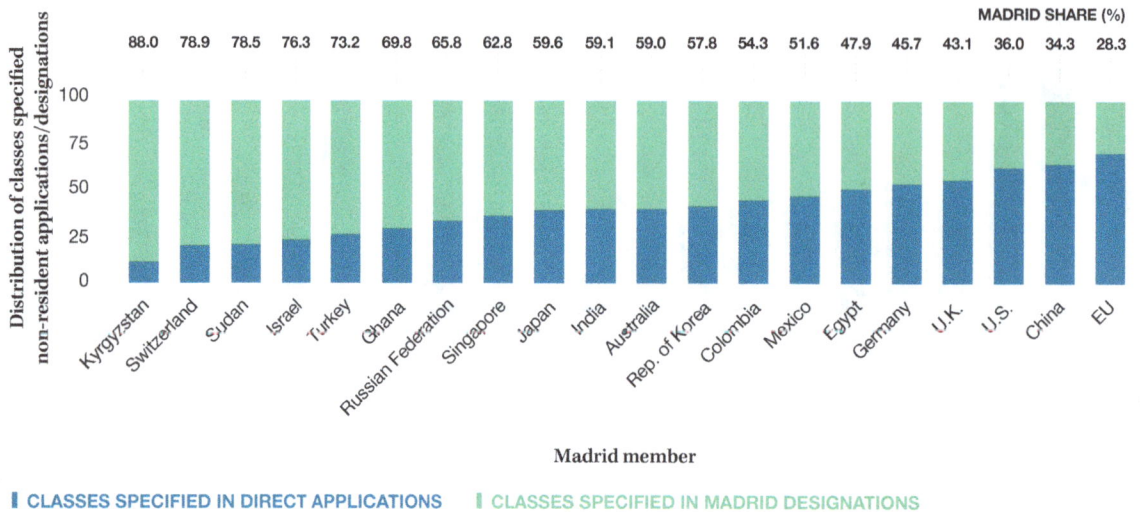

MADRID SHARE (%)

Kyrgyzstan	Switzerland	Sudan	Israel	Turkey	Ghana	Russian Federation	Singapore	Japan	India	Australia	Rep. of Korea	Colombia	Mexico	Egypt	Germany	U.K.	U.S.	China	EU
88.0	78.9	78.5	76.3	73.2	69.8	65.8	62.8	59.6	59.1	59.0	57.8	54.3	51.6	47.9	45.7	43.1	36.0	34.3	28.3

Distribution of classes specified non-resident applications/designations

Madrid member

▌CLASSES SPECIFIED IN DIRECT APPLICATIONS   ▌CLASSES SPECIFIED IN MADRID DESIGNATIONS

Note: EU indicates trademark activity occurring at the European Union Intellectual Property Office (EUIPO) and not within the IP offices of individual EU member states. The direct route refers to classes specified in applications filed only by non-residents of all origins – irrespective of Madrid membership – directly with the Madrid member office. The Madrid route refers to classes specified in designations received by the Madrid member office.

Source: WIPO Statistics Database, September 2017.

Statistical tables

Figure B47
Trademark applications by office and origin, 2016

Name	Application class count by office			Application class count by origin	Equivalent application class count by origin	Madrid international applications	
	Total	Resident	Non-resident	Total (a)	Total (a)	Origin (h)	Designated Madrid member
Afghanistan	..	..	..	179	341	..	n.a.
African Intellectual Property Organization	12,487	3,281	9,206	n.a.	n.a.	n.a.	2,015
African Regional Intellectual Property Organization	487	134	353	n.a.	n.a.	n.a.	n.a.
Albania	7,808	918	6,890	1,019	2,639	1	2,216
Algeria (b,c)	26,448	14,483	11,965	14,639	14,930	3	2,675
Andorra	2,387	618	1,769	941	5,266	4	n.a.
Angola	..	..	..	53	447	..	n.a.
Antigua and Barbuda (d)	1,718	4	1,714	38	146	1	676
Argentina	71,058	55,739	15,319	58,895	63,751	2	n.a.
Armenia	9,133	2,356	6,777	2,881	3,233	18	2,289
Aruba	..	..	..	1	1	..	n.a.
Australia	135,073	81,399	53,674	120,400	209,640	2,060	13,407
Austria	23,230	14,689	8,541	47,596	304,638	1,095	2,523
Azerbaijan	11,584	2,817	8,767	3,358	3,779	6	2,984
Bahamas	1,406	425	981	1,802	4,982	15	n.a.
Bahrain	11,215	371	10,844	727	1,238	1	2,193
Bangladesh	12,375	8,580	3,795	8,765	9,040	..	n.a.
Barbados	1,094	202	892	1,287	4,446	3	n.a.
Belarus	18,759	4,652	14,107	7,011	8,222	143	4,458
Belgium (e)	n.a.	n.a.	n.a.	38,870	251,563	696	n.a.
Belize	..	..	..	904	2,281	20	n.a.
Benelux Office for Intellectual Property (f)	66,514	56,190	10,324	n.a.	n.a.	n.a.	2,607
Benin (j)	n.a.	n.a.	n.a.	215	3,511	..	n.a.
Bermuda	..	..	..	867	4,074	5	n.a.
Bhutan (d)	1,746	..	1,746	25	25	..	673
Bolivia (Plurinational State of)	7,923	3,000	4,923	3,116	3,251	..	n.a.
Bonaire, Sint Eustatius and Saba (d)	1,612	..	1,612	3	84	..	609
Bosnia and Herzegovina	10,543	797	9,746	1,275	1,986	22	3,031
Botswana	3,271	537	2,734	578	578	..	828
Brazil	166,368	137,878	28,490	142,667	155,168	1	n.a.
Brunei Darussalam	..	..	..	274	706	..	n.a.
Bulgaria	18,166	14,243	3,923	23,958	76,151	248	1,305
Burkina Faso (j)	n.a.	n.a.	n.a.	141	2,381	..	n.a.
Cabo Verde	..	..	..	1	1	..	n.a.
Cambodia (d)	4,099	..	4,099	49	157	1	1,647
Cameroon (j)	n.a.	n.a.	n.a.	716	11,518	2	n.a.
Canada	153,722	81,540	72,182	107,636	184,022	65	n.a.

TRADEMARKS

Name	Application class count by office			Application class count by origin	Equivalent application class count by origin	Madrid international applications	
	Total	Resident	Non-resident	Total (a)	Total (a)	Origin (h)	Designated Madrid member
Central African Republic (j)	n.a.	n.a.	n.a.	45	109	..	n.a.
Chad (j)	n.a.	n.a.	n.a.	29	461	..	n.a.
Chile	45,368	31,820	13,548	35,567	39,205	2	n.a.
China	3,697,916	3,526,953	170,963	3,722,426	4,199,467	3,820	22,491
China, Hong Kong SAR	71,715	27,064	44,651	44,340	119,680	..	n.a.
China, Macao SAR	11,507	1,684	9,823	2,129	2,955	..	n.a.
Colombia	42,737	24,299	18,438	27,579	30,002	39	4,156
Comoros	..	..	..	4	4	..	n.a.
Congo (j)	n.a.	n.a.	n.a.	49	625	..	n.a.
Cook Islands	..	..	..	47	506	..	n.a.
Costa Rica	14,173	6,797	7,376	7,683	8,196	1	n.a.
Côte d'Ivoire (j)	n.a.	n.a.	n.a.	899	15,055	..	n.a.
Croatia	8,333	4,334	3,999	6,988	18,251	139	1,399
Cuba	9,858	2,242	7,616	2,432	3,026	2	1,787
Curaçao	2,809	0	2,809	414	3,114	11	694
Cyprus	2,982	1,090	1,892	10,451	60,239	162	680
Czech Republic	24,414	19,301	5,113	32,372	128,566	322	1,532
Democratic People's Republic of Korea (d)	2,517	..	2,517	159	439	5	985
Democratic Republic of the Congo	..	..	..	18	290	..	n.a.
Denmark	11,147	7,596	3,551	27,818	177,103	600	1,221
Djibouti	..	..	..	5	86	..	n.a.
Dominica	..	..	..	106	278	1	n.a.
Dominican Republic	13,012	7,446	5,566	7,906	8,770	3	n.a.
Ecuador	15,890	9,254	6,636	9,813	10,438	..	n.a.
Egypt	35,122	12,750	22,372	13,990	16,164	19	4,358
El Salvador	10,620	3,621	6,999	4,172	4,285	..	n.a.
Equatorial Guinea (j)	n.a.	n.a.	n.a.	8	153	..	n.a.
Eritrea	..	..	..	3	3	..	n.a.
Estonia	4,411	1,999	2,412	4,027	29,591	50	989
Ethiopia	..	..	..	11	38	..	n.a.
European Union Intellectual Property Office (g)	369,970	273,213	96,757	n.a.	n.a.	n.a.	22,012
Fiji	..	..	..	64	145	5	n.a.
Finland	10,405	7,516	2,889	25,725	166,956	537	997
France	274,201	258,090	16,111	379,619	1,088,225	4,124	3,289
Gabon (j)	n.a.	n.a.	n.a.	60	476	..	n.a.
Gambia (b,c)	544	45	499	78	526	..	488
Georgia	9,425	2,217	7,208	2,828	4,536	30	2,478
Germany	209,983	190,216	19,767	466,730	2,300,068	7,544	4,055
Ghana	5,519	900	4,619	939	1,255	..	1,305

Name	Application class count by office			Application class count by origin	Equivalent application class count by origin	Madrid international applications	
	Total	Resident	Non-resident	Total (a)	Total (a)	Origin (h)	Designated Madrid member
Greece (d)	2,362	1	2,361	4,588	70,199	113	1,113
Grenada	635	18	617	30	30	..	n.a.
Guatemala	..	..	..	2,180	2,369	..	n.a.
Guinea (j)	n.a.	n.a.	n.a.	243	4,019	..	n.a.
Guinea-Bissau (j)	n.a.	n.a.	n.a.	36	612	..	n.a.
Guyana (i)	905	..	..	14	14	1	n.a.
Haiti	..	..	..	15	19	..	n.a.
Honduras	7,548	2,185	5,363	2,412	2,466	..	n.a.
Hungary	13,237	9,318	3,919	14,337	55,425	138	1,429
Iceland	9,074	1,521	7,553	2,289	5,318	38	2,280
India	313,623	264,662	48,961	276,155	294,598	175	11,608
Indonesia	63,721	48,756	14,965	50,413	51,911	1	n.a.
Iran (Islamic Republic of)	190,762	177,538	13,224	179,778	183,764	39	3,974
Iraq	..	..	..	463	598	..	n.a.
Ireland (i)	6,999	..	..	10,684	91,233	181	879
Israel	18,815	3,463	15,352	9,902	36,548	281	4,682
Italy	94,037	83,358	10,679	182,269	1,037,759	3,079	3,136
Jamaica	5,349	2,742	2,607	2,820	2,928	..	n.a.
Japan	451,320	390,525	60,795	477,616	622,072	2,412	14,965
Jordan	7,346	3,013	4,333	3,708	5,499	..	n.a.
Kazakhstan	22,924	8,495	14,429	9,848	10,199	90	4,640
Kenya (b,c)	10,870	4,684	6,186	4,936	5,670	11	1,901
Kiribati	..	..	..	3	3	..	n.a.
Kuwait (b,i)	13,051	..	..	478	1,855	..	n.a.
Kyrgyzstan	6,357	269	6,088	342	342	5	2,189
Lao People's Democratic Republic (d)	1,686	..	1,686	17	44	..	709
Latvia	5,296	2,214	3,082	3,944	14,166	98	1,148
Lebanon (b,c)	1,537	1,253	284	2,194	6,928	1	n.a.
Lesotho (d)	1,715	..	1,715	6	6	..	655
Liberia (d)	2,039	..	2,039	2	2	..	793
Libya	..	..	..	39	93	..	n.a.
Liechtenstein	8,756	490	8,266	4,199	12,062	90	2,336
Lithuania	6,773	3,851	2,922	6,150	25,533	114	1,138
Luxembourg (e)	n.a.	n.a.	n.a.	30,437	157,815	466	n.a.
Madagascar	6,050	2,757	3,293	2,784	2,784	3	937
Malawi	1,167	499	668	506	506	..	n.a.
Malaysia	39,107	18,527	20,580	24,791	29,283	4	n.a.
Maldives	..	..	..	21	21	..	n.a.
Mali (j)	n.a.	n.a.	n.a.	245	3,829	..	n.a.
Malta	602	435	167	5,549	41,896	53	n.a.

TRADEMARKS

Name	Application class count by office			Application class count by origin	Equivalent application class count by origin	Madrid international applications	
	Total	Resident	Non-resident	Total (a)	Total (a)	Origin (h)	Designated Madrid member
Marshall Islands	..	..	..	259	858	2	n.a.
Mauritania (j)	n.a.	n.a.	n.a.	75	844	..	n.a.
Mauritius	2,328	1,110	1,218	2,560	4,719	9	n.a.
Mexico	141,726	98,739	42,987	111,067	126,225	74	9,360
Monaco	9,249	1,624	7,625	4,313	22,103	74	2,288
Mongolia	12,040	7,629	4,411	7,746	7,935	2	1,521
Montenegro (d)	7,236	..	7,236	1,091	3,768	21	2,495
Morocco	29,046	15,173	13,873	16,680	24,659	111	3,930
Mozambique	5,337	1,291	4,046	1,324	1,648	..	1,133
Myanmar	..	..	..	63	63	..	n.a.
Namibia (c,i)	4,849	..	..	1,792	1,840	..	1,029
Nauru	..	..	..	8	24	..	n.a.
Nepal	5,078	3,215	1,863	3,298	3,357	..	n.a.
Netherlands (e)	n.a.	n.a.	n.a.	86,851	533,201	1,492	n.a.
New Zealand	45,830	16,577	29,253	25,467	43,503	409	6,994
Nicaragua	..	..	..	336	336	..	n.a.
Niger (j)	n.a.	n.a.	n.a.	69	965	..	n.a.
Nigeria	..	..	..	196	932	..	n.a.
Norway	43,127	11,788	31,339	18,128	56,673	300	8,535
Oman (d)	5,551	..	5,551	191	779	..	2,165
Pakistan	36,126	27,017	9,109	27,864	29,257	..	n.a.
Palau	..	..	..	10	10	..	n.a.
Panama	12,607	5,082	7,525	8,293	14,422	8	n.a.
Papua New Guinea	861	108	753	120	147	..	n.a.
Paraguay	..	..	..	319	346	..	n.a.
Peru	30,708	19,356	11,352	20,963	22,296	..	n.a.
Philippines	47,953	22,357	25,596	23,565	24,333	28	5,168
Poland	46,387	39,420	6,967	58,964	332,798	447	2,178
Portugal	30,474	24,750	5,724	31,634	120,556	220	1,436
Qatar	..	..	..	1,179	3,328	..	n.a.
Republic of Korea	231,978	183,620	48,358	240,683	324,516	941	11,526
Republic of Moldova	11,067	3,049	8,018	3,789	4,216	47	2,502
Romania	24,984	20,575	4,409	24,092	78,125	97	1,560
Russian Federation	251,549	193,213	58,336	222,993	249,933	1,178	15,194
Rwanda	2,377	194	2,183	201	201	..	717
Saint Kitts and Nevis	..	..	..	64	280	..	n.a.
Saint Lucia	..	..	..	128	128	..	n.a.
Saint Vincent and the Grenadines	..	..	..	16	97	1	n.a.
Samoa	218	31	187	328	787	..	n.a.
San Marino (d)	3,240	..	3,240	415	2,602	9	1,122

Name	Application class count by office			Application class count by origin	Equivalent application class count by origin	Madrid international applications	
	Total	Resident	Non-resident	Total (a)	Total (a)	Origin (h)	Designated Madrid member
Sao Tome and Principe	1,439	23	1,416	24	24	..	533
Saudi Arabia (b,c)	18,254	7,423	10,831	10,099	17,015	..	n.a.
Senegal (j)	n.a.	n.a.	n.a.	576	9,264	..	n.a.
Serbia	16,410	3,431	12,979	7,583	12,082	240	3,912
Seychelles	..	..	..	1,825	3,766	12	n.a.
Sierra Leone (d)	1,874	..	1,874	78	78	..	752
Singapore	45,332	9,721	35,611	33,057	56,517	490	9,035
Sint Maarten (Dutch Part) (d)	1,724	..	1,724	..	..	..	672
Slovakia	14,169	9,436	4,733	13,079	45,407	121	1,202
Slovenia (d)	2,714	..	2,714	4,913	32,912	169	1,120
Solomon Islands	..	..	..	33	33	..	n.a.
Somalia	..	..	..	5	32	..	n.a.
South Africa	37,976	22,734	15,242	24,982	36,095	4	n.a.
Spain	79,795	71,312	8,483	121,242	753,076	1,327	2,631
Sri Lanka	10,828	6,893	3,935	7,399	9,358	1	n.a.
Sudan	4,772	1,332	3,440	1,341	1,341	..	1,169
Suriname	1,358	545	813	602	705	1	n.a.
Swaziland (b,i)	2,462	..	..	169	250	..	746
Sweden	20,730	16,570	4,160	45,559	307,884	695	1,364
Switzerland	89,670	36,762	52,908	156,180	487,130	3,068	14,299
Syrian Arab Republic (i)	10,473	..	..	578	2,820	7	1,215
T F Y R of Macedonia (d)	7,842	..	7,842	837	2,349	62	2,683
Tajikistan	5,205	160	5,045	163	163	..	1,863
Thailand	56,131	35,720	20,411	40,832	46,931	6	n.a.
Timor-Leste	..	..	..	1	1	..	n.a.
Togo (j)	n.a.	n.a.	n.a.	240	3,568	..	n.a.
Tonga	..	..	..	4	4	..	n.a.
Trinidad and Tobago	2,907	929	1,978	1,047	1,128	..	n.a.
Tunisia (i)	11,667	..	..	617	3,488	27	2,435
Turkey	227,159	193,824	33,335	220,517	277,870	1,281	8,959
Turkmenistan (d)	4,625	..	4,625	20	20	..	1,890
Uganda	3,044	1,291	1,753	1,313	1,340	..	n.a.
Ukraine	69,611	45,880	23,731	51,755	58,406	409	6,472
United Arab Emirates	18,777	5,199	13,578	12,459	33,689	19	n.a.
United Kingdom	142,147	114,722	27,425	246,810	1,223,673	3,012	5,358
United Republic of Tanzania	..	..	..	48	48	..	n.a.
United States of America	545,587	388,504	157,083	716,175	1,611,311	7,730	21,647
Uruguay (b,c)	9,463	3,655	5,808	4,511	5,834	..	n.a.
Uzbekistan	12,215	6,457	5,758	6,578	6,610	4	1,950
Vanuatu	..	..	..	54	297	..	n.a.

TRADEMARKS

Name	Application class count by office			Application class count by origin	Equivalent application class count by origin	Madrid international applications	
	Total	Resident	Non-resident	Total (a)	Total (a)	Origin (h)	Designated Madrid member
Venezuela (Bolivarian Republic of)	..	..	..	610	1,015	2	n.a.
Viet Nam	82,041	54,965	27,076	57,260	58,584	100	6,073
Yemen	4,403	2,561	1,842	2,720	2,720	..	n.a.
Zambia (d)	2,417	..	2,417	33	33	..	997
Zimbabwe	3,232	155	3,077	163	244	..	812
Others/Unknown	5	0	5	68,053	166,634	15	4
Total (k)	9,768,200	7,798,600	1,969,600	9,768,200	n.a.	53,493	362,210

a. Data on application class count by origin are incomplete, because some offices do not report detailed statistics containing the origin of application class counts.

b. 2015 data are reported for application class count by office.

c. 2015 data are reported for application class count by origin.

d. Only Madrid designation data are available, so application class count by office and origin data may be incomplete.

e. This country does not have a national trademark office. All applications for trademark protection are filed at the Benelux Office for Intellectual Property or the European Union Intellectual Property Office.

f. Resident applications include those filed by residents of Belgium, Luxembourg and the Netherlands.

g. Resident applications include those filed by residents of EU member states.

h. Origin is defined as the country/territory of the stated residence of the applicant in an international application.

i. Total includes an aggregate direct application class count that cannot be broken down into direct and non-resident components.

j. The African Intellectual Property Office (OAPI) is the competent office for processing applications.

k. Totals are estimated for application class counts by office and origin.

n.a. indicates not applicable.

.. indicates not available.

Source: WIPO Statistics Database, September 2017.

Figure B48
Trademark registrations by office and origin, and trademarks in force, 2016

Name	Registration class count by office			Registration class count by origin	Equivalent registration class count by origin	Madrid international registrations	In force by office
	Total	Resident	Non-resident	Total (a)	Total (a)	Origin (i)	Total
Afghanistan	..	..	..	101	236	..	..
African Intellectual Property Organization (d)	5,177	..	5,177	n.a.	n.a.	n.a.	..
African Regional Intellectual Property Organization (e)	422	139	283	n.a.	n.a.	n.a.	1,377
Albania	8,118	794	7,324	873	1,467	4	..
Algeria (b,c,e)	11,226	3,335	7,891	3,460	3,759	5	37,044
Andorra	2,394	623	1,771	896	4,168	7	21,932
Angola	..	..	..	43	637	1	..
Antigua and Barbuda (d)	1,766	4	1,762	39	174	1	8,314
Argentina	59,065	43,674	15,391	46,045	50,589	2	739,449
Armenia	9,120	2,436	6,684	2,989	3,640	21	18,870
Aruba	..	..	..	3	3	..	..

Name	Registration class count by office			Registration class count by origin	Equivalent registration class count by origin	Madrid international registrations	In force by office
	Total	Resident	Non-resident	Total (a)	Total (a)	Origin (i)	Total
Australia	97,660	50,695	46,965	82,485	156,185	1,667	607,871
Austria	19,498	12,397	7,101	43,204	261,176	973	103,090
Azerbaijan	10,812	2,225	8,587	4,720	7,411	2	..
Bahamas	768	32	736	1,341	4,635	14	..
Bahrain (b,c)	9,085	119	8,966	253	496	1	..
Bangladesh	3,378	704	2,674	791	953	..	49,179
Barbados	402	18	384	720	2,504	1	..
Belarus	16,514	3,117	13,397	5,559	7,405	111	125,335
Belgium (f)	n.a.	n.a.	n.a.	34,908	229,107	606	n.a.
Belize	..	..	..	789	1,798	22	3,536
Benelux Office for Intellectual Property (g)	58,661	49,551	9,110	n.a.	n.a.	n.a.	612,245
Benin (k)	n.a.	n.a.	n.a.	9	90	..	..
Bermuda	..	..	..	1,029	5,489	6	..
Bhutan (d)	1,531	..	1,531	2	2	..	..
Bolivia (Plurinational State of)	6,975	2,277	4,698	2,346	2,400	..	45,934
Bonaire, Sint Eustatius and Saba (d)	1,457	..	1,457	..	..	..	..
Bosnia and Herzegovina	9,941	604	9,337	1,068	1,605	21	15,752
Botswana	2,581	108	2,473	115	115	..	..
Brazil	99,938	71,303	28,635	75,434	88,337	2	..
Brunei Darussalam	..	..	..	184	535	..	..
Bulgaria	13,665	9,959	3,706	14,605	54,550	156	51,091
Cabo Verde	..	..	..	1	1	..	..
Cambodia (d)	3,812	..	3,812	79	268	..	..
Cameroon (k)	n.a.	n.a.	n.a.	5	59	..	..
Canada	95,798	51,430	44,368	70,277	137,276	44	555,571
Central African Republic (k)	n.a.	n.a.	n.a.	11	11	..	..
Chad (k)	n.a.	n.a.	n.a.	3	3	..	..
Chile	34,107	20,707	13,400	23,985	27,468	1	390,803
China	2,270,810	2,119,151	151,659	2,242,284	2,620,631	2,961	12,376,357
China, Hong Kong SAR	70,484	25,495	44,989	38,554	100,734	..	382,688
China, Macao SAR	11,021	1,348	9,673	1,727	2,429	..	97,210
Colombia	30,061	13,874	16,187	16,609	19,129	24	293,314
Comoros	..	..	..	5	5	..	..
Congo (k)	n.a.	n.a.	n.a.	4	4	..	..
Cook Islands	..	..	..	21	75	..	..
Costa Rica	11,644	4,427	7,217	5,012	5,525	1	188,263
Côte d'Ivoire (k)	n.a.	n.a.	n.a.	27	405	..	..
Croatia	7,007	3,320	3,687	6,018	16,583	127	121,843
Cuba	6,243	1,015	5,228	1,243	1,540	1	38,827
Curaçao	2,877	0	2,877	318	2,667	5	23,098
Cyprus	2,957	1,107	1,850	9,737	45,862	123	58,520
Czech Republic	28,767	23,886	4,881	36,622	115,561	276	123,039

TRADEMARKS

Name	Registration class count by office			Registration class count by origin	Equivalent registration class count by origin	Madrid international registrations	In force by office
	Total	Resident	Non-resident	Total (a)	Total (a)	Origin (i)	Total
Democratic People's Republic of Korea (d)	2,067	..	2,067	213	375	8	..
Democratic Republic of the Congo	..	..	..	27	189	1	..
Denmark	9,696	6,410	3,286	25,202	142,481	473	139,420
Djibouti	..	..	..	2	2	..	..
Dominica	..	..	..	92	210	1	..
Dominican Republic	11,233	5,646	5,587	5,951	6,653	4	121,161
Ecuador	5,354	3,992	1,362	4,420	4,957	..	..
Egypt (e)	16,938	3,139	13,799	3,836	5,341	17	115,646
El Salvador	8,116	2,165	5,951	2,548	2,683	..	83,909
Estonia	3,630	1,246	2,384	2,923	24,003	48	56,900
Ethiopia	..	..	..	6	6	..	..
European Union Intellectual Property Office (h)	330,379	244,634	85,745	n.a.	n.a.	n.a.	1,043,466
Fiji	..	..	..	80	80	2	..
Finland	8,892	5,835	3,057	22,164	135,897	430	102,293
France (d)	6,100	8	6,092	125,559	790,590	3,718	840,000
Gabon (k)	n.a.	n.a.	n.a.	18	18	..	..
Gambia (b,c,e)	582	45	537	46	46	..	402
Georgia	8,213	1,082	7,131	1,667	2,916	27	..
Germany	163,130	147,191	15,939	400,016	2,013,265	6,462	938,344
Ghana	4,429	150	4,279	167	167	..	45,606
Greece (d)	2,270	1	2,269	3,659	52,302	96	..
Grenada (b,c)	569	9	560	12	12	..	293
Guatemala (b,c)	9,415	3,981	5,434	5,076	5,184	..	..
Guinea (k)	n.a.	n.a.	n.a.	12	12	..	..
Guyana (j)	585	..	..	20	20	1	669
Haiti	..	..	..	30	34	..	..
Holy See	..	..	..	25	700	..	..
Honduras (e)	5,944	1,305	4,639	1,493	1,574	..	81,523
Hungary	9,657	5,942	3,715	10,272	42,042	121	55,242
Iceland	8,642	1,287	7,355	1,958	3,875	24	59,147
India	201,988	158,415	43,573	168,075	182,797	107	1,328,383
Indonesia	19,622	13,854	5,768	15,316	16,528	1	605,397
Iran (Islamic Republic of)	89,444	74,482	14,962	77,054	80,975	44	..
Iraq	..	..	..	287	422	..	..
Ireland (j)	5,454	..	..	9,926	84,905	175	81,890
Israel	17,864	2,584	15,280	7,854	28,702	211	129,226
Italy	41,992	34,414	7,578	129,943	896,763	2,664	406,297
Jamaica (e)	4,195	2,114	2,081	2,204	2,204	..	16,797
Japan (j)	198,015	..	..	82,280	206,781	1,975	1,850,288
Jordan (e)	7,248	2,123	5,125	2,848	4,717	..	15,293
Kazakhstan	21,737	6,704	15,033	7,986	8,046	66	..
Kenya (b,c,e)	10,722	3,268	7,454	3,477	3,828	3	43,865

Name	Registration class count by office			Registration class count by origin	Equivalent registration class count by origin	Madrid international registrations	In force by office
	Total	Resident	Non-resident	Total (a)	Total (a)	Origin (i)	Total
Kiribati	..	..	..	1	1	..	..
Kuwait (b,j)	7,670	..	..	429	2,940	..	..
Kyrgyzstan	6,106	271	5,835	296	296	2	10,090
Lao People's Democratic Republic (d)	1,211	..	1,211	11	11	..	..
Latvia	4,966	2,209	2,757	3,833	11,074	85	25,166
Lebanon (b,c)	9,527	4,098	5,429	4,678	6,783	1	..
Lesotho (d)	1,636	..	1,636	..	..	..	..
Liberia (d)	1,896	..	1,896	22	22	..	..
Libya	..	..	..	16	70	..	..
Liechtenstein (d)	6,598	5	6,593	3,151	9,748	56	..
Lithuania	6,597	3,673	2,924	5,337	21,290	83	36,166
Luxembourg (f)	n.a.	n.a.	n.a.	22,698	133,205	419	n.a.
Madagascar	6,304	2,783	3,521	2,795	2,795	2	..
Malawi	1,247	344	903	345	345	..	..
Malaysia	32,806	12,686	20,120	16,834	20,684	4	294,772
Maldives	..	..	..	2	2	..	..
Mali (k)	n.a.	n.a.	n.a.	18	18	..	..
Malta	578	365	213	4,472	34,531	36	22,165
Marshall Islands	..	..	..	278	899	..	..
Mauritania (k)	n.a.	n.a.	n.a.	22	76	..	..
Mauritius	2,061	914	1,147	1,826	3,489	5	..
Mexico	120,357	79,053	41,304	87,651	100,811	49	1,098,227
Monaco	8,288	1,554	6,734	3,389	14,780	53	10,428
Mongolia	9,247	4,878	4,369	4,982	5,063	1	12,114
Montenegro (d)	7,319	..	7,319	421	1,289	8	48,659
Morocco	23,758	10,849	12,909	11,997	17,283	89	107,158
Mozambique	5,198	1,042	4,156	1,055	1,217	..	20,302
Myanmar	..	..	..	97	97	..	..
Namibia (b,c)	2,951	3	2,948	180	207	..	1,825
Nepal (e)	2,786	1,169	1,617	1,196	1,196	..	39,017
Netherlands (f)	n.a.	n.a.	n.a.	81,699	473,266	1,247	n.a.
New Zealand	39,415	12,840	26,575	19,819	35,085	342	252,768
Nicaragua	..	..	..	217	244	..	..
Niger (k)	n.a.	n.a.	n.a.	11	11	..	..
Nigeria	..	..	..	75	480	..	..
Norway	35,351	7,643	27,708	13,545	45,602	223	214,702
Oman (d)	5,916	..	5,916	114	384	..	..
Pakistan	12,578	5,579	6,999	6,178	7,723	..	125,315
Palau	..	..	..	1	1	..	..
Panama	7,272	2,615	4,657	5,679	12,439	8	144,876
Papua New Guinea	1,136	107	1,029	139	139	..	10,564
Paraguay	..	..	..	223	223	..	..
Peru	26,189	15,542	10,647	16,562	17,750	..	..

TRADEMARKS

Name	Registration class count by office			Registration class count by origin	Equivalent registration class count by origin	Madrid international registrations	In force by office
	Total	Resident	Non-resident	Total (a)	Total (a)	Origin (i)	Total
Philippines	44,643	19,830	24,813	20,592	20,925	16	..
Poland	26,816	20,876	5,940	37,599	277,257	336	227,304
Portugal	24,511	20,246	4,265	26,643	99,473	194	201,545
Qatar	..	..	..	1,219	2,947	..	..
Republic of Korea	161,106	117,181	43,925	159,542	256,259	843	1,096,481
Republic of Moldova (e)	8,972	1,617	7,355	2,486	2,906	52	19,526
Romania	19,644	15,539	4,105	18,557	60,318	79	81,669
Russian Federation	149,187	91,676	57,511	119,631	140,549	825	557,405
Rwanda (e)	2,288	140	2,148	147	147	..	2,335
Saint Kitts and Nevis	..	..	..	127	594	1	..
Saint Lucia	..	..	..	95	122	..	..
Saint Vincent and the Grenadines	..	..	..	18	153	1	..
Samoa	470	18	452	526	1,120	..	4,120
San Marino (d)	2,756	..	2,756	312	2,769	9	2,155
Sao Tome and Principe (d)	1,238	..	1,238	..	..	..	..
Saudi Arabia (b,c)	18,631	7,482	11,149	9,377	13,238	..	..
Senegal (k)	n.a.	n.a.	n.a.	8	8	..	..
Serbia	15,210	2,890	12,320	6,348	10,158	223	28,238
Seychelles	..	..	..	819	1,845	7	..
Sierra Leone (d)	1,965	..	1,965	10	10	..	..
Singapore	49,609	10,449	39,160	27,605	49,456	414	297,846
Sint Maarten (Dutch Part) (d)	1,729	..	1,729	..	..	..	..
Slovakia	12,687	8,220	4,467	11,923	38,292	110	48,696
Slovenia (d)	2,380	..	2,380	4,761	28,195	160	..
Solomon Islands	..	..	..	10	10	..	..
South Africa	11,281	6,139	5,142	7,978	18,364	1	339,452
Spain	66,049	59,002	7,047	109,242	717,669	1,179	784,606
Sri Lanka	22,492	7,359	15,133	7,696	9,181	1	22,492
Sudan	3,643	387	3,256	407	407	..	2,209
Suriname	1,019	446	573	513	618	..	10,280
Swaziland (b,e,j)	2,296	..	..	358	358	..	1,358
Sweden	17,310	13,627	3,683	40,733	265,103	604	130,092
Switzerland	82,235	34,403	47,832	133,485	417,722	2,561	233,270
Syrian Arab Republic (j)	5,866	..	..	288	1,719	3	..
T F Y R of Macedonia (d)	7,645	..	7,645	618	1,930	30	..
Tajikistan (d)	4,455	..	4,455	20	20	..	..
Thailand	35,809	19,319	16,490	23,292	28,017	2	375,852
Togo (k)	n.a.	n.a.	n.a.	15	15	..	..
Tonga	..	..	..	3	3	..	..
Trinidad and Tobago	2,582	597	1,985	698	733	..	21,450
Tunisia (j)	12,598	..	..	337	1,305	19	..
Turkey	218,137	183,371	34,766	206,677	257,054	934	863,582

Name	Registration class count by office			Registration class count by origin	Equivalent registration class count by origin	Madrid international registrations	In force by office
	Total	Resident	Non-resident	Total (a)	Total (a)	Origin (i)	Total
Turkmenistan (d)	4,374	..	4,374	78	78	..	..
Uganda	2,094	763	1,331	771	798	..	10,356
Ukraine	40,199	19,829	20,370	25,540	31,600	315	172,015
United Arab Emirates	16,727	3,674	13,053	8,900	28,044	21	197,664
United Kingdom	117,852	97,228	20,624	213,060	1,155,447	2,443	612,691
United Republic of Tanzania	..	..	..	43	91	1	..
United States of America	326,481	221,500	104,981	509,700	1,310,250	6,671	2,121,508
Uruguay (b,c,e)	6,390	2,421	3,969	3,291	4,506	1	92,931
Uzbekistan	8,344	2,733	5,611	2,800	2,800	2	19,930
Vanuatu	..	..	..	24	78	..	..
Venezuela (Bolivarian Republic of)	..	..	..	543	1,056	2	..
Viet Nam	41,348	20,466	20,882	22,070	23,185	73	215,054
Yemen	2,014	1,198	816	1,248	1,248	..	..
Zambia (d)	2,327	..	2,327	3	3	..	..
Zimbabwe	3,311	155	3,156	163	244	..	60,889
Others/Unknown	..	..	..	53,836	153,953	15	..
Total [l]	6,549,100	4,813,300	1,735,800	6,549,100	n.a.	44,726	39,093,100

a. Data on registration class count by origin are incomplete, because some offices do not report detailed statistics containing the origin of registration class counts.

b. 2015 data are reported for registration class count by office.

c. 2015 data are reported for registration class count by origin.

d. Only Madrid designation data are available, so registration class count by office and origin data may be incomplete.

e. 2015 data are reported for trademarks in force.

f. This country does not have a national trademark office. All trademark registrations for this country are issued by the Benelux Office for Intellectual Property or the European Union Intellectual Property Office.

g. Resident registrations include those issued to residents of Belgium, Luxembourg and the Netherlands.

h. Resident registrations include those issued to residents of EU member states.

i. Origin is defined as the country/territory of the stated residence of the holder of an international registration.

j. Total includes an aggregate direct registration class count that cannot be broken down into direct and non-resident components.

k. The African Intellectual Property Office (OAPI) is the competent office for issuing registrations.

l. Totals are estimated for registration class counts by office and origin and for total registrations in force.

n.a. indicates not applicable.

.. indicates not available.

Source: WIPO Statistics Database, September 2017.

Industrial designs

Highlights

Applications are approaching the 1 million mark

An estimated 963,100 applications were filed worldwide in 2016, representing annual growth of 10.4%. This was the second consecutive year of growth in filings worldwide, following a 10.2% drop in 2014 (figure 15). Increased filings in China accounted for 90% of the total growth in 2016.

The design count worldwide doubled between 2005 and 2016. As was the case with industrial design applications, the number of designs contained in applications (design count) increased sharply, rising 8.3% to reach a total of 1.24 million (figure 16).

Figure 15
Industrial design applications worldwide

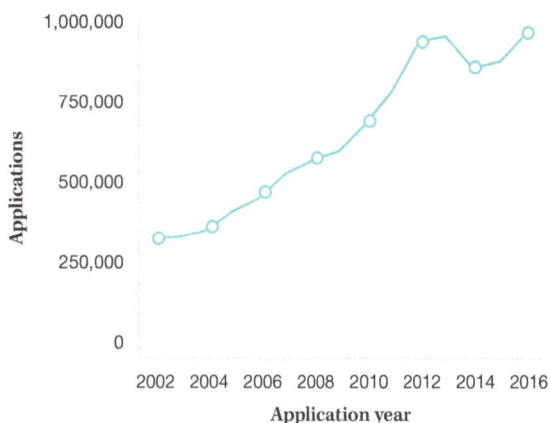

Source: Standard figure C1.

Figure 16
Number of designs in industrial design applications worldwide

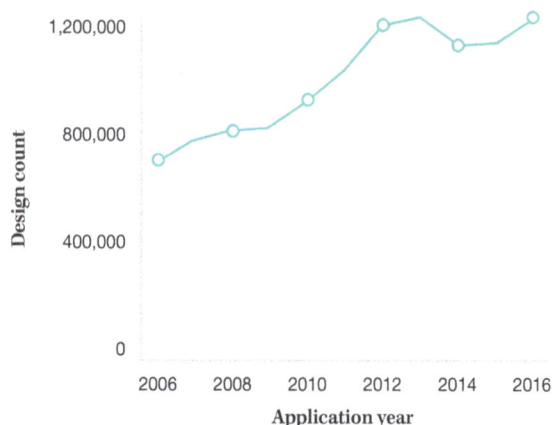

Source: Standard figure C2.

More than half of all designs were contained in applications filed at China's office

The State Intellectual Property Office of China (SIPO) received applications containing 52% of all designs in applications filed worldwide in 2016. The application design count at SIPO grew by 14.3% on the previous year to reach 650,344 designs – a particularly notable surge after almost zero growth in 2013 and 2015, and a 14.4% drop in 2014. Nonetheless, the 2016 volume remained slightly below the figure for 2012 four years earlier. SIPO was followed by the European Union Intellectual Property Office (EUIPO; 104,522), the Korean Intellectual Property Office (KIPO; 69,120), and the offices of Germany (56,188) and Turkey (46,305) (figure 17).

The top 20 offices combined accounted for 93% of designs in all applications. Of these, 14 saw increases in their application design count.[1] The offices of the Islamic Republic of Iran (+34.8%), Ukraine (+17.4%), China (+14.3%) and the United States of America (U.S.; +12.1%) saw double-digit growth, while those of the Russian Federation (+9.4%), the EUIPO (+6.5%), Canada (+5.5%) and France (+5.4%) likewise experienced notable increases. Of the four offices that received fewer designs in applications, those of Switzerland (-9.1%) and the Republic of Korea (-4.6%) saw significant decreases.

Among those offices located in low- and middle-income countries, annual growth in 2016 was particularly high in Guatemala (+70.4%), the Philippines (+42.2%) and Belarus (+41.9%). The offices of Pakistan, South Africa and Viet Nam saw double-digit growth of between 12% and 18%.

Designs contained in resident applications accounted for 89.3% of the world total design count in 2016. This represented at least one-third of all designs in applications at each of the top 20 offices, with the exception of the office of Canada (14.8%). The offices with the highest resident design count shares were those of the Islamic Republic of Iran (98.9%), Italy (98.6%) and China (97.2%).

An increase in the number of designs contained in resident applications had a positive impact on the overall annual growth rates of 12 of the top 20 offices and was the primary driver of growth at six of them, making a particularly high contribution in China and Ukraine. Increasing resident and non-resident design counts contributed almost equally to overall growth at the office of the Russian Federation. An increase in the non-resident design count was the main or sole driver of growth at the offices of Australia, India, Japan and the U.S.

Design count

Some offices allow industrial design applications to contain more than one design for the same good or in the same class; others allow only one design per application. To capture the differences in application filing systems across offices, one needs to compare their respective application and registration design counts.

Figure 17
Application design counts for the top 10 offices, 2016

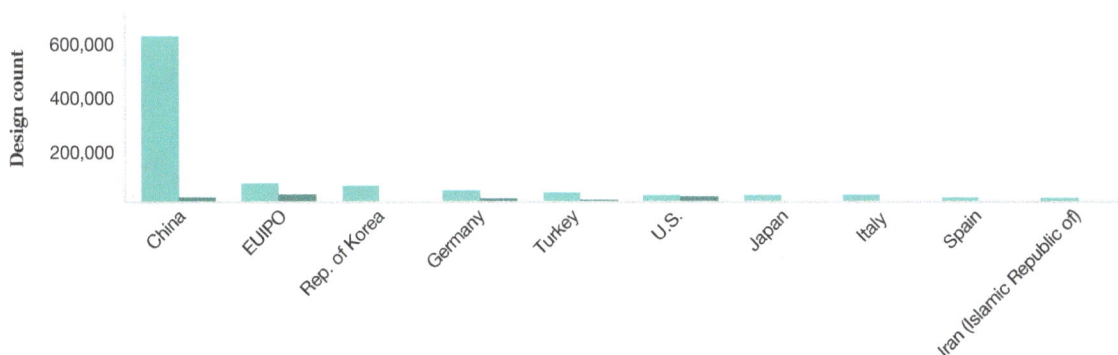

I RESIDENT I NON-RESIDENT

Source: Standard figure C10.

Equivalent design count

Designs in applications filed at regional offices are equivalent to multiple designs in applications filed in the respective member states of those offices. To calculate the number of equivalent designs for the African Intellectual Property Organization (OAPI, which has 17 member states), the Benelux Office for Intellectual Property BOIP, (3) and the EUIPO (28), each design is multiplied by the corresponding number of member states. However, the African Regional Intellectual Property Organization (ARIPO) does not register industrial designs with automatic region-wide applicability. Therefore, for this office, each application is counted as one application abroad if the applicant does not reside in a member state or as one resident application and one application abroad if the applicant resides in a member state.

The offices of all upper middle-income countries combined received 60.5% of all designs contained in applications filed in 2016 (figure 18). China accounted for the vast majority of this share, with the other upper middle-income countries generating only 8.1% of the world total. The share of the high-income countries stood at 35.5%. Offices of lower middle-income countries received 3.8% of the total, and those of low-income countries only 0.2%.

Between 2006 and 2016, average annual growth in design counts was 12.4% for China and 3.6% for the other upper middle-income countries combined. Over the same period, offices in high-income (+1.6%) and

lower middle-income (+1.7%) economies had much lower growth rates in comparison, while those of low-income (-4.5%) countries decreased sharply.

Asia accounted for more than two-thirds (69.3%) of all designs in applications filed worldwide in 2016 (figure 19). It was followed by Europe (23.2%) and North America (4.1%). Of all geographical regions, only Asia (+9%), North America (+5.3%) and Europe (+1.3%) experienced average annual growth between 2006 and 2016. In contrast, Oceania (0%), Africa (-0.3%) and Latin America and the Caribbean (LAC; -0.3%) had zero or negative average annual growth rates.

Figure 18
Application design counts by income group

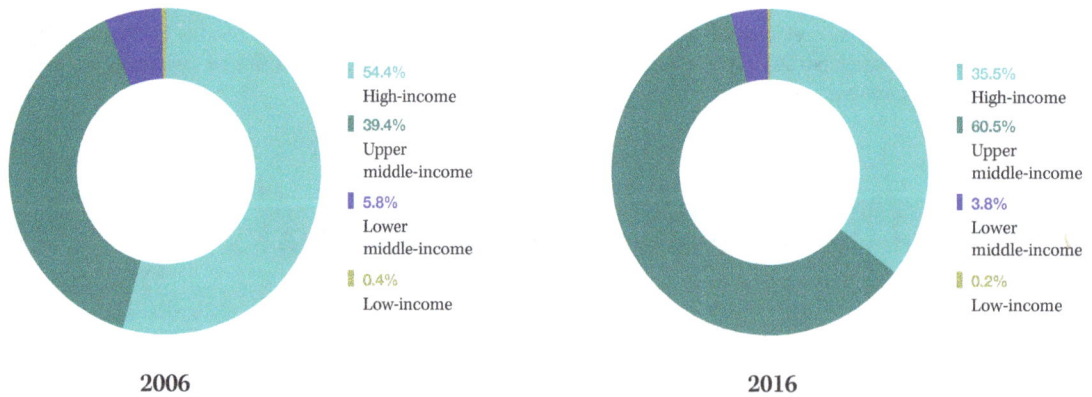

2006

- 54.4% High-income
- 39.4% Upper middle-income
- 5.8% Lower middle-income
- 0.4% Low-income

2016

- 35.5% High-income
- 60.5% Upper middle-income
- 3.8% Lower middle-income
- 0.2% Low-income

Source: Standard figure C7.

Figure 19
Application design counts by region

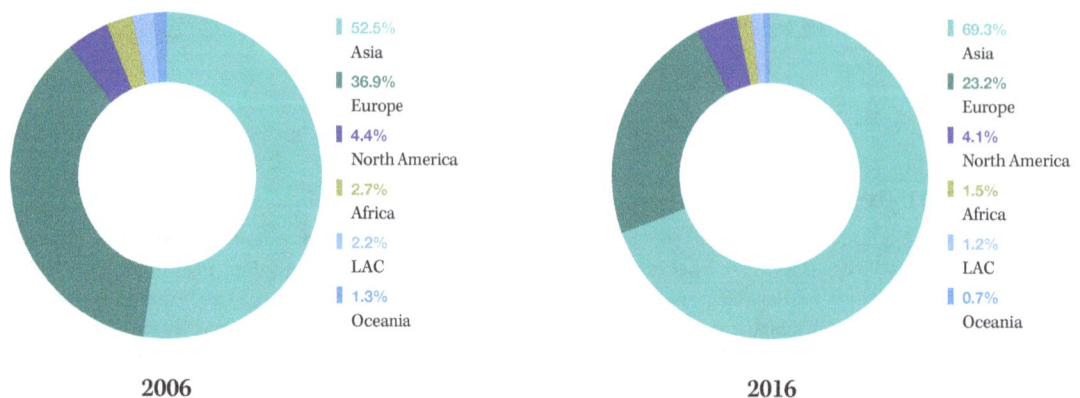

2006

- 52.5% Asia
- 36.9% Europe
- 4.4% North America
- 2.7% Africa
- 2.2% LAC
- 1.3% Oceania

2016

- 69.3% Asia
- 23.2% Europe
- 4.1% North America
- 1.5% Africa
- 1.2% LAC
- 0.7% Oceania

Source: Standard figure C8.

INDUSTRIAL DESIGNS

Industrial design applications filed since 1883

Between 1883 and the early 1950s, the Japan Patent Office (JPO) and the United States Patent and Trademark Office (USPTO) averaged similar numbers of applications, rarely exceeding 10,000. The JPO received the largest number of applications from the 1950s to the late 1990s, reaching approximately 50,000 annual filings at its peak. SIPO began receiving applications in 1985 and saw unprecedented growth, from 640 in 1985 to 660,000 in 2013. It experienced its first and unique drop in 2014. KIPO surpassed the JPO in 2004, and has remained the second-largest office since then. In 2012, the USPTO moved ahead of the JPO to become the third largest. The fifth-largest office is the EUIPO, which began receiving applications in 2003. Unlike the other four offices, the EUIPO has a multiple design system. Applications filed at the EUIPO contained 104,522 designs in 2016.

Trend in industrial design applications for the top five offices

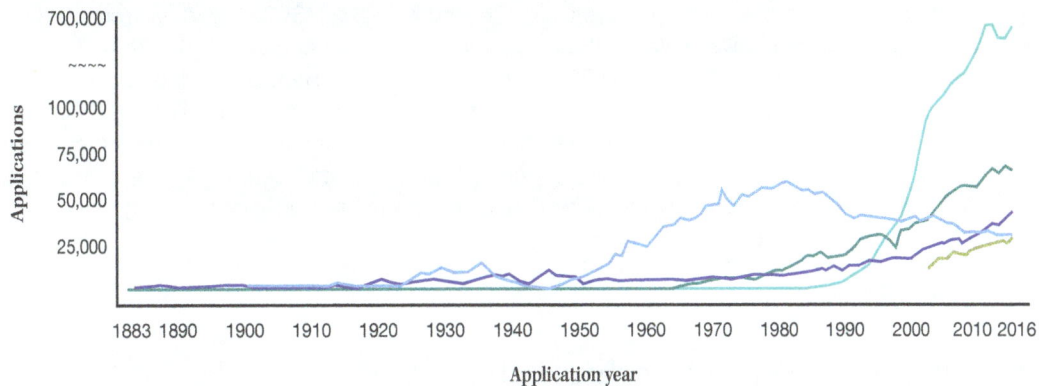

CHINA   REP. OF KOREA   U.S.   JAPAN   EUIPO

Source: Standard figure C9.

Applicants from China reinforce their top position in filings

Applications received by offices from resident and non-resident applicants are referred to as office data, whereas applications filed by applicants at a national/regional office (resident applications) or at foreign offices (applications abroad) are referred to as origin data. Here, industrial design statistics based on the origin of the residence of the first named applicant are reported in order to complement the picture of industrial design activity worldwide.

Applicants from China had the highest equivalent design count in 2016, numbering almost 800,000 (map 3). They were followed by applicants residing in Germany (636,395), Italy (364,944), the U.S. (320,395) and France (213,873). Equivalent designs in applications filed abroad accounted for between 89% and 93% of the total for applicants from all of these countries except for those from China, whose designs in applications filed in China accounted for 80% of the total.

Equivalent design counts increased for 15 origins in 2016, nine of which saw double-digit growth. The sharpest increases came from applicants residing in the Netherlands (+34.1%) and Spain (+20.5%). In contrast, applicants from both Switzerland (-24%) and the Czech Republic (-23.2%) saw sharp decreases in their equivalent design count.

European origins dominate the top 20 origins with 14 countries, followed by five located in Asia and one in North America. In terms of income categories, 18 of the top 20 origins belong to the high-income group, while two upper middle-income countries – China and Turkey – also feature.

Applicants from Germany (569,764), Italy (326,428) and the U.S. (295,965) had the highest number of equivalent designs in applications filed abroad in 2016, and each had growth of between 11% and 20% compared with the previous year. Among the top 10 origins of equivalent designs in applications filed abroad, applicants from Switzerland (-24%) and China (-10.5%) saw the most pronounced declines.

The Republic of Korea tops the ranking when adjusting for GDP and population

The Republic of Korea (3,493) had the highest resident design count per 100 billion US dollars (USD) of gross domestic product (GDP) in 2016 (figure 20). It was followed by China (3,183) and Turkey (2,093). Japan (505) and Mongolia (907) were the two other countries in Asia to rank among the top 20. For Africa, only Morocco (1,559) is listed, ranking seventh. The

14 remaining countries were all located in Europe. In this region, the three countries with the highest count per unit of GDP were Italy (1,836), Germany (1,829) and Ukraine (1,647). The gap between the Republic of Korea and China has reduced since 2006, as the resident design count per USD 100 billion GDP decreased by 355 for the Republic of Korea while increasing by 946 for China.

The Republic of Korea (1,222) was also the country with by far the highest resident design count per million population in 2016. It was followed by Germany (806) and Italy (636). Switzerland fell from third position in 2015 to seventh in 2016 with 457 resident designs per million population, due to a 21% annual fall in its resident design count. The top 20 origins in terms of resident design count per million population comprised countries located in Asia and Europe, and these mostly in the high-income category.

Map 3
Equivalent design counts by origin, 2016

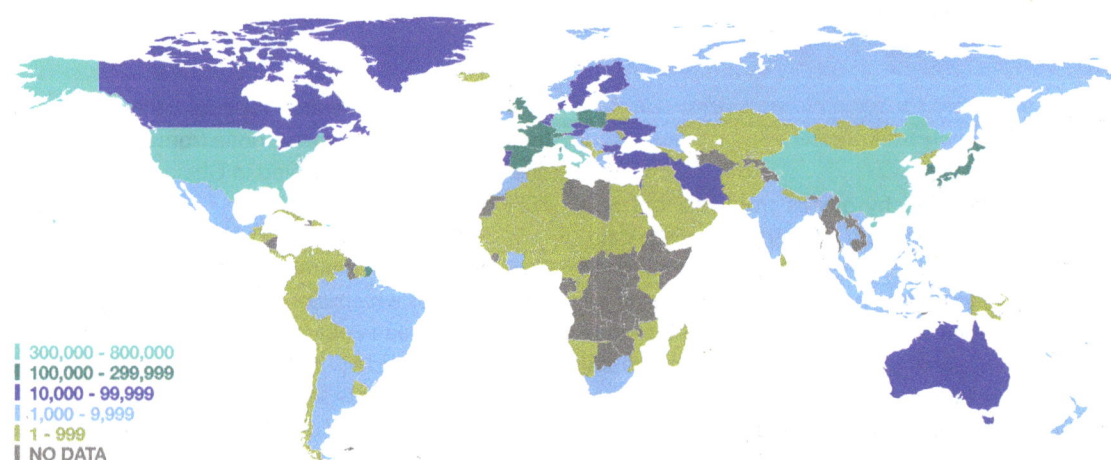

- 300,000 - 800,000
- 100,000 - 299,999
- 10,000 - 99,999
- 1,000 - 9,999
- 1 - 999
- NO DATA

Source: Standard figure C16.

Figure 20
Resident application design counts per USD 100 billion GDP for the top 10 origins

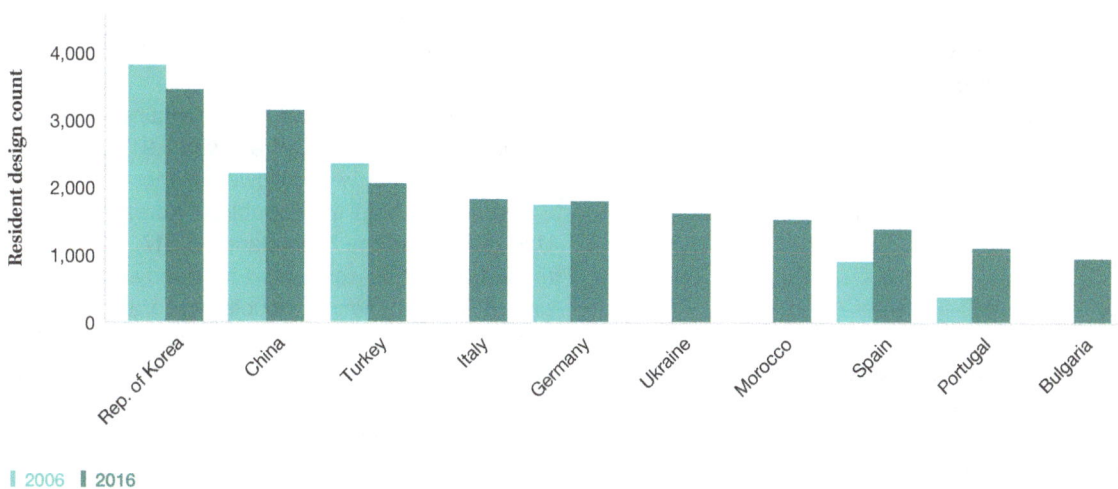

Resident design count (y-axis: 0, 1,000, 2,000, 3,000, 4,000)

Origins: Rep. of Korea, China, Turkey, Italy, Germany, Ukraine, Morocco, Spain, Portugal, Bulgaria

■ 2006 ■ 2016

Source: Standard figure C25.

Furnishing and articles of clothing were the most recorded classes

The Locarno classification includes 32 classes of industrial designs. In 2016, the classes that accounted for the largest shares of the world total remained furnishings (10.8%), articles of clothing (8.6%) and packages and containers (7.3%). More than a quarter (26.7%) of all designs in applications belonged to one of these three classes.

Grouping the Locarno classes into 12 industry sectors highlights the most important sectors for industrial design in each country. For most of the top 10 offices for which data were available, industrial design filing was concentrated in just three sectors, although these top three sectors varied from office to office. For example, textiles and accessories was the main sector at the EUIPO and the offices of Germany, India and the Republic of Korea, while furniture and household goods accounted for the largest share in Australia, the Islamic Republic of Iran, Turkey and the U.K.

In 10 of the top 15 countries of origin, the majority of designs in applications were filed among their top three sectors, with applicants residing in Austria (75.5%) and Switzerland (72.4%) recording the highest level of concentration among their top three sectors. The furniture and household sector was among the top three sectors for 12 of the top origins, whereas textiles and accessories featured in the top three for 10 of them.

Industrial design registrations worldwide fell mainly due to a big drop in China

An estimated 706,300 industrial designs were registered worldwide in 2016. This represents an annual decline of 3.5% following a pronounced 21.5% increase in 2015. This fall was mainly due to a considerable decrease in registrations in China, which registered 36,524 fewer applications than in 2015. The decline in registrations in China may in part be a result of a sharp decrease in filings (-14.4%) observed there in 2014. Nonetheless, registrations in China accounted for 63% of the world total in 2016.

About 974,000 designs were contained in applications registered in 2016, down 2.1% on 2015. China accounted for 46% of all designs in applications registered worldwide, and the top 20 offices combined comprised 91% of the total. Among these offices, eight saw annual growth, including Brazil (+112.2%), the Islamic Republic of Iran (+23.5%), Morocco (+18.3%) and the U.S. (+13.6%). In contrast, the offices of the Russian Federation (-36.2%), Switzerland (-9.7%), China (-7.6%), Spain (-6.3%) and China, Hong Kong SAR (-5.7%) experienced marked decreases.

Industrial design registrations in force shot up to 3.6 million

A record 3.6 million industrial design registrations were in force worldwide in 2016, up 6% on 2015. The number of registrations in force in China increased by over 120,000 to reach 1.36 million – 36% of the world total. China was followed by the Republic of Korea (338,234), the U.S. (307,018), Japan (250,819) and the EUIPO (194,781). Four of these top five offices saw growth of between 4.6% for the U.S. and 9.7% for China. In contrast, Japan saw a slight decrease of 0.1%.

Hague filings grew by 36%

The Hague System offers applicants an advantageous way to seek industrial design protection internationally as an alternative to using the Paris Convention for the Protection of Industrial Property. For further information and statistics on this System, see the *Hague Yearly Review 2017*.

In 2016, the Hague System received 5,562 international applications, up 35.6% on 2015. These applications contained 18,716 designs, representing annual growth of 13.9%. It was the second consecutive year of strong growth, reflecting the recent expansion of the Hague System to include Japan, the Republic of Korea and the U.S.

Applicants residing in Germany remained the largest users of the Hague System with 3,917 designs in applications. They were followed by those residing in Switzerland (2,555), the Republic of Korea (1,882), the U.S. (1,410) and the Netherlands (1,317). Combined, these five origins accounted for nearly 60% of the total. All five experienced double-digit growth in filings except for Switzerland, where they fell by 22.9%. Among the top 20 origins, the strongest growth was among applicants from Cyprus (+138.4%), Turkey (+136.5%) and Japan (+109.2%).

The European Union (EU) has received the largest number of designs contained in designations each year since 2010. In 2016, it recorded 14,952 designs. It was followed by Switzerland (8,811), Turkey (6,137), the U.S. (4,722) and Norway (3,324). Four of the top 20 designated Hague members recorded double-digit annual growth, the highest two being France (+45.9%) and the EU (+12%).

The Hague System accounted for 15.8% of all designs contained in non-resident applications filed worldwide. When considering only non-resident applications filed at offices of Hague members, this share rises to 48%, a decrease of 6 percentage points since 2015. This change in share was due to the inclusion of Japan and the U.S. – two new Hague members – in the calculation.

INDUSTRIAL DESIGNS

Standard figures and tables

INDUSTRIAL DESIGNS

INDUSTRIAL DESIGNS

Industrial design applications and registrations worldwide

Figure C1

Trend in industrial design applications worldwide

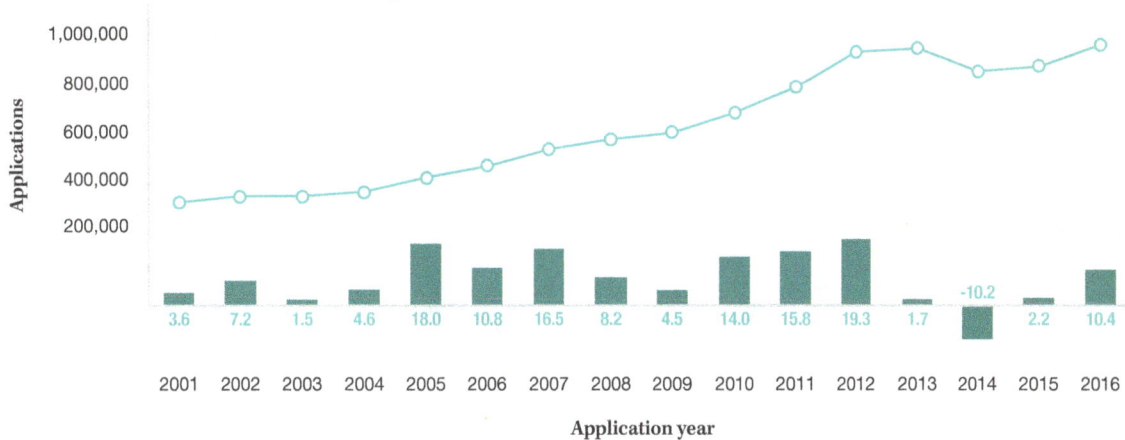

■ APPLICATIONS   ■ GROWTH RATE (%)

Note: World totals are WIPO estimates using data covering 151 IP offices. These totals include the numbers of applications filed directly with national and regional offices (known as the "Paris route") as well as the numbers of designations received via the Hague System (where applicable).

Source: WIPO Statistics Database, September 2017.

Figure C2

Trend in application design counts worldwide

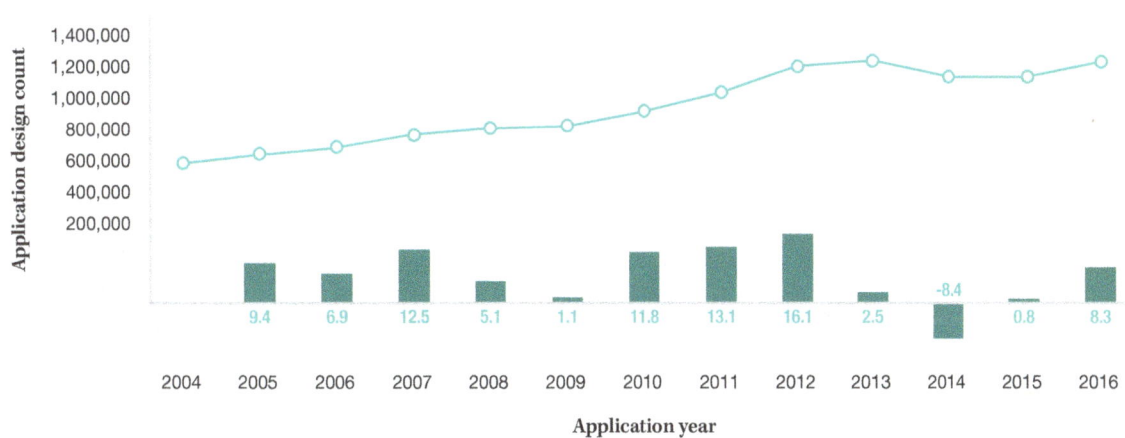

■ APPLICATION DESIGN COUNT   ■ GROWTH RATE (%)

Note: World totals are WIPO estimates using data covering 151 IP offices. These totals include design counts in applications filed directly with national and regional offices (known as the "Paris route") as well as design counts in designations received via the Hague System (where applicable). See the glossary for the definition of design count.

Source: WIPO Statistics Database, September 2017.

Figure C3
Resident and non-resident application design counts worldwide

NON-RESIDENT SHARE (%)

| | 29.4 | 25.1 | 23.3 | 22.1 | 20.1 | 16.2 | 15.3 | 15.0 | 14.2 | 14.6 | 15.5 | 15.7 | 14.8 |

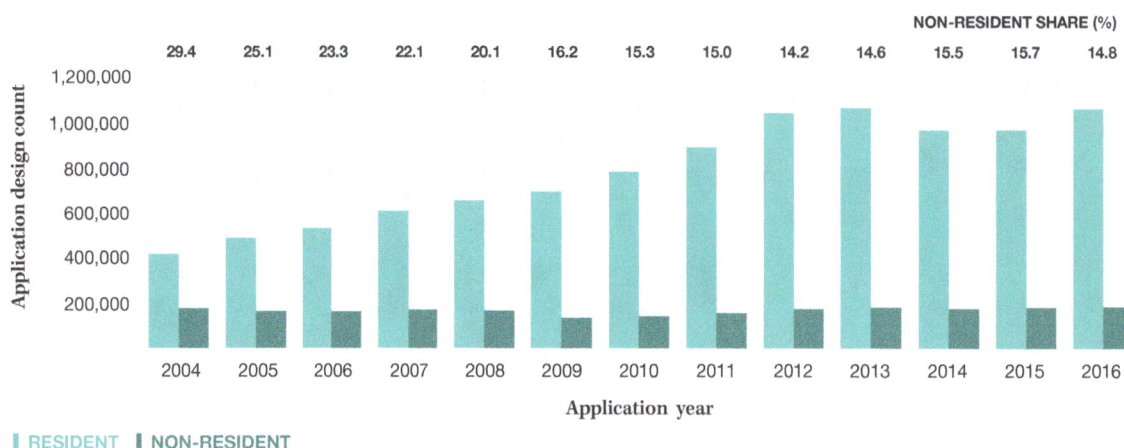

Application year

| RESIDENT | NON-RESIDENT

Note: World totals are WIPO estimates using data covering 151 IP offices. These totals include design counts in applications filed directly with national and regional offices (known as the "Paris route") as well as design counts in designations received via the Hague System (where applicable). See the glossary for the definition of design count.

Source: WIPO Statistics Database, September 2017.

Figure C4
Trend in industrial design registrations worldwide

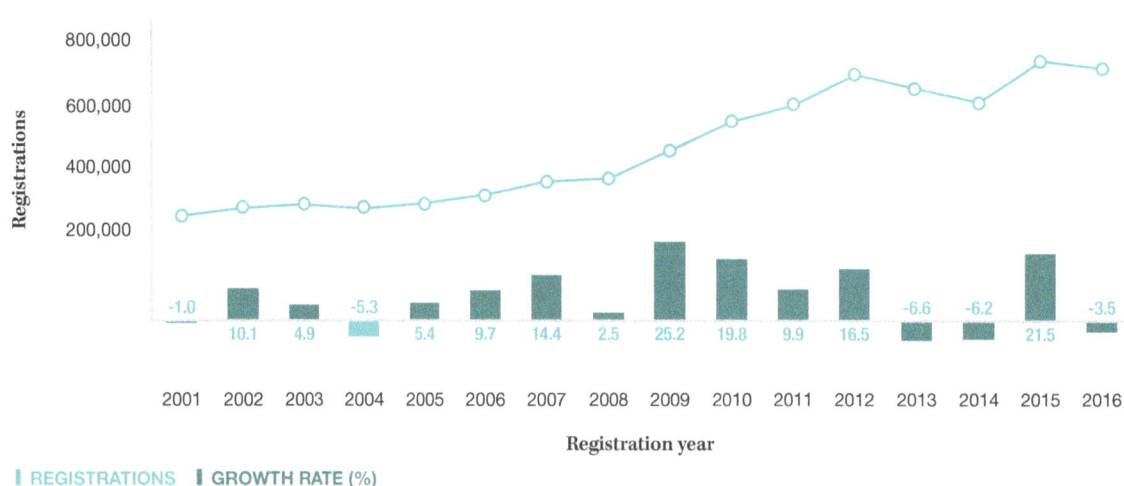

Registration year

| REGISTRATIONS | GROWTH RATE (%)

Note: World totals are WIPO estimates using data covering 147 IP offices. These totals include the numbers of registrations issued by national and regional offices for applications filed directly with offices (known as the "Paris route") as well as for designations received via the Hague System (where applicable).

Source: WIPO Statistics Database, September 2017.

INDUSTRIAL DESIGNS

Figure C5
Trend in registration design counts worldwide

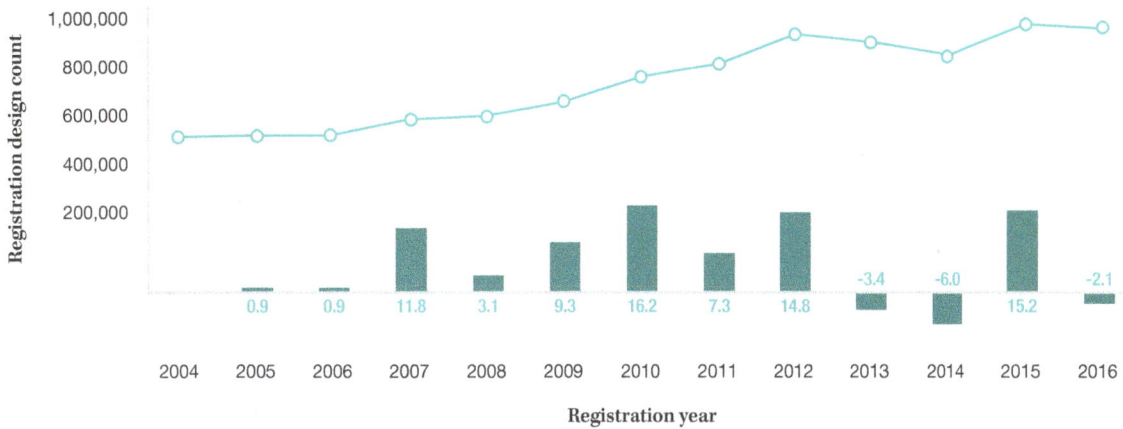

| REGISTRATION DESIGN COUNT | GROWTH RATE (%)

Note: World totals are WIPO estimates using data covering 147 IP offices. These totals include design counts in registrations issued by national and regional offices for applications filed directly with offices (known as the "Paris route") as well as for designations received via the Hague System (where applicable).

Source: WIPO Statistics Database, September 2017.

INDUSTRIAL DESIGNS

Figure C6
Resident and non-resident registration design counts worldwide

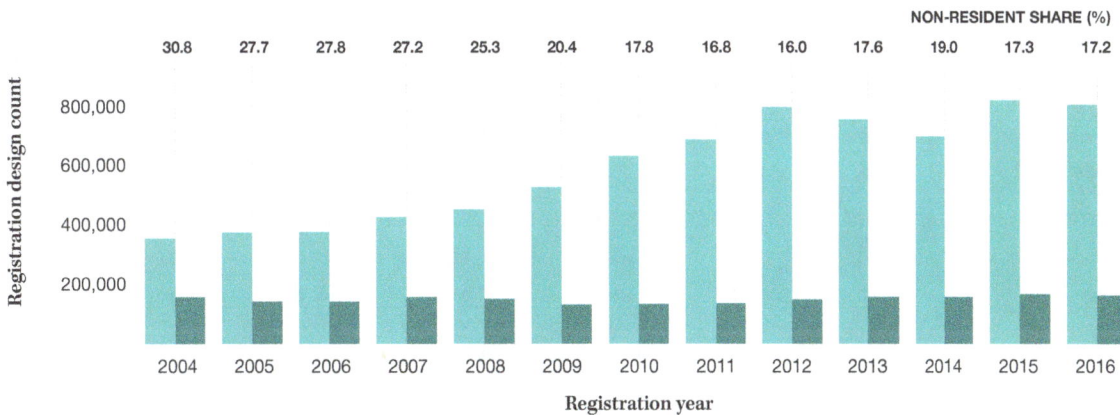

| RESIDENT | NON-RESIDENT

Note: World totals are WIPO estimates using data covering 147 IP offices. These totals include design counts in registrations issued by national and regional offices for applications filed directly with offices (known as the "Paris route") as well as for designations received via the Hague System (where applicable).

Source: WIPO Statistics Database, September 2017.

Industrial design applications and registrations by office

Figure C7
Application design counts by income group

Income group	Number of designs in applications		Resident share (%)		Share of world total (%)		Average growth (%)
	2006	2016	2006	2016	2006	2016	2006-16
High-income	374,600	440,500	72.8	73.1	54.4	35.5	1.6
Upper middle-income	271,800	751,000	86.8	93.8	39.4	60.5	10.7
...Upper middle-income without China	*70,500*	*100,700*	*67.8*	*72.2*	*10.2*	*8.1*	*3.6*
Lower middle-income	40,000	47,400	48.3	61.2	5.8	3.8	1.7
Low-income	2,700	1,700	30.1	42.1	0.4	0.2	-4.5
World	**689,100**	**1,240,600**	**76.7**	**85.2**	**100.0**	**100.0**	**6.1**

Note: Totals by income group are WIPO estimates using data covering 151 IP offices. Each category includes the following number of offices: high-income (57), upper middle-income (43), lower middle-income (37) and low-income (14). Data for the European Union Intellectual Property Office are allocated to the high-income group because most EU member states are high-income countries. For similar reasons, data for the African Regional Intellectual Property Organization and the African Intellectual Property Organization are allocated to the low-income group. For information on income group classification, see the Data description section.

Source: WIPO Statistics Database, September 2017.

Figure C8
Application design counts by region

Region	Number of designs in applications		Resident share (%)		Share of world total (%)		Average growth (%)
	2006	2016	2006	2016	2006	2016	2006-16
Africa	18,200	17,700	44.5	59.0	2.7	1.5	-0.3
Asia	362,000	859,700	88.4	92.8	52.5	69.3	9.0
Europe	254,300	288,400	68.9	73.5	36.9	23.2	1.3
Latin America & the Caribbean	15,500	15,000	41.0	49.7	2.2	1.2	-0.3
North America	30,400	51,100	48.9	49.6	4.4	4.1	5.3
Oceania	8,700	8,700	47.1	35.6	1.3	0.7	0.0
Total	**689,100**	**1,240,600**	**76.7**	**85.2**	**100.0**	**100.0**	**6.1**

Note: Totals by geographical region are WIPO estimates using data covering 151 IP offices. Each region includes the following number of offices: Africa (29), Asia (41), Europe (46), Latin America & the Caribbean (28), North America (2) and Oceania (5). For information on geographical region classification, see the Data description section.

Source: WIPO Statistics Database, September 2017.

Figure C9
Trend in industrial design applications for the top five offices

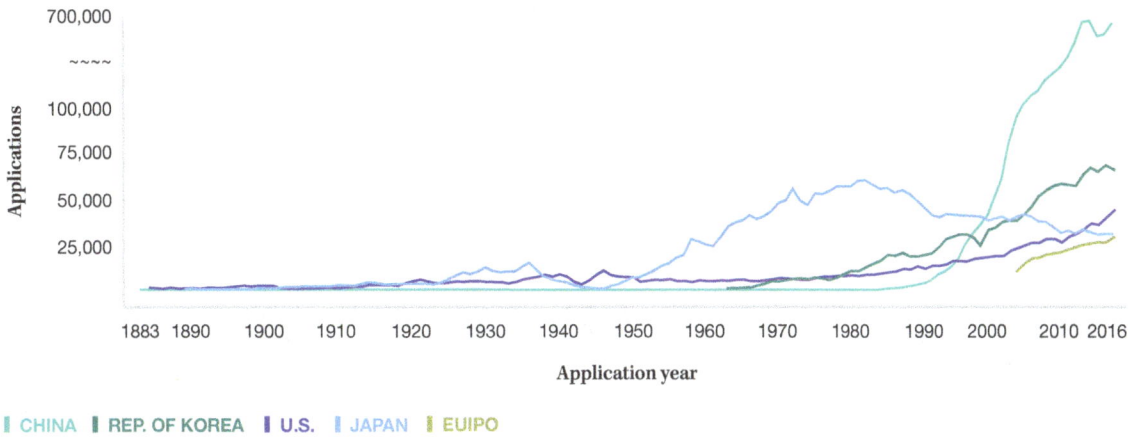

Applications (y-axis): 700,000 / ~~~~ / 100,000 / 75,000 / 50,000 / 25,000

Application year (x-axis): 1883 1890 1900 1910 1920 1930 1940 1950 1960 1970 1980 1990 2000 2010 2016

| CHINA | REP. OF KOREA | U.S. | JAPAN | EUIPO

Note: EUIPO is the European Union Intellectual Property Office. Data are based on the numbers of applications filed; that is, differences between single-design and multiple-design filing systems across IP offices are not taken into account. The top five offices were selected based on their 2016 totals.

Source: WIPO Statistics Database, September 2017.

Figure C10
Application design counts for the top 20 offices, 2016

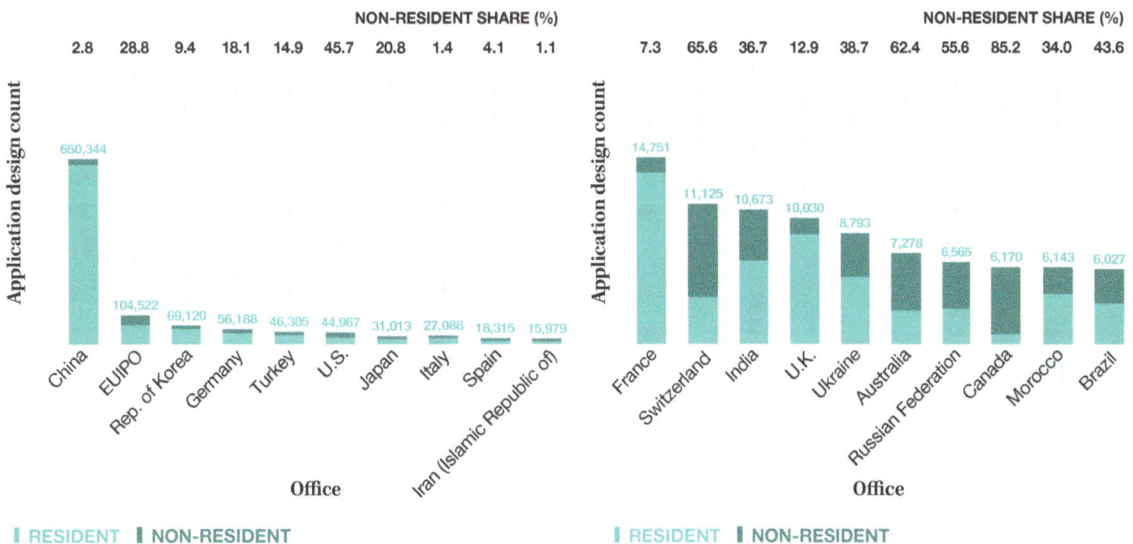

NON-RESIDENT SHARE (%)									
2.8	28.8	9.4	18.1	14.9	45.7	20.8	1.4	4.1	1.1

Application design count:
China 650,344; EUIPO 104,522; Rep. of Korea 69,120; Germany 56,188; Turkey 46,305; U.S. 44,967; Japan 31,013; Italy 27,088; Spain 18,315; Iran (Islamic Republic of) 15,979

Office

| RESIDENT | NON-RESIDENT

NON-RESIDENT SHARE (%)									
7.3	65.6	36.7	12.9	38.7	62.4	55.6	85.2	34.0	43.6

Application design count:
France 14,751; Switzerland 11,125; India 10,673; U.K. 10,030; Ukraine 8,793; Australia 7,278; Russian Federation 6,565; Canada 6,170; Morocco 6,143; Brazil 6,027

Office

| RESIDENT | NON-RESIDENT

Note: EUIPO is the European Union Intellectual Property Office.

Source: WIPO Statistics Database, September 2017.

INDUSTRIAL DESIGNS

Figure C11

Contribution of resident and non-resident application design counts to total growth for the top 20 offices, 2015-16

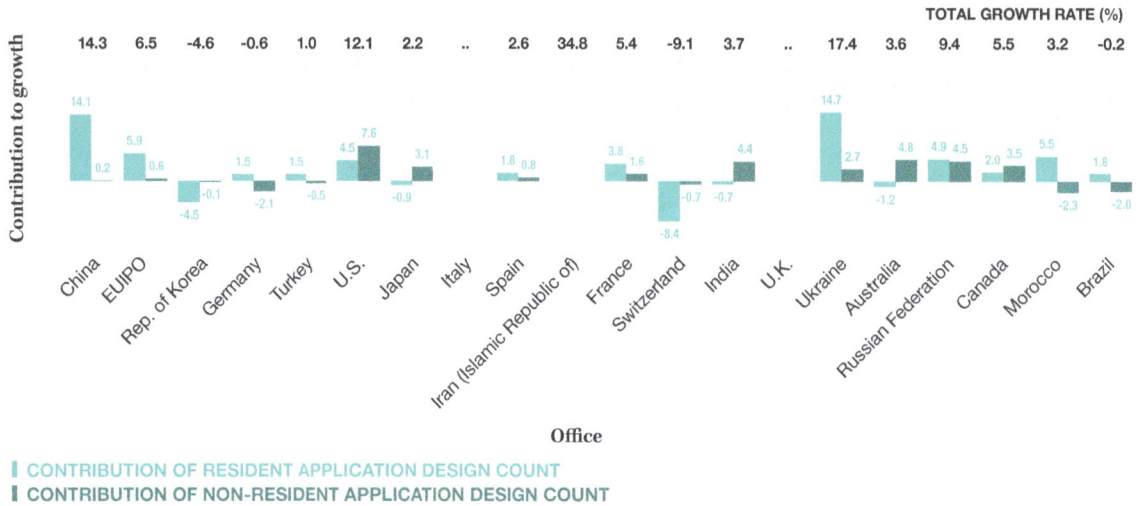

TOTAL GROWTH RATE (%)

14.3	6.5	-4.6	-0.6	1.0	12.1	2.2	..	2.6	34.8	5.4	-9.1	3.7	..	17.4	3.6	9.4	5.5	3.2	-0.2

Contribution to growth (Office)

CONTRIBUTION OF RESIDENT APPLICATION DESIGN COUNT
CONTRIBUTION OF NON-RESIDENT APPLICATION DESIGN COUNT

.. indicates not available.

Note: EUIPO is the European Union Intellectual Property Office. This figure shows total growth in application design counts broken down by the respective contributions of resident and non-resident filings. For example, design counts in Spain grew by 2.6%, and resident applicants contributed 1.8 percentage points to this total growth. The 2015 data for resident and non-resident breakdown were not available for the office of the Islamic Republic of Iran.

Source: WIPO Statistics Database, September 2017.

Figure C12

Application design counts for offices of selected low- and middle-income countries, 2016

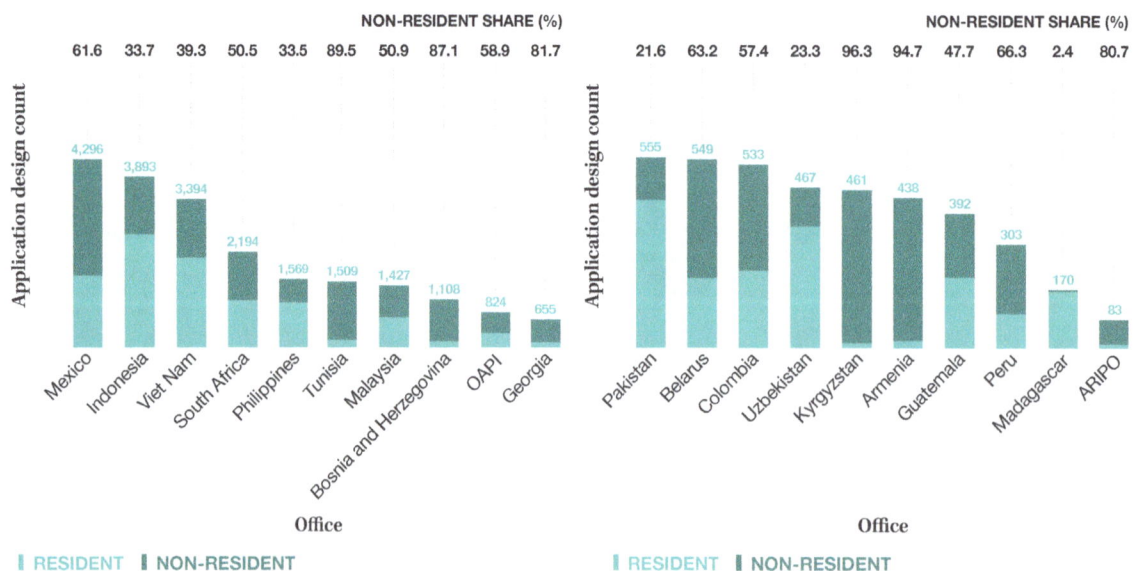

NON-RESIDENT SHARE (%)

61.6	33.7	39.3	50.5	33.5	89.5	50.9	87.1	58.9	81.7

NON-RESIDENT SHARE (%)

21.6	63.2	57.4	23.3	96.3	94.7	47.7	66.3	2.4	80.7

RESIDENT | NON-RESIDENT

Note: ARIPO is the African Regional Intellectual Property Organization. OAPI is the African Intellectual Property Organization. The selected offices are from different world regions and income groups (low-income, lower middle-income and upper middle-income). Where available, data for all offices are presented in the statistical table at the end of this section.

Source: WIPO Statistics Database, September 2017.

Figure C13

Contribution of resident and non-resident application design counts to total growth for offices of selected low- and middle-income countries, 2015-16

TOTAL GROWTH RATE (%)

Mexico	Indonesia	Viet Nam	South Africa	Philippines	Tunisia	Malaysia	Bosnia and Herzegovina	OAPI	Georgia	Pakistan	Belarus	Colombia	Uzbekistan	Kyrgyzstan	Armenia	Guatemala	Peru	Madagascar	ARIPO
7.4	-2.0	17.6	11.9	42.2	-4.4	-19.0	-7.4	3.1	-47.0	13.5	41.9	-25.8	9.1	-46.0	-50.6	70.4	-15.4	-17.5	-33.1

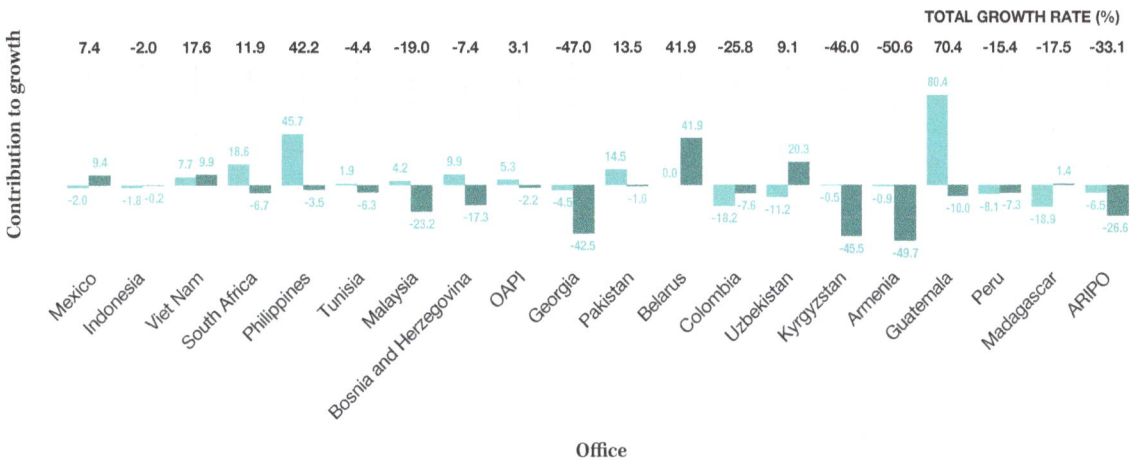

CONTRIBUTION OF RESIDENT APPLICATION DESIGN COUNT
CONTRIBUTION OF NON-RESIDENT APPLICATION DESIGN COUNT

Note: ARIPO is the African Regional Intellectual Property Organization. OAPI is the African Intellectual Property Organization. The selected offices are from different world regions and income groups (low-income, lower middle-income and upper middle-income). Where available, data for all offices are in the statistical table at the end of this section. This figure shows total growth in design counts broken down by the respective contributions of resident and non-resident filings. For example, the design count in Viet Nam grew by 17.6%, and resident applicants contributed 7.7 percentage points to this growth.

Source: WIPO Statistics Database, September 2017.

Figure C14

Registration design counts for the top 20 offices, 2016

GROWTH RATE (%)

China	EUIPO	Rep. of Korea	Germany	Turkey	Italy	U.S.	Japan	Spain	Switzerland
-7.6	7.8	-0.9	-2.8	1.2	..	13.6	-1.4	-6.3	-9.7
446,135	101,817	55,736	50,020	48,687	31,956	31,395	26,813	17,946	10,804

GROWTH RATE (%)

Ukraine	U.K.	India	Brazil	Australia	Morocco	Canada	Russian Federation	Iran (Islamic Republic of)	China, Hong Kong SAR
4.6	49.1	-1.7	112.2	1.2	18.3	-0.4	-36.2	23.5	-5.7
8,546	8,481	7,331	6,972	6,668	6,075	5,703	5,476	5,126	4,432

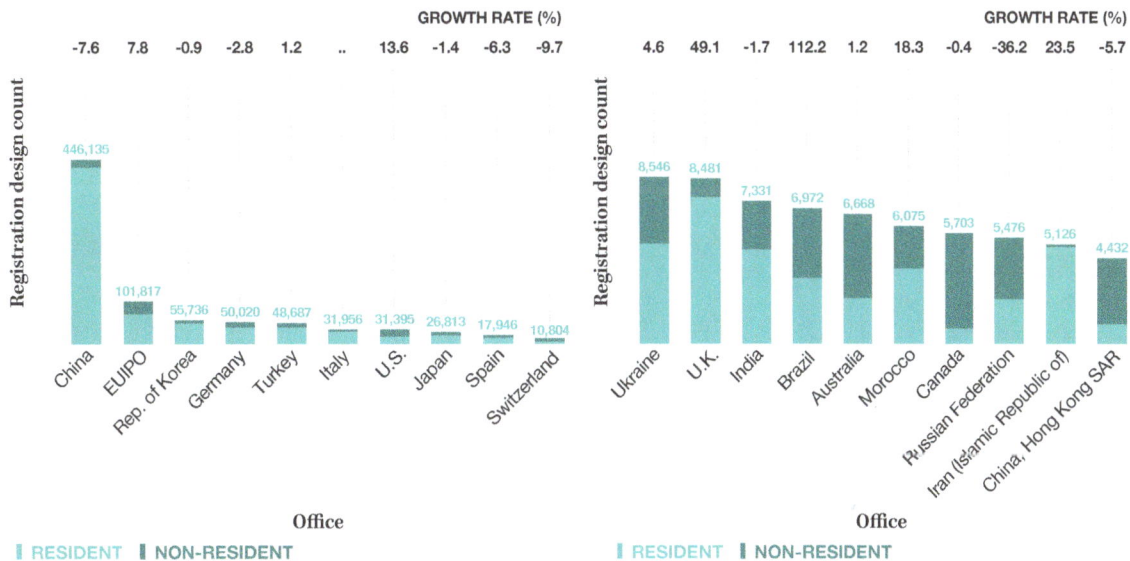

RESIDENT NON-RESIDENT

.. indicates not available.

Note: EUIPO is the European Union Intellectual Property Office. Registration design count data for France were not available.

Source: WIPO Statistics Database, September 2017.

Figure C15
Registration design counts for offices of selected low- and middle-income countries, 2016

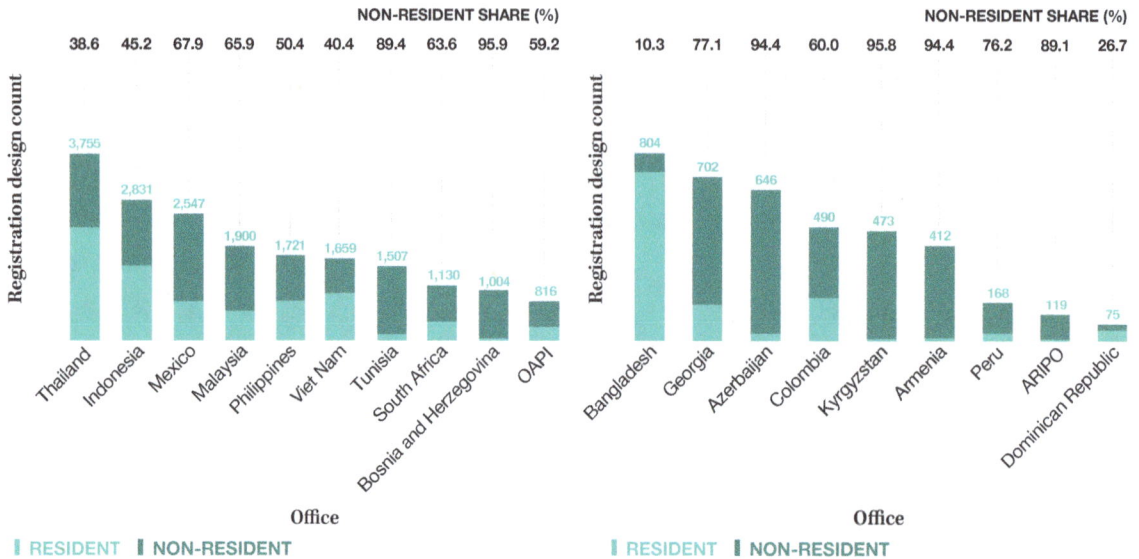

Note: ARIPO is the African Regional Intellectual Property Organization. OAPI is the African Intellectual Property Organization. The selected offices are from different world regions and income groups (low-income, lower middle-income and upper middle-income). Where available, data for all offices are presented in the statistical table at the end of this section.

Source: WIPO Statistics Database, September 2017.

Application design counts by origin

INDUSTRIAL DESIGNS

Figure C16
Equivalent application design counts by origin, 2016

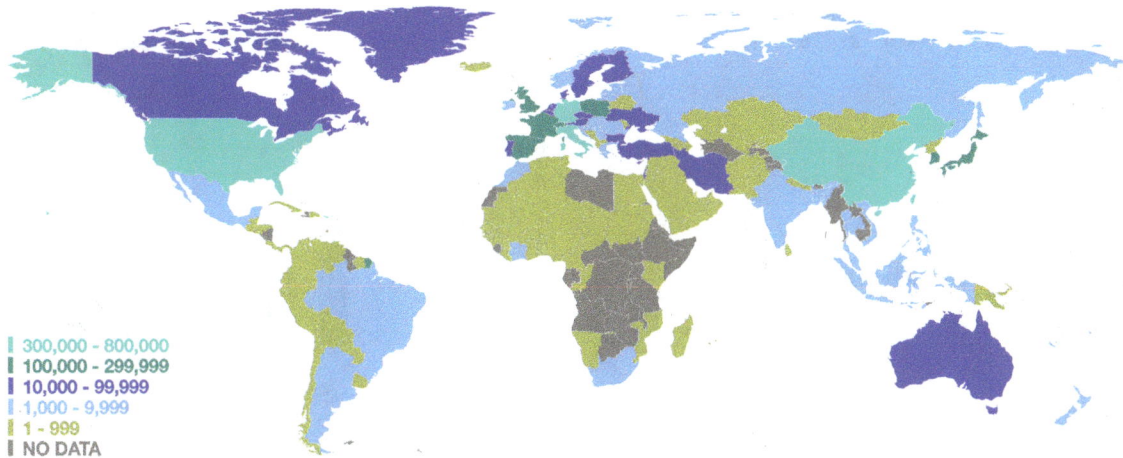

- 300,000 - 800,000
- 100,000 - 299,999
- 10,000 - 99,999
- 1,000 - 9,999
- 1 - 999
- NO DATA

Note: Equivalent application design count includes resident applications and applications filed abroad. The origin of an industrial design application is determined by the residence of the first named applicant. Applications filed at some regional offices are considered equivalent to multiple applications in the member states of those offices. See the glossary for the full definition of equivalent application.

Source: WIPO Statistics Database, September 2017.

Figure C17
Application design counts for the top 20 origins, 2016

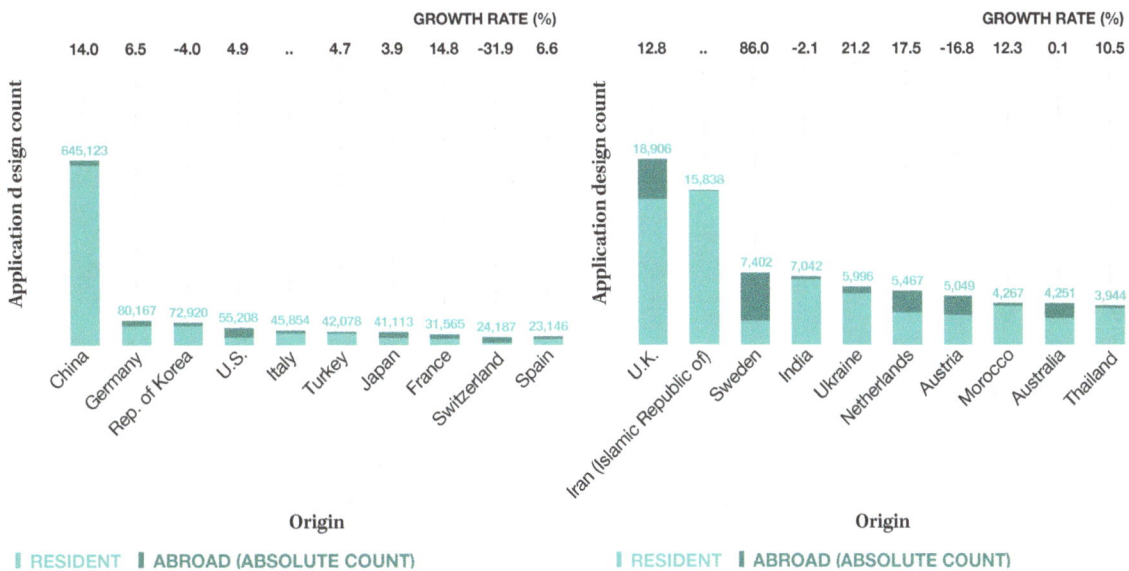

GROWTH RATE (%)

| 14.0 | 6.5 | -4.0 | 4.9 | .. | 4.7 | 3.9 | 14.8 | -31.9 | 6.6 |

Application design count

- China — 645,123
- Germany — 80,167
- Rep. of Korea — 72,920
- U.S. — 55,208
- Italy — 45,854
- Turkey — 42,078
- Japan — 41,113
- France — 31,565
- Switzerland — 24,187
- Spain — 23,146

Origin

RESIDENT | ABROAD (ABSOLUTE COUNT)

GROWTH RATE (%)

| 12.8 | .. | 86.0 | -2.1 | 21.2 | 17.5 | -16.8 | 12.3 | 0.1 | 10.5 |

Application design count

- U.K. — 18,906
- Iran (Islamic Republic of) — 15,836
- Sweden — 7,402
- India — 7,042
- Ukraine — 5,996
- Netherlands — 5,467
- Austria — 5,049
- Morocco — 4,267
- Australia — 4,251
- Thailand — 3,944

Origin

RESIDENT | ABROAD (ABSOLUTE COUNT)

.. indicates not available.

Note: Data are based on absolute count, not equivalent count. The origin of an industrial design application is determined by the residence of the first named applicant. An application filed at a regional office is considered a resident filing if the applicant is a resident of one of that office's member states. See the glossary for the definition of absolute applications.

Source: WIPO Statistics Database, September 2017.

Figure C18
Equivalent application design counts for the top 20 origins, 2016

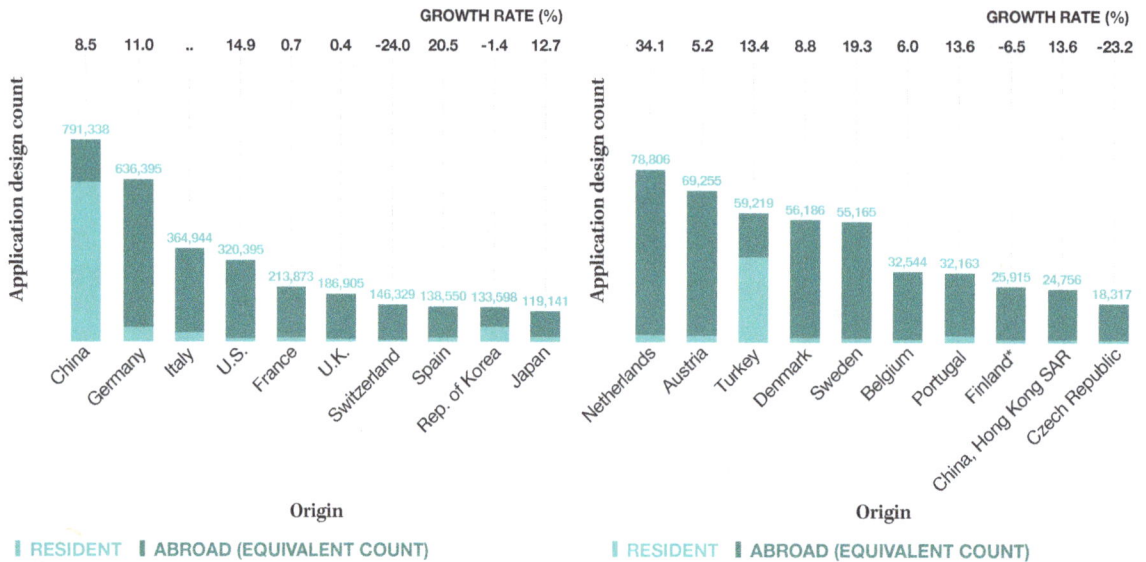

GROWTH RATE (%)

8.5 11.0 .. 14.9 0.7 0.4 -24.0 20.5 -1.4 12.7

Application design count

791,338 China
636,395 Germany
364,944 Italy
320,395 U.S.
213,873 France
186,905 U.K.
146,329 Switzerland
138,550 Spain
133,598 Rep. of Korea
119,141 Japan

GROWTH RATE (%)

34.1 5.2 13.4 8.8 19.3 6.0 13.6 -6.5 13.6 -23.2

Application design count

78,806 Netherlands
69,255 Austria
59,219 Turkey
56,186 Denmark
55,165 Sweden
32,544 Belgium
32,163 Portugal
25,915 Finland*
24,756 China, Hong Kong SAR
18,317 Czech Republic

Origin

| RESIDENT | ABROAD (EQUIVALENT COUNT)

Origin

| RESIDENT | ABROAD (EQUIVALENT COUNT)

.. indicates not available.

* indicates 2015 data.

Note: The origin of an industrial design application is determined by the residence of the first named applicant. An application filed at a regional office is considered a resident filing if the applicant is a resident of one of that office's member states. See the glossary for the definition of equivalent applications.

Source: WIPO Statistics Database, September 2017.

Figure C19
Application design counts for selected low- and middle-income origins, 2016

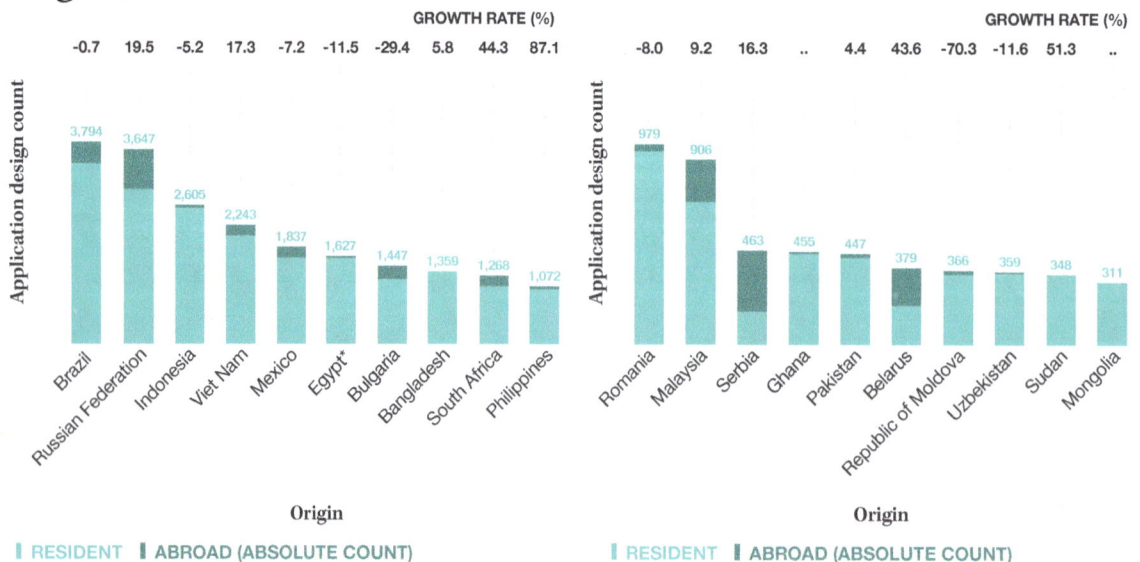

GROWTH RATE (%)

-0.7 19.5 -5.2 17.3 -7.2 -11.5 -29.4 5.8 44.3 87.1

Application design count

3,794 Brazil
3,647 Russian Federation
2,605 Indonesia
2,243 Viet Nam
1,837 Mexico
1,627 Egypt*
1,447 Bulgaria
1,359 Bangladesh
1,268 South Africa
1,072 Philippines

GROWTH RATE (%)

-8.0 9.2 16.3 .. 4.4 43.6 -70.3 -11.6 51.3 ..

Application design count

979 Romania
906 Malaysia
463 Serbia
455 Ghana
447 Pakistan
379 Belarus
366 Republic of Moldova
359 Uzbekistan
348 Sudan
311 Mongolia

Origin

| RESIDENT | ABROAD (ABSOLUTE COUNT)

Origin

| RESIDENT | ABROAD (ABSOLUTE COUNT)

.. indicates not available.

* indicates 2015 data.

Note: Data are based on absolute count, not equivalent count. The selected origins are from different world regions and income groups (low-income, lower middle-income and upper middle-income). Where available, data for all origins are presented in the statistical table at the end of this section. The origin of an industrial design application is determined by the residence of the first named applicant. See the glossary for the definition of absolute application.

Source: WIPO Statistics Database, September 2017.

Figure C20
Flow of non-resident design counts for the top five origins and the top 10 offices of high-income economies, 2016

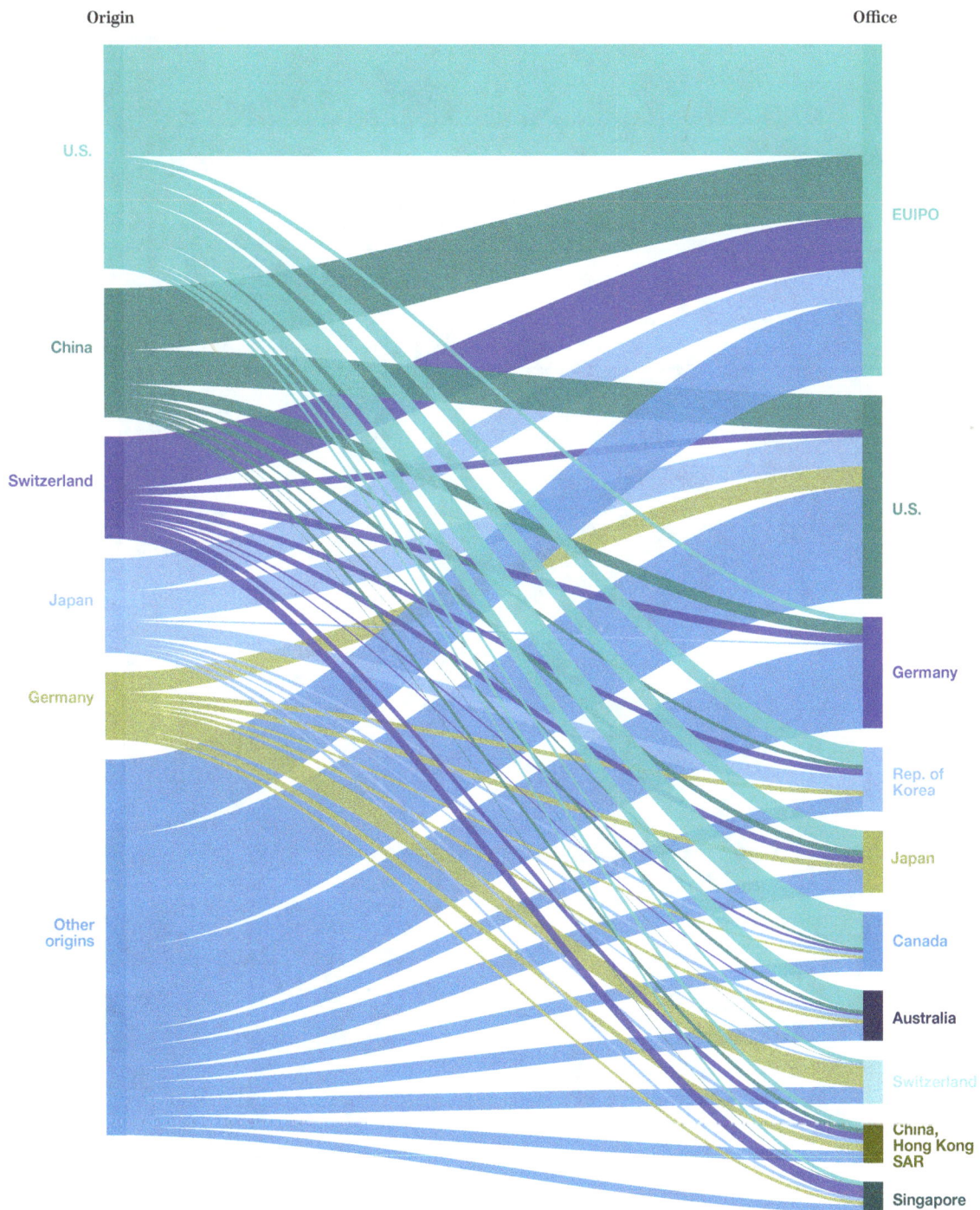

Origin

Office

U.S.

China

Switzerland

Japan

Germany

Other origins

EUIPO

U.S.

Germany

Rep. of Korea

Japan

Canada

Australia

Switzerland

China, Hong Kong SAR

Singapore

INDUSTRIAL DESIGNS

Note: EUIPO is the European Union Intellectual Property Office. Data are based on absolute count, not equivalent count.

Source: WIPO Statistics Database, September 2017.

INDUSTRIAL DESIGNS

Figure C21
Flow of non-resident design counts for the top five origins and the top 10 offices of low- and middle-income economies, 2016

Origin   Office

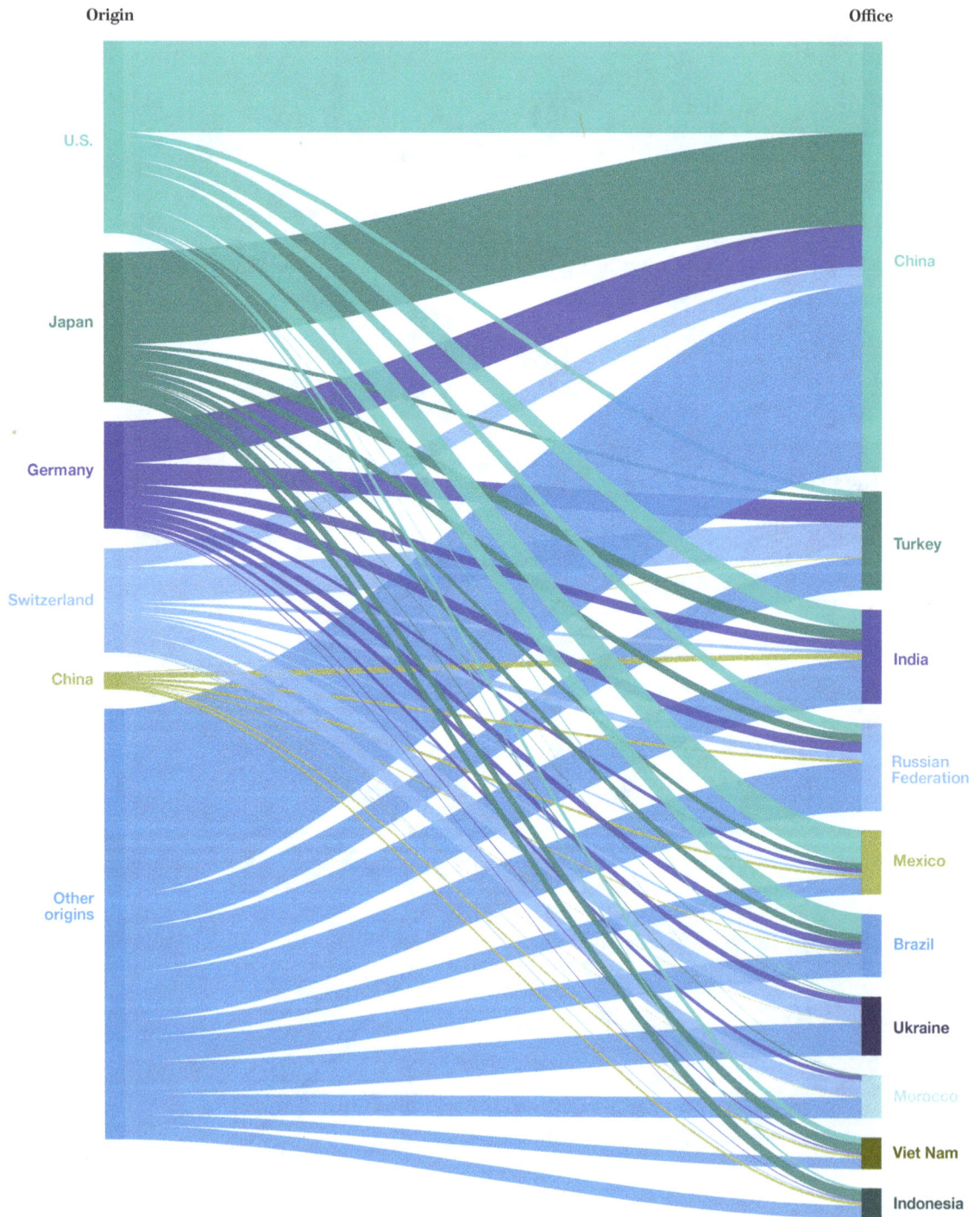

Note: Data are based on absolute count, not equivalent count.

Source: WIPO Statistics Database, September 2017.

Application design counts by Locarno class

Application design counts by Locarno class, 2016

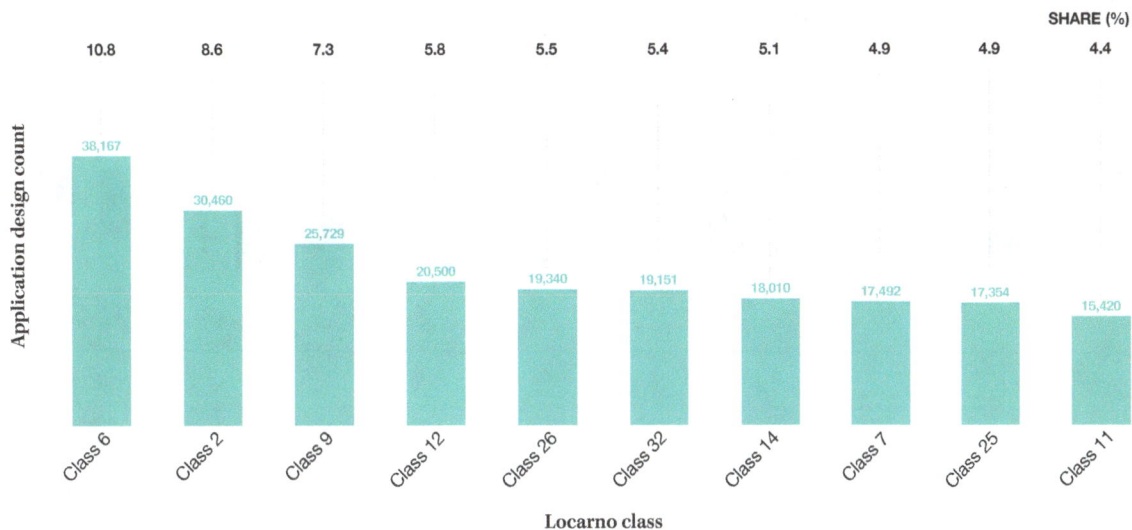

SHARE (%)

| 10.8 | 8.6 | 7.3 | 5.8 | 5.5 | 5.4 | 5.1 | 4.9 | 4.9 | 4.4 |

Application design count

- Class 6: 38,167
- Class 2: 30,460
- Class 9: 25,729
- Class 12: 20,500
- Class 26: 19,340
- Class 32: 19,151
- Class 14: 18,010
- Class 7: 17,492
- Class 25: 17,354
- Class 11: 15,420

Locarno class

Note: See Annex D for class definitions. These figures are based on data from 111 IP offices. Class data are not available or are incomplete for the offices of China, Japan and the U.S.

Source: WIPO Statistics Database, September 2017.

Figure C23

Distribution of application design counts by the top three sectors and for the top 10 offices, 2016

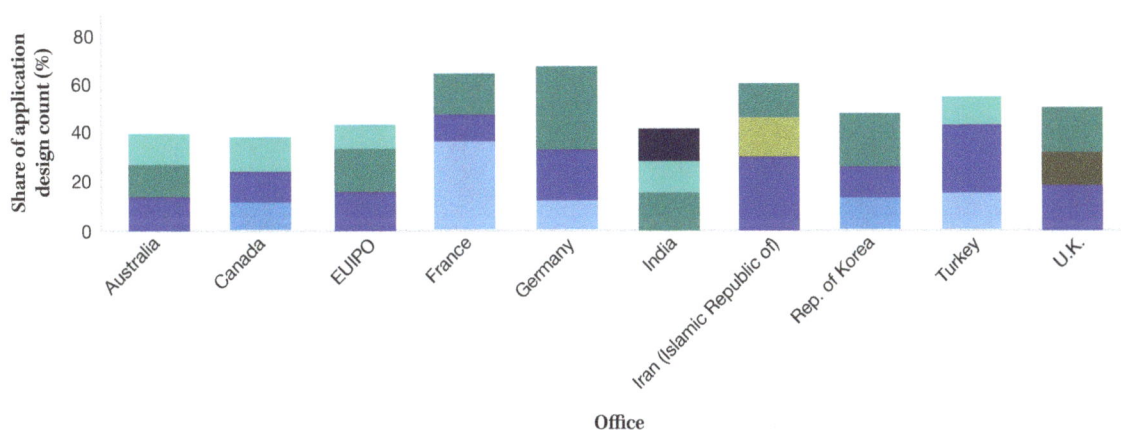

Share of application design count (%)

Offices: Australia, Canada, EUIPO, France, Germany, India, Iran (Islamic Republic of), Rep. of Korea, Turkey, U.K.

Office

| ADVERTISING | CONSTRUCTION | FURNITURE AND HOUSEHOLD GOODS | LEISURE AND EDUCATION
| PACKAGING | TEXTILES AND ACCESSORIES | TOOLS AND MACHINES | TRANSPORT

Note: EUIPO is the European Union Intellectual Property Office. A concordance table produced by the Organisation for Economic Co-operation and Development (OECD) was used to convert the 32 classes into 12 industry sectors (see Annex D for definitions). The top three sectors and top 10 offices were selected based on their 2016 totals. Data for several large offices are not available or incomplete, including the offices of China, Japan and the U.S.

Source: WIPO Statistics Database, September 2017.

INDUSTRIAL DESIGNS

Figure C24

Distribution of application design counts by the top three sectors for the top 15 origins, 2016

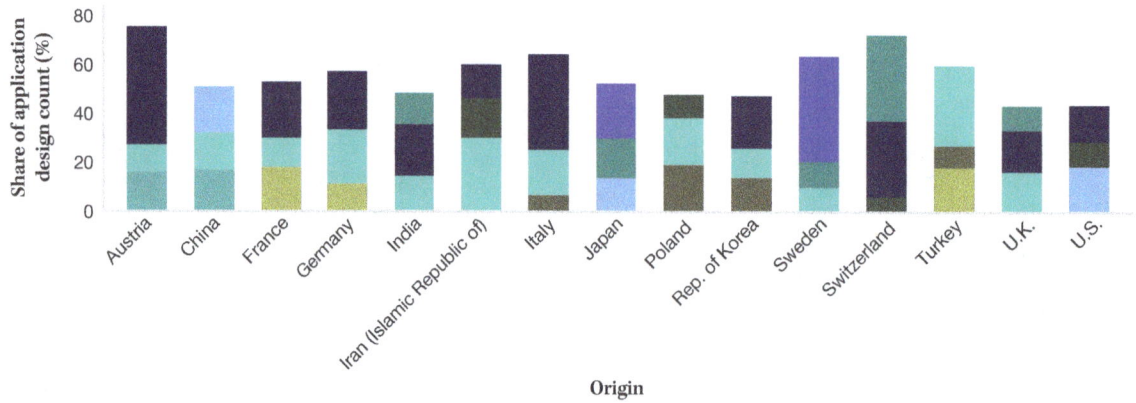

Origin

ADVERTISING | **CONSTRUCTION** | **ELECTRICITY AND LIGHTING** | **FURNITURE AND HOUSEHOLD GOODS**
ICT AND AUDIOVISUAL | **PACKAGING** | **TEXTILES AND ACCESSORIES** | **TOOLS AND MACHINES** | **TRANSPORT**

Note: A concordance table produced by the Organisation for Economic Co-operation and Development (OECD) was used to convert the 32 classes into 12 industry sectors (see Annex D for definitions). The top three sectors and top 15 origins were selected based on their 2016 totals. These figures are based on data from 111 IP offices. Class data were not available or incomplete for the offices of China, Japan and the U.S.

Source: WIPO Statistics Database, September 2017.

INDUSTRIAL DESIGNS

Application design count in relation to GDP and population

Figure C25

Resident application design count per USD 100 billion of GDP for the top 20 origins

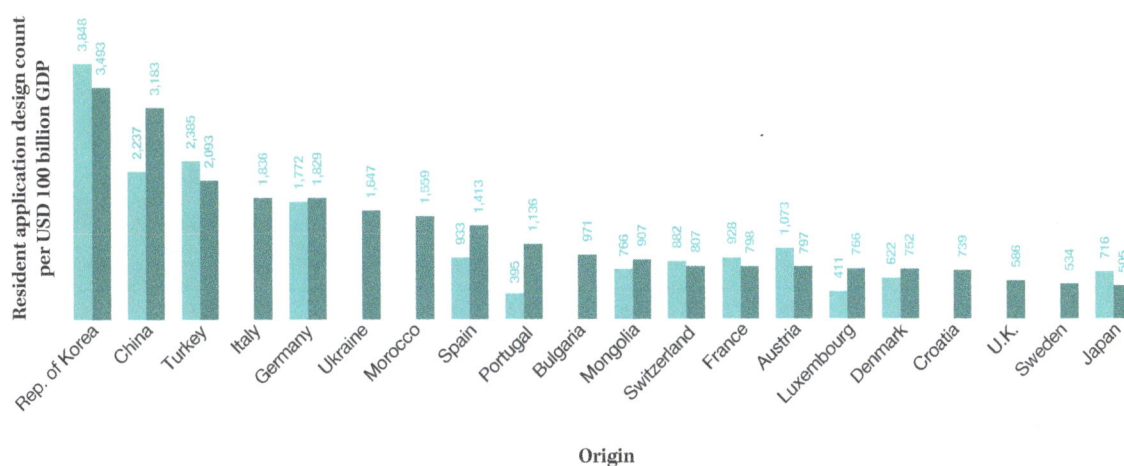

Origin

2006 2016

Note: GDP data are in constant 2011 US PPP dollars. Origins were selected if they had a GDP greater than 25 billion PPP dollars and received resident applications containing more than 100 designs. Due to space constraints, only the top 20 origins that fulfil these criteria are presented.

Sources: WIPO Statistics Database and World Bank, September 2017.

Figure C26

Resident application design count per million population for the top 20 origins

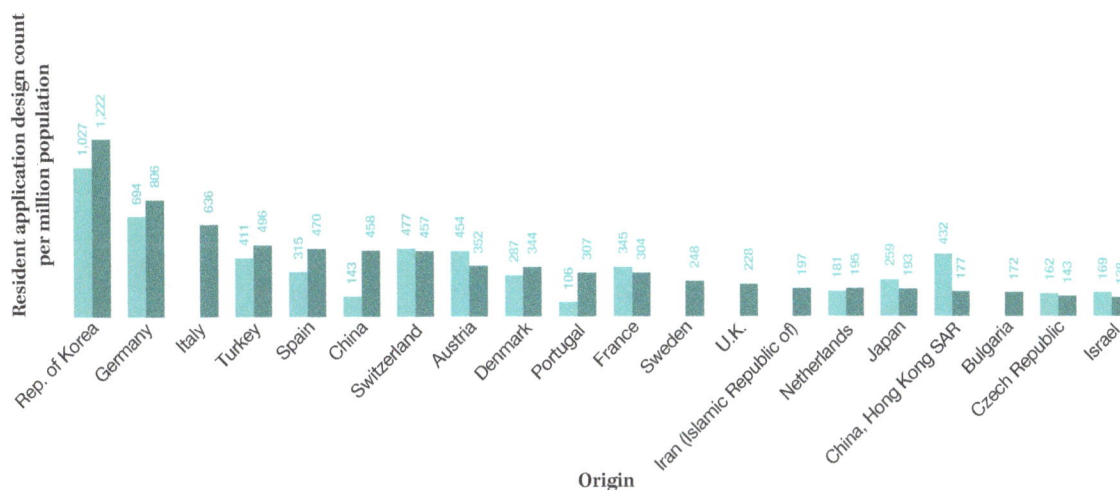

Origin

2006 2016

Note: Origins were selected if they had a population greater than five million and received resident applications containing more than 100 designs. Due to space constraints, only the top 20 origins that fulfil these criteria are presented.

Sources: WIPO Statistics Database and World Bank, September 2017.

Industrial design registrations in force

Figure C27
Trend in industrial design registrations in force worldwide

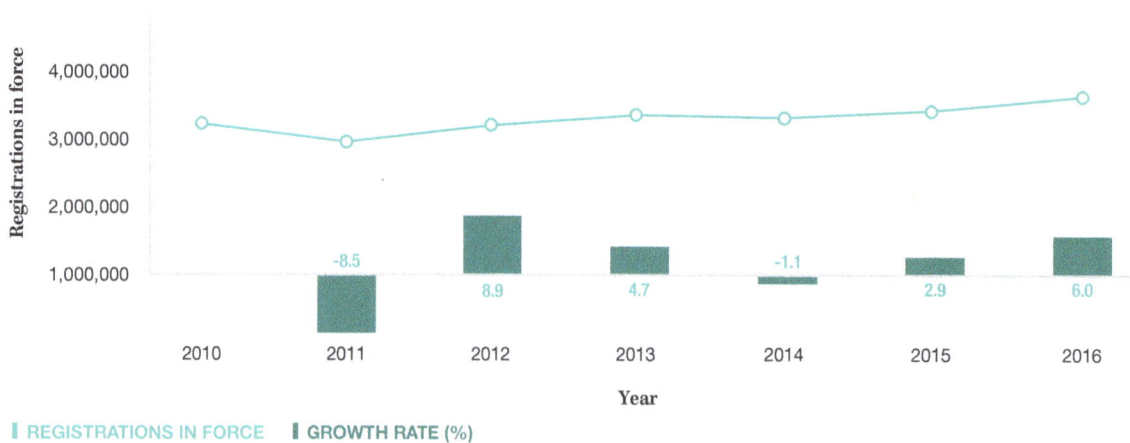

REGISTRATIONS IN FORCE   **GROWTH RATE (%)**

Note: WIPO estimates cover 113 IP offices and include direct national and regional applications as well as designations received via the Hague System. Data refer to the number of industrial design registrations in force and not the number of designs contained in registrations.

Source: WIPO Statistics Database, September 2017.

Figure C28
Industrial design registrations in force for the top 20 offices, 2016

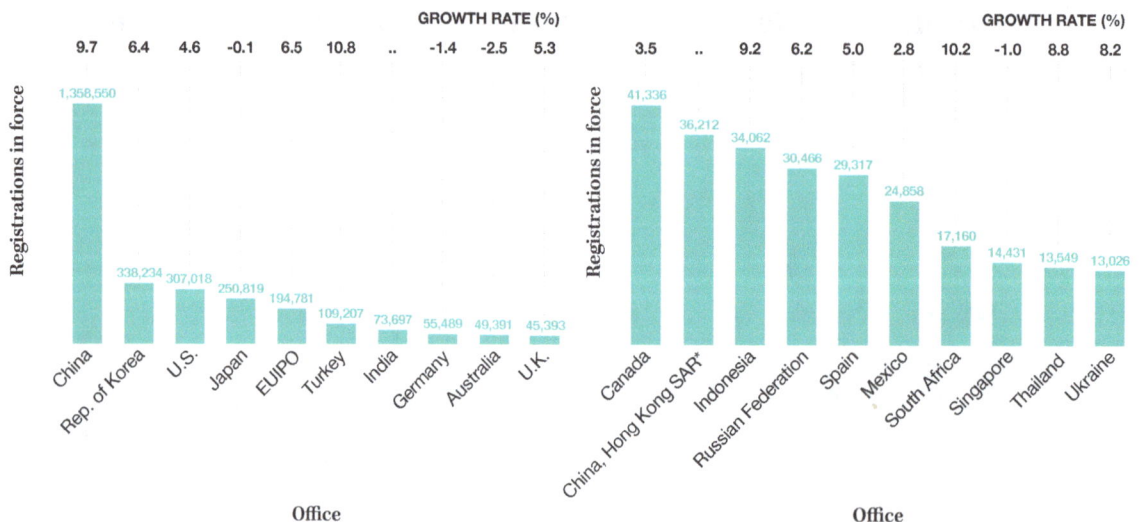

.. indicates not available.

* indicates 2015 data.

Note: EUIPO is the European Union Intellectual Property Office. Data refer to the number of industrial design registrations in force and not the number of designs contained in registrations. Registrations in force data are not available for Brazil, France and Italy.

Source: WIPO Statistics Database, September 2017.

Figure C29
Industrial design registrations in force in 2016 as a percentage of total registrations

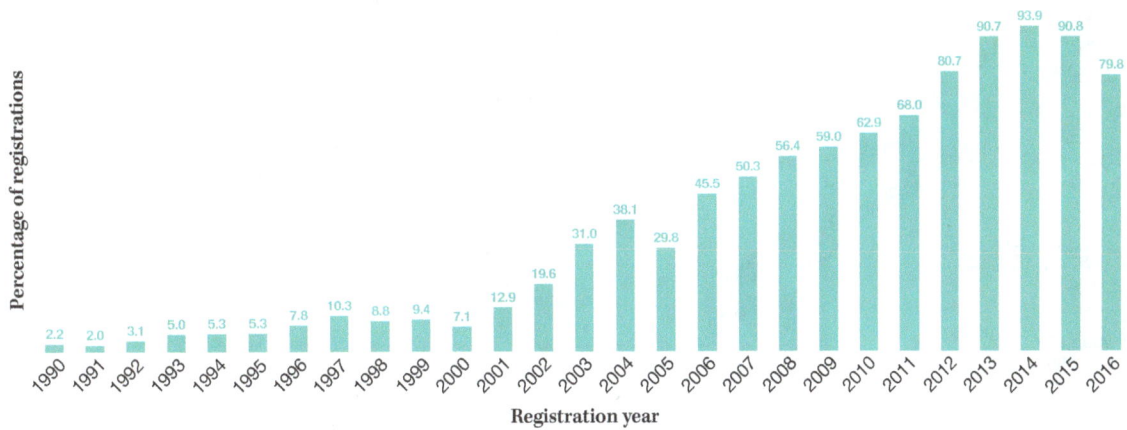

Note: Percentages are calculated using the number of industrial designs registered in year t and in force in 2016 divided by the total number of industrial designs registered in year t. The graph is based on data from 77 offices (including most large offices, with the exception of Brazil, France, Italy and Japan) for which a breakdown of industrial design registrations in force by year of registration was available.

Source: WIPO Statistics Database, September 2017.

Figure C30
Average age of industrial design registrations in force at selected offices

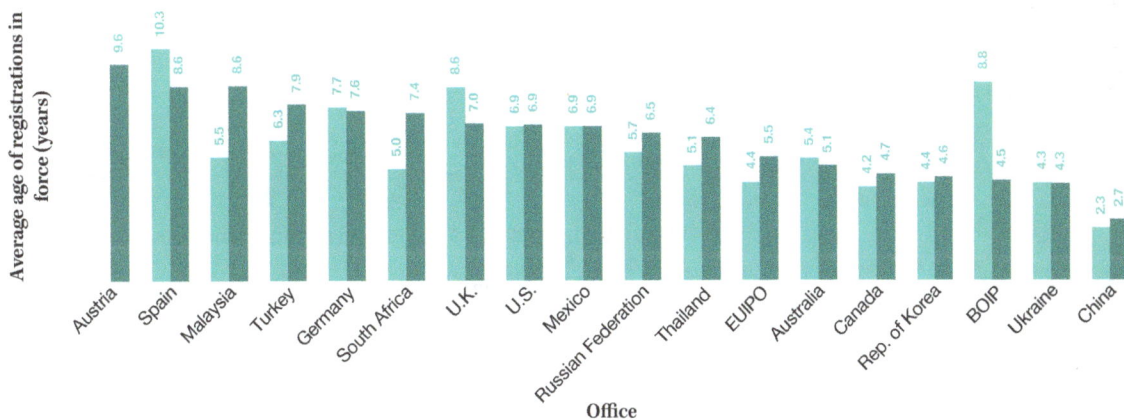

2011 ▮ 2016

Note: BOIP is the Benelux Office of Intellectual Property. EUIPO is the European Union Intellectual Property Office.

Source: WIPO Statistics Database, September 2017.

173

Industrial design applications and registrations through the Hague System

Figure C31
Designs contained in Hague international applications by origin, 2016

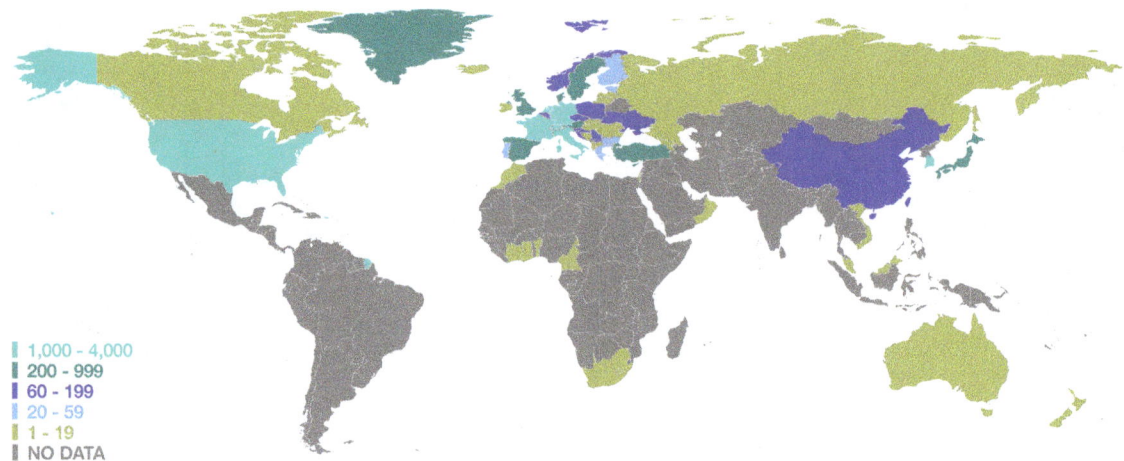

- 1,000 – 4,000
- 200 – 999
- 60 – 199
- 20 – 59
- 1 – 19
- NO DATA

Source: WIPO Statistics Database, September 2017.

Figure C32
Trend in designs contained in Hague international applications

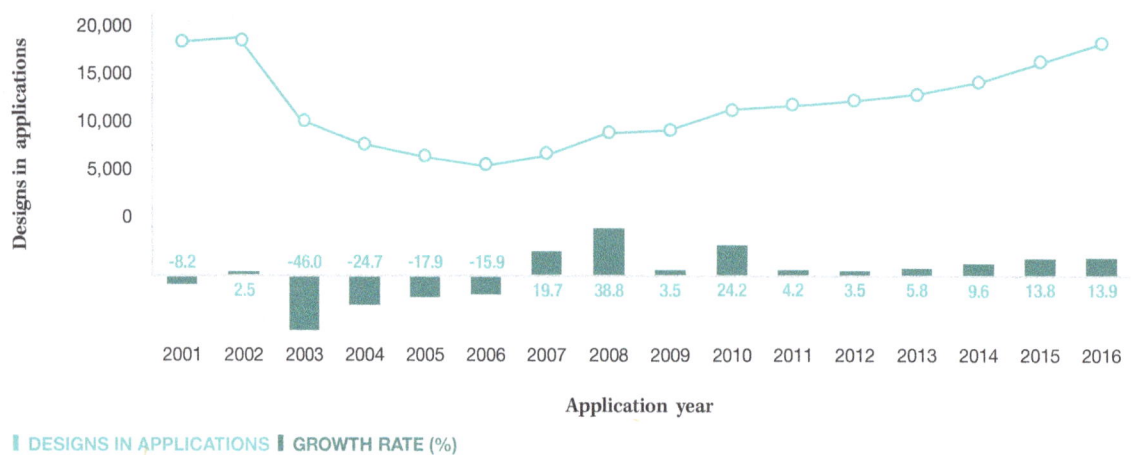

	2001	2002	2003	2004	2005	2006	2007	2008	2009	2010	2011	2012	2013	2014	2015	2016
Growth rate	-8.2	2.5	-46.0	-24.7	-17.9	-15.9	19.7	38.8	3.5	24.2	4.2	3.5	5.8	9.6	13.8	13.9

Application year

Designs in applications

❘ DESIGNS IN APPLICATIONS ❘ GROWTH RATE (%)

Source: WIPO Statistics Database, September 2017.

Figure C33

Designs contained in designations in Hague international applications for the top 20 designated Hague members, 2016

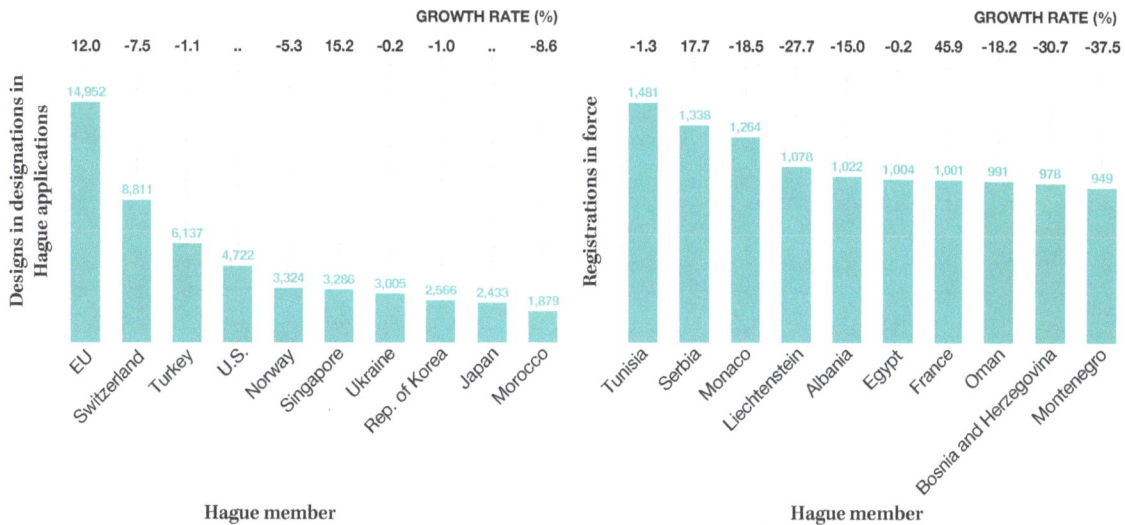

GROWTH RATE (%)

12.0	-7.5	-1.1	..	-5.3	15.2	-0.2	-1.0	..	-8.6

Designs in designations in Hague applications

EU	14,952
Switzerland	8,811
Turkey	6,137
U.S.	4,722
Norway	3,324
Singapore	3,286
Ukraine	3,005
Rep. of Korea	2,566
Japan	2,433
Morocco	1,879

Hague member

GROWTH RATE (%)

-1.3	17.7	-18.5	-27.7	-15.0	-0.2	45.9	-18.2	-30.7	-37.5

Registrations in force

Tunisia	1,481
Serbia	1,338
Monaco	1,264
Liechtenstein	1,078
Albania	1,022
Egypt	1,004
France	1,001
Oman	991
Bosnia and Herzegovina	978
Montenegro	949

Hague member

Note: EU indicates industrial design activity occurring at the European Union Intellectual Property Office (EUIPO) and not within the IP offices of individual EU member states. No growth rate is given for Japan and the U.S. as they are new Hague members and so no historical data are available for comparison.

Source: WIPO Statistics Database, September 2017.

Figure C34

Designs contained in Hague international applications for the top 20 origins, 2016

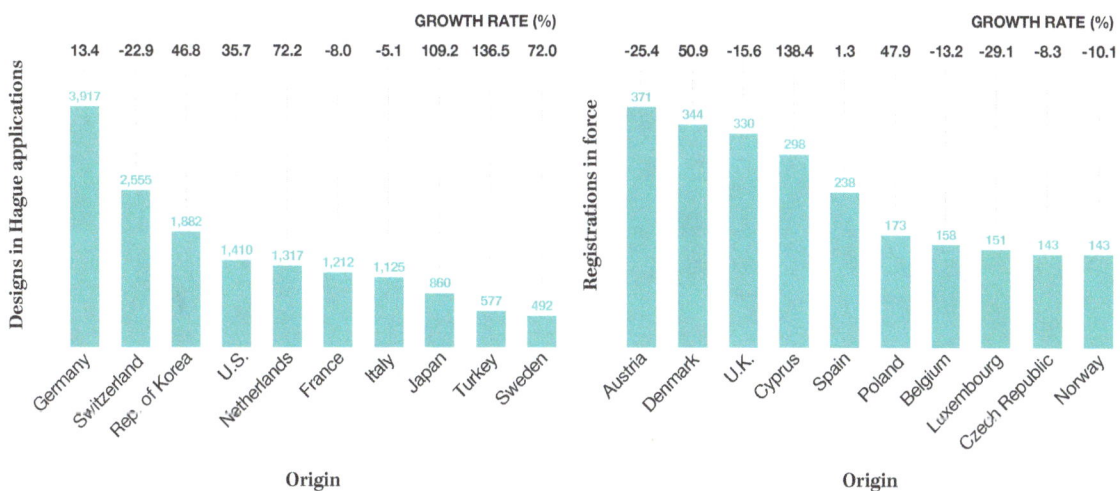

GROWTH RATE (%)

13.4	-22.9	46.8	35.7	72.2	-8.0	-5.1	109.2	136.5	72.0

Designs in Hague applications

Germany	3,917
Switzerland	2,555
Rep. of Korea	1,882
U.S.	1,410
Netherlands	1,317
France	1,212
Italy	1,125
Japan	860
Turkey	577
Sweden	492

Origin

GROWTH RATE (%)

-25.4	50.9	-15.6	138.4	1.3	47.9	-13.2	-29.1	-8.3	-10.1

Registrations in force

Austria	371
Denmark	344
U.K.	330
Cyprus	298
Spain	238
Poland	173
Belgium	158
Luxembourg	151
Czech Republic	143
Norway	143

Origin

Note: Origin is defined as the country of the stated residence of the first named applicant in an international application.

Source: WIPO Statistics Database, September 2017.

INDUSTRIAL DESIGNS

Figure C35

Trend and share of designs contained in non-resident applications by filing route

HAGUE SHARE (%)

| 15.6 | 14.0 | 13.2 | 12.9 | 12.2 | 11.8 | 11.8 | 13.3 | 12.0 | 14.4 | 15.8 |

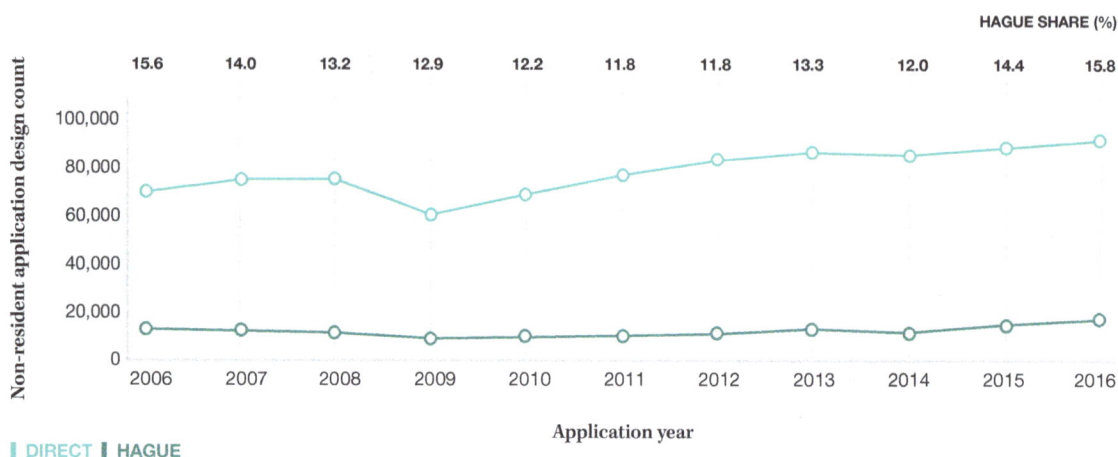

▍ DIRECT ▍ HAGUE

Note: The direct route refers to designs contained in applications filed by non-residents of Hague member origins directly with national or regional IP offices of Hague members. The Hague route refers to designs contained in designations received via the Hague System.

Source: WIPO Statistics Database, September 2017.

Figure C36

Designs contained in non-resident applications by filing route for selected Hague members, 2016

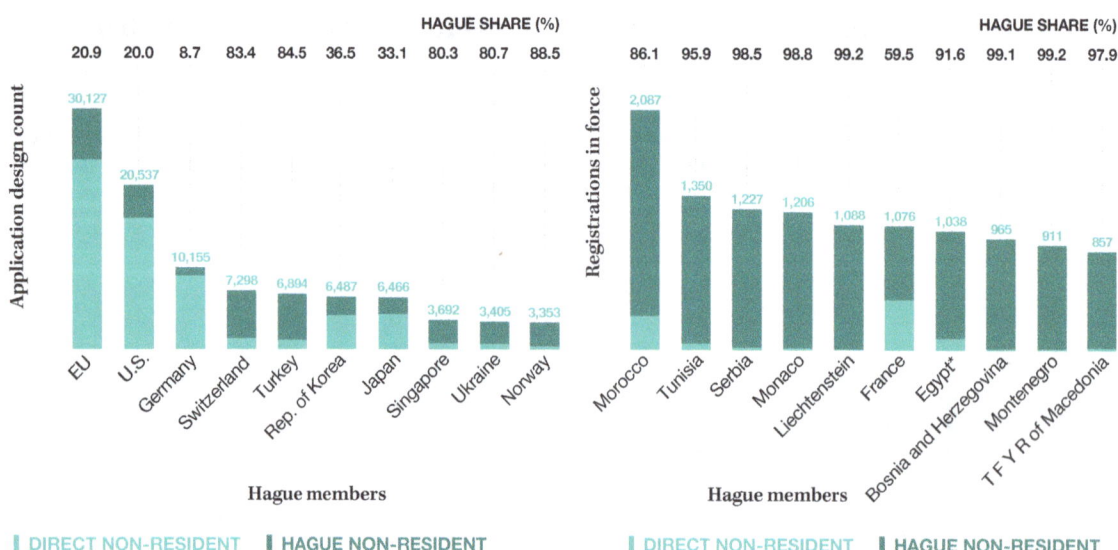

▍ DIRECT NON-RESIDENT ▍ HAGUE NON-RESIDENT

▍ DIRECT NON-RESIDENT ▍ HAGUE NON-RESIDENT

* indicates 2015 data.

Note: EU indicates industrial design activity occurring at the European Union Intellectual Property Office (EUIPO) and not within the IP offices of individual EU member states. The direct route refers to designs contained in applications filed by non-residents of Hague member origins directly with national or regional IP offices of Hague members. The Hague route refers to designs contained in designations received via the Hague System.

Source: WIPO Statistics Database, September 2017.

INDUSTRIAL DESIGNS

Statistical tables

Industrial design applications by office and origin, 2016

Name	Application design count by office			Application design count by origin	Equivalent application design count by origin	Hague international application design count	
	Total	Resident	Non-resident	Total (a)	Total (a)	Origin (e)	Designated Hague member
Afghanistan	..	..	..	1	1	..	n.a.
African Intellectual Property Organization	824	339	485	n.a.	n.a.	n.a.	566
African Regional Intellectual Property Organization	83	16	67	n.a.	n.a.	n.a.	n.a.
Albania (d)	942	1	941	15	69	2	1,022
Algeria	..	..	..	1	1	..	n.a.
Andorra	..	..	..	11	38	..	n.a.
Antigua and Barbuda (b,c)	1	0	1	1	1	..	n.a.
Argentina	1,653	1,115	538	1,154	1,316	..	n.a.
Armenia	438	23	415	34	277	1	485
Australia	7,278	2,739	4,539	4,251	12,000	6	n.a.
Austria	2,140	701	1,439	5,049	69,255	371	n.a.
Azerbaijan	640	22	618	22	22	..	670
Bahamas	..	..	..	22	103	..	n.a.
Bahrain	90	23	67	28	109	..	n.a.
Bangladesh	1,456	1,359	97	1,359	1,359	..	n.a.
Barbados	4	3	1	265	1,750	..	n.a.
Belarus	549	202	347	379	514	..	n.a.
Belgium	n.a.	n.a.	n.a.	1,856	32,544	158	n.a.
Belize	291	0	291	6	168	..	290
Benelux	1,269	946	323	n.a.	n.a.	n.a.	343
Benin (d,f)	n.a.	n.a.	n.a.	7	55	1	54
Bermuda	..	..	..	16	448	..	n.a.
Bolivia (Plurinational State of)	63	40	23	41	41	..	n.a.
Bosnia and Herzegovina	1,108	143	965	145	145	3	978
Botswana (d)	105	..	105	..	..	..	175
Brazil	6,027	3,400	2,627	3,794	8,735	..	n.a.
Brunei Darussalam (d)	108	..	108	..	..	1	155
Bulgaria	925	648	277	1,447	17,069	38	234
Burkina Faso (f)	n.a.	n.a.	n.a.	4	68	..	n.a.
Cambodia (b,c)	69	9	60	23	23	..	n.a.
Cameroon (f)	n.a.	n.a.	n.a.	41	697	2	n.a.
Canada	6,170	916	5,254	2,764	16,669	5	n.a.
Chad (f)	n.a.	n.a.	n.a.	1	17	..	n.a.
Chile	401	89	312	163	244	..	n.a.
China	650,344	631,949	18,395	645,133	791,338	96	n.a.
China, Hong Kong SAR	4,936	1,304	3,632	2,886	24,756	..	n.a.

INDUSTRIAL DESIGNS

Name	Application design count by office			Application design count by origin	Equivalent application design count by origin	Hague international application design count	
	Total	Resident	Non-resident	Total (a)	Total (a)	Origin (e)	Designated Hague member
China, Macao SAR	218	45	173	164	1,433	..	n.a.
Colombia	533	227	306	285	339	..	n.a.
Congo (f)	n.a.	n.a.	n.a.	7	119	..	n.a.
Costa Rica	64	17	47	27	27	..	n.a.
Côte d'Ivoire (d,f)	n.a.	n.a.	n.a.	204	3,452	1	64
Croatia	1,134	573	561	1,014	3,365	64	554
Cuba	8	7	1	7	7	..	n.a.
Cyprus	46	46	0	426	2,694	298	n.a.
Czech Republic	1,098	905	193	2,063	18,317	143	n.a.
Democratic People's Republic of Korea (d)	55	..	55	10	37	..	85
Denmark	405	5	400	3,131	56,186	344	371
Dominican Republic	71	50	21	55	55	..	n.a.
Ecuador	136	71	65	71	71	..	n.a.
Egypt (b,c)	2,663	1,625	1,038	1,627	1,670	..	1,004
El Salvador	40	17	23	18	18	..	n.a.
Estonia	291	58	233	306	3,413	26	284
European Union Intellectual Property Office	104,522	74,395	30,127	n.a.	n.a.	n.a.	14,952
Finland (b,c)	450	310	140	1,912	25,915	42	276
France	14,751	13,675	1,076	31,568	213,873	1,212	1,001
Gabon (d,f)	n.a.	n.a.	n.a.	..	..	..	51
Georgia	655	120	535	160	214	2	604
Germany	56,188	46,033	10,155	80,169	636,395	3,917	862
Ghana	569	453	116	455	482	1	161
Greece	1,113	912	201	1,239	8,718	21	267
Guatemala	392	205	187	216	216	..	n.a.
Guinea (f)	n.a.	n.a.	n.a.	34	578	..	n.a.
Guinea-Bissau (f)	n.a.	n.a.	n.a.	7	119	..	n.a.
Honduras	37	15	22	15	15	..	n.a.
Hungary	994	856	138	1,195	7,183	3	145
Iceland	314	49	265	56	137	1	315
India	10,673	6,753	3,920	7,051	7,882	..	n.a.
Indonesia	3,893	2,581	1,312	2,609	2,700	..	n.a.
Iran (Islamic Republic of)	15,979	15,811	168	15,838	15,838	..	n.a.
Iraq	..	..	..	13	310	..	n.a.
Ireland	181	122	59	470	5,816	4	n.a.
Israel	1,865	1,181	684	2,050	10,312	8	n.a.
Italy	27,088	26,698	390	45,854	364,944	1,125	220
Jamaica	183	178	5	181	181	..	n.a.
Japan	31,013	24,547	6,466	41,126	119,141	860	2,433

Name	Application design count by office			Application design count by origin	Equivalent application design count by origin	Hague international application design count	
	Total	Resident	Non-resident	Total (a)	Total (a)	Origin (e)	Designated Hague member
Jordan	101	53	48	59	59	..	n.a.
Kazakhstan	239	89	150	89	89	..	n.a.
Kenya	104	89	15	89	89	..	n.a.
Kuwait	..	..	..	6	6	..	n.a.
Kyrgyzstan	461	17	444	17	17	..	438
Latvia	242	176	66	372	1,592	3	129
Lebanon	..	..	..	5	48	..	n.a.
Lesotho	..	..	..	2	2	..	n.a.
Liberia	..	..	..	2	2	..	n.a.
Liechtenstein	1,239	151	1,088	445	3,685	61	1,078
Lithuania	423	56	367	221	3,450	9	395
Luxembourg	n.a.	n.a.	n.a.	1,098	11,964	151	n.a.
Madagascar	170	166	4	166	166	..	n.a.
Malaysia	1,427	701	726	906	1,149	1	n.a.
Mali (d,f)	n.a.	n.a.	n.a.	20	228	..	42
Malta	..	..	..	185	4,397	3	n.a.
Marshall Islands	..	..	..	10	172	..	n.a.
Mauritania (f)	n.a.	n.a.	n.a.	1	1	..	n.a.
Mauritius	..	..	..	16	151	..	n.a.
Mexico	4,296	1,651	2,645	1,837	2,377	..	n.a.
Monaco	1,218	12	1,206	108	1,863	30	1,264
Mongolia	823	311	512	311	311	..	564
Montenegro	919	8	911	8	8	..	949
Morocco	6,143	4,056	2,087	4,271	4,417	15	1,879
Mozambique	32	29	3	30	30	..	n.a.
Namibia (d)	118	..	118	1	1	..	199
Nepal	34	11	23	15	15	..	n.a.
Netherlands	n.a.	n.a.	n.a.	5,473	78,806	1,317	n.a.
New Zealand	1,358	358	1,000	908	4,634	3	n.a.
Niger (d,f)	n.a.	n.a.	n.a.	1	17	..	40
Nigeria	..	..	..	7	34	..	n.a.
Norway	3,931	578	3,353	1,116	7,812	143	3,324
Oman (d)	903	1	902	7	34	1	991
Pakistan	555	435	120	447	636	..	n.a.
Panama	52	9	43	59	194	..	n.a.
Papua New Guinea (b,c)	39	3	36	10	10	..	n.a.
Paraguay	..	..	..	13	67	..	n.a.
Peru	303	102	201	102	102	..	n.a.
Philippines	1,569	1,043	526	1,072	1,477	..	n.a.

INDUSTRIAL DESIGNS

Name	Application design count by office			Application design count by origin	Equivalent application design count by origin	Hague international application design count	
	Total	Resident	Non-resident	Total (a)	Total (a)	Origin (e)	Designated Hague member
Poland (d)	138	..	138	5,178	130,123	173	217
Portugal	2,291	2,096	195	3,219	32,163	35	n.a.
Qatar	..	..	..	54	810	..	n.a.
Republic of Korea	69,120	62,633	6,487	72,931	133,598	1,882	2,566
Republic of Moldova	902	351	551	366	447	7	500
Romania	1,337	624	713	979	9,729	8	593
Russian Federation	6,565	2,912	3,653	3,647	5,564	5	n.a.
Rwanda (b,c)	69	5	64	5	5	..	149
Saint Vincent and the Grenadines	..	..	..	22	616	..	n.a.
Samoa	2	2	0	5	5	..	n.a.
San Marino	14	1	13	58	274	..	n.a.
Sao Tome and Principe (d)	88	..	88	..	..	..	138
Saudi Arabia	937	386	551	474	501	..	n.a.
Senegal (d,f)	n.a.	n.a.	n.a.	21	357	..	60
Serbia	1,400	173	1,227	463	1,239	76	1,338
Seychelles	..	..	..	1	1	..	n.a.
Singapore	4,337	645	3,692	1,232	5,649	22	3,286
Slovakia	482	258	224	461	3,836	12	n.a.
Slovenia (d)	540	12	528	482	6,129	85	596
South Africa	2,194	1,087	1,107	1,291	3,100	1	n.a.
Spain	18,315	17,562	753	23,148	138,550	238	315
Sri Lanka	382	237	145	255	309	..	n.a.
Sudan	381	348	33	348	348	..	n.a.
Suriname (d)	38	..	38	5	115	..	57
Swaziland	..	..	..	10	10	..	n.a.
Sweden	750	689	61	7,402	55,165	492	n.a.
Switzerland	11,125	3,827	7,298	24,188	146,329	2,555	8,811
Syrian Arab Republic (c)	211	..	..	276	276	..	171
T F Y R of Macedonia	938	81	857	86	167	3	881
Tajikistan (b,c)	131	0	131	..	..	..	185
Thailand	4,857	3,759	1,098	3,944	5,294	..	n.a.
Togo (f)	n.a.	n.a.	n.a.	3	51	..	n.a.
Trinidad and Tobago	110	70	40	71	71	..	n.a.
Tunisia	1,509	159	1,350	170	353	..	1,481
Turkey	46,305	39,411	6,894	42,082	59,219	577	6,137
Turkmenistan (d)	73	..	73	..	..	..	n.a.
Ukraine	8,793	5,388	3,405	5,996	13,377	97	3,005
United Arab Emirates (d)	3,978	..	..	110	758	..	n.a.
United Kingdom	10,030	8,738	1,292	18,911	186,905	330	n.a.
United States of America	44,967	24,430	20,537	55,213	320,395	1,410	4,722
Uruguay (b,c)	57	8	49	10	10	..	n.a.
Uzbekistan	467	358	109	359	359	..	n.a.

Name	Application design count by office			Application design count by origin	Equivalent application design count by origin	Hague international application design count	
	Total	Resident	Non-resident	Total (a)	Total (a)	Origin (e)	Designated Hague member
Venezuela (Bolivarian Republic of)	..	..	..	14	122	..	n.a.
Viet Nam	3,394	2,060	1,334	2,243	2,567	15	n.a.
Yemen	46	28	18	30	30	..	n.a.
Others/Unknown	..	..	..	28,289	56,511	200	n.a.
Total (g)	1,240,600	1,056,500	184,100	1,240,600	n.a.	18,716	75,121

a. Design count by origin is incomplete, as some offices do not report the origin of applications.

b. 2015 data are reported for application design count by office.

c. 2015 data are reported for application design count by origin.

d. Only Hague designation data are available and/or the office has not reported the origin of applications, so design count by office and origin data may be incomplete.

e. Origin is defined as the country of the stated address of residence of the applicant in an international application.

f. The African Intellectual Property Organization (OAPI) is the competent office for processing applications.

g. Totals are estimated for application design counts by office and origin.

n.a. indicates not applicable

.. indicates not available

Source: WIPO Statistics Database, September 2017.

Figure C38
Industrial design registrations by office and origin, and industrial designs in force, 2016

Name	Registration design count by office			Registration design count by origin	Equivalent registration design count by origin	Hague international registration design count	In force by office
	Total	Resident	Non-resident	Total (a)	Total (a)	Origin (e)	Total
Afghanistan	..	..	..	3	3	..	..
African Intellectual Property Organization	816	333	483	n.a.	n.a.	n.a.	..
African Regional Intellectual Property Organization	119	13	106	n.a.	n.a.	n.a.	749
Albania (d)	942	1	941	12	39	1	24
Algeria	..	..	..	..	..	..	1,474
Andorra	..	..	..	18	45	..	..
Antigua and Barbuda	..	..	..	1	1	..	..
Argentina	1,476	1,014	462	1,049	1,211	..	..
Armenia	412	23	389	33	276	1	54
Australia	6,668	2,438	4,230	3,616	10,517	3	49,391
Austria	2,174	685	1,489	5,211	66,665	389	9,680
Azerbaijan	646	36	610	36	36	..	312
Bahamas	..	..	..	29	110	..	..
Bahrain	91	21	70	25	106	..	234
Bangladesh	804	721	83	721	721	..	..

INDUSTRIAL DESIGNS

Name	Registration design count by office			Registration design count by origin	Equivalent registration design count by origin	Hague international registration design count	In force by office
	Total	Resident	Non-resident	Total (a)	Total (a)	Origin (e)	Total
Barbados	1	1	0	177	1,581	..	..
Belarus	375	172	203	265	400	..	1,494
Belgium	n.a.	n.a.	n.a.	1,819	30,626	129	n.a.
Belize	290	0	290	12	39	..	..
Benelux	1,203	861	342	n.a.	n.a.	n.a.	5,172
Benin (d,f)	n.a.	n.a.	n.a.	7	55	4	..
Bermuda	..	..	..	19	532	..	..
Bolivia (Plurinational State of)	45	9	36	10	10	..	242
Bosnia and Herzegovina	1,004	41	963	42	42	1	389
Botswana (d)	105	..	105	..	..	..	73
Brazil	6,972	3,446	3,526	3,851	8,225	..	..
Brunei Darussalam (d)	108	..	108	..	..	..	..
Bulgaria	681	326	355	1,072	15,074	41	2,306
Burkina Faso (f)	n.a.	n.a.	n.a.	3	51	..	..
Cambodia (b,c)	99	31	68	32	32	..	..
Cameroon (f)	n.a.	n.a.	n.a.	26	442	..	..
Canada	5,703	801	4,902	2,111	14,666	3	41,336
Chad (f)	n.a.	n.a.	n.a.	1	17	..	..
Chile	412	38	374	78	159	..	2,955
China	446,135	429,710	16,425	440,170	578,568	103	1,358,550
China, Hong Kong SAR	4,432	1,078	3,354	2,358	21,852	..	..
China, Macao SAR	79	6	73	93	876	..	873
Colombia	490	196	294	236	290	..	3,885
Congo (f)	n.a.	n.a.	n.a.	1	17	..	..
Costa Rica	27	3	24	4	4	..	623
Côte d'Ivoire (d,f)	n.a.	n.a.	n.a.	222	3,598	..	..
Croatia	1,026	459	567	880	3,231	53	4,780
Cuba	10	9	1	9	9	..	48
Cyprus	46	46	0	367	2,689	153	62
Czech Republic	1,072	999	73	1,928	17,156	190	3,253
Democratic People's Republic of Korea (d)	55	..	55	8	35	..	..
Democratic Republic of the Congo	..	..	..	7	7	..	..
Denmark	540	143	397	3,078	55,944	361	2,149
Dominican Republic	75	55	20	55	55	..	..
Ecuador	187	76	111	79	79	..	..
Egypt (b,c)	1,627	646	981	651	678	..	..
El Salvador	19	3	16	3	3	..	572
Estonia	297	56	241	255	3,441	24	1,373
European Union Intellectual Property Office	101,817	71,997	29,820	n.a.	n.a.	n.a.	194,781
Finland (b,c)	292	190	102	1,856	23,861	57	2,246

| Name | Registration design count by office | | | Registration design count by origin | Equivalent registration design count by origin | Hague international registration design count | In force by office |
	Total	Resident	Non-resident	Total (a)	Total (a)	Origin (e)	Total
France (d)	994	354	640	17,184	195,952	1,157	..
Gabon (d,f)	n.a.	n.a.	n.a.	1	17	..	..
Georgia	702	161	541	172	226	2	275
Germany	50,020	41,641	8,379	73,181	614,530	3,559	55,489
Ghana (d)	116	..	116	4	31	1	1,594
Greece	1,240	1,018	222	1,296	7,398	22	1,455
Guatemala	207	0	207	5	5	..	428
Guinea (f)	n.a.	n.a.	n.a.	35	595	..	..
Guinea-Bissau (f)	n.a.	n.a.	n.a.	5	85	..	..
Honduras (e)	22	7	15	12	12	..	266
Hungary	335	183	152	535	7,117	16	3,938
Iceland	309	44	265	49	103	1	932
India	7,331	4,901	2,430	5,176	5,931	..	73,697
Indonesia	2,831	1,552	1,279	1,654	1,745	..	34,062
Iran (Islamic Republic of)	5,126	5,091	35	5,103	5,103	..	..
Iraq (e)	..	..	..	2	2	..	29
Ireland	116	72	44	389	5,438	5	1,134
Israel	1,388	883	505	1,566	9,342	6	..
Italy	31,956	31,706	250	48,651	364,308	1,163	..
Jamaica	120	116	4	116	116	..	4,513
Japan	26,813	21,246	5,567	36,730	113,185	786	250,819
Jordan	92	44	48	46	46	..	1,920
Kazakhstan	182	72	110	79	79	..	182
Kenya	163	38	125	41	41	..	..
Kuwait	..	..	..	4	4	..	..
Kyrgyzstan	473	20	453	21	21	..	135
Latvia	231	165	66	314	1,858	3	396
Lebanon	..	..	..	4	31	..	..
Liechtenstein (d,e)	1,091	12	1,079	319	3,127	40	85
Lithuania	387	70	317	218	3,285	16	296
Luxembourg	n.a.	n.a.	n.a.	996	13,451	181	n.a.
Madagascar	185	185	0	185	185	..	1,496
Malawi	..	..	..	..	..	..	251
Malaysia	1,900	648	1,252	844	1,060	1	24,299
Maldives	..	..	..	1	1	..	..
Mali (d,f)	n.a.	n.a.	n.a.	27	411	..	..
Malta	..	..	..	153	3,852	3	62
Marshall Islands	..	..	..	13	175	..	..
Mauritius	..	..	..	24	175	..	..
Mexico	2,547	818	1,729	943	1,402	..	24,858

INDUSTRIAL DESIGNS

INDUSTRIAL DESIGNS

Name	Registration design count by office			Registration design count by origin	Equivalent registration design count by origin	Hague international registration design count	In force by office
	Total	Resident	Non-resident	Total (a)	Total (a)	Origin (e)	Total
Monaco	1,220	10	1,210	113	2,651	2	379
Mongolia	641	130	511	130	130	..	2,575
Montenegro	947	9	938	9	9	..	129
Morocco	6,075	3,990	2,085	4,201	4,299	15	..
Mozambique	26	23	3	23	23	..	667
Namibia (d)	118	..	118	2	2	..	..
Nepal (e)	21	10	11	10	10	..	10
Netherlands	n.a.	n.a.	n.a.	4,984	73,071	1,342	n.a.
New Zealand	1,181	249	932	689	3,686	3	10,753
Niger (d,f)	n.a.	n.a.	n.a.	1	17		..
Nigeria	..	..	..	12	12	..	..
Norway	3,874	557	3,317	1,110	7,671	152	9,557
Oman (d)	903	1	902	4	31	1	..
Pakistan	391	272	119	280	388	..	6,103
Panama	1	1	0	38	173	..	599
Papua New Guinea (b,c,e)	28	1	27	5	5	..	4
Paraguay	..	..	..	4	58	..	..
Peru	168	40	128	40	40	..	2,714
Philippines	1,721	853	868	887	1,157	..	..
Poland (d,e)	132	..	132	4,778	121,272	117	10,516
Portugal	2,032	1,917	115	3,022	31,264	41	4,455
Qatar	..	..	..	31	787	..	..
Republic of Korea	55,736	50,263	5,473	61,073	120,626	1,903	338,234
Republic of Moldova	1,427	897	530	902	983	1	3,339
Romania	1,660	961	699	1,263	9,014	12	3,902
Russian Federation	5,476	2,340	3,136	2,773	4,474	5	30,466
Rwanda (b,c,e)	69	5	64	5	5	..	140
Saint Vincent and the Grenadines	..	..	..	14	392	..	..
Samoa (b,c)	1	1	0	5	5	..	11
San Marino	16	0	16	21	453	..	82
Sao Tome and Principe (d)	88	..	88	..	..	..	..
Saudi Arabia	794	337	457	411	438	..	3,781
Senegal (d,f)	n.a.	n.a.	n.a.	19	323	..	..
Serbia	1,376	119	1,257	411	1,160	35	3,801
Seychelles	..	..	..	24	24	..	..
Singapore	4,376	688	3,688	1,202	5,052	21	14,431
Slovakia	353	261	92	422	3,176	4	834
Slovenia (d)	540	12	528	426	5,938	59	..
Solomon Islands	..	..	..	1	1	..	..
South Africa	1,130	411	719	591	2,389	1	17,160

| Name | Registration design count by office | | | Registration design count by origin | Equivalent registration design count by origin | Hague international registration design count | In force by office |
	Total	Resident	Non-resident	Total (a)	Total (a)	Origin (e)	Total
Spain	17,946	17,198	748	21,958	123,304	293	29,317
Sri Lanka	341	272	69	276	276	..	1,296
Sudan	381	348	33	348	348	..	381
Suriname (d)	38	..	38	5	115	..	..
Swaziland	..	..	..	4	4	..	..
Sweden	617	594	23	5,619	54,570	464	5,268
Switzerland	10,804	3,647	7,157	24,336	167,971	2,433	..
Syrian Arab Republic (c)	318	..	..	142	142	..	4,455
T F Y R of Macedonia	893	43	850	48	129	1	2,376
Tajikistan (b,c,e)	135	0	135	..	..	..	48
Thailand	3,755	2,306	1,449	2,438	3,464	..	13,549
Togo (f)	n.a.	n.a.	n.a.	2	34	..	..
Trinidad and Tobago	139	75	64	77	77	..	..
Tunisia	1,507	159	1,348	164	196	..	..
Turkey	48,687	41,508	7,179	44,054	62,072	508	109,207
Turkmenistan (d)	72	..	72	..	..	..	..
Ukraine	8,546	5,196	3,350	5,730	12,949	88	13,026
United Arab Emirates (d)	2,707	..	..	83	785	..	1,736
United Kingdom	8,481	7,577	904	17,174	176,946	289	45,393
United Republic of Tanzania	..	..	..	3	3	..	..
United States of America	31,395	16,235	15,160	45,572	300,407	1,312	307,018
Uruguay (b,c,e)	47	5	42	6	6	..	659
Uzbekistan	131	117	14	117	117	..	514
Venezuela (Bolivarian Republic of)	..	..	..	14	122	..	..
Viet Nam	1,659	988	671	1,088	1,142	15	9,865
Yemen	10	5	5	7	7	..	33
Others/Unknown	..	..	..	27,055	54,710	9	..
Total (g)	**974,000**	**806,100**	**167,900**	**974,000**	**n.a.**	**17,601**	**3,624,700**

a. Design count by origin is incomplete, as some offices do not report the origin of registrations.

b. 2015 data are reported for registration design counts by office.

c. 2015 data are reported for registration design counts by origin.

d. Only Hague designation data are available and/or the office has not reported the origin of registrations, so design count by office and origin data may be incomplete.

e. Origin is defined as the country of the stated address of residence of the holder in an international registration.

f. The African Intellectual Property Organization (OAPI) is the competent office for registering applications.

g. Totals are estimated for registration design counts by office and origin, and for total registrations in force data.

n.a. indicates not applicable

.. indicates not available

Source: WIPO Statistics Database, September 2017.

INDUSTRIAL DESIGNS

Plant varieties

Highlights

Plant variety applications grew at their fastest rate in 15 years

Around 16,510 plant variety applications were filed worldwide in 2016, up 8.3% on 2015 – the largest increase in applications in 15 years (figure 21). The offices of China, the Republic of Korea, Ukraine and the Community Plant Variety Office (CPVO) of the European Union (EU) accounted for most of this growth.

Figure 21
Plant variety applications worldwide

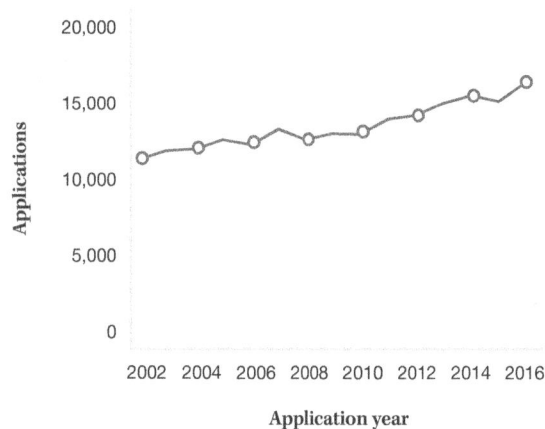

Source: Standard figure D1.

Offices with the most plant variety filings

The CPVO remained the top filing office in 2016, receiving 3,299 applications. China was second with 2,923, followed by the United States of America (U.S.; 1,604), Ukraine (1,274) and Japan (977) (figure 22).[1] Among these top five offices, China (+24.8%), the CPVO (+6.0%), Japan (+6.9%) and Ukraine (+18.5%) experienced growth, while the U.S. (-1.8%) was the only top-five office to experience a decline. Growth in China and at the CPVO was driven by resident filings, whereas a large increase in non-resident filings drove growth in Ukraine. The decline in filings in the U.S. was caused by a decrease in resident filings which outweighed a year-on-year increase in non-resident filings.

The combined share of applications received at the top five offices worldwide increased marginally, from around 60% in 2015 to 61% in 2016, due to the growth experienced by China and Ukraine.

Eight of the top 10 offices received more applications from residents than from non-residents. Among these offices, China's resident share (91.9%) was the highest. In contrast, Australia and Ukraine received more than half their filings from non-resident applicants.

Offices of high-income economies accounted for the largest proportion (57.5%) of plant variety applications received in 2016, but this was down from 73.6% a decade earlier in 2006 (figure 23). Offices in the upper middle-income group, however, saw their combined share increase from 19.6% in 2006 to 31.9% in 2016, mostly driven by the increase in filings in China. The share held by the lower middle-income group likewise increased, from 6.8% in 2006 to 10.6% in 2016.

Figure 22
Plant variety applications for the top 10 offices, 2016

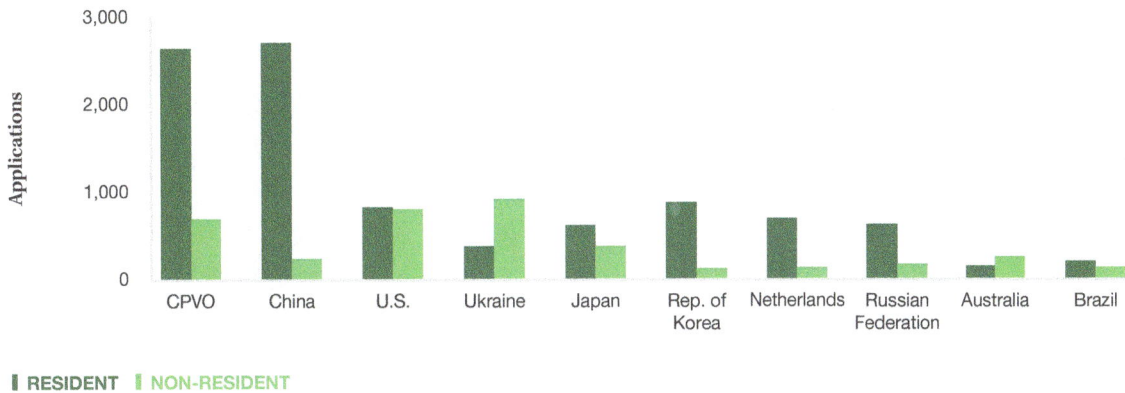

▮ RESIDENT ▮ NON-RESIDENT

Source: Standard figure D5.

Figure 23
Plant variety applications by income group

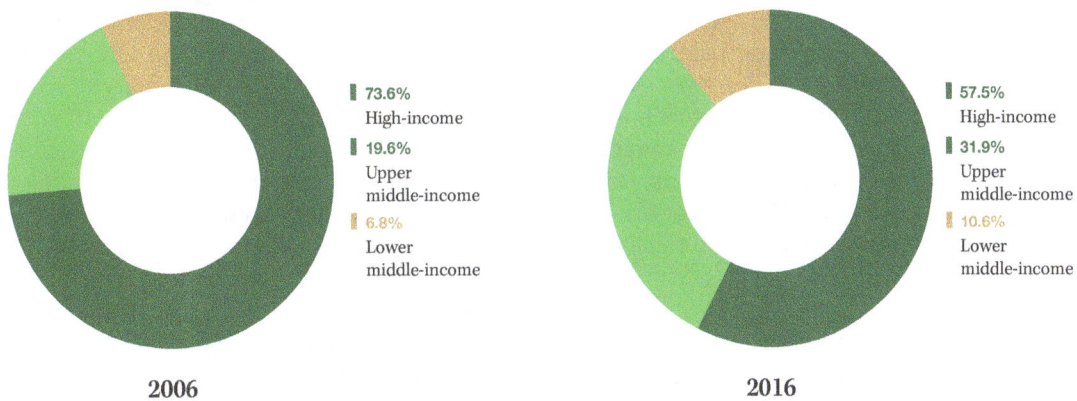

▮ 73.6%
High-income

▮ 19.6%
Upper
middle-income

▮ 6.8%
Lower
middle-income

2006

▮ 57.5%
High-income

▮ 31.9%
Upper
middle-income

▮ 10.6%
Lower
middle-income

2016

Source: Standard figure D3.

Offices in Europe received 42.1% of all plant variety applications in 2016, somewhat less than their share a decade earlier (46.6%) (figure 24). Asia saw its share increase from 22.9% in 2006 to 32.6% in 2016 at the expense of a drop of 4.6 percentage points in North America. Shares for Latin America and the Caribbean (LAC; 7.7%), Africa (3.1%) and Oceania (3.1%) were largely unchanged.

PLANT VARIETIES

Figure 24
Plant variety applications by region

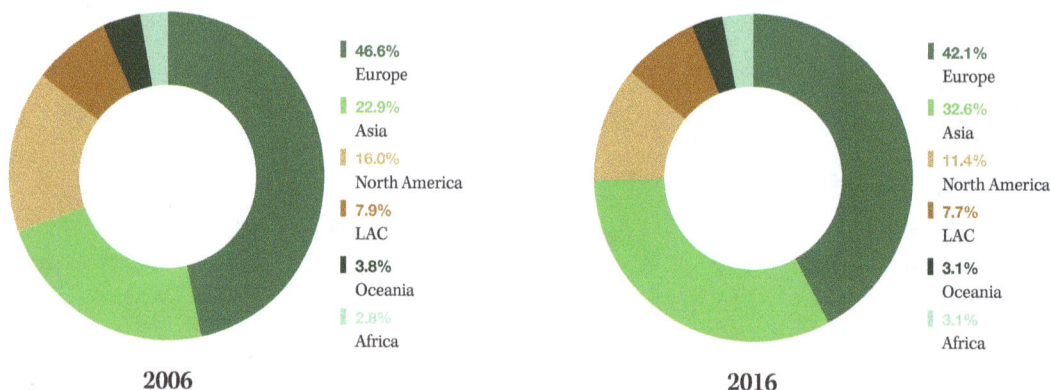

	2006
46.6%	Europe
22.9%	Asia
16.0%	North America
7.9%	LAC
3.8%	Oceania
2.8%	Africa

	2016
42.1%	Europe
32.6%	Asia
11.4%	North America
7.7%	LAC
3.1%	Oceania
3.1%	Africa

2006   **2016**

Source: Standard figure D4.

Applicants from the Netherlands filed the most worldwide

Applications received by offices from resident and non-resident applicants are referred to as office data, whereas applications filed by applicants at a national/regional office (resident applications) or at a foreign office (applications abroad) are referred to as origin data. Here, plant variety statistics based on the origin of residence are reported in order to complement the picture of activity worldwide. Note that for applicants domiciled in EU member states, filing at the CPVO regional office is also regarded as a resident filing.

Applicants from the Netherlands remained the most active applicants in the world in 2016, filing 3,129 plant variety applications at various offices.

They were followed by applicants from China, who filed 2,720 applications. The U.S. (2,035), France (1,050) and Germany (934) were the third, fourth and fifth largest origins, respectively. Among the top five origins, China (+29.5%) and the Netherlands (+15%) experienced the largest annual growth in filings. France (+1.2%) and the U.S. (+0.4%) also saw modest growth, while Germany declined slightly by 0.8%.

While applicants from four of the top five origins filed most of their applications abroad or at the regional office, only those from China filed almost exclusively at home. Similarly, applicants from Japan, the Republic of Korea, the Russian Federation and Ukraine also filed predominantly at their home offices, reflecting lower interest in seeking protection internationally.

PLANT VARIETIES

Equivalent count

Origin data are compiled using two different counting methods – absolute counts and equivalent counts. The difference between the two lies in the treatment of regional office (CPVO) data. For absolute counts, an application received by the CPVO is counted only once. For the equivalent count, a single application filed at the CPVO is equivalent to multiple applications. To calculate the number of equivalent applications at the CPVO in 2016, each application has been multiplied by the corresponding number of member states. If the applicant resided in one of the 28 EU member states, the application was counted as one resident filing and 27 filings abroad. If the applicant did not reside in an EU member state, the application was counted as 28 filings abroad.

Equivalent counts take multiple members of the regional office into account. One would expect to see those country origins whose applicants filed intensively at the CVPO move up the ranking when this counting method is applied. Not surprisingly, European countries and the U.S. topped the list of origins based on equivalent counts. Applicants from the Netherlands remained number one, with 37,716 equivalent applications filed worldwide. They were followed by applicants from France (13,659), Germany (11,599) and the U.S. (10,463). China (3,000) was the only other non-European country among the top 10 origins despite the fact that only 10% of its applicants' filings were equivalent filings abroad. This is in marked contrast to the Netherlands, for which the share was 95%.

Map 4
Equivalent plant variety applications by origin, 2016

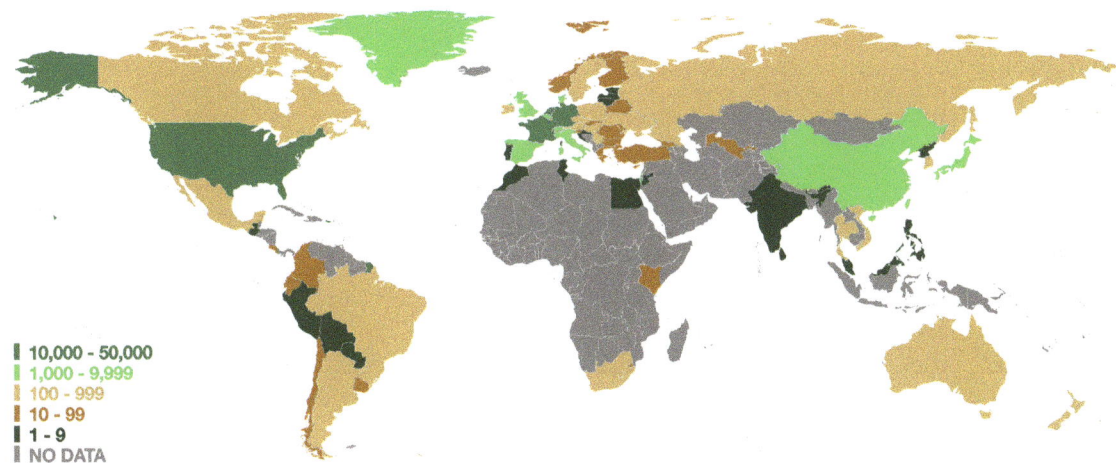

- 10,000 - 50,000
- 1,000 - 9,999
- 100 - 999
- 10 - 99
- 1 - 9
- NO DATA

Source: Standard figure D9.

PLANT VARIETIES

The number of titles issued increased for the fourth consecutive year

The total number of plant variety titles issued rose by 5.2% in 2016 to reach 13,280 (figure 25). China accounted for most of this growth, with titles issued increasing by 34.2%. However, the CPVO issued the largest number of titles (2,980). China (2,132) issued the second most titles, overtaking the U.S. (1,703). They were followed by Japan (941) and the Republic of Korea (834). Together with China, other offices that saw large increases in titles issued were the Republic of Korea (+34.7%), Canada (+26.5%), Brazil (+13.2%) and Japan (+11.1%). The Netherlands (-4.1%) was the only office among the top 10 to issue fewer titles in 2016 than in 2015.

The grant or registration process takes time, so fluctuations in volumes of granted plant variety titles may reflect changes in processing capacities or procedural delays.

Steady growth in plant varieties in force

Around 116,540 plant variety titles were in force at the end of 2016, up 4.8% on 2015. The CPVO (25,148) and the U.S. (24,375) were the two offices with the highest numbers of active titles. Other offices maintaining at least 4,000 active titles included Japan (8,339), the Netherlands (7,937), China (6,781), the Republic of Korea (4,801) and the Russian Federation (4,739).

Figure 25
Plant variety titles issued worldwide

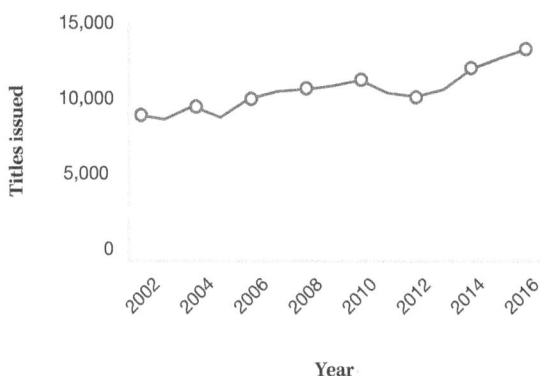

Source: Standard figure D2.

Standard figures and tables

PLANT VARIETIES

Plant variety applications and titles issued worldwide

Figure D1
Trend in plant variety applications worldwide

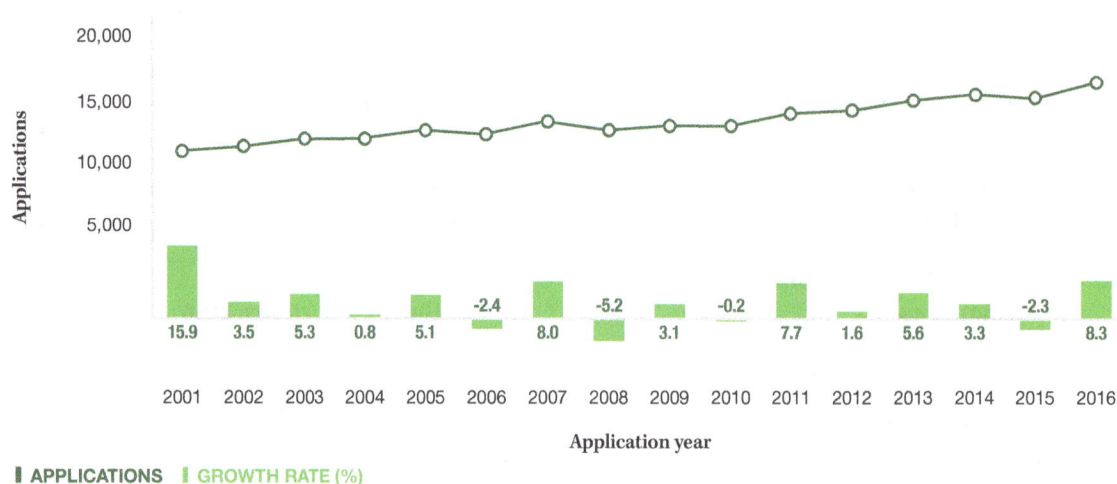

APPLICATIONS   GROWTH RATE (%)

Note: World totals are WIPO estimates using data covering 68 offices.

Source: WIPO Statistics Database, September 2017.

Figure D2
Trend in plant variety titles issued worldwide

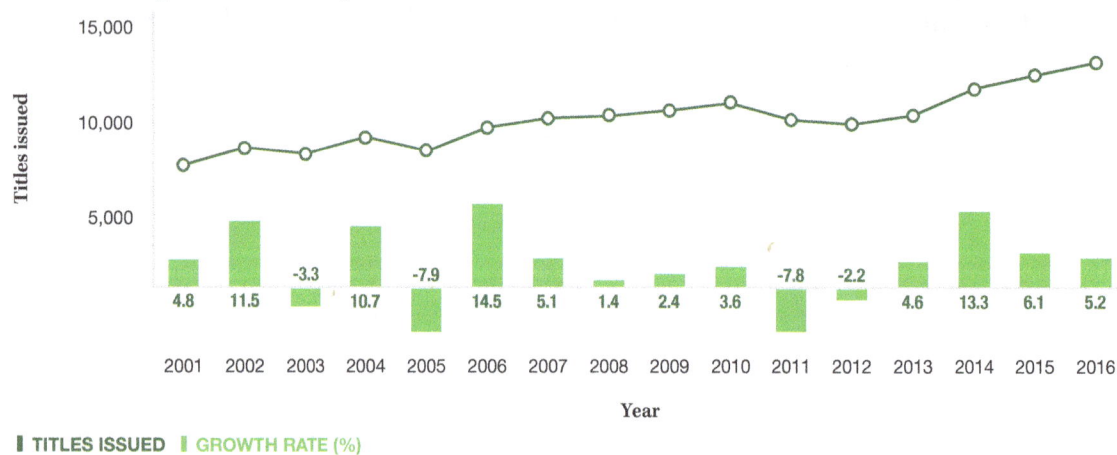

TITLES ISSUED   GROWTH RATE (%)

Note: World totals are WIPO estimates using data covering 68 offices.

Source: WIPO Statistics Database, September 2017.

Plant variety applications and titles issued by office

Figure D3
Plant variety applications by income group

Income group	Number of applications		Resident share (%)		Share of world total (%)		Average growth (%)
	2006	2016	2006	2016	2006	2016	2006-16
High-income	9,122	9,494	64.6	68.2	73.6	57.5	0.4
Upper middle-income	2,430	5,270	73.0	74.0	19.6	31.9	8.0
Lower middle-income	838	1,746	64.0	34.5	6.8	10.6	7.6
World	**12,390**	**16,510**	**66.3**	**66.5**	**100.0**	**100.0**	**2.9**

Note: Totals by income group are WIPO estimates using data covering 68 offices. Each category includes the following number of offices: high-income countries/economies (37), upper middle-income (21) and lower middle-income (10). The EU's Community Plant Variety Office (CPVO) data are allocated to the high-income group because the majority of EU member states are high-income countries. For information on income group classification, see the Data description section.

Source: WIPO Statistics Database, September 2017.

Figure D4
Plant variety applications by region

Region	Number of applications		Resident share (%)		Share of world total (%)		Average growth (%)
	2006	2016	2006	2016	2006	2016	2006-16
Africa	352	511	30.1	10.2	2.8	3.1	3.8
Asia	2,838	5,386	75.7	83.5	22.9	32.6	6.6
Europe	5,767	6,931	79.5	68.9	46.6	42.1	1.9
Latin America & the Caribbean	976	1,277	41.7	45.9	7.9	7.7	2.7
North America	1,980	1,886	36.7	47.4	16.0	11.4	-0.5
Oceania	477	519	46.8	34.1	3.8	3.1	0.8
World	**12,390**	**16,510**	**66.3**	**66.5**	**100.0**	**100.0**	**2.9**

Note: Totals by geographic region are WIPO estimates using data covering 68 offices. Each region includes the following number of offices: Africa (4), Asia (12), Europe (33), Latin America & the Caribbean (14), North America (3) and Oceania (2).

Source: WIPO Statistics Database, September 2017.

PLANT VARIETIES

Figure D5
Plant variety applications for the top 20 offices, 2016

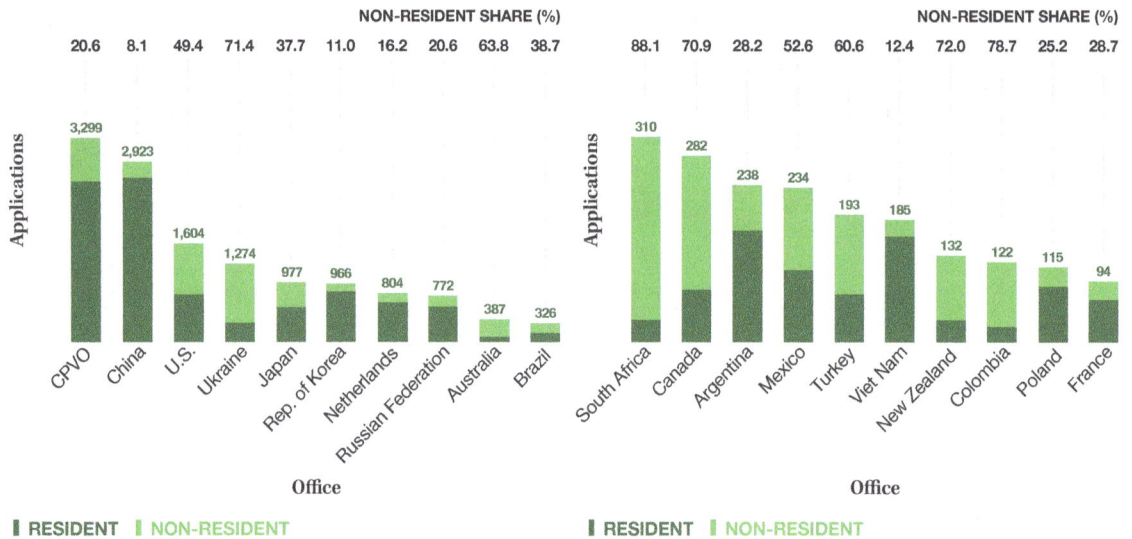

NON-RESIDENT SHARE (%)

| 20.6 | 8.1 | 49.4 | 71.4 | 37.7 | 11.0 | 16.2 | 20.6 | 63.8 | 38.7 |

NON-RESIDENT SHARE (%)

| 88.1 | 70.9 | 28.2 | 52.6 | 60.6 | 12.4 | 72.0 | 78.7 | 25.2 | 28.7 |

Applications (left chart): CPVO 3,299; China 2,923; U.S. 1,604; Ukraine 1,274; Japan 977; Rep. of Korea 966; Netherlands 804; Russian Federation 772; Australia 387; Brazil 326

Applications (right chart): South Africa 310; Canada 282; Argentina 238; Mexico 234; Turkey 193; Viet Nam 185; New Zealand 132; Colombia 122; Poland 115; France 94

Office

■ RESIDENT ■ NON-RESIDENT   ■ RESIDENT ■ NON-RESIDENT

Note: CPVO is the Community Plant Variety Office. In general, national offices of CPVO member states receive lower volumes of applications because applicants may apply via the CPVO to seek protection within any CPVO member state.

Source: WIPO Statistics Database, September 2017.

Figure D6
Contribution of resident and non-resident applications to total growth for the top 20 offices, 2015-16

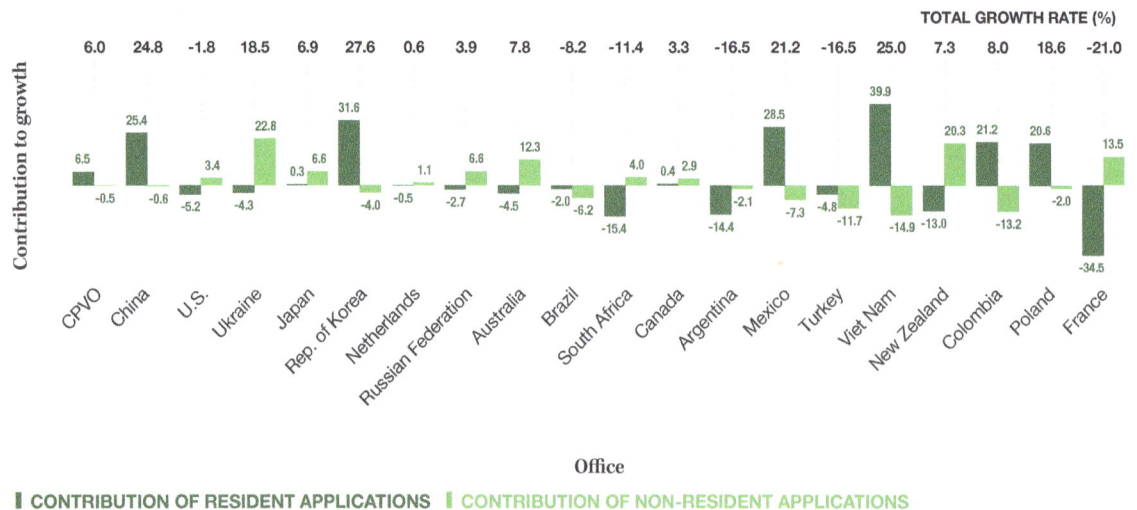

TOTAL GROWTH RATE (%)

| 6.0 | 24.8 | -1.8 | 18.5 | 6.9 | 27.6 | 0.6 | 3.9 | 7.8 | -8.2 | -11.4 | 3.3 | -16.5 | 21.2 | -16.5 | 25.0 | 7.3 | 8.0 | 18.6 | -21.0 |

Contribution to growth:

- CPVO: 6.5, -0.5
- China: 25.4, -0.6
- U.S.: 3.4, -5.2
- Ukraine: 22.8, -4.3
- Japan: 0.3, 6.6
- Rep. of Korea: 31.6, -4.0
- Netherlands: 1.1, -0.5
- Russian Federation: 6.6, -2.7
- Australia: 12.3, -4.5
- Brazil: -2.0, -6.2
- South Africa: 4.0, -15.4
- Canada: 0.4, 2.9
- Argentina: -14.4, -2.1
- Mexico: 28.5, -7.3
- Turkey: -4.8, -11.7
- Viet Nam: 39.9, -14.9
- New Zealand: 20.3, -13.0
- Colombia: 21.2, -13.2
- Poland: 20.6, -2.0
- France: -34.5, 13.5

Office

■ CONTRIBUTION OF RESIDENT APPLICATIONS ■ CONTRIBUTION OF NON-RESIDENT APPLICATIONS

Note: CPVO is the Community Plant Variety Office. This figure shows total growth in plant variety applications broken down by the respective contributions of resident and non-resident filings. For example, applications in Japan grew by 6.9%, and resident applications contributed 0.3 percentage points to this total growth while non-resident applications accounted for the other 6.6 percentage points.

Source: WIPO Statistics Database, September 2017.

Figure D7
Plant variety applications for offices of selected low- and middle-income countries, 2016

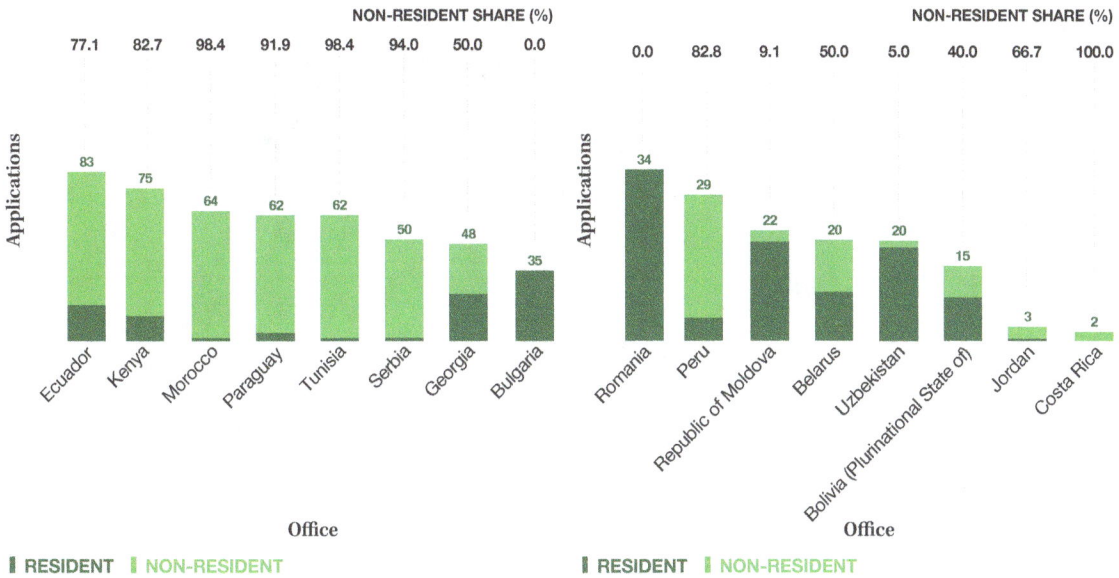

Note: The selected offices are from different world regions and income groups. Where available, data for all offices are in the statistical table at the end of this section.

Source: WIPO Statistics Database, September 2017.

Figure D8
Plant variety titles issued by the top 20 offices, 2016

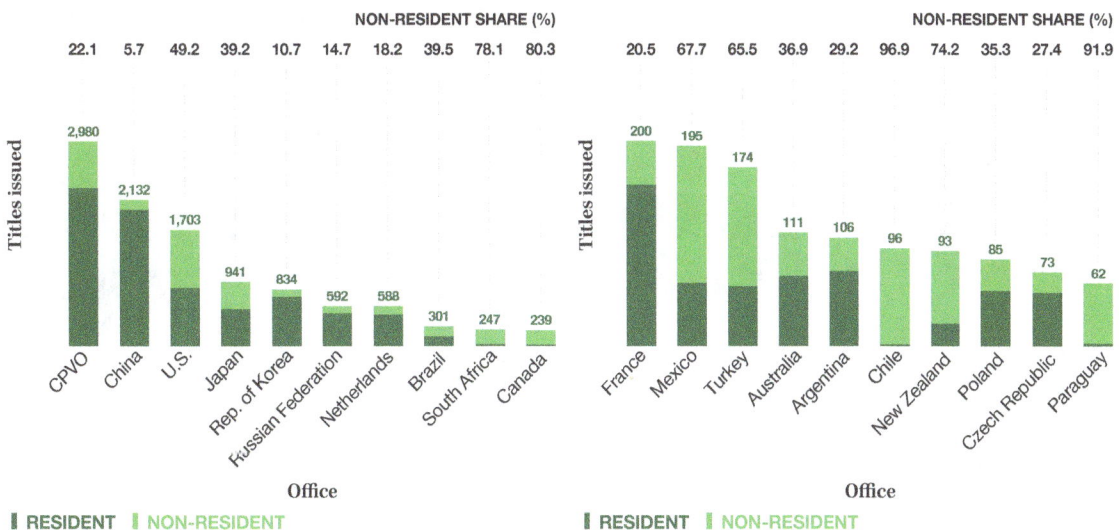

Note: CPVO is the Community Plant Variety Office. The procedure for issuing titles varies across offices, and differences in the numbers of titles issued between offices depend on factors such as examination capacity and procedural delays, so there is a time lag between application and title issue dates. For this reason, data on applications for a given year should not be compared with data on titles issued for the same year.

Source: WIPO Statistics Database, September 2017.

195

PLANT VARIETIES

Plant variety applications and titles issued by origin

Figure D9
Equivalent plant variety applications by origin, 2016

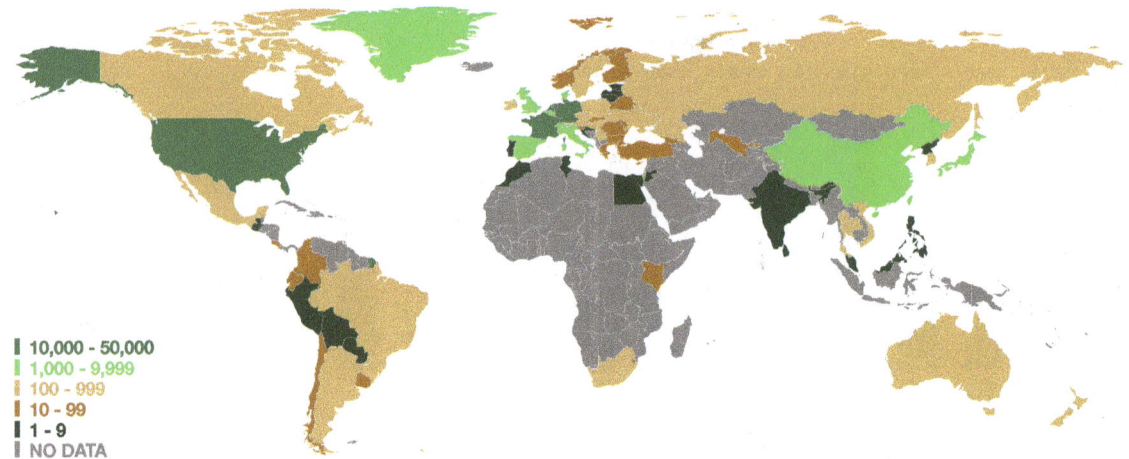

- 10,000 - 50,000
- 1,000 - 9,999
- 100 - 999
- 10 - 99
- 1 - 9
- NO DATA

Note: Equivalent plant variety applications by origin include resident applications and applications filed abroad. The origin of an application is determined by the residence of the applicant. Applications filed at regional offices are considered equivalent to multiple applications in the relevant member states. See the glossary for the definition of equivalent application.

Source: WIPO Statistics Database, September 2017.

Figure D10
Plant variety applications for the top 20 origins, 2016

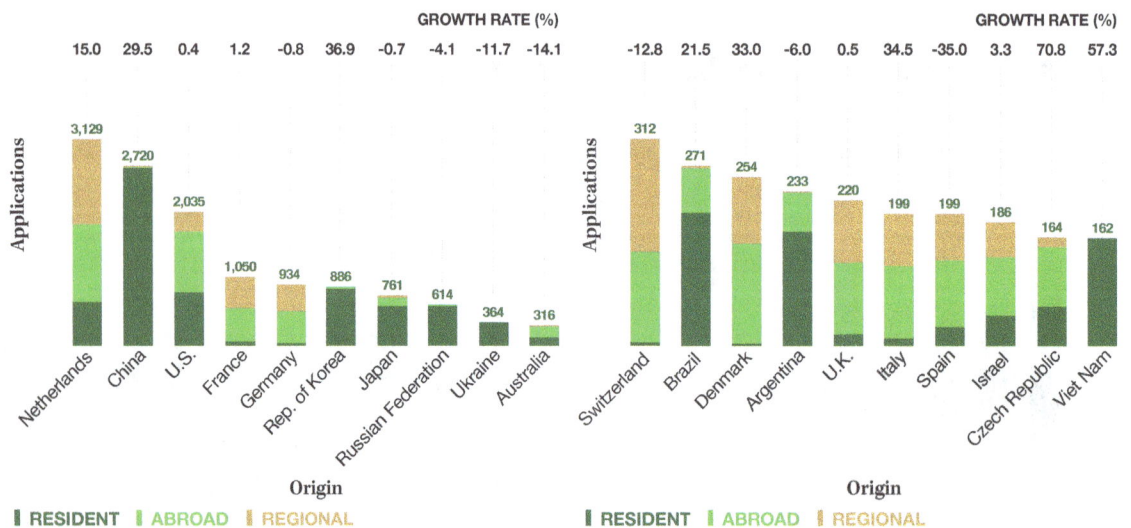

GROWTH RATE (%)

| 15.0 | 29.5 | 0.4 | 1.2 | -0.8 | 36.9 | -0.7 | -4.1 | -11.7 | -14.1 |

GROWTH RATE (%)

| -12.8 | 21.5 | 33.0 | -6.0 | 0.5 | 34.5 | -35.0 | 3.3 | 70.8 | 57.3 |

Left chart (Applications):
- Netherlands: 3,129
- China: 2,720
- U.S.: 2,035
- France: 1,050
- Germany: 934
- Rep. of Korea: 886
- Japan: 761
- Russian Federation: 614
- Ukraine: 364
- Australia: 316

Right chart (Applications):
- Switzerland: 312
- Brazil: 271
- Denmark: 254
- Argentina: 233
- U.K.: 220
- Italy: 199
- Spain: 199
- Israel: 186
- Czech Republic: 164
- Viet Nam: 162

Origin

RESIDENT   ABROAD   REGIONAL

Note: Data are based on absolute count, not equivalent count. Applications by origin include resident applications and applications filed abroad. The origin of an application is determined by the residence of the applicant. Regional refers to applications filed at the EU's Community Plant Variety Office.

Source: WIPO Statistics Database, September 2017.

PLANT VARIETIES

Figure D11
Plant variety applications abroad for the top 20 origins, 2016

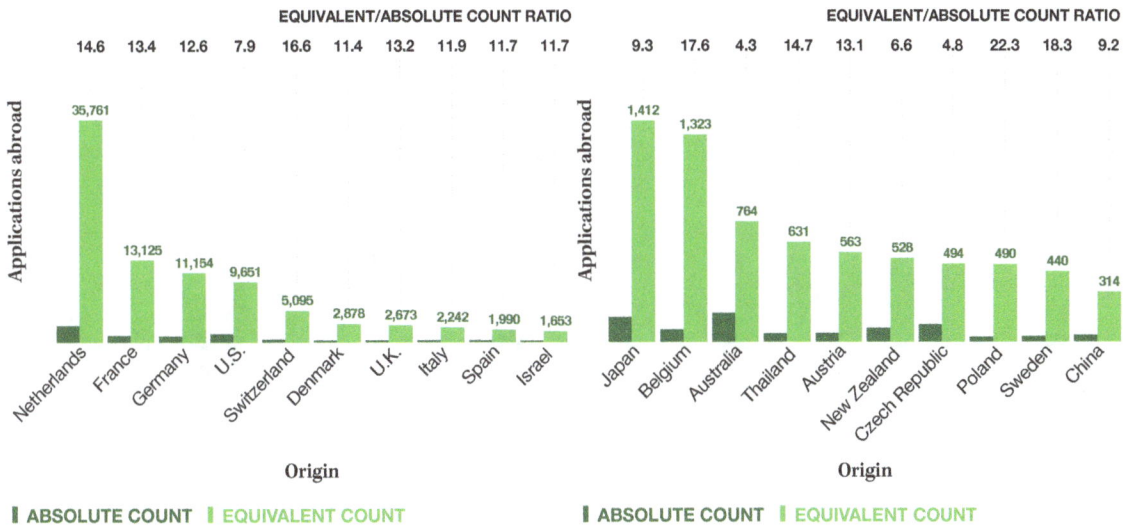

EQUIVALENT/ABSOLUTE COUNT RATIO

| 14.6 | 13.4 | 12.6 | 7.9 | 16.6 | 11.4 | 13.2 | 11.9 | 11.7 | 11.7 |

EQUIVALENT/ABSOLUTE COUNT RATIO

| 9.3 | 17.6 | 4.3 | 14.7 | 13.1 | 6.6 | 4.8 | 22.3 | 18.3 | 9.2 |

Applications abroad: Netherlands 35,761; France 13,125; Germany 11,154; U.S. 9,651; Switzerland 5,095; Denmark 2,878; U.K. 2,673; Italy 2,242; Spain 1,990; Israel 1,653

Japan 1,412; Belgium 1,323; Australia 764; Thailand 631; Austria 563; New Zealand 528; Czech Republic 494; Poland 490; Sweden 440; China 314

ABSOLUTE COUNT   EQUIVALENT COUNT

Note: The origin of an application is determined by the residence of the applicant. Applications filed at regional offices are considered equivalent to multiple applications in the relevant member states. See the glossary for the definition of equivalent applications.

Source: WIPO Statistics Database, September 2017.

Figure D12
Plant variety titles issued for the top 20 origins, 2016

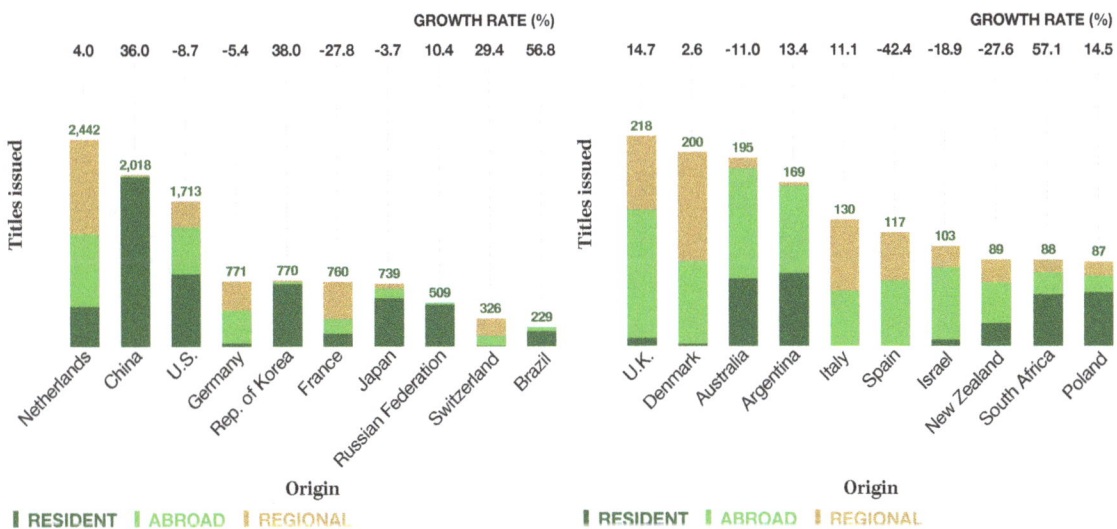

GROWTH RATE (%)

| 4.0 | 36.0 | -8.7 | -5.4 | 38.0 | -27.8 | -3.7 | 10.4 | 29.4 | 56.8 |

GROWTH RATE (%)

| 14.7 | 2.6 | -11.0 | 13.4 | 11.1 | -42.4 | -18.9 | -27.6 | 57.1 | 14.5 |

Titles issued: Netherlands 2,442; China 2,018; U.S. 1,713; Germany 771; Rep. of Korea 770; France 760; Japan 739; Russian Federation 509; Switzerland 326; Brazil 229

U.K. 218; Denmark 200; Australia 195; Argentina 169; Italy 130; Spain 117; Israel 103; New Zealand 89; South Africa 88; Poland 87

RESIDENT   ABROAD   REGIONAL

Note: Data are based on absolute count, not equivalent count. The origin of titles issued is determined by the residence of the applicant. Regional refers to titles issued by the EU's Community Plant Variety Office.

Source: WIPO Statistics Database, September 2017.

PLANT VARIETIES

Figure D13
Plant variety titles issued abroad for the top 20 origins, 2016

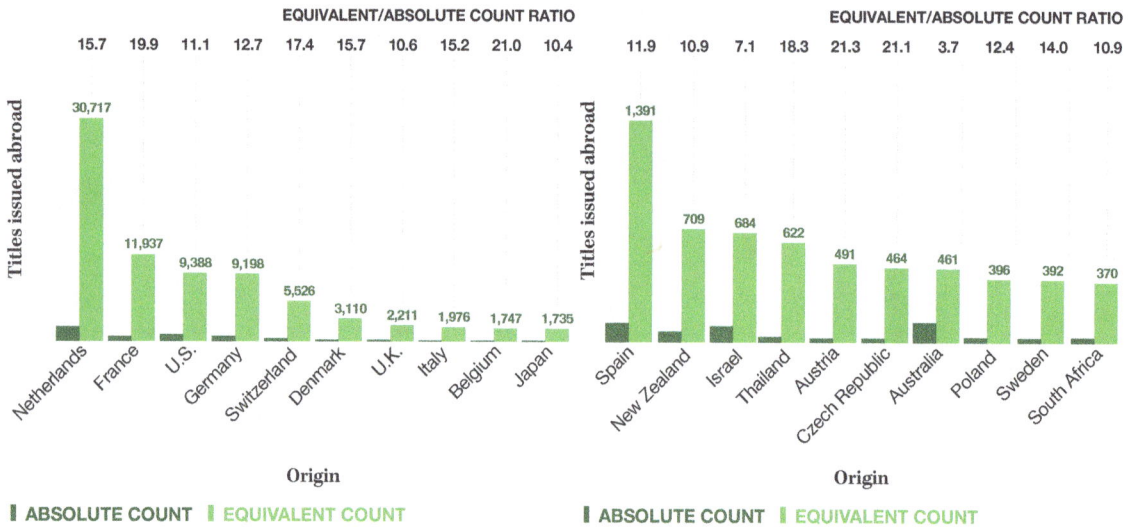

Note: The origin of titles issued is determined by the residence of the applicant. Titles issued by regional offices are considered equivalent to multiple titles in the relevant member states. See the glossary for the definition of equivalent count.

Source: WIPO Statistics Database, September 2017.

Plant varieties in force

Figure D14
Trend in plant varieties in force worldwide

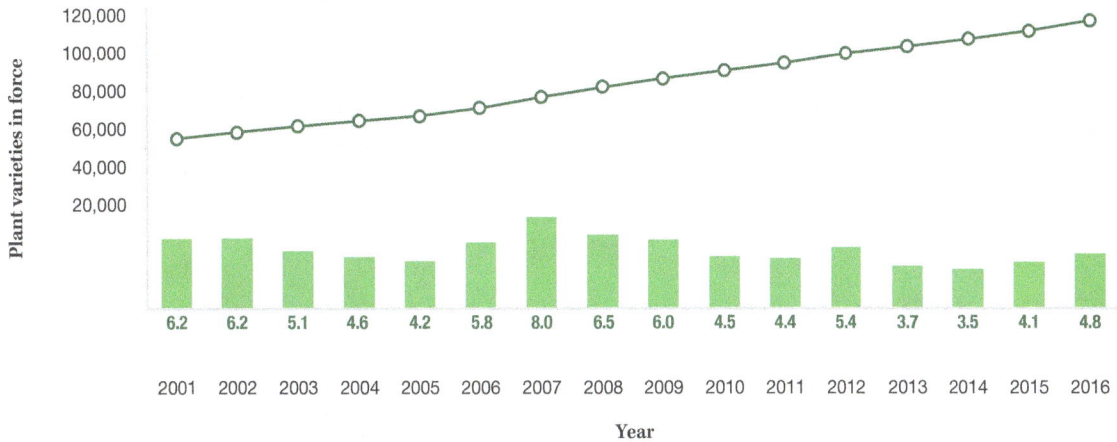

	2001	2002	2003	2004	2005	2006	2007	2008	2009	2010	2011	2012	2013	2014	2015	2016
Growth rate	6.2	6.2	5.1	4.6	4.2	5.8	8.0	6.5	6.0	4.5	4.4	5.4	3.7	3.5	4.1	4.8

Year

▌ PLANT VARIETIES IN FORCE   ▌ GROWTH RATE (%)

Note: World totals are WIPO estimates using data covering 68 offices.

Source: WIPO Statistics Database, September 2017.

Figure D15
Plant varieties in force at selected offices, 2016

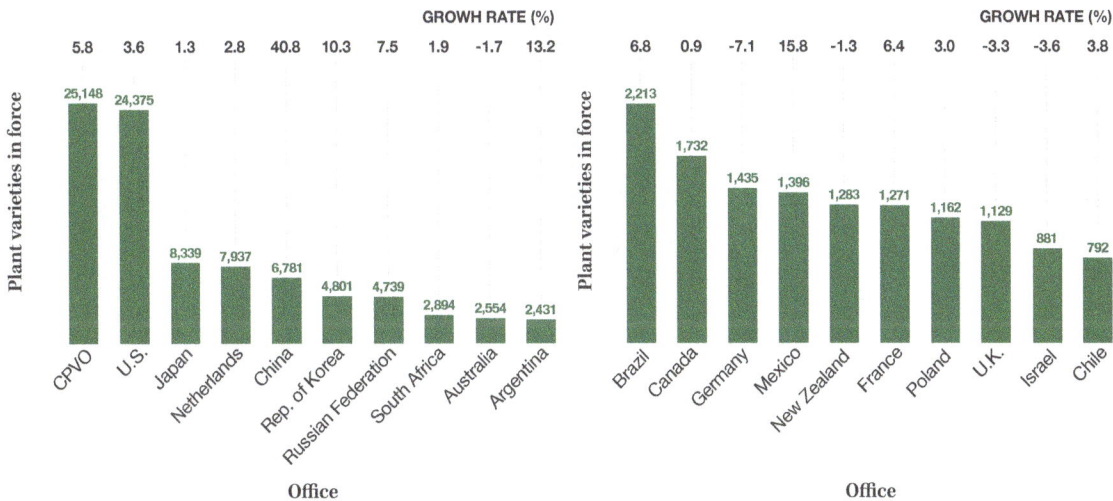

GROWH RATE (%)

5.8	3.6	1.3	2.8	40.8	10.3	7.5	1.9	-1.7	13.2

CPVO	U.S.	Japan	Netherlands	China	Rep. of Korea	Russian Federation	South Africa	Australia	Argentina
25,148	24,375	8,339	7,937	6,781	4,801	4,739	2,894	2,554	2,431

Office

GROWH RATE (%)

6.8	0.9	-7.1	15.8	-1.3	6.4	3.0	-3.3	-3.6	3.8

Brazil	Canada	Germany	Mexico	New Zealand	France	Poland	U.K.	Israel	Chile
2,213	1,732	1,435	1,396	1,283	1,271	1,162	1,129	881	792

Office

Note: CPVO is the Community Plant Variety Office.

Source: WIPO Statistics Database, September 2017.

Statistical table

Figure D16
Plant variety applications and titles issued by office and origin, 2016

Name	Applications by office			Applications by origin	Equivalent applications by origin	Grants by office			Plant varieties in force
	Total	Resident	Non-resident	Total	Total	Total	Resident	Non-resident	Office
African Intellectual Property Organization (a)	..	..	..	..	..	..	..	..	49
Argentina	238	171	67	233	261	106	75	31	2,431
Australia	387	140	247	316	904	111	70	41	2,554
Austria	2	2	0	45	585	..	..	..	24
Belarus	20	10	10	11	39	28	18	10	252
Belgium	4	4	0	79	1,375	1	1	0	53
Bolivia (Plurinational State of)	15	9	6	9	9	15	9	6	57
Brazil	326	200	126	271	327	301	182	119	2,213
Bulgaria	35	35	0	44	44	21	21	0	391
Canada	282	82	200	110	278	239	47	192	1,732
Chile	90	10	80	23	51	96	3	93	792
China	2,923	2,686	237	2,720	3,000	2,132	2,011	121	6,781
Colombia	122	26	96	27	27	42	0	42	561
Community Plant Variety Office	3,299	2,621	678	n.a.	..	2,980	2,320	660	25,148
Costa Rica	2	0	2	6	34	2	1	1	13
Croatia	6	6	0	6	6	10	10	0	58
Czech Republic	68	60	8	164	569	73	53	20	761
Democratic People's Republic of Korea (b)	..	..	..	1	1	..	..	..	..
Denmark	3	2	1	254	2,981	3	2	1	102
Ecuador	83	19	64	24	24	39	4	35	273
Egypt (b)	..	..	..	2	2	..	..	..	..
Estonia	10	3	7	3	3	13	1	12	97
Finland	7	5	2	16	16	21	14	7	206
France	94	67	27	1,050	13,659	200	159	41	1,271
Georgia	48	24	24	24	24	47	37	10	166
Germany	56	50	6	934	11,599	54	49	5	1,435
Greece (b)	..	..	..	2	56	..	..	..	..
Guatemala (b)	..	..	..	2	2	..	..	..	..
Hungary	15	14	1	37	199	17	16	1	151
India (b)	..	..	..	2	2	..	..	..	..
Ireland (a)	..	..	..	23	158	..	..	..	..
Israel	56	45	11	186	1,698	39	7	32	881
Italy	12	11	1	199	2,332	..	..	..	..
Japan	977	609	368	761	2,021	941	572	369	8,339
Jordan	3	1	2	1	1	1	0	1	48
Kenya	75	13	62	19	19	24	1	23	387
Kyrgyzstan (a)	..	..	..	..	..	..	..	..	5
Latvia	10	9	1	9	9	2	1	1	196
Lithuania	2	2	0	2	2	6	2	4	76
Luxembourg (b)	..	..	..	95	95	..	..	..	..
Malaysia (b)	..	..	..	1	1	..	..	..	..
Mexico	234	111	123	125	209	195	63	132	1,396
Morocco	64	1	63	1	1	13	2	11	314
Netherlands	804	674	130	3,129	37,716	588	481	107	7,937
New Zealand	132	37	95	117	565	93	24	69	1,283
Norway	8	2	6	4	32	21	8	13	215
Panama	1	0	1	..	..	..	..	..	19
Paraguay	62	5	57	5	5	62	5	57	461
Peru	29	5	24	7	7	7	4	3	97
Philippines (b)	..	..	..	1	1	..	..	..	..
Poland	115	86	29	108	594	85	55	30	1,162

Name	Applications by office			Applications by origin	Equivalent applications by origin	Grants by office			Plant varieties in force
	Total	Resident	Non-resident	Total	Total	Total	Resident	Non-resident	Office
Portugal	3	3	0	3	3	1	0	1	12
Republic of Korea	966	860	106	886	970	834	745	89	4,801
Republic of Moldova	22	20	2	24	24	37	33	4	184
Romania	34	34	0	43	70	26	24	2	335
Russian Federation	772	613	159	614	614	592	505	87	4,739
Serbia	50	3	47	10	150	38	3	35	246
Singapore	1	0	1	2	2	5	2	3	5
Slovakia	21	20	1	26	26	27	24	3	443
Slovenia (a)	..	..	..	6	60	..	..	..	..
South Africa	310	37	273	88	312	247	54	193	2,894
Spain	40	29	11	199	2,089	..	..	..	321
Sri Lanka (b)	..	..	..	1	1	..	..	..	..
Swaziland (b)	..	..	..	21	21	..	..	..	..
Sweden	5	1	4	25	457	6	2	4	137
Switzerland	72	5	67	312	5,100	62	8	54	691
Thailand (b)	..	..	..	43	631	..	..	..	..
Tunisia	62	1	61	1	1	13	2	11	128
Turkey	193	76	117	99	99	174	60	114	737
Ukraine	1,274	364	910	364	364	..	..	..	..
United Kingdom	54	17	37	220	2,785	33	9	24	1,129
United Republic of Tanzania (a)	..	..	..	..	..	..	..	..	73
United States of America (PPA) (c)	1,177	468	709	n.a.	..	1,235	474	761	16,942
United States of America (PVPA)	427	344	83	2,035	10,463	468	391	77	7,433
Uruguay	48	14	34	16	44	58	12	46	576
Uzbekistan	20	19	1	19	19	10	9	1	67
Viet Nam	185	162	23	162	162	56	35	21	280
Others/Unknown	..	..	..	28	196	..	..	..	..
Total (2016 estimates)	**16,510**	**11,000**	**5,510**	**16,510**	**n.a.**	**13,280**	**7,900**	**4,000**	**116,540**

(a) This office did not report data, so applications by origin data may be incomplete.

(b) This country or organization is not a member of the International Union for the Protection of New Varieties of Plants (UPOV).

(c) Applications by origin are reported under "United States of America (PVPA)", as statistics by origin do not distinguish between applications under the Plant Variety Protection Act and those under the Plant Patent Act.

n.a. indicates not applicable

.. indicates not available

Sources: WIPO Statistics Database, September 2017.

PLANT VARIETIES

Geographical indications

At present, there is a notable lack of global statistics on geographical indications (GIs).[1] The collection of reliable GI statistics could enable researchers to conduct empirical research and promote evidence-based policymaking.

In 2016, WIPO initiated a survey to collect GI data and invited national and regional intellectual property (IP) offices and/or other competent authorities to share these data. A pilot survey for reference year 2015 was launched in 2016. Based on the response rate and inputs received from respondents, the questionnaires were revised and sent to national/regional authorities in 2017 inviting them to share their 2016 GI data with WIPO. In response, 54 national/regional authorities provided their data to WIPO in 2017.

It is important to note that responsibility for protecting GIs is often shared among different authorities within a country. This can make it challenging to obtain a complete picture of all GIs protected in any particular country. WIPO has made substantial efforts to gather data from all sources, but in many instances it has not been possible to obtain data from every source. Therefore, caution should be exercised when interpreting the GI data here presented. Notwithstanding data limitations, this is the first time WIPO has reported GI data covering a large number of countries. We encourage countries unable to share their GI data with us to provide relevant statistics in the near future.

What is a geographical indication?

A GI is a sign identifying a good as originating in a specific geographical area and possessing a given quality, reputation or other characteristic that is *essentially attributable* to that geographical origin. Thus, the main function of a GI is to indicate a connection between that quality, characteristics or reputation of the good and its territory of origin.

World-renowned examples of GIs include Café de Colombia (Colombia), Bordeaux (France), Kampot Pepper (Cambodia), Penja Pepper (Cameroon) and Scotch whisky (UK).

GIs are mainly used for agricultural and food products, which typically tend to have a close natural link with their place of origin. There are, however, also many GIs for other kinds of products. The specific qualities of the product may derive from traditional manufacturing skills or from a combi-

nation of local know-how and natural resources. Examples of such GIs include Bohemia Crystal (Czech Republic), Solingen Cutlery (Germany), Kilim Carpets (Turkey), Swiss Watches (Switzerland) and Yangzhou Lacquerware (China).

Although GIs are commonly names of places, under many systems they may consist of non-geographical terms with a traditional geographical connotation. Reblochon (France) and Argan oil (Morocco) serve as GIs although they are not geographical names.

Geographical indications can only be used by producers, whose goods conform to the applicable requirements concerning the area of origin, processing method and typicity of the product. Production sites located outside the area of origin and goods that do not meet the applicable requirements are prevented from using the protected indication.

What is an appellation of origin?

An appellation of origin (AO) is a special kind of geographical indication. It generally consists of a geographical name or a traditional denomination which serves to designate a product as originating therein, where the quality or characteristics of the product are due *exclusively or essentially* to the geographical environment, including natural and human factors, and which have given the good its reputation. The most important difference between AOs and other GIs is that the link with the place of origin should be stronger in the case of an AO. In other words, AOs are a more restrictive sub-category of GIs.

How are GIs protected?

At the national and regional levels, GIs are protected through a variety of legal means. These include *sui generis* systems – laws specifically designed to protect geographical indications,[2] often based on a registration procedure. *Sui generis* systems generally provide protection against any direct and indirect commercial use of the GI as well as against its imitation. *Sui generis* systems for GI protection are used in many countries and also by two regional intergovernmental organizations: the African Intellectual Property Organization (OAPI) and the European Union (EU).

GIs are also protected on the basis of trademark law, commonly through the use of collective and certification marks. Because trademarks incorporating geographical terms are typically not recorded by IP offices as a separate category of trademarks, and because not all trademarks incorporating geographical terms can be considered GIs, it may be difficult to determine the exact number of registered GIs within those jurisdictions. It is also worth noting that GI protection via trademark and *sui generis* systems are not mutually exclusive but often coexist, under many legal frameworks, and are available to the benefit of GI holders.

Finally, GIs are typically also protected under unfair competition and consumer protection laws and administrative and judicial decisions as well as under specific laws or decrees recognizing individual GIs.

The effects of a GI right obtained in a particular jurisdiction are limited to the territory of that jurisdiction. Thus, where a right over a GI is obtained in one jurisdiction, it is protected there but not abroad. In order to obtain protection in a foreign jurisdiction, GI holders must, in principle, seek protection under the relevant national laws prevailing in the jurisdiction in question. However, international agreements can facilitate the acquisition of GI rights abroad. In particular, many bilateral and regional trade agreements have incorporated lists of GIs that are to be protected in the relevant parties to the agreement. The listed GIs may relate to existing or subsequent registrations of GI rights, but protection may also emanate from the trade agreements themselves.

Another way of obtaining GI protection abroad is through two international registration systems administered by WIPO: the Lisbon System and the Madrid System.

The Lisbon System

The Lisbon System was established in 1958 to facilitate the international protection of appellations of origin through a single registration procedure.[3] Registration with the WIPO International Bureau ensures protection in all Lisbon contracting parties, without need for renewal and as long as the appellation of origin remains protected in its contracting party of origin. However, the decision whether to protect a newly registered appellation of origin at the national level remains the prerogative of each contracting party, and each Lisbon member can refuse protection based on any ground within one year of being notified of a new appellation of origin by the WIPO International Bureau. The Lisbon System is flexible as regards the means by which countries may provide protection for the registered appellation of origin (e.g., *sui generis* systems, trademark laws or specific ad hoc decrees as well as judicial and administrative decisions).

Globally-renowned examples of appellations of origin protected under the Lisbon System include Tequila (Mexico), Chianti for wines (Italy), Habanos for cigars (Cuba) and handicrafts such as Chulucanas for ceramics (Peru), Herend for porcelain (Hungary) and Kraslice musical instruments (Czech Republic). The scope of the System extends to non-geographical traditional names such as Reblochon (France) and Vinho Verde (Portugal).

In 2015, with the adoption of the Geneva Act of the Lisbon Agreement on Appellations of Origin and Geographical Indications, which will enter into force after five ratifications or accessions, Lisbon contracting parties modernized the System to attract a wider membership, while preserving its principles and objectives. The Geneva Act formally extends the scope of the Lisbon System to the general category of geographical indications in addition to appellations of origin. The new Act also opens the Lisbon System to accession by intergovernmental organizations such as the EU and OAPI.

The Madrid System

GIs can also be protected in several countries as collective and certification marks through the Madrid System, an international registration system legally governed by the Madrid Agreement (1891) and the Madrid Protocol (1989) and administered by WIPO.[4] Famous examples of collective and certification marks registered under the Madrid System include Napa Valley for wine (U.S.) and Parmigiano Reggiano for cheese (Italy). As at June 2017, there were more than 1,200 collective and certification marks registered under the Madrid System. However, collective and certification marks protecting GIs are not separately recorded, so it is difficult to determine their exact number.

How many GIs are in force worldwide?

Data received from the 54 national/regional authorities that shared their data with WIPO (figure 29) reveals the existence of approximately 42,527 protected GIs. Approximately 49% of these were in force domestically and the remaining 51% in foreign jurisdictions (figure 26). Germany had the largest number of GIs in force (9,499), followed by China (7,566), the EU (4,914), the Republic of Moldova (3,442) and Bosnia and Herzegovina (3,147). The top five authorities accounted for 67% of the 2016 total (figure 27).

These figures should be interpreted with caution, however. Not only are the data limited to the 54 countries that shared their data with WIPO, but the submissions made by many countries were incomplete. The questionnaire underlying the data collection asked for information regarding GIs protected through *sui generis* systems, the trademark system and trade agreements. As can be seen from figure 29, many countries were unable to provide statistics on the number of GIs protected through the trademark system, reflecting the difficulty of identifying such GIs among all collective and certification trade-

marks registered. In addition, several countries could not provide data on the number of GIs protected through trade agreements. Finally, there is likely to be double-counting of GIs protected through two or more legal means.[5]

Figure 26
Geographical indications in force worldwide, 2016

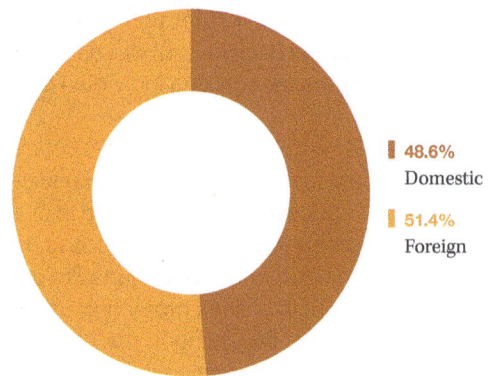

- 48.6% Domestic
- 51.4% Foreign

Source: WIPO Statistics Database, September 2017.

Figure 27
Geographical indications in force by national/regional authority, 2016

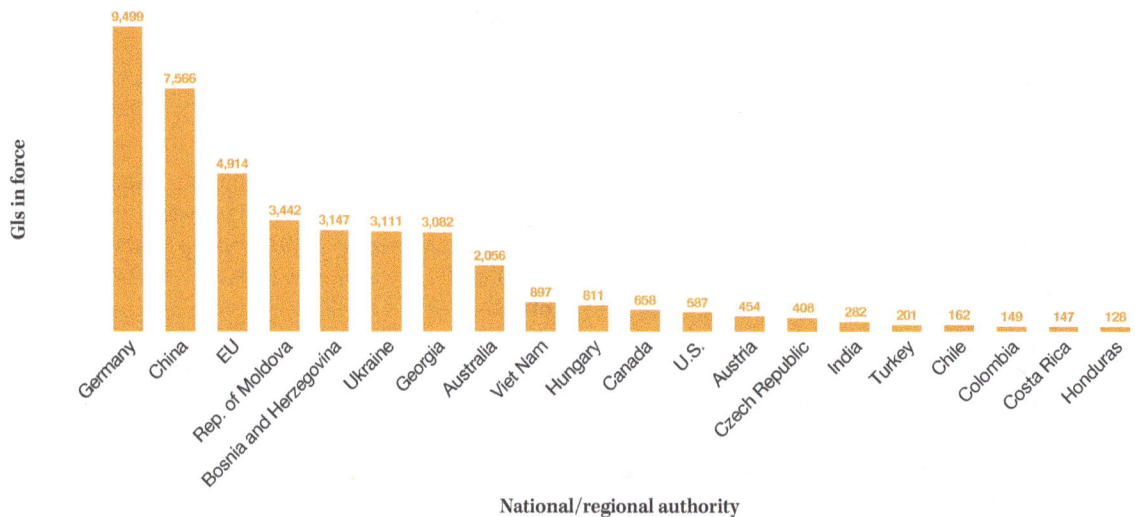

Source: WIPO Statistics Database, September 2017.

Figure 28

Appellations of origin in force by origin, 2016

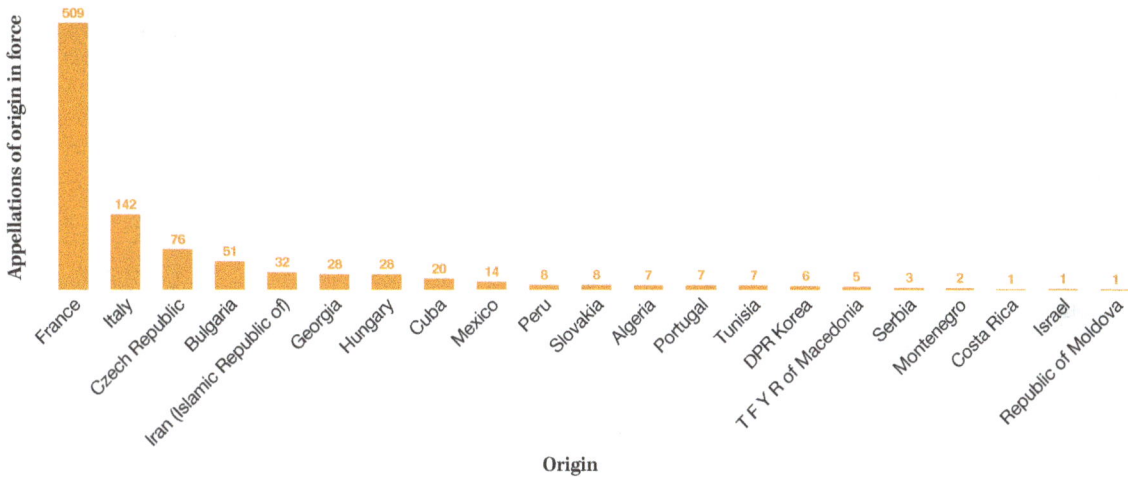

Source: WIPO Statistics Database, September 2017.

Use of the Lisbon System to protect appellations of origin

The Lisbon System consists of 28 member countries, many of which are European. In 2016, there were 956 appellations of origin in force via the Lisbon System (figure 28). France accounted for 53.2% of this total, followed by Italy (14.9%), the Czech Republic (7.9%) and Bulgaria (5.3%).

Conclusions

This is the first time WIPO has compiled and reported GI data covering a large number of national/regional authorities. Although the data are incomplete and partial, this initiative should be seen as an initial step in creating more comprehensive and accurate data sets regarding GIs.

WIPO will continue to collect these data and it is hoped that data coverage will improve over time.

We are grateful to all those authorities that shared their data, and encourage authorities unable to share their data at present to make efforts to share them in the future.

Figure 29
Geographical indications in force in 2016

National/regional authority	Total	Domestic	Foreign	*Sui generis*	Trademarks	Agreements
Argentina	7	7		7		
Armenia	8	1	7		8	
Australia	2,056	122	1,934	116	68	1,872
Austria*	454					454
Azerbaijan	18	10	8			
Bangladesh	1	1		1		
Belarus	31	1	31	31	1	
Bosnia and Herzegovina	3,147	13	3,134	13		3,134
Brazil	56	48	8	56		
Bulgaria*	122	122		122		
Cambodia	2	2		2		
Canada	658	25	633	646		12
Chile	162	146	16	162		
China	7,566	7,416	150			
China, Hong Kong SAR	36		36		36	
China, Macao SAR	11		11	1	10	
Colombia	149	25	124	30		119
Costa Rica	147	5	142	5		142
Croatia	3	3		3		
Cuba	29	25	4	25		4
Czech Republic*	408	200	208	200		208
Estonia*	6	6		6		
European Union	4,914	3,356	1,558	3,383		1,531
Finland*	0	0	0			
France*	1	1		1		
Georgia	3,082	47	3,035	47		3,035
Germany*	9,499	7,276	2,223	7,275	1	2,223
Greece*	0	0	0			
Guatemala	32		32			32
Honduras	128	10	118		128	
Hungary*	811	23	788	23		788
India	282	270	12	282		
Iran (Islamic Republic of)	33	33		33		
Israel	0	0	0			
Italy*	0	0		0		
Japan	39	32	7			
Kazakhstan	1		1	1		
Latvia*	2	2		2		
Malaysia	74	67	7			
Mongolia	4	4		4		
Morocco	79	79		36	43	
Peru	123	10	113	10		113
Philippines	0	0	0			
Portugal*	14	14		14		
Republic of Moldova	3,442	9	3,433	16		3,426
Romania*	23	23		23		
Serbia	69	55	14			
Singapore	0	0	0			
Slovakia*	2	2		2		
Trinidad and Tobago	0	0	0			
Turkey	201	195	6	198		3
Ukraine	3,111	17	3,094	21		3,090
United States of America	587	314	273		587	
Viet Nam	897			56	841	

Note: * indicates EU member states. For certain products, protection of GIs in member states falls within the competence of the EU.

Source: WIPO Statistics Database, September 2017.

GEOGRAPHICAL INDICATIONS

Additional information

Data description

Data sources

Intellectual property (IP) data are taken from the WIPO Statistics Database and are based primarily on WIPO's annual IP statistics survey (see below) and on data compiled by WIPO in processing international applications/registrations through the Patent Cooperation Treaty (PCT) and the Madrid and Hague Systems.

Data are available from WIPO's Statistics Data Center at *www.wipo.int/ipstats*.

Patent family and technology data are extracted from the WIPO Statistics Database and from the 2017 autumn edition of the European Patent Office's PATSTAT database.

Gross domestic product and population data are from the World Bank's World Development Indicators database.

This report uses the World Bank's income classifications. Economies are classified according to 2016 gross national income per capita as calculated using the World Bank Atlas method. The classifications are low-income (USD 1,005 or less), lower middle-income (USD 1,006 to USD 3,955), upper middle-income (USD 3,956 to USD 12,235) and high-income (over USD 12,235).

This report uses United Nations (UN) definitions of regions and sub-regions, although the geographical terms used in the report may differ slightly from those defined by the UN.

WIPO's annual IP statistics survey

WIPO collects data from national and regional IP offices around the world through an annual survey consisting of multiple questionnaires, and enters these data into the WIPO Statistics Database. When possible, data published on IP offices' websites or in annual reports are used to supplement questionnaire responses in cases where IP offices do not provide statistics. Efforts are ongoing to improve the quality and availability of IP statistics, and to gather data for as many IP offices and countries as possible. The questionnaires are available in English, French and Spanish at *www.wipo.int/ipstats/en/data_collection/questionnaire*.

In addition to its regular IP survey covering patents, utility models, trademarks, industrial designs and plant varieties, WIPO launched a new survey in 2017 to collect data on geographical indications. Around 54 national and regional authorities shared their 2016 data on geographical indications in force with WIPO. Furthermore, WIPO also launched a new questionnaire to compile patent office operations data covering application process times, examination capacity and examination outcome. A large number of IP offices shared operations data with WIPO. The Special section chapter of this report is based on the data collected via this new survey.

Data are broken down by IP office, origin, resident and non-resident applications, applications abroad, class count, design count and other factors. See the glossary for definitions of key concepts used in this publication.

Offices are requested to report data by the origin (country or territory) of applications, grants or registrations. However, some offices are unable to provide a detailed breakdown. Instead, these offices report either an aggregate total or a simple breakdown by total resident and total non-resident. For this reason, the totals for each origin are underreported. However, the unknown origin shares of the 2016 totals are low – only 1.1% for patent applications, 0.8% for trademark application class counts and 2.7% for application design counts.

Table 1
IP applications data coverage by IP type

IP type	Number of offices on which 2016 world totals are based	Number of offices for which 2016 data are available	Data coverage (%)
Patents	154	119	99.2
Utility models	74	62	99.9
Trademarks (a)	166	116	97.7
Industrial designs (b)	151	124	99.8
Plant varieties	68	60	99.7

a. refers to the number of trademark applications based on class count (that is, the number of classes specified in applications).

b. refers to the number of industrial design applications based on design count (that is, the number of designs contained in applications).

Estimating world totals

World totals for applications for, and grants/registrations of, patents, utility models, trademarks, industrial designs and plant varieties are WIPO estimates. Data are not available for all IP offices for every year. Missing data are estimated using methods such as linear extrapolation and averaging adjacent data points. The estimation method used depends on the year and office in question. When an office provides data not broken down by origin, WIPO estimates the resident and non-resident counts using the historical shares of that office. Data are available for most of the larger offices; only small shares of world totals are estimated. For example, the estimate of the total number of patent applications worldwide covers 154 offices. Data are available for 119 of them which account for 99.2% of the estimated world total. Table 1 shows the availability and coverage of data on applications for different types of IP.

National and international data

Application and grant/registration data include data on both direct filings and filings through WIPO-administered international systems (where applicable). For patents and utility models, data include direct filings at national patent offices as well as PCT national phase entries. For trademarks, data include filings at national and regional offices and designations received by relevant offices through the Madrid System. For industrial designs, data include national and regional applications combined with designations received by relevant offices through the Hague System.

International comparability of indicators

Every effort has been made to compile IP statistics based on the same definitions and to facilitate international comparability. Although data are collected from offices using questionnaires from WIPO's harmonized annual IP survey, national laws and regulations for filing IP applications or for issuing IP rights as well as statistical reporting practices may differ among jurisdictions. Due to continual updating of data and the revision of historical statistics, data in this report may differ from data in previous editions and from data available on WIPO's website.

IP systems at a glance

The patent system

A patent is a set of exclusive rights granted by law to applicants for an invention that meets the standards of novelty, non-obviousness and industrial applicability. It is valid for a limited period (generally 20 years), during which time the patent holder can commercially exploit the invention on an exclusive basis. In return, applicants are obliged to disclose their inventions to the public, so that others skilled in the art may replicate them. The patent system is designed to encourage innovation by providing innovators with time-limited exclusive legal rights, thus enabling them to appropriate the returns from their innovative activity.

The procedures for acquiring patent rights are governed by the rules and regulations of national and regional patent offices. These offices are responsible for issuing patents, and the rights are limited to the jurisdiction of the issuing authority. To obtain patent rights, applicants must file an application describing the invention with a national or regional office.

Applicants can also file an international application through the Patent Cooperation Treaty (PCT) System, an international treaty administered by WIPO that facilitates the acquisition of patent rights in multiple jurisdictions. The PCT System simplifies the process of multiple national patent filings by delaying the requirement to file a separate application in each jurisdiction in which protection is sought. However, the decision whether to grant a patent remains the prerogative of national or regional patent offices, and patent rights are limited to the jurisdiction of each patent-granting authority.

The PCT application process begins with the international phase, during which an international search and optional preliminary examination and supplementary international search are performed. It concludes with the national phase, during which national (or regional) patent offices decide on the patentability of an invention according to national law. Further information about the PCT System is available at *www.wipo.int/pct.*

The utility model system

Like a patent, a utility model (UM) confers a set of rights to an invention for a limited period, during which the UM holder can commercially exploit their invention on an exclusive basis. The terms and conditions for granting a UM differ from those for granting a traditional patent. For example, UMs are issued for a shorter period (6-10 years), and at most offices protection is granted without substantive examination. As with patents, procedures for granting UM rights are governed by the rules and regulations of national intellectual property (IP) offices, and rights are limited to the jurisdiction of the issuing authority.

Approximately 75 countries provide protection for UMs. In this report, the term "utility model" refers to UMs and other types of protection similar to UMs, such as innovation patents in Australia and short-term patents in Ireland.

Microorganisms under the Budapest Treaty

The Budapest Treaty on the International Recognition of the Deposit of Microorganisms for the Purposes of Patent Procedure plays an important role in relation to biotechnological inventions. Disclosing an invention is a generally recognized requirement for receiving a patent. When an invention involves microorganisms, national laws in most countries require the applicant to deposit a sample at a designated International Depositary Authority (IDA).

To eliminate the need to deposit a microorganism in every country in which patent protection is sought, the Budapest Treaty provides that depositing a microorganism with any IDA will suffice for the purposes of patent procedures at national patent offices of all contracting states and at regional patent offices that recognize the treaty. An IDA is a scientific institution – typically a "culture collection" – capable of storing microorganisms. Currently, there are 46 IDAs around the world. Further information about the Budapest Treaty is available at *www. wipo.int/treaties/en/registration/budapest.*

ADDITIONAL INFORMATION

The trademark system

A trademark is a distinctive sign that identifies certain goods or services as those produced or provided by a specific person or enterprise. Trademarks can be registered for both goods and services. In the latter case, the term "service mark" is sometimes used. For simplicity, this report uses "trademark" regardless of whether the registration concerns goods or services. The holder of a registered trademark has the exclusive right to use the mark in relation to the goods or services for which it is registered, and can block unauthorized use of the trademark, or a confusingly similar mark, to prevent consumers from being misled. Unlike patents, trademark registrations can be maintained indefinitely provided the trademark holder pays the required renewal fees.

The procedures for registering trademarks are governed by the rules and regulations of national and regional IP offices. Therefore, trademark rights are limited to the jurisdiction of the authority in which a trademark is registered. Trademark applicants can file an application with the relevant national or regional IP office or an international application through the Madrid System. However, when an applicant files internationally via the Madrid System, the decision to issue a trademark registration remains the prerogative of the national or regional IP office concerned, and trademark rights remain limited to the jurisdiction of the authority issuing that registration.

The Madrid System is governed legally by the Madrid Agreement (1891) and the Madrid Protocol (1989) and is administered by WIPO. It simplifies multinational trademark registration by allowing an applicant to apply for a trademark in a large number of countries by filing a single application through a national or regional IP office that is party to the System. This eliminates the requirement to file an individual application in each jurisdiction in which protection is sought. The System also simplifies subsequent management of the trademark, since it is possible to centrally request and record further changes, or to renew the registration through a single procedure. A registration recorded in the International Register yields the same effect as a registration made directly with each designated Contracting Party (Madrid member) if no refusal is made by the competent authority of that jurisdiction within a specified time limit. Further information about the Madrid System is available at *www.wipo.int/madrid*.

The industrial design system

Industrial designs are applied to a wide variety of industrial products and handicrafts.[1] They refer to the ornamental or aesthetic aspects of a useful article, including compositions of lines or colors or three-dimensional forms that give a special appearance to a product or handicraft. The holder of a registered industrial design has exclusive rights over the design and can prevent unauthorized copying or imitation of the design by others.

The procedures for registering industrial designs are governed by national or regional laws. An industrial design can be protected if it is new or original, and rights are limited to the jurisdiction of the issuing authority. Registrations can be obtained by filing an application with a relevant national or regional IP office or by filing an international application through the Hague System. Once a design is registered, the term of protection is generally five years and may be renewed for additional periods of five years up to a total of 15 years in most cases. In some countries, industrial designs are protected through the delivery of a design patent rather than design registration.

The Hague System comprises two international treaties – the Hague Act and the Geneva Act. The System makes it possible for an applicant to register industrial designs in multiple countries by filing a single application with the International Bureau of WIPO, thus simplifying multinational registration. Moreover, by allowing the filing of up to 100 different designs per application, the System offers considerable opportunities for efficiency gains. It also streamlines the subsequent management of industrial design registration, since it is possible to record changes or renew a registration through a single procedure. Further information about the Hague System is available at *www.wipo.int/hague*.

Plant variety protection

To obtain protection, a plant breeder must file an individual application with each authority entrusted with granting breeders' rights. A breeder's right is granted only when a variety is new, distinct, uniform and stable, and has a suitable denomination.

In the United States of America (U.S.), two legal frameworks protect new plant varieties: the Plant Patent Act (PPA) and the Plant Variety Protection Act (PVPA). Under the PPA, whoever invents or discovers and asexually reproduces any distinct and new variety of plant – including cultivated sports, mutants, hybrids and newly-found seedlings other than a tuber-propagated plant (in practice, Irish potato and Jerusalem artichoke), or a plant found in an uncultivated state – may obtain a patent. Under the PVPA, the U.S. protects all sexually reproduced plant varieties and tuber-propagated plant varieties, excluding fungi and bacteria.

Glossary

This glossary provides definitions of key technical terms and concepts. Many of the these terms are defined generically (for example, "application") but apply to several or all of the various forms of intellectual property (IP) covered in this report.

Applicant

An individual or other legal entity that files an application for a patent, utility model, trademark or industrial design. There may be more than one applicant in an application. For the statistics in this publication, the name of the first named applicant is used to determine the origin of the application.

Application

The procedure for requesting IP rights at an office which then examines the application and decides whether to grant protection. Also refers to a set of documents submitted to an office by the applicant.

Application abroad

For statistical purposes, an application filed by a resident of a given state or jurisdiction with the IP office of another state or jurisdiction. For example, an application filed by an applicant domiciled in France with the Japan Patent Office (JPO) is considered an application abroad from the perspective of France. This differs from a "non-resident application," which describes an application

filed by a resident of a foreign state or jurisdiction from the perspective of the office receiving the application: the example above would be a non-resident application from the JPO's point of view.

Application date

The date on which the IP office receives an application that meets the minimum requirements. Also referred to as the filing date.

Budapest Treaty

Disclosure of an invention is a requirement for granting a patent. Normally, an invention is disclosed by means of a written description. Where an invention involves a microorganism or the use of a microorganism, disclosure is not always possible in writing but can sometimes only be effected by depositing a sample of the microorganism with a specialized institution. To eliminate the need to deposit a microorganism in each country in which patent protection is sought, the Budapest Treaty provides that the deposit of a microorganism with any International Depositary Authority (IDA) suffices for the purposes of patent procedure at the national patent offices of all contracting states and at any regional patent office that recognizes the treaty.

Class

May refer to the classes defined in either the Locarno Classification or the Nice Classification. Classes indicate the categories of products and services (where applicable) for which industrial design or trademark protection is requested. See "Locarno Classification" and "Nice Classification."

Class count

The number of classes specified in a trademark application or registration. In the international trademark system and at certain national and regional offices, an applicant can file a trademark application that specifies one or more of the 45 goods and services classes of the Nice Classification. Offices use a single- or multi-class filing system. For example, the offices of Japan, the Republic of Korea and the United States of America (U.S.) as well as many European IP offices have multi-class filing systems. The offices of Brazil,

ADDITIONAL INFORMATION

Mexico and South Africa follow a single-class filing system, requiring a separate application for each class in which an applicant seeks trademark protection. To capture the differences in application and registration numbers across offices, it is useful to compare their respective application and registration class counts.

Certification trademark

Certification marks are usually given for compliance with defined standards, but are not confined to any membership. They may be used by anyone who can certify that the products involved meet certain established standards. In many countries, the main difference between collective marks and certification marks is that collective marks may only be used by a specific group of enterprises, for example, members of an association, while certification marks may be used by anybody who complies with the standards defined by the owner of the certification mark.

Collective trademark

Collective marks are usually defined as signs which distinguish the geographical origin, material, mode of manufacture or other common characteristics of goods or services of different enterprises using the collective mark. The owner may be either an association of which those enterprises are members or any other entity, including a public institution or a cooperative.

Community Plant Variety Office (CPVO) of the European Union (EU)

An EU agency that manages a system of plant variety rights covering all EU member states.

Design count

The number of designs contained in an industrial design application or registration. Under the Hague System for the International Registration of Industrial Designs, it is possible for an applicant to obtain protection for up to 100 industrial designs for products belonging to one and the same class by filing a single application. Some national or regional IP offices allow applications to contain more than one design for the same product or within the same class, while others allow only one design per application. In order to capture the differences in application and registration numbers across offices, it is useful to compare their respective application and registration design counts.

Designation

Designation in an international application or registration means the request by which the applicant/international registration holder specifies the jurisdiction(s) in which they seek to protect their industrial designs (Hague System) or trademarks (Madrid System).

Direct filing

See "National route."

Equivalent application

Applications at regional offices are equivalent to multiple applications, one in each of the states that is a member of those offices. To calculate the number of equivalent applications for the Benelux Office for Intellectual Property (BOIP), the Eurasian Patent Organization (EAPO), the African Intellectual Property Organization (OAPI), the Patent Office of the Cooperation Council for the Arab States of the Gulf (GCC Patent Office) and the European Union Intellectual Property Office (EUIPO), each application is multiplied by the corresponding number of member states. For European Patent Office (EPO) and African Regional Intellectual Property Organization (ARIPO) data, each application is counted as one application abroad if the applicant does not reside in a member state or as one resident and one application abroad if the applicant resides in a member state. The equivalent application concept is used for reporting data by origin.

Equivalent grant (registration)

Grants (registrations) at regional offices are equivalent to multiple grants (registrations), one in each of the states that is a member of those offices. To calculate the number of equivalent grants (registrations) for BOIP, EAPO, the EUIPO, the GCC Patent Office or OAPI, each grant (registration) is multiplied by the corresponding number of member states. For EPO and ARIPO data, each grant is counted as one grant abroad if the applicant does not reside in a member state or as one resident and one grant abroad if the applicant resides in a member state. The equivalent grant (registration) concept is used for reporting data by origin.

European Patent Office (EPO)

The EPO is the regional patent office created under the European Patent Convention, in charge of granting European patents for EPC member states. Under Patent Cooperation Treaty (PCT) procedures, the EPO acts as a receiving office, an International Searching Authority and an International Preliminary Examining Authority.

European Union Intellectual Property Office (EUIPO)

The EUIPO is the office responsible for managing the EU trademark and the registered community design. The validity of these two intellectual property rights extends across the jurisdictions of the EU's 28 member states.

Filing

See "Application."

Foreign-oriented patent families

A special subset of patent families that comprises foreign-oriented patent families: this includes only patent families that have at least one filing office different from the office of the applicant's country of origin. Some foreign-related patent families include only one filing office, because applicants may choose to file directly with a foreign office. For example, if a Canadian applicant files a patent application directly with the United States Patent and Trademark Office (USPTO) without previously filing with the patent office of Canada, that application and applications filed subsequently with the USPTO will form a foreign-oriented patent family.

Geographical indication

A geographical indication (GI) is a sign identifying a good as originating in a specific geographical area and possessing a given quality, reputation or other characteristic that is *essentially attributable* to that geographical origin. Thus, the main function of a GI is to indicate a connection between that quality,

characteristics or reputation of the good and its territory of origin.

Grant

A set of exclusive rights legally accorded to the applicant when a patent or utility model is granted or issued.

Gross domestic product (GDP)

The total unduplicated output of economic goods and services produced within a country as measured in monetary terms.

Hague international application

An application for the international registration of an industrial design filed under the WIPO-administered Hague System.

Hague international registration

An international registration issued via the Hague System, which facilitates the acquisition of industrial design rights in multiple jurisdictions. An application for international registration of an industrial design leads to its recording in the International Register and the publication of the registration in the *International Designs Bulletin*. If the registration is not refused by the IP office of a designated Hague member, the international registration will have the same effect as a registration made in that jurisdiction.

Hague member (Contracting Party)

A state or intergovernmental organization that is a member of the Hague System. Includes any state or intergovernmental organization party to the 1999 Act and/or the 1960 Act of the Hague Agreement. Entitlement to file an international application under the Hague Agreement is limited to natural persons or legal entities having a real and effective industrial or commercial establishment, or a domicile, in at least one of the Contracting Parties to the Agreement, or being a national of one of those Contracting Parties or of a member state of an intergovernmental organization that is a Contracting Party. In addition – but only under the 1999 Act – an international application may be filed on the basis of habitual residence in the jurisdiction of a Contracting Party.

Hague route

An alternative to the Paris route (i.e., the direct national or regional route), the Hague route enables an application for international registration of industrial designs to be filed using the Hague System.

Hague System

The abbreviated form of the Hague System for the International Registration of Industrial Designs. This System comprises two international treaties: the Hague Act of 1960 and the Geneva Act of 1999. The Hague System makes it possible for an applicant to register up to 100 industrial designs in multiple jurisdictions by filing a single application with the International Bureau of WIPO. It simplifies multi national registration by reducing the requirement to file separate applications with each IP office. The System also simplifies the subsequent management of the industrial design, since it is possible to record changes or renew a registration through a single procedural step.

In force

Refers to IP rights that are currently valid or, in the case of trademarks, active. To remain in force, IP protection must be maintained.

Industrial design

Industrial designs are applied to a wide variety of industrial products and handicrafts. They refer to the ornamental or aesthetic aspects of a useful article, including compositions of lines or colors or any three-dimensional forms that give a special appearance to a product or handicraft. The holder of a registered industrial design has exclusive rights against unauthorized copying or imitation of the design by third parties. Industrial design registrations are valid for a limited period. The term of protection is usually 15 years in most jurisdictions. However, differences in legislation exist, notably in China (which provides for a 10-year term from the application date) and the U.S. (which provides for a 14-year term from the date of registration).

Intellectual property (IP)

Creations of the mind: inventions, literary and artistic works, symbols, names, images and designs used in commerce. IP is divided into two categories: industrial property – which includes patents, utility models, trademarks, industrial designs and geographical indications of source – and copyright, which includes literary and artistic works such as novels, poems, plays, films, musical works, artistic works (such as drawings, paintings, photographs and sculptures) and architectural designs. Rights related to copyright include those of performing artists in their performances, those of producers of sound recordings in their recordings and those of broadcasters in their radio and television programs.

International Depositary Authority (IDA)

A scientific institution – typically a culture collection – capable of storing microorganisms that has acquired the status of an International Depositary Authority under the Budapest Treaty and provides for the receipt, acceptance and storage of microorganisms and the furnishing of samples thereof. Currently, 46 such authorities exist around the world.

International Patent Classification (IPC)

An international recognized patent classification system, the IPC has a hierarchical structure of language-independent symbols and is divided into sections, classes, sub-classes and groups. IPC symbols are assigned according to the technical features in patent applications. A patent application that relates to multiple technical features can be assigned several IPC symbols.

International Union for the Protection of New Varieties of Plants (UPOV)

An intergovernmental organization established by the International Convention for the Protection of New Varieties of Plants (the UPOV Convention), which was adopted on December 2, 1961. UPOV provides and promotes an effective system of plant variety protection with the aim of encouraging the development of new varieties of plants for the benefit of society.

Invention

A new solution to a technical problem. To qualify for patent protection, the invention must be novel, involve an inventive step and be industrially applicable, as judged by a person skilled in the art.

Lisbon System

The Lisbon System was established in 1958 to facilitate the international protection of appellations of origin through a single registration procedure. Registration with the WIPO International Bureau ensures protection in all Lisbon contracting parties, without need for renewal and as long as the appellation of origin remains protected in its contracting party of origin. However, the decision whether to protect a newly registered appellation of origin at the national level remains the prerogative of each contracting party, and each Lisbon member can refuse protection based on any ground within one year of being notified of a new appellation of origin by the WIPO International Bureau. The Lisbon System is flexible as regards the means which countries may provide protection for the registered appellation of origin (e.g., *sui generis* systems, trademark laws or specific ad hoc decrees as well as judicial and administrative decisions).

Locarno Classification (LOC)

The abbreviated form of the International Classification for Industrial Designs under the Locarno Agreement, used for registering industrial designs. The LOC comprises a list of 32 classes and their respective subclasses with explanatory notes plus an alphabetical list of the goods in which industrial designs are incorporated and an indication of the classes and subclasses into which they fall.

Madrid international application

An application for international registration under the Madrid System, which is a request for protection of a trademark in one or more Madrid members. An international application must be based on a basic mark – prior application or registration of a mark in a Madrid member.

Madrid international registration

An application for international registration of a mark leads to its recording in the International Register and the publication of the international registration in the *WIPO Gazette of International Marks*. If the international registration is not refused protection by a designated Madrid member, it will have the same effect as a national or regional trademark registration made under the law applicable in that Madrid member's jurisdiction.

Madrid member (Contracting Party)

A state or intergovernmental organization – for example the European Union (EU) or the African Intellectual Property Organization (OAPI) – that is party to the Madrid Agreement and/or the Madrid Protocol.

Madrid route

The Madrid route (the Madrid System) is an alternative to the direct national or regional route (also called the Paris route).

Madrid System

An abbreviation describing two procedural treaties for the international registration of trademarks, namely the Madrid Agreement for the International Registration of Marks and the Protocol relating to that Agreement. The Madrid System is administered by the International Bureau of WIPO.

Maintenance

An act by the applicant to keep an IP grant/registration valid (in force), primarily by paying the required fee to the IP office of the state or jurisdiction providing protection. That fee is also known as a "maintenance fee." A trademark can be maintained indefinitely by paying renewal fees; however, patents, utility models and industrial designs can be maintained for only a limited number of years.

Microorganism deposit

The transmittal of a microorganism to an International Depositary Authority (IDA), which receives and accepts it, the storage of such a microorganism by the IDA, or both transmittal and storage.

National phase under the PCT

The phase that follows the international phase of the PCT procedure and that consists of the entry and processing of the international application in the individual countries or regions in which the applicant seeks protection for an invention.

National route

Applications for IP protection filed directly with the national office of, or acting for, the relevant state or jurisdiction (see also "Hague route," "Madrid route" and "PCT route"). The national route is also called the "direct route" or "Paris route."

Nice Classification (NCL)

The abbreviated form of the International Classification of Goods and Services for the Purposes of Registering Marks, an international classification established under the Nice Agreement. The Nice Classification consists of 45 classes, which are divided into 34 classes for goods and 11 for services. (See also "Class" above.)

Non-resident

For statistical purposes, a "non-resident" application refers to an application filed with the IP office of, or acting for, a state or jurisdiction in which the first-named applicant in the application is not domiciled. For example, an application filed with the Japan Patent Office (JPO) by an applicant residing in France is considered a non-resident application from the perspective of the JPO. Non-resident applications are sometimes referred to as foreign applications. A non-resident grant or registration is an IP right issued on the basis of a non-resident application.

Origin (country or region)

For statistical purposes, the origin of an application means the country or territory of residence of the first named applicant in the application. In some cases (notably in the U.S.), the country of origin is determined by the residence of the assignee rather than that of the applicant.

Paris Convention

The Paris Convention for the Protection of Industrial Property, signed on March 20, 1883, is one of the most important treaties, as it establishes general principles applicable to all IP rights. It establishes the "right of priority" that enables an IP applicant, when filing an application in countries other than the original country of filing, to claim priority of an earlier application filed up to 12 months previously for patents and utility models, and up to six months previously for trademarks and industrial designs.

Paris route

An alternative to the Hague, Madrid or PCT routes, the Paris route (also called the "direct route" or "national route") enables individual IP applications to be filed directly with an office that is a signatory to the Paris Convention.

Patent

A set of exclusive rights granted by law to applicants for inventions that are new, non-obvious and commercially applicable. A patent is valid for a limited period of time (generally 20 years), during which patent holders can commercially exploit their inventions on an exclusive basis. In return, applicants are obliged to disclose their inventions to the public in a manner that enables others skilled in the art to replicate the invention. The patent system is designed to encourage innovation by providing innovators with time-limited exclusive legal rights, thus enabling them to appropriate the returns from their innovative activity.

Patent Cooperation Treaty (PCT)

An international treaty administered by WIPO, the PCT allows applicants to seek patent protection for an invention simultaneously in a large number of countries (PCT contracting states) by filing a single PCT international application. The granting of patents, which remains under the control of national or regional patent offices, is carried out in what is called the "national phase" or "regional phase."

Patent family

Applicants often file patent applications in multiple jurisdictions, so some inventions are recorded more than once. To take this into account, WIPO has indicators related to patent families, defined as patent applications interlinked by one or more of: priority claim, Patent Cooperation Treaty national phase entry, continuation, continuation-in-part, internal priority and addition or division. WIPO's patent family definition includes only those associated with patent applications for inventions and excludes patent families associated with utility model applications.

PCT application

A patent application filed through the WIPO-administered PCT, also known as an international application.

PCT-Patent Prosecution Highway (PCT-PPH) Pilots

A number of bilateral agreements signed between patent offices that enable applicants to request an accelerated examination procedure because of positive patentability findings made by the international searching and/or international preliminary examining authority, in the written opinion by an International Searching Authority, the written opinion of an International Preliminary Examining Authority or the international preliminary report on patentability.

PCT route

A patent application filed through the WIPO-administered PCT, also known as an international application.

PCT System

The PCT, an international treaty administered by WIPO, facilitates the acquisition of patent rights in a large number of jurisdictions. The PCT System simplifies the process of multiple national patent filings by reducing the requirement to file a separate application in each jurisdiction. However, the decision whether to grant patent rights remains in the hands of national and regional patent offices, and patent rights remain limited to the jurisdiction of the patent-granting authority. The PCT application process starts with the international phase, during which an international search and possibly a preliminary examination are performed, and concludes with the national phase, during which a national or regional patent office decides on the patentability of an invention according to national law.

Pending patent application

In general, this refers to a patent application filed with a patent office for which no patent has yet been granted or refused, and for which the application has not been withdrawn. In jurisdictions where a request for examination is required to start the examination process,

a pending application may refer to an application for which a request for examination has been received or one for which no patent has been granted or refused, and for which the application has not been withdrawn.

Plant Patent Act (PPA) of the U.S.

Under the law commonly known as the "Plant Patent Act," whoever invents or discovers and asexually reproduces any distinct and new variety of plant, including cultivated sports, mutants, hybrids and newly-found seedlings, other than a tuber-propagated plant or a plant found in an uncultivated state, may obtain a patent therefor.

Plant variety

According to the UPOV Convention, plant variety means a plant grouping within a single botanical taxon of the lowest known rank which, irrespective of whether the conditions for the grant of a breeder's right are fully met, can be defined by the expression of the characteristics resulting from a given genotype or combination of genotypes, distinguished from any other plant grouping by the expression of at least one of the said characteristics and considered as a unit with regard to its suitability for being propagated unchanged.

Plant variety grant

Under the UPOV Convention, the breeder's right is granted (title of protection is issued) only when the variety is new, distinct, uniform, stable and has a suitable denomination.

Plant Variety Protection Act (PVPA) of the U.S.

Under the PVPA, the U.S. protects all sexually reproduced plant varieties and tuber-propagated plant varieties, excluding fungi and bacteria.

Prior art

All information disclosed to the public about an invention, in any form, before a given date. Information on prior art can assist in determining whether the claimed invention is new and involves an inventive step (i.e., is nonobvious) for the purposes of international searches and international preliminary examination.

217

Priority date

The filing date of the application on the basis of which priority is claimed. (See "Paris Convention" above.)

Publication date

The date on which an IP application is disclosed to the public. On that date, the subject matter of the application becomes prior art.

Regional application/grant (registration)

An application filed with or granted (registered) by an IP office having regional jurisdiction over more than one country. There are currently seven regional offices: the African Intellectual Property Organization (OAPI), the African Regional Intellectual Property Organization (ARIPO), the Benelux Office for Intellectual Property (BOIP), the Eurasian Patent Organization (EAPO), the European Patent Office (EPO), the European Union Intellectual Property Office (EUIPO) and the Patent Office of the Cooperation Council for the Arab States of the Gulf (GCC Patent Office).

Registered Community design

A registration issued by the EUIPO based on a single application filed directly with the office by an applicant seeking protection within the EU as a whole.

Registration

An exclusive set of rights legally accorded to the applicant when an industrial design or trademark is registered or issued. See "Industrial design" or "Trademark." Registrations are issued to applicants to make use of and exploit their industrial design or trademark for a limited period of time and can, in some cases (particularly in the case of trademarks), be renewed indefinitely.

Renewal

The process by which the protection of an IP right is maintained (i.e., kept in force). Usually consists of paying renewal fees to an IP office at regular intervals. If renewal fees are not paid, the registration may lapse. See also "Maintenance."

Resident

For statistical purposes, a resident application refers to an application filed with the IP office of, or acting for, the state or jurisdiction in which the first named applicant in the application has residence. For example, an application filed with the JPO by a resident of Japan is considered a resident application for the JPO. Resident applications are sometimes referred to as "domestic applications." A resident grant/registration is an IP right issued on the basis of a resident application.

Trademark

A sign used by the owner of specific goods or services to distinguish them from those of others. Depending on the jurisdiction, a trademark can consist of words and combinations of words (for instance, slogans), names, logos, figures and images, letters, numbers, smells, sounds and moving images, or a combination thereof. The procedures for registering trademarks are governed by the legislation and procedures of national and regional IP offices and WIPO. Trademark rights are limited to the jurisdiction of the IP office that registers the trademark. Trademarks can be registered by filing an application at the relevant national or regional office(s), or by filing an international application through the Madrid System.

Utility model

A special form of patent right granted by a state or jurisdiction to an inventor or the inventor's assignee for a fixed period of time. The terms and conditions for granting a utility model are slightly different from those for normal patents (including a shorter term of protection and less stringent patentability requirements). The term can also describe what are known in certain countries as "petty patents," "short-term patents" or "innovation patents."

World Intellectual Property Organization (WIPO)

A United Nations specialized agency dedicated to the promotion of innovation and creativity for the economic, social and cultural development of all countries through a balanced and effective international IP system. WIPO was established in 1967 with a mandate to promote the protection of IP throughout the world through cooperation among states and in collaboration with other international organizations.

List of abbreviations

ARIPO	African Regional Intellectual Property Organization
BOIP	Benelux Office for Intellectual Property
CPVO	Community Plant Variety Office of the European Union
EAPO	Eurasian Patent Organization
EPO	European Patent Office
EU	European Union
EUIPO	European Union Intellectual Property Office
GCC Patent Office	Patent Office of the Cooperation Council for the Arab States of the Gulf
GDP	Gross Domestic Product
GI	Geographical Indication
IDA	International Depositary Authority
IP	Intellectual Property
IPC	International Patent Classification
JPO	Japan Patent Office
KIPO	Korean Intellectual Property Office
OAPI	African Intellectual Property Organization
PCT	Patent Cooperation Treaty
PPA	Plant Patent Act of the United States of America
PVPA	Plant Variety Protection Act of the United States of America
Rep. of Korea	Republic of Korea
SIPO	State Intellectual Property Office of the People's Republic of China
U.K.	United Kingdom
UM	Utility Model
UPOV	International Union for the Protection of New Varieties of Plants
U.S.	United States of America
USPTO	United States Patent and Trademark Office
WIPO	World Intellectual Property Organization

Annex A
IPC-technology concordance table

FIELD OF TECHNOLOGY	IPC CODES
Electrical engineering	
Electrical machinery, apparatus, energy	F21H%, F21K%, F21L%, F21S%, F21V%, F21W%, F21Y%, H01B%, H01C%, H01F%, H01G%, H01H%, H01J%, H01K%, H01M%, H01R%, H01T%, H02B%, H02G%, H02H%, H02J%, H02K%, H02M%, H02N%, H02P%, H02S%, H05B%, H05C%, H05F%, H99Z%
Audio-visual technology	G09F%, G09G%, G11B%, H04N 3%, H04N 5%, H04N 7%, H04N 9%, H04N 11%, H04N 13%, H04N 15%, H04N 17%, H04N 19%, H04N 101%, H04R%, H04S%, H05K%
Telecommunications	G08C%, H01P%, H01Q%, H04B%, H04H%, H04J%, H04K%, H04M%, H04N 1%, H04Q%
Digital communication	H04L%, H04N 21%, H04W%
Basic communication processes	H03B%, H03C%, H03D%, H03F%, H03G%, H03H%, H03J%, H03K%, H03L%, H03M%
Computer technology	G06C%, G06D%, G06E%, G06F%, G06G%, G06J%, G06K%, G06M%, G06N%, G06T%, G10L%, G11C%
IT methods for management	G06Q%
Semiconductors	H01L%
Instruments	
Optics	G02B%, G02C%, G02F%, G03B%, G03C%, G03D%, G03F%, G03G%, G03H%, H01S%
Measurement	G01B%, G01C%, G01D%, G01F%, G01G%, G01H%, G01J%, G01K%, G01L%, G01M%, G01N 1%, G01N 3%, G01N 5%, G01N 7%, G01N 9%, G01N 11%, G01N 13%, G01N 15%, G01N 17%, G01N 19%, G01N 21%, G01N 22%, G01N 23%, G01N 24%, G01N 25%, G01N 27%, G01N 29%, G01N 30%, G01N 31%, G01N 35%, G01N 37%, G01P%, G01Q%, G01R%, G01S%, G01V%, G01W%, G04B%, G04C%, G04D%, G04F%, G04G%, G04R%, G12B%, G99Z%
Analysis of biological materials	G01N 33%
Control	G05B%, G05D%, G05F%, G07B%, G07C%, G07D%, G07F%, G07G%, G08B%, G08G%, G09B%, G09C%, G09D%
Medical technology	A61B%, A61C%, A61D%, A61F%, A61G%, A61H%, A61J%, A61L%, A61M%, A61N%, H05G%
Chemistry	
Organic fine chemistry	A61K 8%, A61Q%, C07B%, C07C%, C07D%, C07F%, C07H%, C07J%, C40B%
Biotechnology	C07G%, C07K%, C12M%, C12N%, C12P%, C12Q%, C12R%, C12S%
Pharmaceuticals	A61K 6%, A61K 9%, A61K 31%, A61K 33%, A61K 35%, A61K 36%, A61K 38%, A61K 39%, A61K 41%, A61K 45%, A61K 47%, A61K 48%, A61K 49%, A61K 50%, A61K 51%, A61K 101%, A61K 103%, A61K 125%, A61K 127%, A61K 129%, A61K 131%, A61K 133%, A61K 135%, A61P%
Macromolecular chemistry, polymers	C08B%, C08C%, C08F%, C08G%, C08H%, C08K%, C08L%
Food chemistry	A01H%, A21D%, A23B%, A23C%, A23D%, A23F%, A23G%, A23J%, A23K%, A23L%, C12C%, C12F%, C12G%, C12H%, C12J%, C13B 10%, C13B 20%, C13B 30%, C13B 35%, C13B 40%, C13B 50%, C13B 99%, C13D%, C13F%, C13J%, C13K%
Basic materials chemistry	A01N%, A01P%, C05B%, C05C%, C05D%, C05F%, C05G%, C06B%, C06C%, C06D%, C06F%, C09B%, C09C%, C09D%, C09F%, C09G%, C09H%, C09J%, C09K%, C10B%, C10C%, C10F%, C10G%, C10H%, C10J%, C10K%, C10L%, C10M%, C10N%, C11B%, C11C%, C11D%, C99Z%
Materials, metallurgy	B22C%, B22D%, B22F%, C01B%, C01C%, C01D%, C01F%, C01G%, C03C%, C04B%, C21B%, C21C%, C21D%, C22B%, C22C%, C22F%
Surface technology, coating	B05C%, B05D%, B32B%, C23C%, C23D%, C23F%, C23G%, C25B%, C25C%, C25D%, C25F%, C30B%
Micro-structural and nano-technology	B81B%, B81C%, B82B%, B82Y%
Chemical engineering	B01B%, B01D 1%, B01D 3%, B01D 5%, B01D 7%, B01D 8%, B01D 9%, B01D 11%, B01D 12%, B01D 15%, B01D 17%, B01D 19%, B01D 21%, B01D 24%, B01D 25%, B01D 27%, B01D 29%, B01D 33%, B01D 35%, B01D 36%, B01D 37%, B01D 39%, B01D 41%, B01D 43%, B01D 57%, B01D 59%, B01D 61%, B01D 63%, B01D 65%, B01D 67%, B01D 69%, B01D 71%, B01F%, B01J%, B01L%, B02C%, B03B%, B03C%, B03D%, B04B%, B04C%, B05B%, B06B%, B07B%, B07C%, B08B%, C14C%, D06B%, D06C%, D06L%, F25J%, F26B%, H05H%
Environmental technology	A62C%, B01D 45%, B01D 46%, B01D 47%, B01D 49%, B01D 50%, B01D 51%, B01D 52%, B01D 53%, B09B%, B09C%, B65F%, C02F%, E01F 8%, F01N%, F23G%, F23J%, G01T%

FIELD OF TECHNOLOGY	IPC CODES
Mechanical engineering	
Handling	B25J%, B65B%, B65C%, B65D%, B65G%, B65H%, B66B%, B66C%, B66D%, B66F%, B67B%, B67C%, B67D%
Machine tools	A62D%, B21B%, B21C%, B21D%, B21F%, B21G%, B21H%, B21J%, B21K%, B21L%, B23B%, B23C%, B23D%, B23F%, B23G%, B23H%, B23K%, B23P%, B23Q%, B24B%, B24C%, B24D%, B25B%, B25C%, B25D%, B25F%, B25G%, B25H%, B26B%, B26D%, B26F%, B27B%, B27C%, B27D%, B27F%, B27G%, B27H%, B27J%, B27K%, B27L%, B27M%, B27N%, B30B%
Engines, pumps, turbines	F01B%, F01C%, F01D%, F01K%, F01L%, F01M%, F01P%, F02B%, F02C%, F02D%, F02F%, F02G%, F02K%, F02M%, F02N%, F02P%, F03B%, F03C%, F03D%, F03G%, F03H%, F04B%, F04C%, F04D%, F04F%, F23R%, F99Z%, G21B%, G21C%, G21D%, G21F%, G21G%, G21H%, G21J%, G21K%
Textile and paper machines	A41H%, A43D%, A46D%, B31B%, B31C%, B31D%, B31F%, B41B%, B41C%, B41D%, B41F%, B41G%, B41J%, B41K%, B41L%, B41M%, B41N%, C14B%, D01B%, D01C%, D01D%, D01F%, D01G%, D01H%, D02G%, D02H%, D02J%, D03C%, D03D%, D03J%, D04B%, D04C%, D04G%, D04H%, D05B%, D05C%, D06G%, D06H%, D06J%, D06M%, D06P%, D06Q%, D21B%, D21C%, D21D%, D21F%, D21G%, D21H%, D21J%, D99Z%
Other special machines	A01B%, A01C%, A01D%, A01F%, A01G%, A01J%, A01K%, A01L%, A01M%, A21B%, A21C%, A22B%, A22C%, A23N%, A23P%, B02B%, B28B%, B28C%, B28D%, B29B%, B29C%, B29D%, B29K%, B29L%, B33Y%, B99Z%, C03B%, C08J%, C12L%, C13B 5%, C13B 15%, C13B 25%, C13B 45%, C13C%, C13G%, C13H%, F41A%, F41B%, F41C%, F41F%, F41G%, F41H%, F41J%, F42B%, F42C%, F42D%
Thermal processes and apparatus	F22B%, F22D%, F22G%, F23B%, F23C%, F23D%, F23H%, F23K%, F23L%, F23M%, F23N%, F23Q%, F24B%, F24C%, F24D%, F24F%, F24H%, F24J%, F25B%, F25C%, F27B%, F27D%, F28B%, F28C%, F28D%, F28F%, F28G%
Mechanical elements	F15B%, F15C%, F15D%, F16B%, F16C%, F16D%, F16F%, F16G%, F16H%, F16J%, F16K%, F16L%, F16M%, F16N%, F16P%, F16S%, F16T%, F17B%, F17C%, F17D%, G05G%
Transport	B60B%, B60C%, B60D%, B60F%, B60G%, B60H%, B60J%, B60K%, B60L%, B60M%, B60N%, B60P%, B60Q%, B60R%, B60S%, B60T%, B60V%, B60W%, B61B%, B61C%, B61D%, B61F%, B61G%, B61H%, B61J%, B61K%, B61L%, B62B%, B62C%, B62D%, B62H%, B62J%, B62K%, B62L%, B62M%, B63B%, B63C%, B63G%, B63H%, B63J%, B64B%, B64C%, B64D%, B64F%, B64G%
Other fields	
Furniture, games	A47B%, A47C%, A47D%, A47F%, A47G%, A47H%, A47J%, A47K%, A47L%, A63B%, A63C%, A63D%, A63F%, A63G%, A63H%, A63J%, A63K%
Other consumer goods	A24B%, A24C%, A24D%, A24F%, A41B%, A41C%, A41D%, A41F%, A41G%, A42B%, A42C%, A43B%, A43C%, A44B%, A44C%, A45B%, A45C%, A45D%, A45F%, A46B%, A62B%, A99Z%, B42B%, B42C%, B42D%, B42F%, B43K%, B43L%, B43M%, B44B%, B44C%, B44D%, B44F%, B68B%, B68C%, B68F%, B68G%, D04D%, D06F%, D06N%, D07B%, F25D%, G10B%, G10C%, G10D%, G10F%, G10G%, G10H%, G10K%
Civil engineering	E01B%, E01C%, E01D%, E01F 1%, E01F 3%, E01F 5%, E01F 7%, E01F 9%, E01F 11%, E01F 13%, E01F 15%, E01H%, E02B%, E02C%, E02D%, E02F%, E03B%, E03C%, E03D%, E03F%, E04B%, E04C%, E04D%, E04F%, E04G%, E04H%, E05B%, E05C%, E05D%, E05F%, E05G%, E06B%, E06C%, E21B%, E21C%, E21D%, E21F%, E99Z%

Note: For definitions of IPC symbols, see *www.wipo.int/classifications/ipc*. For an electronic version of the IPC technology concordance table, visit *www.wipo.int/ipstats*.

Source: WIPO.

Annex B
Definitions for selected energy-related technology fields

Energy-related technologies	International patent classification (IPC) symbols
Solar energy technology	F24J 2/00, F24J 2/02, F24J 2/04, F24J 2/05, F24J 2/06, F24J 2/07, F24J 2/08, F24J 2/10, F24J 2/12, F24J 2/13, F24J 2/14, F24J 2/15, F24J 2/16, F24J 2/18, F24J 2/23, F24J 2/24, F24J 2/36, F24J 2/38, F24J 2/42, F24J 2/46, F03G 6/06, G02B 5/10, H01L 31/052, E04D 13/18, H01L 31/04, H01L 31/042, H01L 31/18, E04D 1/30, G02F 1/136, G05F 1/67, H01L 25/00, H01L 31/00, H01L 31/048, H01L 33/00, H02J 7/35, H02N 6/00
Fuel cell technology	H01M 4/00, H01M 4/86, H01M 4/88, H01M 4/90, H01M 8/00, H01M 8/02, H01M 8/04, H01M 8/06, H01M 8/08, H01M 8/10, H01M 8/12, H01M 8/14, H01M 8/16, H01M 8/18, H01M 8/20, H01M 8/22, H01M 8/24
Wind energy	F03D 1/00, F03D 3/00, F03D 5/00, F03D 7/00, F03D 9/00, F03D 11/00, B60L 8/00
Geothermal energy	F24J 3/08, F03G 4/00, F03G 7/05

Note: For definitions of IPC symbols, see *www.wipo.int/classifications/ipc*. The correspondence between IPC symbols and technology fields is not always clear-cut, and so it is difficult to capture all patents in a specific technology field. Nonetheless, the IPC-based definitions of the four technologies presented above are likely to capture the vast majority of related patents.

Source: WIPO.

Annex C
International Classification of Goods and Services under the Nice Agreement

Class heading	Goods or services
Class 3	Bleaching preparations and other substances for laundry use; cleaning, polishing, scouring and abrasive preparations; soaps; perfumery, essential oils, cosmetics, hair lotions; dentifrices
Class 5	Pharmaceutical and veterinary preparations; sanitary preparations for medical purposes; dietetic substances adapted for medical use, food for babies; plasters, materials for dressings; material for stopping teeth, dental wax; disinfectants; preparations for destroying vermin; fungicides, herbicides
Class 9	Scientific, nautical, surveying, photographic, cinematographic, optical, weighing, measuring, signaling, checking (supervision), life-saving and teaching apparatus and instruments; apparatus and instruments for conducting, switching, transforming, accumulating, regulating or controlling electricity; apparatus for recording, transmission or reproduction of sound or images; magnetic data carriers, recording discs; automatic vending machines and mechanisms for coin-operated apparatus; cash registers, calculating machines, data processing equipment and computers; fire-extinguishing apparatus
Class 25	Clothing, footwear, headgear
Class 29	Meat, fish, poultry and game; meat extracts; preserved, frozen, dried and cooked fruits and vegetables; jellies, jams, compotes; eggs; milk and milk products; edible oils and fats
Class 30	Coffee, tea, cocoa, sugar, rice, tapioca, sago, artificial coffee; flour and preparations made from cereals, bread, pastry and confectionery, ices; honey, treacle; yeast, baking-powder; salt, mustard; vinegar, sauces (condiments); spices; ice
Class 35	Advertising; business management; business administration; office functions
Class 41	Education; providing of training; entertainment; sporting and cultural activities
Class 42	Scientific and technological services and research and design relating thereto; industrial analysis and research services; design and development of computer hardware and software
Class 43	Services for providing food and drink; temporary accommodation

Note: See *www.wipo.int/classifications/nice* for a complete list of all classes and further information on the International Classification of Goods and Services under the Nice Agreement.

Source: WIPO.

Industry sector	Abbreviation (where applicable)	Nice classes
Agricultural products and services	Agriculture	29, 30, 31, 32, 33, 43
Management, Communications, Real estate and Financial services	Business services	35, 36
Chemicals	-	1, 2, 4
Textiles – Clothing and Accessories	Clothing	14, 18, 22, 23, 24, 25, 26, 27, 34
Construction, Infrastructure	Construction	6, 17, 19, 37, 40
Pharmaceuticals, Health, Cosmetics	Health	3, 5, 10, 44
Household equipment	-	8, 11, 20, 21
Leisure, Education, Training	Leisure & Education	13, 15, 16, 28, 41
Scientific research, Information and Communication Technology	Research & Technology	9, 38, 42, 45
Transportation and Logistics	Transportation	7, 12, 39

Source: Edital®.

Annex D
International Classification for Industrial Designs
(Locarno Classification)

Class Heading	Goods
Class 2	Articles of clothing and haberdashery
Class 6	Furnishing
Class 7	Household goods, not elsewhere specified
Class 9	Packages and containers for the transport or handling of goods
Class 11	Articles of adornment
Class 12	Means of transport or hoisting
Class 14	Recording, communication or information retrieval equipment
Class 25	Building units and construction elements
Class 26	Lighting apparatus
Class 32	Graphic symbols and logos, surface patterns, ornamentation

Note: See www.wipo.int/classifications/locarno for a complete list of all classes and further information.

Source: WIPO.

Locarno classes	Sector
20, 32	Advertising
1, 27, 31	Agricultural products and food preparation
23, 25, 29	Construction
13, 26	Electricity and lighting
6, 7, 30	Furniture and household goods
24, 28	Health, pharma and cosmetics
14, 16, 18	ICT and audiovisual
17, 19, 21, 22	Leisure and education
9	Packaging
2, 3, 5, 11	Textiles and accessories
4, 8, 10, 15	Tools and machines
12	Transport

Source: Organisation for Economic Co-operation and Development (OECD).

Notes

Preliminary

1. The products and handicrafts to which industrial designs are applied range from technical and medical instruments to watches, jewelry and other luxury items, and from housewares, electrical appliances, vehicles and construction materials to textile designs and leisure goods.

Special section

1. Benjamin Mitra-Kahn, Alan Marco, Michael Carley, Paul D'Agostino, Peter Evans, Carl Frey, Nadiya Sultan (2013). *Patent Backlogs, Inventories and Pendency: An International Framework.* Newport, United Kingdom: United Kingdom Intellectual Property Office/ United States Patent and Trademark Office.

Gaétan de Rassenfosse and Alexandra K. Zaby (2016). *The Economics of Patent Backlog.*

Wesley M. Cohen and Stephen A. Merrill (eds.) (2003). *Patents in the Knowledge-Based Economy.* Washington, D.C.: National Academies Press.

Adam B. Jaffe and Josh Lerner (2004). *Innovation and Its Discontents: How Our Broken Patent System is Endangering Innovation and Progress, and What to Do About It.* Princeton, N.J.: Princeton University Press.

The Economist. "Getting serious about patents," November 3, 2012; "Patently absurd," May 5, 2011; "Patent fiction," December 11, 2014.

2. Having an adequate number of examiners is essential for the timely processing of applications. However, other factors, such as IT infrastructure, greater cooperation among offices and so on can contribute to the efficient processing of applications.

3. Richard A. Posner, "Why there are too many patents in America," *The Atlantic,* July 12, 2012.

4. Michael D. Frakes and Melissa F. Wasserman (2015). "Does the U.S. Patent and Trademark Office grant too many bad patents? Evidence from a quasi-experiment," 67 *Stanford Law Review,* 613-676.

5. In order to work out the grant rate of all applications filed in 2016, one would need to wait between 5 and 10 years. Reporting data with a 5 to 10-year lag has limited value for policy-making.

Trademarks

1. Equivalent application class counts differ from the absolute class counts, which are presented in figure B20 and do not take into account the multiplying effect of regional offices.

Plant varieties

1. Throughout this section, U.S. data refer to a combination of Plant Variety Protection Act and Plant Patent Act data. However, separate data relating to each Act are given in statistical table D16.

Geographical indications

1. Recently, the Organization for an International Geographical Indications Network (oriGIn), which is a non-governmental organization (NGO), published GI data for a large number of countries: *www.origin-gi.com.*

2. The terminology used at national and regional levels to refer to *sui generis* rights over GIs is not uniform. Different terms such as appellations of origin, controlled appellations of origin, protected designations of origin, protected geographical indications, (qualified) indications of source or simply geographical indications are used in different legislations. Despite the different terminology, however, the common denominator shall remain the link between the specific quality, characteristics or reputation of the product and its territory of origin. For simplicity, the present text generally uses "geographical indication (GI)" regardless of the different national and regional terminology.

3. The Lisbon System is administered by WIPO and comprises the Lisbon Agreement for the Protection of Appellations of Origin and their International Registration (1958), as revised at Stockholm in 1967 and amended in 1979, and the Geneva Act of the Lisbon Agreement on Appellations of Origin and Geographical Indications (2015), which has not yet entered into force.

4. For more information about the Madrid System, please see the *Madrid Yearly Review 2017.*

5. In principle, double-counting of the same subject matter protected by different IP rights also occurs in patent, trademark and industrial design statistics. However, the inclusion of GIs covered in trade agreements adds a layer of complexity, as relevant GIs may, in some case, only have legal effect once registered at the national level.

Additional information

1. The products and handicrafts to which industrial designs are applied range from technical and medical instruments to watches, jewelry and other luxury items, and from housewares, electrical appliances, vehicles and construction materials to textile designs and leisure goods.